Jewish Heritage Reader

Selected, with Introduction by

RABBI MORRIS ADLER

Lily Edelman, Editor

A B'NAI B'RITH BOOK

Taplinger Publishing Co., Inc.
New York

The B'nai B'rith Department of Adult Jewish Education, organized in 1954, has as its purpose to stimulate and promote the study of Judaism among adult Jews. Through annual Institutes of Judaism, year-round discussion groups, and authoritative and readable publications, it helps individuals and groups plan study programs on the religious and cultural heritage of the Jewish people.

Acknowledgments

The selections in this Reader are culled from *Jewish Heritage,* the illustrated quarterly published by B'nai B'rith's Commission on Adult Jewish Education, and now in its seventh year.

Appreciation must be here recorded to all authors included, each of whom has generously given permission for reprinting. Grateful acknowledgment must also be made to Dr. Louis L. Kaplan, Chairman of the *Jewish Heritage* Editorial Committee, and the members of that committee: Martin D. Cohn, Rabbi Arthur Hertzberg, Rabbi Benjamin M. Kahn. To Rabbi Morris Adler, Chairman of the Commission and member of the Editorial Committee, who conceived and structured this volume and made the selections for it, our thanks are beyond measure.

It must also be recorded that Ruth Nussbaum and Ephraim Fischoff translated from the German Lion Feuchtwanger's "The Jew's Sense of History."

God the Accused by Elie Wiesel is reprinted from the author's novel *Night,* with permission of Hill and Wang. *When Is A Jew Not a Jew* is extracted and reprinted from *The Jerusalem Post* Law Report, December 14, 1962.

L.E.

Contents

CONTENTS

V. CREATIVE JEWS OF OUR TIME

VI. ISRAEL—REBORN

VII. JEWISH LIFE IN THE UNITED STATES

VIII. DILEMMAS, CHALLENGES, REAPPRAISALS

The Creative Uses of the Past

An Introduction

Morris Adler

MAN's present is the upward thrust of all his yesterdays. In him and through him course forces that had their origin in a period beyond his capacity to isolate precisely or to delineate as to character, reenforced and altered by all that has transpired since. Manifold impacts of man's past unite to endow him with capacities and attributes that give him ascendancy over the other creatures in nature.

But man does not live solely in the frame of the physical world. From the milieu of history and culture which serves as the matrix for his life as a member of the human family, he derives his identity as man. "Tradition is the only way we have of knowing who we are," Mark Van Doren says. Culture and civilization are man's human heritage, even as his physical and creaturely traits are the product of his animal heredity. Language, art, religion, group customs, values and memories extend and enrich the environment into which man the creature is born and in which he develops and matures into man the human.

Man therefore cannot be understood without considering the two worlds which join to form the universe in which he moves and has his essential being. The controversy as to which is more decisive, nature or nurture, has long waged without resolution. Judaism did not make the mistake, common to some other religions and philosophic systems, of minimizing the one or ignoring the other. The first vague sounds which the ears of the infant absorb, the first sights which the tiny pupils of his eyes bring into uncertain focus, the first tender caresses to which he responds—these are part of his human inheritance. Their interpenetration of the roots out of which the child's personality will subsequently flower can never thereafter be fully exorcised. The child has begun to accumulate the past out of which his future, as from a womb, will emerge.

Detachment from one's fellow men, an ancient Jewish sage taught, spells death (human not physical) for the individual. "Associate or perish" is an inviolable law of human life. The association is not only on the horizontal plane of fellowship with one's contemporaries but includes also the vertical relatedness to the history and culture which shaped them. Without the ample legacy granted to man almost at birth, human life would with each new generation revert to its earliest and most primitive form. We are truly "the pensioners of the past." Were the human past not accessible to us, we would, to take only the matter of speech and therefore of thought, be reduced to little more than gurgles, roars and bleatings—the only sounds we could develop in the short span of a single life.

Culture pours the accumulated strivings, experience, advances, creations of many lifetimes, extending over many centuries, into the life stream of the individual and group presently existing. In the capacity to conserve the accretions of past centuries and to communicate them to new generations, perhaps more than in any other single factor, is to be sought the human differential which sets man apart from and above all other known creatures.

No man can escape the past. The most modern "avant garde" individual cannot dispense with it, and he continues to reveal in his own acts and views its presence and influence. Men have on occasion resented and renounced the past and have sometimes made of their negation the dominant philosophy of their life. The very force and vehemence of their revolt betrayed the hold it had upon them, since only that which deeply enters and colors one's life can excite such intensity of rejection. But there are many who recline peacefully in the maternal arms of the past and suckle contentedly at its breast. Some absorb it without the awareness that every time they speak a word, read a line, shake hands with a neighbor or cast a vote, they are paying tribute to it.

History, however, does not always move in peaceful channels or pleasant paths. There are social, political, cultural upheavals, conflicts and revolutions in history, comparable to the tidal floods, earthquakes and volcanic eruptions in nature. Discontinuities appear on the landscape of human life that have their counterpart in the chasms and canyons of the earth. Yet even in such eventualities the past preserves its hold upon men. Only the upsurge of a wild barbarism in society would attempt to erase it, and then only to return to a more distant and primitive past.

In such periods of stress and disruption, man is forced to face the past consciously, to evaluate and select from it that which appears to be precious and relevant. Such a time is now upon us. Much of the uncertainty and confusion in contemporary life is a consequence of our unwillingness or inability to face our past with adequate wisdom and insight. Uncertain of our past, we are confused about our present and are thus alienated from ourselves. The fantastic rapidity of change in our society and its continuing acceleration make the very ground under us quake with frantic movement, appearing to dissolve all the stabilities upon which we formerly built our lives. There is left for some moderns no terra firma upon which to stand.

In the absence of a tradition modern man stands denuded before the immediate. Without a past he is the captive of each solitary moment or day or year. Uprooted he sways with every impulse and fugitive whim. His existence disintegrates into episodic and disparate clots, and his life is an improvised series of unrelated variations. He is uncertain and apprehensive because the pin-point in time which he occupies is isolated and solitary. The eminent American critic Van Wyck Brooks has observed: "No one in this country has roots anywhere; we don't live in America, we board here; we are like spiders that move over the surface of the water." Of Franz Kafka, the writer who reveals modern man in all his nakedness and dark pathos, one critic has written, "he suffered the pangs of the absent God in his life."

Contemporary man is at sea because he has lost his sense of history as well as his relatedness to it. He tends to forget that while human history may seem to take a new turn, man never really starts over. In reacting against the encrustments, irrelevancies and follies of the past, he turns his back upon its entirety and has thus cut himself off from a vital resource of strength, continuity and wisdom.

Modern man can find a way toward wholeness by examining the abundant bequests of the past reverently but critically and with mature independence. He can suffuse his life with its echoes without losing his own voice in the process. It cannot be either-or, either the past or the present. It must be both in behalf of the future.

The necessity for creative confrontation with the past is perhaps most evident in the case of the modern Jew. For him centuries of history have been telescoped into a few decades. The transition was abrupt, sharp and not infrequently shattering. Several millions of Jews alive today were born in a pre-modern, pre-technological, pre-scientific and pre-democratic era. In their own life-span they have been hurtled across a chasm of time which took their non-Jewish peers four hundred years or more to negotiate. Where others could walk leisurely, the Jew was compelled to leap instantaneously. One day he lived in the medieval world, the next in the modern West.

In the face of such upheaval casualties were inevitable. The holocaust which engulfed him in apocalyptic darkness stirred apprehension and anguish. From the depths questions arose within him, doubts, denials, resistances. It was not easy to continue to believe in the teachings of the Jewish tradition that the cosmic order rests on justice, that the Jew has a role in the redemption of mankind, that every individual is invested with high and inalienable dignity.

The rise of the State of Israel helped bolster his sagging faith. The

Jew as victim began to appear as the Jew the builder, the fighter, the pioneer. Here was a place on the world map called Israel, built by Jews, governed by Jews, regenerated by Jews. "Jewishness" now meant a people, a national will, a language and literature, self-respect, a calendar, a geography, a history, a faith, an ethic, memories, hopes, a vision of redemption. Out of this "concreteness" might come once again a word meant for all mankind. From it too there might radiate to Jews in other lands influences to revitalize and stimulate the will to Jewish knowledge and the Jewish way of life.

Other powerful forces have also been at work. Today, half the Jews of the world live in the free world, in a society which, with increasingly minor reservations, welcomes their integration into its economy, culture and civic life. As fascinating interests and opportunities outside of the Jewish community invite the Jew, his relationship to his tradition is once more at stake. Living in the heart of the open society, like his non-Jewish peers, he too is the object of forces that act as dissolvents of tradition, blunt the sense of history and continuity and assault the distinctive and the singular.

The Jew as an individual has won equality and freedom. What will now happen to the individual as Jew? The history of the Jew in the world is that of a marginal man. Will the history of the modern Jew be that of a marginal tradition? Will the larger circumference of his naturalization into the modern world obscure the smaller circle of his Jewish affiliation?

Or will the modern Jew remaining fully rooted in his particular tradition bring into his broader life as a member of society the liberating perspective, the passion for study, the ethical sensitivities with which that tradition is so richly seeded? Will he know now how to integrate his membership in the larger society with a Jewish identification of meaningful depth and intensity? Will he learn how to blend his historic culture as a Jew with the new learning in philosophy, science, art, and with the prevailing forms, habits and daily preoccupations? Will he be able to communicate the faith of his fathers with such devotion and understanding that it can serve as the faith of his children born under the new dispensation of freedom and integration?

One could hardly draw up a catalogue of more perplexing problems than those which the contemporary informed and affirmative Jew is called upon to grapple with, if not to resolve. The comment of André Malraux is profoundly pertinent: "A heritage is not transmitted, it must be conquered."

This publication presents a sampling of the many elements of the Jewish past that have shaped the Jewish present and the issues that grow out of the modern Jew's confrontation with them. Implied in its very title are both affirmation and challenge. The affirmation is that the Jewish heritage is significant and enriching and, like all great heritages of the human spirit, relevant and modern. The challenge is to transmute the many yesterdays incarnate in the experience of the Jew into the resource for fashioning a multitude of tomorrows.

The creative artist drawing from Jewish springs of inspiration can, without losing his universality, gain in fervor, depth and vitality. The thinker and scientist, incorporating into their thought a tradition in which reason, learning and the adventurous quest for truth are prominent, need sacrifice neither intellectual integrity nor philosophic breadth. The professional, student, businessman or worker can within the framework of his life in the modern world enrich and invigorate his "humanity" through a positive relationship with a tradition instinct with a universal vision, a faith in the meaning and worth of life, a high estimate of man, his dignity and potentiality.

What the prophet Obadiah counselled many centuries ago—"Let the house of Jacob possess its inheritance"—applies with equal pertinence to all men who would be creative users of the past.

I

Portraits and Definitions

The Jew—A Profile

Morris Adler

There has been much discussion in recent years as to what is the authentic and proper definition of a Jew. With diffidence I submit the following profile as the distillation of one man's lifetime encounter with Jews.

A JEW is a man who never sees another Jew for the first time. Even at the initial meeting when two Jews are introduced to each other, a vague consciousness of having met before is stirred in each. Memory cannot with any definiteness specify or describe the time, place or nature of the earlier association, but that there has been such an association seems assured. It may have been at Sinai, where, according to tradition, all the unborn souls of the children of Israel were assembled.

When a Jew travels abroad and sits in the lobby of a hotel he responds with radar-like awareness to the presence of other Jews and warms at their nearness. His sense of strangeness and of remoteness from home is immediately blunted or dispelled. He may or may not strike up an acquaintance with those he recognizes as fellow-Jews. The knowledge of their proximity suffices.

A Jew is often a man who speaks with animation and apparent determination about his desire "to withdraw to a farm and live in rural seclusion" but who rarely implements his intention. The Jew is not built for isolation or withdrawal. He is the product of a history that has always stressed community life. Though he may envy his holiday fishing guide, who seems to live a carefree solitary existence, he could no more emulate him than fly to the moon on his tallit.

A Jew is a man whose historic experience of dispersion leads him to feel fully strange nowhere in the world, yet whose enforced wanderings for many centuries make it difficult to relax in a feeling of complete at-homeness anywhere. No one enjoys a farther-flung kinship than he, and hence distant places are tinged with a degree of familiarity. On the other hand, memories deeply imbedded in his subconscious alert him to the most subtle tensions in the familiar surroundings in which he lives.

A Jew is often a man who is practical and knows full well the value and power of those realities which offer stability, security and status. He appreciates the role possession and position can play in himself and his family with protections and satisfactions. Yet however

3

calloused and corrupt he may become by such a view, he never entirely frees himself from a gnawing conviction that the ultimate values lie elsewhere. An occasional experience, a moment of rare illumination agitates that conviction into greater vitality. He may feel haunted—however briefly—by a sense that his accomplishments, though impressive in a conventional way, do not reflect the abidingly important goods of life.

A Jew is a person who has been raised by the collective experience and memory of his group to a sustained compassion for all in the world who suffer deprivation and oppression. This concern for the submerged transcends his political affiliation or economic grouping. It is a permanent aspect of his outlook and does not flicker on or off with his own changing fortunes. Hence it is that Jews are to be found in extraordinary proportions in movements devoted to social betterment, liberation and human welfare.

And in the Jew there functions deep in his marrow a respect for learning. Even if an individual Jew may himself have been denied a higher education, he will always bemoan this lack and will strive unrelentingly to make it possible for his children to advance in their schooling. This regard for knowledge is the fruit of a long history in which learning was a prominent factor in the life of a people deprived of political power and social acceptance. Learning for the Jew is not an acquisition by which to ornament one's life. Indeed, the Jew feels that without it, life is not fully life.

When Is a Jew Not a Jew?

Israeli Court Decision

*On December 6, 1962, the Israel Supreme Court ruled that
Brother Daniel, a Jewish-born Roman Catholic monk, now
residing in Haifa, could not be called a Jew under the Law of
Return. This decision was a step toward clarifying the term
"Jew" and its relationship to "Israeli" and "convert." Some of
the questions with which the case deals are:*
—Is anyone who calls himself a Jew automatically Jewish?
—Does a Jew who converts to Christianity remain a Jew?
—Can one be a Jew and a Christian at the same time?
—Is it true that "once a Jew—always a Jew"?

The decision of Supreme Court of Israel
in the case of:
OSWALD RUFEISEN, Petitioner
vs. MINISTER OF INTERIOR, Respondent

The High Court, by majority decision, discharged an order nisi
calling on the Minister of Interior to show cause why he should not
grant the petitioner an immigrant's visa under the Law of Return,
1950.

The petitioner, Oswald Rufeisen, known as Father Daniel, a
Carmelite monk, was born in Poland to Jewish parents. He was
brought up as a Jew, and belonged to a Zionist youth movement.
During the Nazi occupation of Poland he rescued hundreds of his
fellow-Jews from the Gestapo in legendary feats of daring. While hiding from the Nazis in a Catholic convent, he was converted to Catholicism. In 1945, when the war had ended, he joined the Carmelite Order
in the hope that he would be transferred to one of its monasteries in
Palestine. In 1958, he was finally permitted by the Order to come to
Israel. In his application to the authorities to be allowed to leave
Poland he gave as his reason for wishing to go to Israel the fact that he
was a Jew, albeit of the Catholic religion, and had always wanted to
live in his ancestral homeland.

His application to leave was granted only after he had renounced
his Polish nationality. He was given a travel document similar to those
given to all Jews emigrating from Poland to Israel.

When Father Daniel arrived in Israel, he applied for an immigrant's

5

certificate and declared himself a Jew for purposes of registration in the Register of Inhabitants. He was not registered as a Jew and his application for a certificate was refused by the then Minister of Interior, Mr. Bar Yehuda, who wrote to him saying that in his own personal opinion he was fully entitled to be recognized as a Jew but that he was powerless to grant him the certificate he sought in view of a decision of the Government that only a person who in good faith declares himself to be a Jew and has no other religion should be registered as a Jew. Mr. Bar Yehuda concluded his letter to Father Daniel with the apologetic explanation that a Minister may not act according to his own lights and concepts but must act within the existing lawful limitations while continuing to press for their amendment.

Father Daniel eventually petitioned the High Court for an order nisi which was granted him.

Section 2 of the Law of Return provides that every Jew has the right to come to Israel as an immigrant, while section 3(a) lays down that "a Jew who has come to Israel and subsequent to his arrival has expressed his desire to settle in Israel may, while still in Israel, receive an immigrant's certificate."

The opinion of the majority by JUSTICE MOSHE SILBERG

We were confronted at the outset, in this most unusual of cases, with the psychological paradox that we felt that we, as Jews, owed the petitioner, an apostate, all our admiration and thanks. For this man risked his own life times beyond number, during the dark days of the holocaust in Europe, to rescue his brother Jews from the very jaws of the Nazi beasts. It was difficult to envisage how such a man could be deprived of his life's aspiration to identify himself completely with the people whom he loves and to become a citizen of the country of his dreams as of right, as a Jew, and not as an accepted stranger.

But we dared not allow our appreciation and gratitude to betray us into desecrating the name and content of the concept "Jew." For the petitioner has asked no less of us than to ignore the historical and sanctified meaning of the designation "Jew" and to forget about those spiritual values for which we were massacred at various times during our long exile. If we were to accede to his request, the aura of glory and splendor surrounding our martyrs of the Middle Ages would pale and vanish without trace and our history would lose its continuity and begin to count its days from the beginning of the emancipation, after the French Revolution. No man is entitled to demand such a sacrifice from us, even though he have as much to his credit as the petitioner.

The concrete question before us is what is the meaning of the term

"Jew" in the Law of Return, and can it be so interpreted as to include an apostate who regards and feels himself to be a Jew despite his religious conversion? The answer to this question depends on whether the "Jew" of the Law of Return must be given a secular or a religious meaning. The ruling opinion in Jewish law is that an apostate remains a Jew for all purposes save (perhaps) in certain marginal cases which do not affect the general principle. This may be seen from the writings and opinions of leading Talmudic commentators and scholars [*from whom Justice Silberg quoted extensively*]. In other words, according to Jewish religious law a Jew remains a Jew, for all practical purposes, even though he may deliberately change his religion.

But here comes the rub—if rub there be. The term "Jew" in the Law of Return does not refer to the "Jew" of Jewish religious law, but to the "Jew" of secular law. For the Law of Return, with all its historical importance, is a secular law which must be interpreted in the light of the legislative purpose behind it. And as this law is an original Israel law, drafted in Hebrew and not translated, its terminology must be given the ordinary everyday meaning which the ordinary Israel man in the street would attach to it. And the ordinary everyday meaning of the designation "Jew," in my opinion, undoubtedly precludes the inclusion of an apostate.

It is not my intention to preach any religious philosophy or to take up the cudgels for any specific view on what path the future development of the Jewish people should follow. I am well aware of the fact that opinions on this score are divided into all the shades of the spiritual rainbow. There is, however, one thing which all Israel has in common: we do not wish to sever ourselves from our historical past or deny our heritage.

Whatever the theological outlook of a Jew in Israel may be—whether he be religious, irreligious or anti-religious—he is inextricably bound by an umbilical cord to historical Jewry from which he draws his language and his festivals and whose spiritual and religious martyrs have nourished his national pride. An apostate cannot possibly identify himself completely with a people which has suffered so much from religious persecution, and his sincere affection for Israel and its people cannot possibly take the place of such identification.

At this stage Justice Silberg went on to emphasize, in order to obviate any misunderstanding, that he had no quarrel with the modern Catholic Church nor did he intend, for one moment, to compare the petitioner with some of the notorious apostates of the Middle Ages. But he felt that the petitioner's personal decency and humanity did not affect the question of whether he was entitled to arrogate to himself the designation of "Jew."

As to the petitioner's Counsel's argument that only a theocratic State could refuse to recognize the petitioner as a Jew, it is completely unfounded. Israel is not a theocratic state as it is not religion but the law which regulates the daily life of its citizens, as witness the very case under consideration. For if religious doctrine were to be applied to the petitioner, he would be regarded as a Jew. On the other hand, the fundamental conception that "Jew" and "Christian" are a contradiction in terms is something which is unreservedly accepted by all, as can be seen from the quotations submitted by the State Attorney. Furthermore, the healthy instinct and urge for survival of the Jewish people also contribute toward this general conception, as experience has shown that apostates are eventually lost completely to the national family tree for the simple reason that their children intermarry. As for the petitioner's Counsel's frivolous remark that there is no fear that the petitioner's children would intermarry as he is a monk sworn to celibacy, it was, to put it euphemistically, not in the best of taste.

The order nisi should be discharged.

Justice Moshe Landau and Eliyahu Many concurred with Justice Silberg.

Minority dissenting opinion by *JUSTICE HAIM COHN*

I agree with Justice Silberg that according to Jewish law an apostate remains a Jew. I agree also that the Law of Return should not be construed according to the rules and principles of interpretation generally applied by the courts of Israel to enactments of the Knesset. I wish to add that, in my opinion, all the traditional religious tests applicable to the question of who is a Jew are irrelevant to the interpretation of the Law of Return. For the law of Israel is that religious laws are applicable to matters of marriage and divorce only. It is the demarcation line between obligatory law and non-obligatory religion which symbolizes the rule of law and ensures the citizen of his fundamental rights.

I agree also with Justice Silberg that we cannot cut ourselves off from our historical past nor deny our heritage. I would add that a basic law such as the Law of Return, which translates from theory into practice the "I believe" of the State, demands an interpretation in keeping with the background to, and the idea behind, the establishment of the State of Israel. But I cannot agree that such an interpretation of the Law of Return demands that the petitioner be denied the right to be called a Jew.

It is true that throughout our history tens of thousands of our people have been tortured, slaughtered and burnt at the hands of the

Catholic Church. Not even the latest catastrophe of the Nazi holocaust can wipe out the memory of those murdered in the Crusades, in the Inquisition, and in pogroms, ostensibly in the name of God.

If I have correctly understood my honorable colleague, he cannot, for historical reasons, ever envisage the possibility of regarding as a Jew a person who has allied himself to the Catholic Church, even though this Church is no longer, either in theory or in practice, an enemy of the Jewish people. I for my part, however, feel that change and progress are the very breath of historical continuity. The establishment of the State was a revolutionary event in the history of dispersed Israel. If in the Diaspora we have been either a tolerated or persecuted minority, in our own State we have become a nation like all other nations, standing on our own feet. This revolution demands a change in values and in attitude, a revision in our *galut* thinking.

The petitioner is knocking on the gates of the homeland which, in the words of the Declaration of the Establishment of the State, were to be "opened wide to every Jew," and the Minister of the Interior refuses him entry because he is wearing the robes of a Catholic priest, because a cross hangs from his neck, and because he declares that he believes in the faith of the gentiles. If, however, he had packed away his robes, hidden his cross and concealed his faith, the gates would have been opened wide to him and no one would have barred his way. One cannot but recall, in this context, those Jews (Marranos) who only by concealing their Jewishness had found the gates open to them.

Times have changed and the wheel has come round full circle. Should a man who regards Israel as his homeland, who is passionately imbued with the desire to live here, but who is a Christian by religion, be denied entrance through the portals of the country for that reason only? Should the State of Israel, which is "based on freedom, justice and peace as envisaged by the prophets of Israel," behave toward those returning to her shores as the Catholic monarchies behaved? And did not the prophets of Israel envisage that the gates will be opened so that "the righteous gentile who keepeth the truth may enter in"?

If it had not been for the petitioner's faith, no one would have denied that he is a Jew. But only because he is of another religion does the edict of the Government make him a non-Jew. I, for my part, am willing to accept only the first part of the Government's definition of a Jew: a person who in good faith declares himself to be Jewish. I am not prepared to accept their proviso that he must not have any other religion. In the absence of any objective yardstick in the Law of Return itself, there is no alternative but to assume that the legislator wished to make do with a subjective yardstick: that is that the right to return to Israel is reserved to every person who declares he is a Jew returning to his homeland and wishing to settle there. The addition of the demand that that person should have no other religion goes beyond the powers of the Government and is therefore invalid and not binding.

For all the above reasons, the order nisi should be made absolute. *By majority decision, order nisi discharged without costs. Decision given on December 6, 1962.*

Israel, a Religious People

Eugene B. Borowitz

ON EACH of his recent visits to the United States David Ben Gurion brought a simple and a single message: "Come to Israel. Those of you who wish to fulfill yourselves as Jews, those of you to whom Jewishness is significant, come and settle in our ancestral land."

What Ben Gurion offered is palpable enough. He held out to us the possibility of living in a real Jewish community, where almost everyone is a Jew, and where Jewish life is culturally predominant. Children learn Hebrew as naturally as they grow. The Bible is a school text-book and a national craze. Schools and factories close not only for Shabbat and the High Holy Days but in celebration of every Jewish holiday. In short, it is an atmosphere in which by simply living in one's neighborhood and being concerned with issues that confront the community one is already involved in Jewish affairs. Here is normal, natural Jewishness, without the strain, the unnatural tension that characterize the effort to be a Jew in the Diaspora.

Yet only if we understand the thinking that lies behind this challenge can we know how to respond to it. The critical question is: Who really is "Israel"? What are we Jews, and where may true Jewishness be lived?

It was not by chance that the founders of the Jewish state in what was once called Palestine chose as its name "Israel." (Or, "The State of Israel"—the ambiguity is important!) But is Israel primarily that political entity which exists today on the soil of what was once called Palestine? The word "Israel," at least for many centuries, had no political connotations. To this day when Jews rise to the Shema— "Hear O Israel"—they are not calling to a state. They mean the Jewish people as a whole. From Ben Gurion's and the classical Zionist's point of view, Israel is the Jewish people centered around its state, in its land. Jewishness, therefore, is sharing in the life of that people, now happily revivified and restored in the full dimensions of land, language and political form. The logical deduction from this point of view is indeed Ben Gurion's invitation. A full Jewish life can be lived only on the land and in the State—and Jews who have merited to reach this happy day in Jewish history should take advantage of an opportunity denied their ancestors for centuries.

But are we prepared to say that Israel the State is the same as Israel the people?

Jewish history itself would raise this question, even if Diaspora Jews did not. Are the past two thousand years of Jewish struggle and suffering, of creativity and consecration, meaningless? Were the Jews of those years, most of whom did *not* live on the land and did *not* speak its language, not authentically Jewish? Shall we dismiss as Jewishly insignificant the Golden Age both of Eastern and Western Islam, with their giants Saadia and Maimonides? Were Babylonia, Franco-Germany and Poland not truly Jewish in their varying cultural expressions?

Logic would require Ben Gurion to deprecate these epochs, and he has not flinched from doing so. He has said that the current generation of Israelis has more in common with what the Israelites felt at the time of Joshua than it has with the Jews of the past two thousand years. Yet it is difficult to believe that, as the generations go by, scholars and even ordinary Jews living in the State of Israel will not study the products of Diaspora Jewry and find them not just the archeological remains of truncated Jewish living, but meaningful expressions of Jewishness that still speak to them. Time and security will surely permit them to recognize that there was an authentic Jewish existence not only outside of the land but in other languages as well.

Our first response to Ben Gurion's message is that two thousand years of Jewish experience have demonstrated the possibility of Jewishness outside the land. While our conditions today may pose special problems in living up to that standard—and special opportunities as well—the past indicates to us that at least our position has Jewish legitimacy.

A second approach may be taken by examining how our tradition conceived of the Jews. How have Jews thought of themselves down through the ages? It is true that the source material from which we have to draw today is biased. It is all religious material which therefore understands the Jews in this special way. But the very word "religious" needs to be understood in its unique Jewish connotation. The Jewish tradition depicts the Jewish people, particularly in its beginnings, as a people like all other peoples. They are described for us, without hesitation, as a small Semitic group like so many others in the Near East, subjected to the same vicissitudes as other peoples, carried by the normal streams and patterns of history, with the same difficulties in establishing their monarchy and watching it break up, being subjected to the domination of larger powers, of watching economies come and go, expand and contract. The Jews are a folk, an ethnic entity, a land-language-literature-destiny group like so many others in human history.

Only one thing is different about the Jewish people. But the difference is decisive. This people has the fortune, the grace, the uniqueness of having found God. Not a god, but God—the one and only God. And it found Him first. And it has been influenced by this discovery-revelation ever since.

We cannot limit the impact of this discovery-revelation to Moses and the Jews traveling through the wilderness. After Moses a prophetic tradition arose that continued not for a few generations but for centuries; new voices were speaking in a fresh way, evoking the same original depth of divine understanding found earlier in the Mosaic leadership. Thus, over the course of centuries, the life and character of the Jewish people changed. While it began as a people like all other peoples it has become different from all other peoples; it is the only people whose peoplehood is determined by its knowledge of God. The tradition says that what gave the Jewish people its unique character was its relationship with God. This relationship it called *b'rit,* the covenant, the promise, the pledge, the pact between God and this people which had come to know Him.

This Jewish people, having found Him, pledged itself through all of history to remember God and serve Him. It might do what every other people does in history—work, marry, create, migrate—but in and through and underneath the life of mankind was its unique motif— the service of God in loyalty to a pledge.

This people promised to remind mankind of Him by living by His law until they all came to know Him too, to acknowledge Him as God, to live by His law. In turn they believed that God would protect, watch over and eventually vindicate this people "in the end of days."

This was not a guarantee. Individual Jews, families or even communities inevitably might suffer and die. But the people would survive and be vindicated in their service to God.

The people of this covenant is Israel—and it is always truly Israel when it lives up to its obligations under that covenant.

This is the special sense of the word "religious" when applied to Jews. It necessarily has a double meaning—folk *and* faith, community *and* covenant, people *and* pledge. It must not disturb us that Protestantism and Catholicism do not know this intimate fusion of people and religion. The history of religions knows many other social forms for organizing religious groups, and we have no reason not to accept our own. Indeed, without it we could not have survived as we did, nor yet hope to fulfill the covenant in history.

Contrast this traditional view (though expressed in modern terms) with that held by Ben Gurion. By his understanding of Jewishness it would be possible to have an "Israel" which claimed to be the heartland of all the Jewish people and which might at the same time be completely atheistic. This is no idle fancy. The overwhelming majority of Israelis today is not religious in the generally accepted sense. Most Israelis feel no particular attachment to Orthodox Judaism, which is almost their only religious option. Since their Jewishness is national by his definition, they do not have to be Jews by religion. Is it too far-fetched to inquire whether conversions to Christianity would still leave their Jewishness unimpaired?

Clearly "Israel" is not simply to be identified with a particular state. Israel is the community of the covenant wherever it is and under whatever circumstances.

With emancipation from the ghetto, a unique and bewildering division has come upon Jewish life. Before, there was no division between what it meant to be a member of the people and, at the same time, to take on its religious commitment. Every Jew was a religious Jew and a member of the Jewish people at the same time.

But since his admittance to the modern world, the Jew has faced the problem of identifying himself in some form which is deemed both modern and acceptable in terms of contemporary government. The Jews of the Western world chose "religion," and to be a Jew today in the Western democracies is to be a member of a "religious" group.

But the Jews of Central and Eastern Europe could not follow this path. Their emancipation had to take a different form, for in their states and with their religious leadership "religion" was not a means of entering modern times and contemporary culture while still remaining Jewish. They therefore identified themselves as a nationality, a group united by land and language, and perhaps by ethos as well. In a nationality one might be religious if one wanted—a concession to Jewish history and practice—but the dominating factor of what it meant to be a Jew was to be a member of the Jewish nation, preferably in its own land.

This deep and unfortunate cleavage in Jewish life, forced upon us not of our own will but by the differing societies in which we found ourselves, still determines, in large part, the confusion in communication between the American Jewish community and its Israeli brothers.

If the Jews are the covenant people, the people of the pledge, how does that help us to understand the Jewish place, value and significance of the State of Israel? To begin with, it should provide direct religious motivation to be a Zionist. The oldest, most authentic form of living out the covenant was setting up one's own community on one's own land, establishing a society which would show God's kingdom in action, which would be a model for the rest of mankind. That, after all, is what the Torah directs the Jews to do.

Today, we can see in the State of Israel a magnificent possibility of living out the covenant. A Jew who is deeply concerned about his Jewish religious responsibilities might very well say to himself that he ought to spend his life creating that indigenous covenant community of which so much of the Bible speaks. From this religious point of view there is not only good reason for building, supporting, strengthening and understanding the State of Israel, but there is also motivation for *aliyah* as well. Ben Gurion is not altogether without justice.

But if this is our criterion, we also have to judge the present State of Israel by it.

It is not enough for Jews to build a state. The covenant calls for Jews to be not just a people like all other people, but a people with a Messianic mission. While Ben Gurion accepts this Messianic obliga- tion, no voices rise from other leaders in the State of Israel, most conspicuously not from the younger ones, that this is indeed their people's task. But if this is not the task, then there is no more, indeed in a way less, Jewishness to be found in such a "normal" State of Israel than in an "abnormal" Diaspora existence which is made aware of and accepts the religious commitments of our people. Only when the State of Israel seeks to be Zion, when nationalism becomes indeed Zionism in the siddur's centuries-old, hallowed, Messianic sense, does it evoke and command a special sense of Jewish respect and concern.

This is the continuing contribution that the Diaspora Jew can make to his Israeli brother. He can remind him of the religious roots from which he sprang, of that other part of his Jewish heritage which he may be inclined to forget. Out of our spiritual experience, both our failures and successes, as well as with our means, we can aid, strengthen and encourage those tendencies within the State of Israel which seek in their own way to develop the religious spirit implicit there.

After all, how can a people long read the Bible without becoming religious? It would be difficult to be concerned with the prophetic imperatives, standards of righteousness and justice without sooner or later coming to wonder why. And when a people is willing to sacrifice to bring in its brothers from all over the world, to subject itself to all forms of austerity, to feed the hungry, clothe the naked, plead for the widow, judge for the orphan, such a people is close to God.

The most important point still needs to be made. Life in the State of Israel is not the only genuine way of expressing the covenant or of living by it. The last two thousand years of Jewish history, seen in proper focus, testify that there are other modes of being an authentic Jew. In many geographic, political and social circumstances Jews have found it possible to live by the covenant and thus to be recognizably and legitimately Jewish.

How extraordinary a prospect opens up if we visualize the American Jew, now groping for a sense and style of Jewish living, accepting for his life the conclusion that we are indeed the inheritors of a promise. What if, like other generations in the past, we American Jews could, in sincerity, pledge ourselves to the task which our people have carried on historically and which we will do our best to bequeath to our children to carry to the end of time?

If we would recognize this as our responsibility, if we would commit our means, our leisure, our intelligence, the power which has been given into our hands as American Jews, could we not build a Jewish civilization, culture and religious expression, a covenant community as Jewishly true as anything our tradition has yet known?

To be sure, it would be expressed in forms somewhat different from those Jews have used before. For no Jewry has ever been in the situation that American Jews are in.

In being part of the most technically advanced civilization known to mankind, we are required Jewishly to come to grips with the moral problems it is creating for man, most notably his dehumanization.

From this point of view—as hopeful as Judaism and Zionism themselves—it is important to have a Jewish state seeking its own roots, expressing itself in its own culture, holding high the standard of Jewish self-determination.

But it is also desirable, perhaps even necessary, to have another pole— Jews who live outside the State of Israel, who establish Jewish outposts in the great cultures, in the great societies of the times, who must therefore ever seek to understand the implications of their covenant in new terms to meet the new conditions.

The Jews in the small land of Israel will benefit by the cross-fertilization of ideas and concepts from those Jews who willingly take a precarious stand on the periphery so that they may transmit the lessons learned while participating in the driving movement of human history. And as these Diaspora Jews face the danger of being lost in their great societies, of bartering away their Jewishness for supposed gains, they can be reminded by that center in the State of Israel of what Jewish knowledge and Jewish self-respect imply.

Is it too much to believe that there are two ways of living out the covenant, each as legitimate as the other, each facing certain risks, each capable of fructifying Judaism?

If it is not, and if we can find the kind of Jew who accepts the covenant as his own, then the most important contribution we can truly make to the State of Israel and, more important by far, to the God of Israel, whom we both should serve, is to make Judaism alive and vital and significant here in the United States.

The Jew's Sense of History

Lion Feuchtwanger

WHAT is it that has distinguished Jews from all other peoples since time immemorial and up to this day? I believe that their most distinctive characteristic is an enduring vital awareness of a common history. More than four thousand years ago, this consciousness served to unite a few small nomadic tribes to such a degree that they were able to establish first one state and later on another. This same awareness held the Jews together during the dispersion of an almost two-thousand-year exile and has enabled them to establish, in our day, a third commonwealth.

There is no other people whose spirit and evolution are so saturated with history. All the deeds of the Jewish people have been wrought in the name of their history, and it is by this rather than by race that they have felt and still feel themselves to be united. The God of Israel is not a nature God but one who proves Himself by His deeds. He is the God of the perpetual flow of creation and action; His name is interpreted as "I Am Who I Shall Be." He is the God of history. Each experience Israel undergoes is viewed as a continuation of previous events and a link to future ones. No other people has felt so deeply the flow, the dynamics of what they experienced as a community; nor has any other people experienced as intensively the ever-enduring, the permanence within this eternal change. The waves roll on, the river remains the same.

No other people remembers its progenitors as often as the Jewish people in its confessions and prayers, none clings, even in deepest distress, so steadfastly to its faith in a blissful Messianic future. The entire land of Israel is full of history; there is no river, no mountain, no city where the fathers and their God have not manifested themselves. The faith of the Jews is based on historical events. The children of Israel have a covenant involving clearly defined reciprocal commitments: God continuously manifests Himself through Israel's history; Israel must prove itself in the same manner.

Accordingly, to the people of Israel, its chronicles are not a barren past, but endure and continue to be effective. Abraham's obedient readiness to sacrifice his son, the Exodus from Egypt—these are not events that occurred in legendary, primeval times. They are alive, contemporary, living within the consciousness of Jews, inspiring them in happiness, sustaining them in despair. Moses did not lead the Israelites out of Egypt some thirty-four hundred years ago—he liberates them on every fourteenth day of Nissan. Jerusalem was not destroyed nineteen hundred years ago; it is destroyed every ninth day of Av.

Mohammed termed the Jews "the People of the Book"—and rightly so. The Book, the Great Book, their Holy Scriptures, is the foundation of their existence. The skeleton of this book is the presentation and interpetation of the history of Israel.

The Israelites were the first people to write history. Long before the Greeks, they wove their traditions and records into one meaningful, continuous record. Their God had shown them the way, and all events depended on how faithfully they followed that direction and guarded the covenant. They felt they were "sons of the covenant," *b'nai b'rit*, and they continue to feel this. Each Jew is a link in the chain connecting the children of Israel with God, each one an instrument of the group's collective history.

History is the innermost nucleus of Jewish thinking and feeling. The first writer to present the chronicles of a people with continuity was that great poet and storyteller termed the *Yahvist* by critical Biblical scholarship. Three hundred years prior to Thucydides, he created his great historical work. Eleven hundred years before Plutarch, a man of genius, presumably Ebiatar, chancellor to King David, created the first rounded picture of an historical personage embedded in his time —namely, the story of the aging David and his successor. "Do not forget it," warns the Bible, as it tells of the malicious attack by King Amalek on the rear-guard of the Israelites; and day after day, for twenty-five hundred years, the Jew remembers in his prayers this little desert king and his malice.

The great poets connected their own tales with annals of their people. The magnificently simple tale of Ruth the Moabite, with its lesson of tolerance, was probably born out of the political experiences of the author who flourished around the time of Ezra. But the editor enhanced the credibility of the story by fitting it into the early history of his people and by making the heroine the ancestress of David. The masterful story of the miraculous rescue of the Persian Jews by Queen Esther avoids with high wisdom any pious interpretation, and indeed even avoids the mention of God. Instead it adorns the narrative with innumerable frills of Persian courtly tradition so that it appears to be a purely factual report, precise to the last detail. It is as organic parts of Israel's history that these great literary creations—the Books of Ruth and Esther—continue to live in the consciousness of the Jewish people.

Most Jews are named after great historical figures; this is calculated to remind them of their ancestors. Year in, year out, on every Shabbat, his forefathers' experiences are imprinted on the mind of the Jew so as to become a living portion of his being. To feel his historical roots brings the Jew profound tranquillity, and a firm belief in the inevitability and the meaningful course of all history. This faith has fortified him in times of distress so that he has preferred to suffer death rather than abandon the connection with his people.

The conviction of the Messianic mission is also anchored in Israel's history. The figure of the Messiah himself is not vague or utopian; it is firmly planted into the historical sequence of the generations: he is to be an offspring of David. It is Israel's mission to continue its great past undeviatingly until the Messianic age. In the earlier history of Israel there were Messiahs too, even genuine Messiahs, one of them being the Persian King Cyrus, who permitted the Jews to return to Palestine. The expected Messiah is to be the last and supreme one, and his age will mark the conclusion of a long preparation and development.

The proudest event of contemporary Jewish history, the establishment of the third commonwealth in the land of Israel, also has its source in this living consciousness of historical continuity. Had they listened merely to promptings of expediency, the men who were devoting their lives to the establishment of a Jewish homeland would have accepted the British Government's offer of Uganda; instead, they followed their sense of history, which pointed toward Zion, and Zion alone.

Like all their other concepts, the Jews' understanding of immortality is colored by this same perpetual consciousness of an historical mission. In the Bible the dying father summarizes the meaning of his life in a charge to his son, and entrusts him with the continuation of his life. "We have been enjoined to advance the work—but not to finish it." ("The work is not upon thee to finish, nor art thou free to desist from it" [*Pirke Avot* 2:21].) Isaac carries on the life and ideas of Abraham; Solomon fulfills the dream and work of David, building what David was not privileged to build, eradicating the father's enemies, and rounding out the kingdom. The dead live on in the deeds of sons and grandsons, and in their names. A sense of history prevails.

II

Backgrounds and Influences

The Bible as History

William F. Albright

OF ALL the sacred books in the legacy of mankind, the Hebrew Bible is one of the best sources for our knowledge of the past. In recent years, archeologists working in Israel and surrounding countries have dug up an enormous amount of evidence which proves the Bible historically accurate.

This does not mean that every detail can be taken as literally true, or that the traditional picture always agrees with the emerging archeological discovery. The scribes who copied the Biblical documents sometimes made mistakes; the scholars who studied those documents occasionally erred in their interpretation of the tradition; the transmitters of oral tradition re-interpreted and often misunderstood the material which they handed down from generation to generation. Despite this, however, we can say that the Bible is a unique literary legacy which faithfully records the background of past events and often the events themselves.

Up until very recently, an archeologist was thought of mainly as a kind of treasure hunter, always off to far-away places digging up ancient monuments, buildings and tombs. The Biblical scholar, on the other hand, sat in his library, poring over ancient Hebrew texts. Today the disciplines have met, and no Biblical archeologist can really function without a knowledge of Hebrew and many other related languages and a grounding in the sacred texts and history. Nor can any scholar's knowledge of the Bible be complete without a thorough understanding of recent archeological discoveries.

By digging up the Middle East and reconstructing the ancient world, archeologists have made us increasingly certain that the Bible is a living thing and not a gigantic fossil projecting from antiquity. As short a time ago as the beginning of the last century, we knew nothing about the background and world of the Bible except what little we could gather from contemporary Greek and Latin writers. None of the ancient languages of the countries adjacent to Palestine were understood, and a great silence surrounded the origins of the Scriptures. But today, thanks to our ability to decipher those languages and get at the meaning of texts, we can be certain that the Bible is a faithful record of events that really took place in human history and of persons who really walked the face of the ancient world.

For one thing, we have learned that the history and culture of Israel form part of the organic continuity of Western civilization, which

originated in the ancient Orient, spread westward in the Mediterranean basin, and then flowered in Europe. No philosopher of history
can henceforth dissociate the Bible from the historical evolution of our
own race and culture. With our new knowledge of the period preceding the Bible, we can better understand Judaism, which is itself the
resultant of many earlier forces and tendencies. All evidence points to
the unalterable fact that the Jewish tradition is a great unbroken
continuum of ideas.

Twenty years ago the archeological chronology of Palestine was in a
state of chaos, with scholars differing in their dates by centuries and
even by thousands of years before the second millennium. During the
past two decades, the findings of archeologists have dwarfed the sum of
all previous discoveries in their total impact on our knowledge of the
Biblical period. It is now possible to understand the Bible and place it
in its true historical perspective by setting events and cultures in their
correct time relationships.

To begin at the beginning, archeologists have demonstrated beyond
doubt the substantial accuracy of the patriarchal tradition. In contrast
with the peoples of Egypt, Assyria, Babylonia, Greece and Rome, the
Israelites preserved in the Bible an unusually clear picture of their
own simple beginnings and their early migrations, which plunged
them from their favored status under Joseph to bitter oppression after
his death.

We now know that, in accordance with the tradition of Genesis, the
ancestors of Israel were closely related to the nomadic and semi-
nomadic peoples who roamed over North Arabia and its surroundings
in the last centuries of the second millennium B.C.E. and the first
centuries of the first millennium. Genesis derives the ancestors of Israel
from Mesopotamia—archeological evidence agrees. We have extensive
documentation about the ancestral home of Abraham—Ur of the
Chaldees—as a highly prosperous commercial center. Trade was widespread, and caravans of merchants were among the commonest sights.
From excavations in the city of Mari on the Middle Euphrates we can
also speak emphatically about the existence at that time of Nahor (the
ancestral home of Rebekah's parents) and Haran, where Abraham and
his family settled after leaving Ur.

We know too that Abraham and the patriarchs were semi-nomadic
rather than nomadic—that is, though they wandered about with their
flocks, they also settled down and cultivated the land for long periods
at a stretch. In this way, the present-day Bedouins in Israel, who are
gradually becoming sedentary, are in direct line with the patriarchs.
In Palestine, towns were scattered thinly through the hill country and

settlements were largely restricted to the coastal plains and the broad alluvial valleys of Jezreel and the Jordan. The wanderings of the patriarchs are thus correctly limited by tradition to the hill country and the Negev. Records also prove that Egypt then controlled Palestine and southern Syria, and traded actively with them.

Though there has been a persistent effort by many scholars to discredit the Israelite tradition of a prolonged sojourn in Egypt before the time of Moses, evidence now exists of great Semitic influence during the Twelfth Dynasty, which had so increased by the end of the eighteenth century that the Semites had made themselves masters of a large section of Egypt. The Hyksos conquerors are now known to have been mainly of Northwest Semitic stock, closely related to the Hebrews. Jacob and Joseph were undoubtedly members of this group; names like theirs recur in Hyksos documents. The "king who knew not Joseph" and who oppressed the Israelites was probably a pharaoh of the New Empire, after the expulsion of the hated Hyksos from Egypt.

The account of the Exodus follows the actual geography of the area. Further proof of the historic accuracy of the Exodus story, which seems to have taken place around 1200 B.C.E., and of the journey in the region of Sinai, Midian and Kadesh can be supplied without great difficulty, thanks to our growing knowledge of ancient geography.

As for the Mosaic tradition itself, we have come to recognize that Israelite law and religious institutions tend to be older and more continuous than we had earlier supposed. Much of our documentation for this comes from the discovery, in 1929, of a thousand tablets known as Ugaritic, after the town of Ugarit in Syria where they were found. Hundreds of these were written in a dialect closely related to early Hebrew; when deciphered they turned out to be epic poems, some containing far-reaching parallels to the early poetic style of the Bible. This discovery was very important because it was the first time any significant literary remains had been found written in the same language as the Bible.

This earlier dating of Biblical material leads us to an important conclusion about Moses. It is clear now that he played a highly original role in sifting and organizing earlier Semitic and specifically Hebrew concepts and practices. Much of the Mosaic law is based on earlier patterns, which he ingeniously brought together. Moses emerges as a revolutionary figure, creating a great new code out of many divergent and fragmentary strands.

What then do we know about Moses as a leader? We can confidently assume that he was a Hebrew (despite Freud) who was born in Egypt and reared under strong Egyptian influence. All evidence emphasizes that he was actually the founder of the Israelite Common-wealth and the framer of Israel's religious system.

Thanks to an enormous increase in the archeological materials at our disposal since 1930, our picture of Canaanite history and civiliza-tion at the time of the Hebrew Conquest has become far clearer than it was. Excavations suggest that the Israelite invasion was not a charac-teristic incursion of nomads, who continued to live in tents for genera-tions after their first inroads. Neither was the Israelite conquest a gradual infiltration, as some modern scholars have insisted. On the contrary, it was rapid, widespread, devastating. This is conclusively demonstrated by recent findings at Hazor, in northern Israel, the site of a large and elaborate "dig" conducted in Israel, under Yigael Yadin, of The Hebrew University and formerly Army Chief of Staff. We now know, from the dates of pottery uncovered there, that the Israelites (led by an individual like Joshua) conquered Canaan in the thirteenth century B.C.E., within a short period. Later tradition recog-nized that the destruction of a large part of the Canaanite population saved Israel from a process of acculturation and assimilation which might have had far-reaching consequences.

In succeeding periods, Biblical tradition continues to be more relia-ble than other contemporary historical documents. Certain events re-corded in Kings, for example, have been found to be actually more exact than in contemporary Assyrian annals. Between 1200 and 900 B.C.E., the Israelites managed to attain national unity despite many hostile forces operating to break up the confederation. Saul (ca. 1020–1000), the first king, was unable, it is true, to advance beyond a loose political confederacy, mainly, as would appear from our sources, be-cause of innate weakness of character. But his successor, David (ca. 1000–960), effected a true unity, cementing it by a victory over the palace revolt led by his son Absalom in the later years.

David made no attempt, so far as we know, to establish a centralized state; the needs of his personal and official treasury were presumably met by the spoils of war and by regular levies from the conquered Canaanites, from the vassal border-states of Edom, Moab and Ammon, as well as from the tributary Philistines and Aramaeans. His son Solo-mon (ca. 960–922) soon found himself in a difficult position, since he undertook a series of elaborate building operations throughout the country and also established a powerful standing army of chariotry, both of which occur for the first time in the history of Israel.

Scholars used to belittle the tradition preserved in Kings, and re-duced Solomon's building operations to very modest dimensions. However, archeological discovery at Megiddo since 1929 has shown that a single one of his "chariot-cities" included well-constructed stables with cement floors for at least four hundred, and perhaps many more, horses. At Hazor and Tell el-Hesi (a famous site excavated by Egyptian archeologist Sir Flinders Petrie, working in Palestine at the end of the last century) similar installations from the Solomonic age have also been found. Moreover, Nelson Glueck's work at Ezion-geber on the Red Sea since 1938 has demonstrated that Solomon built an elaborate copper refinery there, covering an acre and a half and surrounded by a strong brick wall. Nothing like it is otherwise known from the ancient Near East—yet it was so relatively insignificant an enterprise that it is not even mentioned in our sources.

As we can see, the Bible arose in a world of Mesopotamian and Egyptian culture; streams of influence from the entire civilized world of that day poured into it and were transformed by the faith of Moses and the prophets.

In short, thanks to our recent findings, all handbooks on the Bible, early Christianity and the history of Judaism will soon be in need of drastic revision. With the help of archeologists, the Bible, in addition to being a literary masterpiece and the source of the Judeo-Christian religions, emerges also as an historical document bringing to life the early days of the Jews.

The Pharisees
Jacob B. Agus

THE Pharisees are one of the most misunderstood groups in all of human history. Unfortunately, the very name of Pharisees has for centuries been a principal source of misunderstanding between the Christian and Jewish worlds. To a Christian reader of the New Testament, the Pharisees combine in themselves all the vices against which Jesus protested. They stand for the shell of piety as opposed to its kernel, the shadow rather than the substance of faith. In the Christian stereotype, the Pharisees are hypocrites who know only the external rituals of religion; all their faith consists of cunning calculation, a smart bargain with the deity, while their spirit is cold and petty.

The typical Pharisee, in this view, is vain, puritanical and "holier than thou." When he comes to pray, he says, "O God, I thank Thee for having made me a perfect man, a saint." Faith consists of keeping accounts, accumulating disjointed merits by "hook or crook" on the black side of the ledger so as to be solvent religiously as well as financially.

What is the truth? Who really were the Pharisees? One of the three religious parties in Palestine during the second and first centuries B.C.E., the Pharisees were actually responsible for the foundation of Jewish law as it exists today. Because of the paucity of authentic Jewish sources of that period, it is difficult to determine their precise contribution. But we do know that through their labors Israel and Torah were welded into an indissoluble unity, and the synagogue was endowed with the capacity to assure survival of the Jewish people despite their loss of government, land and Temple.

The Pharisaic movement had a double character in that it consisted of both an inner core of scholars and the broad masses of the people. Jesus was himself a Pharisee, in the broad sense of the term, and many of the arguments between Jesus and the Pharisaic scholars were actually arguments inside Judaism, and, in fact, inside Pharisaism. In its strict sense, the term "Pharisee" stands for the inner core of teachers and pietists who undertook to observe strictly the laws of ritual "purity," to contribute the various priestly tithes, and to avoid the loose ways of the people.

The Pharisees were also teachers and preachers, interpreting the Law. Jesus was a popular preacher who shared the basic beliefs of the Pharisees concerning God's love for man and man's duty to love God with all his heart, soul and might. But he was also critical of some

Pharisaic leaders and their practices. He belonged not to the inner circle of Pharisaic society but to its outer popular fringe. Consequently, nearly all the debates were reported in the New Testament as though they had been held between Pharisees and non-Pharisees, whereas actually they took place within the broad belt of the Pharisaic movement itself.

The Pharisees differed from other groups in ancient Judaism. The Sadducees, for example, descendants of the High Priest Zadok, whom King Solomon had established in the Temple, were members of the controlling social class.

At the opposite pole were the Essenes, the people who shunned all worldly goods in their desire to serve God exclusively and dedicate their entire life to Him; in order to accomplish this, they seceded from the community and established strictly graded societies marked by severe and exacting disciplines. They regarded money as a major source of evil, believing that man cannot serve both God and Mammon. They gave up the pleasures and responsibilities of family life, adopting the communist principle of one for all and all for one. They had their meals in common, abided by strict "purity" rules, practiced charity, meditated on the Law and various mystic doctrines, and dedicated themselves to attaining the perfection of sainthood.

The Pharisees differed from both these groups. The word "Pharisee" derives from root words meaning "separation" and "interpretation." We do not know which meaning was primary and which secondary. Although they were a sect, the Pharisees aimed to transcend sectarian bounds and to make the entire people over in their image. To be a *haver* (friend or member) meant to belong to the inner Pharisaic group and to abide by certain ritualistic rules. In the first place, one had to refrain from eating non-kosher food. The *haverim,* members of the inner society, could not eat in the house of an ordinary Jew (*am ha-aretz*) whose ritualistic piety was uncertain.

In addition, the *haverim* had to abide by certain laws of ritual purity. The first principle was to wash the hands before and after each meal. A man was not permitted in ancient times to study Torah or participate in prayer until after he had gone through his ritual ablutions. This extreme emphasis on ritualism grew out of a worthy spiritual purpose—namely, the attempt to endow all Jews with the dignity of priesthood. All should stand directly before God and all should undertake the sweet yoke of living in accord with priestly regulations. Thus the Pharisees, in their eagerness to stress the principle of equality, called upon all Jews to abide by the priestly rules of "purity" and ritualistic holiness.

Pharisaic democracy was not abstract, doctrinaire or utopian. It insisted that all are equal potentially; the ideal of equality is made a "reality" only if people accept the duties as well as the rights of the nobility. They preached a form of democracy in which all men were urged to emulate the aristocrats of the spirit. They sought to level up rather than to level down. And they began their uplifting efforts by themselves assuming extra duties and burdens. This very effort led the scholars to refrain from entering into close contact with the masses, whose food they could not eat and into whose homes they could not enter.

But this inner circle of pietists and scholars represented only one side of Pharisaism. The other side was oriented in the opposite direction, toward the community. The Pharisees saw it as their mission to separate themselves from the people in order to educate and lead them toward prophetic inwardness and priestly meticulousness. In their societies, the Pharisees cultivated the virtues of learning and piety so as to be worthy of teaching the rest of the people. Though they separated themselves initially, they returned to the people later; they elevated themselves in order to elevate the masses.

There was undoubtedly considerable ill feeling on the part of the ordinary people toward the *haverim,* though this resentment was mixed with sentiments of admiration and reverence. In the Talmud, which was composed during a much later period, we find echoes of such mixed feelings. For instance, Rabbi Akiba said, "When I belonged to the ignorant masses before I became a scholar, I said to myself, 'Give me a scholar, and I will tear him to pieces, like a fish.'" In other words, there was a certain hostility between the inner society and the masses because the latter resented the separation of the former, even though the Pharisees presumably isolated themselves in order to guide and instruct the people.

The Pharisees separated themselves for the sake of bringing all the people to God. They did not associate with sinners, not out of pride, but in order to maintain an inner core of dedicated people within the community. If there can be said to be one dynamic impulse within Pharisaism, it is the ambition to raise all men and women to the level of priests and prophets. They aimed to build an ideal community of God—dedicated people, first within their inner circle, then within all Israel, finally within all mankind. While they recognized that the Essenes were very pious—observing the Sabbath so strictly that they did not move out of their seats from Friday evening to sunset on Saturday—the Pharisees criticized their isolationism. "He who separates himself from the community denies the one God," they said.

The Pharisaic movement reflected the inescapable paradox of all organized religions—tension between the feelings of humility and sim-

plicity, between pride in learning and the mitzvot. The worth of ceremonial observances cannot be taught without getting some people to
believe that ritual is the substance of faith. For some, however, ritual
became a substitute for genuine spirituality. For others, the divine
choice of Israel out of the nations had its counterpart in the choice of
their tight little group out of all Israel. There were those among the
Pharisees who, regarding self-segregation as the best safeguard of their
superiority, sought to raise even higher the barriers within Israel and
between Israel and the nations. Some of the Rabbis went so far as to
declare that every gentile was "impure" from birth, and wanted to
separate Jews from gentiles by establishing barriers against social
mixing.

The liberal rabbis among the Pharisees, the School of Hillel, did
not favor such barriers. They protested when some of the ultra-
Orthodox laws were adopted, but the mood of hostility toward the
Roman oppressors was then too strong to be resisted. A vicious circle of
self-segregation, contempt for gentiles, persecutions and pogroms was
set into motion. Every now and then riots took place between Jews
and Greeks, between Jews and Syrians, between Jews and Romans—
the Jew felt himself surrounded by enemies—with the result that
segregationist barriers were raised higher and higher, and a mighty
though invisible ghetto-wall was established, despite the protests of
those Pharisees who were humanists and did not want such separation.

Nor were all Pharisees alike insofar as their attitude toward Roman
power was concerned. Some were Zealots, who brought about the destruction of Jerusalem, the burning of the Temple and the devastation
of the Holy Land. Wherever the Zealots were dispersed as captive
prisoners or as slaves in Alexandria, in Cyrenaica, in Cyprus, they
stirred up rebellions. They launched desperate revolts even when
there seemed to be no earthly prospect for success. The Zealots—on the
whole—were Pharisees in that they believed in the Oral Law, the
sanctity of the individual, divine providence, the resurrection of the
dead, and the hope of Messianic redemption. But they were also
"activists," believing that it is man's duty to fight, hoping and praying
for divine help, but assured that God would determine the outcome in
His own due time.

Along with the Zealots, the Pharisees also included in their ranks
"quietists," who were, for the most part, the sages of the academies.
The latter generally followed the principle of sole reliance on divine
providence. If God wants man to suffer he must suffer; but he has to
accept life as it is, and must not go banging his head against a wall. In
the fifth chapter of the Babylonian Tractate of Gittin, where the sages
discuss the great tragedy of the destruction of the Temple, they preface

their remarks with the following phrase: "Happy is the man that is always afraid." Of course, they referred primarily to "fear of God," but they also favored ordinary physical fear because people who are afraid will not take unnecessary chances. They taught this doctrine because they had seen the tragedy the Zealots had brought upon the Jewish people.

Once the rebellion was started, however, the Rabbis joined the people. Only when there was no longer any hope did Rabbi Johanan ben Zakkai seek escape; his disciples carried him out of the city in a casket, and there he was able to establish an academy at Jamnia (Yavneh).

The Pharisees were animated by high ideals. They separated themselves from the people in order to teach them. They insisted on the divinity of the total human personality—every human being was sacred, not only in his soul, but in his body as well. Hence, the Law which they molded sought to stamp every phase of life with holiness. They believed that God directs the affairs of men in love and justice, and that all men are free to choose between good and evil. A man's character is his fate. The reality of human freedom meant that man was designed to be "a partner in the work of creation." Even the Law was human in interpretation and divine in inspiration. They believed that all accounts are settled in the world-to-come, following the resurrection of the dead.

Though the Pharisees taught the principle of the inwardness of the divine service of God, this principle was overlaid with so many other teachings that it was easily forgotten. The Pharisaic rabbis taught the discipline of the Law as norms for the community as a whole. They also taught that the Law in itself is not enough: it provides the foundation and undergirding of communal life, but the individual must aim beyond it toward the summits of spiritual perfection.

When Jesus said, "When a person smites you on one cheek, turn the other cheek," he was uttering a Pharisaic teaching. "When a person is insulted and does not insult in return, when he is hurt but does not hurt others, of him does the verse say, 'Those who love God are like the sun when it shines in its mighty power.' " Similarly, when Jesus spoke of the inwardness and simplicity of serving God, he was giving utterance to a Pharisaic ideal. His argument was directed against the abuses of Pharisaism and its excessive emphasis on external forms of ritual.

Apart from faith in his own Messianic character, Jesus demanded a way of life that derived from the conception of love as self-sacrifice and self-giving. To love God is to give up all things for His sake. The Pharisaic scholars bequeathed to us a different and much more fruitful conception of love—love as the building of "the kingdom of heaven" on earth. When a man loves, he builds; such is the healthy expression of a man's love toward wife and family. To the Pharisees, the love of God and man consisted in the building of an ideal community wherein justice and charity, dignity and piety would prevail. A community is based on a structure of laws and on ideals that loom "beyond the line of Law." Hence, their emphasis on deeds, on an endless climb toward perfection, on works of piety and the labor of learning.

In sum, the legacy of Pharisaism is to be sought in two directions— in the life of the Jewish people whose character and destiny they fashioned, and in a pattern of ideas that is universal in scope. For within Christianity, as within Judaism, the prophetic-priestly aims of Pharisaism found expression from time to time in movements of religious rebirth, reasserting the high destiny of every human being in the sight of God and the "priesthood of all believers." Our modern, democratic way of life is a translation in social terms of the Pharisaic philosophy and its ethical teachings.

Teachers of the Midrash

Judah Goldin

IN THE Western world and in some parts of the East too, the Bible enjoys a distinction which no other literary classic has ever enjoyed, at least up to modern times. Until about the beginning of the middle of the eighteenth century, the Bible was the only book familiar to both learned and simple people, old and young, rich and poor. While Plato, Dante and Shakespeare were read either by scholars or devotees of literature, the Bible was consulted by the John Bunyans as well as the John Miltons.

The Bible's popularity was in large measure due to its inherent qualities. However, it proved to be every man's book because, in addition to its own virtues, it had the good fortune of falling into the hands of some of the most extraordinary teachers that we have ever had in history, men who understood how to translate a book from parchment or paper into the common property of all kinds of people.

This "translation" was carried out through an activity called Midrash, a word derived from the Hebrew root meaning literally "to seek out," "to investigate," "to search." In classical Hebrew times men spoke of seeking out, investigating, searching the Bible, the only book which they deemed worthy of meditating day and night. Indeed, some of the sages looked with disfavor on the multiplication of books. Of the making of books there is no end, Ecclesiastes said somewhat satirically.

The first-century sage Hillel urged men to devote themselves to the one book, namely, the Scriptures, because he, like all the ancients, was truly convinced that in this book one could find everything—laws of purity and impurity, the historical narrative of the Jewish people, philosophy, prophetic words, and comfort in the time of tribulation. Like the lover who tries to read between the lines of a letter from his beloved, wondering about what she did not say or why she did say what she said at a particular place, the sages felt that the words of the Lord called for constant attentiveness and exploration. As the sages explored the words of the text, they found ways of interpreting and explaining its meaning; and since their minds were far from lazy, a wealth of interpretations soon developed. Ceasing to mean merely the investigation, Midrash came rapidly to mean the explanation and interpretation of Bible text.

It is impossible to say when Midrash first began. But from about the fourth century B.C.E. on, this activity of searching out and interpreting Scriptures gathered momentum and became one of the dominant activities of intellectual and spiritual life in Palestine, continuing in each generation, one teacher stimulating another disciple, one father stimulating his son, and the son his son in turn. Possibilities occasionally overlooked in one generation were discovered in the next.

Originally the Midrash was not a literary performance, but simply a study activity going on orally in academies, homes, synagogues and in the market place. This oral exercise took on such huge proportions that ultimately people felt that they simply had to record at least in shorthand some of these interpretations and explorations. That is how some of the Midrashim were recorded in the texts we have today. But it is through the Midrashic activity that the Scriptures became known by the common people.

Actually, it was a religious obligation for everyone to know the Bible. In ancient times, however, learning its content was no easy matter. Today, if we read a book on page 12, let us say, and we want to look up something on page 512, it is a matter of seconds to turn the pages forward, and then back again. But in earlier times, readers were dependent on scrolls; if they were reading in the Book of Genesis and suddenly wanted to refer to Deuteronomy, it was a clumsy matter to keep rolling the scroll forward and back for reference.

Furthermore, since Scripture was accepted as the record of God's revealed will, no one could allow himself the luxury of skipping even a sentence or a section, let alone a whole narrative. In reading the record of God's will, how could anyone say that a sentence was trivial? Or that a certain passage was really of secondary significance? Did the Lord speak superfluously? Was what God ordained something of only tertiary importance? Obviously not, and hence it was important to learn everything contained in the scroll. But how in the world could an ordinary person do this, if the scroll itself was so difficult to handle physically as well as intellectually? Here is where the Rabbis used the Midrashim to teach and interpret the Scriptures for the people.

How did the Midrash function? In the Biblical story of Moses and the burning bush, for example, the passage opens with the verse that Moses was a shepherd. One might of course ask what difference it made how Moses earned his living, and probably many people did. But the Rabbis were convinced that if Scripture had gone to the trouble to include this detail, it must be important.

They proceeded therefore to tell the following story: Once upon a time as Moses was taking care of his father-in-law's flock in the wilderness, one of the lambs ran away. Moses pursued but could not overtake the lamb until it reached a stream, where it began to lap up the water. Moses said, "So it was because of thirst that you ran away. How utterly obtuse of me." He waited for the lamb to drink, and then carried it all the way back to the flock, saying, "I do not want you to walk back. You must be worn out from so much running." All this time the Holy One, blessed be He, had been observing from on high what was taking place, and He cried out, "Moses, you have proven yourself a shepherd of the flock of flesh and blood. By My oath, you shall be the shepherd of My folk Israel."

That is the whole story, a story of utter simplicity and without affectation. Yet it taught a very important lesson. By means of this anecdote the Rabbis were able to impress upon an entire congregation the criteria for leadership, describing the leader as someone who takes care of his flock, even the least of it, someone who can recognize that sometimes he overlooks the needs of that flock and then he must have the humility to say he was wrong and make amends, even as Moses did by carrying the lamb back in his bosom. In addition, everybody who sat in that congregation remembered ever after that Moses was a shepherd.

In another verse, one of the prophets says, "For I desire mercy and not sacrifice." Toward the end of the first century or the beginning of the second, a homilist or teacher explained this verse to his congregation by recalling an historic incident. Once upon a time, he said, Rabbi Joshua ben Hananya and his teacher Rabbi Johanan ben Zakkai, walking in the streets of Jerusalem, came to the spot where the Temple had formerly stood. Joshua burst into tears.

"Why are you weeping?" Rabbi Johanan asked. To which Joshua replied, "How shall I not weep when I see the place where the sins of our people used to be atoned, now lying in ruins?"

"Do not weep," said his teacher. "We now have a means of atonement as effective as this—acts of loving-kindness, as it is said by the prophets, 'For I desire mercy and not sacrifice.'"

In this Midrash, as in the one described above, the skillful teaching is noteworthy. By taking a verse of Scripture, and by using a little history and a great deal of pedagogy, the homilist introduced a radical doctrine into the religious culture, namely, that Judaism for its survival does not depend upon the cultic-sacrificial system. Secondly, he taught the noble idea that acts of loving-kindness, though they have nothing ritualistic about them, have an atoning power; and who is not in need of atonement? Above all, nobody in that congregation could ever forget the verse, "For I desire mercy and not sacrifice."

Another Midrash deals with the passage in which God tells Abraham, "Go, leave your father's country, leave your father's homeland, and walk on in the direction which I am going to point out"; Abraham obeyed by moving on, bag and baggage, with "all the souls they had made." The Rabbis wanted the people to remember the extraordinary accomplishments of Abraham, so they commented on the peculiar expression, "all the souls that they had made." How is it possible to make a soul? If all mankind collaborated and tried to create as much as one mosquito, they could not do it! Yet here we speak of souls being made. This passage teaches, the Rabbis concluded, that Abraham and Sarah used to bring people close to the divine, or as we might say in our terms, toward the realization of the truth. One who draws a person toward the divine is regarded as though he had actually created him.

What happened as a result of Midrash was that a series of lessons was impressed cumulatively in a deep way upon the congregation, the people, old and young. These impressions in the course of time literally became second nature to the folk Israel.

Thus the Rabbis went through the Scriptural text, deriving, searching out and explaining. Through the Midrashim the Bible became in the course of time the book of the entire Jewish people, and this people became in turn the People of the Book.

Judaism's Central Affirmation

Morris Adler

THE Rabbis boldly crowned a single verse out of the 5,845 in the Torah with a significance shared by no other. Though it is not set apart in any way within the text, the Rabbis presumed to suggest that in this one verse was concentrated the essence of the whole, almost as though it were the divine will to condense the entire tradition to a single affirmation without diminishing its spiritual intensity and comprehensiveness.

This verse found its way into the prayer book—that most widespread and most frequently invoked volume in Jewish literature—and was likewise accepted almost spontaneously as the key sentence of the tradition by all subsequent generations. The prayer book appears in a diversity of versions, Ashkenazi, Sefardi, Italian, Yemenite, Moroccan; in more recent times it has undergone revision, sometimes drastic, to conform to changing conceptions and interpretations. But no group or individual editor has deleted or modified this sentence.

The reference can be to no other verse than "Hear O Israel: the Lord our God, the Lord is One." The Shema (six words in Hebrew) was usually the first line of the tradition a child was taught even before he had mastered fully the power of speech; they were the words on the lips of martyrs led to their death. Who can estimate their impact upon the consciousness and spirit of a people?

The Shema also symbolized the unity of that people in its far-flung dispersion as well as the kinship of the various elements that united in a single community. Spanish and German; East European and Oriental; poor and rich; learned and untutored; young and old; proud and humble—all were as one in the devout and deeply emotional response which the Shema elicited.

In addition, the Shema suggested the basic content of Jewish belief, to which all else is commentary. It has often been pointed out that Judaism avoided a dogmatic formulation of its creed. No single statement of belief is binding upon all. Leo Baeck describes this aspect of Judaism as follows:

> The dominant form of Judaism always remained that of a religious philosophy of inquiry, a philosophy which produced method rather than system . . . There was always tolerance and even indifference toward modes of expression; it was the idea which was held to be central. Judaism, and the Jew as well, re-

tained an unorthodox air; they neither would nor could rest in the easy comfort of dogma . . . Jewish religious philosophy had as its purpose the constant renewal of the content of religion by means of which it was best preserved and protected from the deadening rigidity of formula. It was a religion which constantly imposed upon its adherents new labors of thought.

The absence of dogmas, however, must not be regarded as a lack of specificity and conviction. Judaism is no amorphous or characterless tradition. It developed around a cluster of ideas which were open to interpretation, to be sure, but which could not be stretched to limits that would dissolve the core pattern. Judaism has an inner integrity which sets bounds upon flexibility. This inner integrity—which in another context might be called its theology, though Hebrew thought and language possess neither the term nor the idea—is concisely and powerfully expressed in the Shema.

Though it embodies the main theme of Judaism, the Shema is not presented as the grand climax of a subtle intellectual process of speculation and thought. For the Jew did not reach his belief in God and his conception of the nature of God as the result of a painstaking rational investigation, moving step by step from observation to conclusion to conviction. Intuitively and with surging moral imaginativeness, the Hebrews first conceived of God as a Reality and Presence and only subsequently refined and organized that overwhelming initial insight by the use of reason. In the words of the non-Jewish scholar, A. B. Davidson: "The Hebrew thinker came down from his thoughts of God upon the world rather than rose from the world up to his thoughts of God." Thus, the Shema is not a theological formula involving only the mind but an impassioned declaration claiming total commitment.

The Shema is the leit-motif of the Jewish faith, its dominant and central theme. In order to prepare the worshipper for the great affirmation, the Rabbis, wise and creative teachers that they were, introduced two benedictions to precede the Shema (*B'rakhot* I:4). In the first benediction, known as the *Yotzer* prayer, God is Creator of the world, Source of the universe, its immensities and power, its galaxies and intricacies, its design and order. This theme recurs in many forms throughout the Bible.*

Creation is not a completed event, permitting God to withdraw into a cosmic vastness outside of it. Creation is a dynamic, ongoing process. The *Yotzer* benediction includes one of the most profoundly religious

* See Psalm 19, Psalm 104 (which is read in the synagogue on Sabbath afternoons during winter), and Job 38.

ideas: "Who daily in His goodness reneweth continually the work of Creation."

The modern Jewish philosopher Hermann Cohen suggests the richness of this concept:

> Thus this idea of the continuousness of renewal was made into a cardinal doctrine whereas the older doctrine of creation at the beginning receded in importance. Every day is a new beginning. The mystery of the initial creation is assimilated into the daily miracle of renewal and consequently into that of the maintenance of the world. The Creator becomes the Maintainer. The uniqueness of God fulfills itself in divine Providence.*

The second benediction introducing the Shema, known as the *Ahavah Rabbah,* opens with the words: "With abounding love hast Thou loved us O Lord our God, with exceeding compassion hast Thou revealed Thy mercy unto us." Israel Abrahams has described it as "one of the most beautiful in the liturgies of the world." God is not only the omnipotent Creator, the just Ruler; He is also the loving Father who reveals Himself through His Torah to His children. He instructs His children in the "law of life." He is near and ever-present. In this prayer God's compassion and mercy are invoked, not through a plea that His children be granted material gifts and personal safety but that they be imbued "with the will to understand, to discern, to hearken and to learn, to teach and to obey, to practice and to fulfill in love all the teachings of Thy Torah." We ask for the spirit that will lead men to obey His commandments and to serve Him with an undivided heart. The concept of God as the Teacher and Father of mankind is celebrated more fully and more fervently than that of God as Creator.

Once our awareness of God as the mighty Ruler and the loving Teacher has been renewed and deepened, we are prepared to recite the Shema with a better understanding of its meaning.

"Hear O Israel: the Lord our God, the Lord is One" (Deuteronomy 6:4). (The newest translation of the Torah by Jews offers the rendering "Hear, O Israel, the Lord our God, the Lord alone.") Both the Oneness and Uniqueness of God are projected, opposing every type of polytheism, dualism, pantheism. God is Creator but is apart from His creation; God is One not in an arithmetical sense alone but primarily in His unduplicated singularity. He is above and beyond and yet in His providence near and accessible. With this declaration, say the

---

* Quoted in *Contemporary Jewish Thought,* B'nai B'rith Book Series, Volume IV, p. 138.

Rabbis, we accept the kingship of God and subject ourselves to His rule.

The Shema, "the watchword of Israel's faith," is followed immediately both in the Torah and in our prayer book by the paragraph:

> And thou shalt love the Lord thy God with all thy heart and with all thy soul and with all thy might. And these words which I command thee this day, shall be upon thy heart; and thou shalt teach them diligently unto thy children, and shalt talk of them when thou sittest in thy house, and when thou walkest by the way and when thou liest down and when thou risest up. And thou shalt bind them for a sign upon thy hand and they shall be for frontlets between thine eyes. And thou shalt write them upon the door posts of thy house and upon thy gates.

An attempt to bring these words closer to our contemporary idiom has been made by Rabbi Shamai Kanter.

> Now hear this Israel, the Lord our God, the only One. You shall love the Lord your God with all your mind, and with all the strength of your whole being. And these words, I command you today, shall remain in your heart. Repeat them over and over to your children. Talk about them when you sit in your house, when you travel, when you lie down to sleep, when you get up. Wear them proudly, like an insignia on your shoulder; like a crown upon your head. Write them on the doorway of your private dwelling, and upon the entrance to your courts of public law.

These words are directed to all the people. Upon each devolves the duty of fulfilling the law of God; to each is given the privilege of relating himself in love to God. Man, created in the image of God, is endowed with an innate capacity to respond to God with his total being. Man's faith in and love of God are to be reflected in every aspect of his life, to govern and inspirit every relationship and activity.

Religion is an attitude and a quality which should permeate the whole of life. To love God and obey His words has implications for man's conduct within his family circle; his relationship to neighbors; his responsibility to the community; his practices in his business and at his leisure; in the daytime and at night. Incumbent upon the man of faith too are his own study and the training of his children. Thus human existence even in its most mundane and physical aspects becomes transposed to a higher key of sensibility and spirituality, mirroring the reality of a God who loves us and expressing the love we have for Him. Man is not and cannot become pure spirit. His body and physical needs have their place and are not to be suppressed. "The Torah," say the Rabbis, "was not given to ministering angels." It was given to men. Its purpose is to release all the potentialities for being human that flow from man's kinship with God.

The second section of the Shema (Deuteronomy 11:13–21) voices the Jewish belief in the dependability of the moral order of the universe. To be sure, virtue is not always rewarded in immediate sequence. The large plan of God's universe is fulfilled through obedience to God's will. Wickedness and evil are a rebellion against the moral character of the cosmos and will ultimately reap the whirlwind of punishment. One cannot contravene the laws of nature with impunity; health is the fruit of conformity to them. In the moral realm, one who breaks the basic principles will be broken by his own misdeeds.

While the rewards enumerated in this section employ a terminology suited to an agricultural society, the principle that they establish remains valid. Man's vision may be too limited to see the operation of this law of reward and punishment and his life-span too brief to recognize its unfolding ("For a thousand years in Thy sight are but as a day that is past and as a watch in the night" [Psalm 90])—yet the law is as certain and as inexorable as any natural law discovered by science.

But reward and punishment are not to be taken as the motivation for man's conduct. They are included to suggest the view of the universe that derives from the belief in a God of justice. Early in the Mishnah of the *Ethics of the Fathers* we are told, "Be not like servants who serve their master for the sake of reward, but be like servants who serve their master without thought of reward" (I:3). Ben Azzai said, "the reward of mitzvah is mitzvah (since one good deed paves the way for another) and the reward of sin is sin" (IV:2). In a moral world man cannot escape this iron-clad consequence; he stoops to wrongdoing and diminishes himself; he rises to virtue and fulfills himself.

The third paragraph that forms part of the *Kriat Shema* (Numbers 15:37–41) deals with one specific Jewish practice, namely the wearing of *tzitzit* or fringes. The law of God which we accept as part of His divine sovereignty is supported by the cosmic order which He created and is evidenced by the life of personal holiness which each individual is to lead. Man, frail, mortal, exposed to temptation from without and to the pressure of impulses and drives from within, is asked to follow disciplines (symbolized by the *tzitzit*) which will keep him from following the dictates of a rebellious heart and from straying in obedience to his senses—"that ye may remember and do all My commandments. Be ye holy unto your God." The last sentence in this section makes reference to the fact that God brought Israel out of Egypt in order that He might "be your God. I am the Lord your God." Thus liberated, man is free to live on the highest level of his potentialities.

The Shema is concluded with a benediction known as the *Geullah* prayer. He who has guided His children in the past and has brought them forth from bondage into freedom is the promise of that redemption of Israel and all mankind which will climax man's history. The last syllable of recorded time is not futility; the last accent of human history is not destruction. Redemption of man from his own and the world's evil will not spring into being as a sudden and unrelated culmination. It will reveal, so that all may see, the deep divine design which underlies all of life as it ushers in the day "when all the earth will be filled with knowledge even as the waters cover the sea" and "the Lord shall be King over all the earth; in that day shall the Lord be One and His name One."

The Mystic Quest

Louis Jacobs

KABBALAH is the name given to the mystic trend in Jewish life and thought. The word is derived from a root meaning "to receive," i.e., the tradition of mystic lore *received* from earlier generations. Though its subject matter is identical with that of all mystic experience, Kabbalah includes more than the testimonies of Jewish mystics; the term embraces the whole body of speculation on mystical themes.

Kabbalah is frequently divided into the theoretical and the practical. Theoretical Kabbalah is the discussion and exposition of theosophical themes, of the nature of the deity and His relation to the world. Partly oral and partly recorded in scores of books, this aspect finds its best-known expression in the *Zohar*.

Practical Kabbalah is the attempt to influence the higher worlds in man's favor by a kind of white magic, which makes use of various combinations of divine names and of certain spiritual and ascetic exercises. In the popular view the Kabbalist is rather like the medieval alchemist searching with his potations and magic circles for the elixir of life.

Because, however, the practical Kabbalah was generally frowned upon by rabbinic authorities, its practitioners were few and their activities rarely enjoyed full respectability. Theoretical Kabbalah, on the other hand, long enjoyed a place of significance as a legitimate esteemed branch of Jewish thought.

The Kabbalists believed that the basic doctrines of the secret lore were revealed to its initiates from the earliest times; the medieval *Book of Raziel* claims to be a work brought to Adam by the angel Raziel to comfort him after he had been driven from paradise and to save him from further sin.

From the point of view of modern historical scholarship it is possible to trace Kabbalist tendencies differing in emphasis and expression according to the temperament of their authors and the influence of the non-Jewish environment. According to Gershom Scholem of The Hebrew University, whose massive researches into Kabbalah have created a new "school" of Jewish learning and whose *Major Trends in Jewish Mysticism* is by far the best work on the subject, Kabbalah enjoyed several major periods of development.

The first important period (aside from numerous mystic passages in the Bible) extends from the first century B.C.E. to the tenth century C.E. The two chief themes discussed by mystics of this period are the accounts of the Heavenly Chariot given in the first chapter of the Book of Ezekiel and of the Creation in the early chapters of Genesis.

The second period took place in Germany in the twelfth and thirteenth centuries, when a group of men (called the Pious) introduced a new regimen of severe asceticism and uncompromising altruism through which they endeavored to attach themselves to God's holiness and greatness. They believed that the saint was endowed with magical powers so that he could influence events; they also held that in order to repent, the sinner is obliged to mortify his flesh in order to counter-balance with self-inflicted torments whatever pleasure is present in the sin.

A great name of this period in the history of Kabbalah is Abraham Abulafia (b. 1240), who developed the idea of *devukut*, "adhesion" or "cleaving" to God, a perpetual "being with God," in which the mystic's every action and thought are concentrated on the divine will. In spite of his great influence on later writers, Abulafia's writings did not appear in print until the nineteenth century.

The golden age of Kabbalah was ushered in with the "discovery" of the *Zohar* (*Light*) by Moses de Leon at the end of the thirteenth century, who alleged that this work was a description of mystical discussions held in the circle of the second-century saint and miracle-worker R. Simeon ben Yohai, and became the Bible of Kabbalism to be quoted together with the Talmud and Scripture itself as revealed doctrine. Scholem's argument that the bulk of this work, at least, was actually written by Moses de Leon himself is now accepted by most experts in this field.

The *Zohar* is a collection of books, generally published in five volumes, three of which are *Zohar* proper—a running commentary to the Pentateuch—a fourth volume called *Supplements to the Zohar* (*Tikkune Zohar* or *Tikkunim*) and a fifth volume, *The New Zohar* (*Zohar Hadash*). Written in a highly colored, somewhat artificial Aramaic, the latter is difficult reading even for the seasoned Talmudist familiar with the Aramaic language. In style, language and content, the *Zohar* is an esoteric rather than popular work.

In post-*Zoharic* times the greatest name in Kabbalah is Isaac Luria, the Safed teacher who died at the early age of thirty-eight (in 1572) and whose doctrines are recorded in the writings of his disciples, particularly those of Hayyim Vital. Safed rather than Jerusalem became the center in Palestine of Kabbalistic learning after the expulsion of the Jews from Spain. It was favored by the mystics because of its elevated situation and the clarity of its air, which were especially suited to the contemplative life. Moreover, the reputed graves of famous mystics of the past were situated around the town.

Luria and his teacher Moses Cordovero were among the prominent members of a mystic brotherhood in Safed which also included Joseph Karo, the author of the *Shulhan Arukh,* and Solomon Alkabetz, author of the hymn *Leho Dodi,* " Come my beloved," now recited in synagogues all over the world but originally composed for the Safed brethren who would go out into the fields on the eve of the Sabbath, clad in white, to welcome the "bride Sabbath."

We learn from a diary kept by Cordovero that members of the circle would visit the graves of the ancient mystics to discourse on the profundities of Kabbalah in the belief that proximity to the last resting places of the great masters powerfully assisted in generating mystic ideas. These peregrinations were known as *gerushim,* "divorces" (i.e., from hearth and home), in order to pursue mystic truth.

The mystic brotherhood in Safed was composed of men of austere piety. Among the moral precepts to which they pledged themselves, they were enjoined to make their hearts the abode of the divine presence by banishing all profane thoughts and concentrating on holy things. They were not to speak evil of any creature, become angered or curse anyone. They were to speak only the truth, never allowing falsehood to escape their lips.

They were to behave in a kindly spirit toward their fellow men, even the transgressors. They were to confess their sins before every meal and before retiring. Only Hebrew, the sacred tongue, was to be used in their conversations with one another. Each night they were to sit on the ground and mourn the destruction of the Temple and weep over the sins which postponed their redemption. No day was to pass without the giving of alms.

The Lurianic school had as its chief aim the bringing of the Messiah by a series of spiritual exercises. Through their performance the "sparks of holiness" scattered in all created things could be returned to their source in God when the redemption of the world would be at hand. The Lurianic doctrine had great influence on Orthodox Kabbalists, but it also resulted in various types of mystic heresy, the most notorious of which was the pseudo-Messianic movement of Sabbatai Z'vi in the seventeenth century. From the idea that the "sparks of holiness" have to be reclaimed before the Messiah can come, it was but a step to the belief that these sparks resided even in forbidden things and that only by committing these sins could all the sparks be returned to their source. When Sabbatai Z'vi embraced Islam, some of his followers still believed in him, confident that this too was part of the process of redemption.

The apostasy of Sabbatai Z'vi and the shameful excesses and immoralities of many of his followers produced a fierce reaction against the study of Kabbalah. It was not until the Hasidic movement, founded by Israel Baal Shem Tov in the eighteenth century, that the subject once again came into its own. The Hasidim succeeded in making Kabbalist ideas accessible to many, even to the untutored. Indeed, Hasidism has been described, not without justice, as "mysticism for the masses."

The Lurianic ideas were adopted by the Hasidim in a new way. The sparks of holiness, they taught, could only be reclaimed by joy. Asceticism was not only unnecessary, it was positively harmful. By partaking of the things of this world in a spirit of consecration, the Hasid believed that he brought about the union of the higher and lower realms. Hasidic teachers were fond of quoting the old legend that Enoch was a cobbler and in sewing the upper to the lower part of his shoes in a spirit of devotion he united the world of the spirit with the world of matter!

The central problem of theoretical Kabbalah is how the good and perfect God could have produced this world of imperfection. How account for the finite world seeing that God is infinite? How did the limited and confined emerge from the limitless and the unbounded?

Two different answers are given in Kabbalistic literature (though actually the Kabbalists themselves look upon the two doctrines as supplementary rather than contradictory). The first is the *Sefirot,* derived from the *Zohar,* holding that God created the world by means of ten emanations. The second doctrine of *Tzimtzum* (from Lurianic sources) explains that God withdrew "from Himself into Himself" in order to leave room for the world to emerge.

The doctrine of the *Sefirot* (the best interpretation of this word is "numbers," though some connect it with the word "spheres") is based on the neo-Platonic distinction between God as He is in Himself and God as He reveals Himself. God as He is in Himself is completely unknown. He (though the Kabbalists prefer "It" to denote this aspect of the deity, i.e., that to which no name or description can be applied) is called *En Soph,* the One without Limit. *En Soph* is so far above human comprehension that nothing may be postulated of it; there cannot even be a reference to It in the Bible. *En Soph* is limited to the universe by means of ten emanations, the highest of which—the crown—represents the emergence of a will in that which is above willing. This, in turn, becomes a will to create, which gives rise to further emanations, until the emergence of sovereignty, which represents the divine power as manifested in the world.

This doctrine was a threat to pure Jewish monotheism, and, over the centuries, produced many opponents of Kabbalistic teaching. But the Kabbalists themselves never tired of emphasizing the essential unity of *En Soph* and the *Sefirot*. A favorite illustration of this unity is that of water poured into colored bottles. The water remains the same though for the moment it partakes of the color of the bottle into which it is poured. Another illustration is that of the soul of man which, though a unity and "hidden," manifests itself in different ways of thought, feeling and action.

This latter illustration points to one of the most characteristic implications of the *Sefirot* doctrine. It is a cardinal principle of Kabbalah that the world of the *Sefirot* is mirrored in man, i.e., every aspect of man's life here on earth has its counterpart in the upper worlds. This is how Kabbalah understands the Biblical teaching of man as created in God's image. In the world of the *Sefirot*, for instance, the *Sefirah* (singular) of Loving-kindness denotes divine mercy, while the *Sefirah* of Power denotes divine justice. The light of God's mercy is too strong by itself, and would cause all things to merge into nothingness, absorbed by it, were it not controlled by the *Sefirah* of Power.

But power, on the other hand, needs to be tempered with mercy if the world is to endure. Both loving-kindness and power merge, therefore, into a third *Sefirah* known as Beauty. When man creates beauty here on earth he is, in fact, engaging in the same process in miniature which takes place in the upper worlds, for beauty is the result of harmony established between the unduly severe and the sugary sentimental.

It follows that the life of man is of the utmost significance for by reproducing, in a spirit of sanctity, the life of the upper worlds he causes the divine grace to flow down from above. Special attention is called to the sexual life of man. The *Sefirah* of Loving-kindness, for instance, is called "masculine" (because it represents the *active* principle at work, as it were, in the upper worlds), the *Sefirah* of Power is "feminine" (representing a *passive* principle). This symbolism is applied to various other *Sefirot*. When man and his wife are united in a spirit of consecration they both mirror the cosmic process and influence it. Hence even those Kabbalists who lived a severely ascetic life generally led a normal sex life as Jewish tradition enjoins.

The *Tzimtzum* doctrine starts from the premise that God withdrew into Himself in order to leave room for the world. (According to Kabbalah, all creative activity is the result of withdrawal, as in the concentration of the thinker, the freedom from distraction of the artist, the attempt of the teacher to put himself in his pupil's place.) This withdrawal left a primordial "empty space" into which the world and time and space as we know them could emerge.

But the withdrawal cannot be complete, for nothing can exist without God. A thin "line" of divine light penetrated into the "open space" in order to sustain creation. At first, however, this light was too strong and shattered the vessels containing it. Only after this "breaking of the vessels" could the finite world emerge. As a result of the "breakage" there are "holy sparks" in all created things. The task of man is to live in the material world in a spirit of consecration and so reclaim the lost sparks and return them to their Source. The Messiah will come when this work of restoration is complete.

This *Tzimtzum* doctrine received a refined interpretation by Hasidism, particularly the *Habad* school. (*Habad* is formed from the initial letters of *Hokhmah*, "Wisdom," *Binah*, "Understanding," *Da'at*, "Knowledge.") As its name implies, the *Habad* movement stressed intellect rather than emotions, believing that authentic mystic feeling is the fruit of profound contemplation engaging the whole mind. In this view *Tzimtzum* or "withdrawal" does not really take place in God but only appears to do so. This finite world is, in fact, from the standpoint of God, only an illusion. In reality only God exists.

In modern times many of the basic assumptions of Kabbalah have been challenged, and it is therefore exceedingly rare to find an orthodox Kabbalist today. Perhaps the last great practicing Kabbalist was the late Chief Rabbi of Palestine, Abraham Kuk, who made a valiant attempt to interpret modern scientific and technological advances in the light of mystic teaching, and infused certain Kabbalistic insights into his Zionist philosophy of "the Return." Rabbi Kuk, for instance, welcomed evolutionary theories, pointing out that the idea of a development from the lower to the higher is basic to the Kabbalistic outlook. But most students of Kabbalah today are critical, objective scholars who use modern methods of investigation to elucidate the problems connected with this branch of Jewish thought.

On the other hand, there is simultaneously a growing interest among present-day thinkers in mysticism. With the breakdown of dogmatic systems and the weakening of religious authority there is a fresh·concern with the religion of the personal life and with the kind of first-hand religious experience exemplified in the lives of the mystics.

Can we hope for anything more? Is it possible that the spirit of Kabbalah can be rekindled? In the words of Professor Scholem: "The story is not ended, it has not yet become history, and the secret life it holds can break out tomorrow in you or in me. Under what aspects this invisible stream of mysticism will come again to the surface we cannot tell."

Guide to Practice
Norman E. Frimer

FROM the very beginning of its publication, the *Shulhan Arukh* was the center of great controversy. No other book in Jewish tradition since the time of Maimonides has been more maligned or more praised. For the Orthodox, the *Shulhan Arukh* is the "Blackstone of Jewish law." No Orthodox rabbi can receive ordination without mastering certain portions and being conversant with all of it. For the non-Orthodox it has frequently been the target for condemnation as the frozen tombstone of medievalism.

The author of the *Shulhan Arukh* was Rabbi Joseph Karo, born in Spain in 1488, who died in 1575 in Palestine, then the center of Talmudic learning and mysticism. With the tragic expulsion of Jews from Spain in 1492 his family was forced to flee first to Portugal, then to Bulgaria, and again from Bulgaria to Turkey. Karo, like his spiritual forebear Maimonides, had received his basic education from his father. He continued his rabbinic studies under several eminent scholars and at the age of thirty-five became the head of his own yeshiva.

By that time he had already begun to grapple with the problem of bringing Jewish law up to date for his time. The earliest medieval code before his was Maimonides' *Mishneh Torah*. Following it, there had been another major compilation by Rabbi Jacob ben Asher, in the fourteenth century, called the *Four Rows*. But in the 150 to 200 years which had elapsed, many new interpretations had been made to meet new situations. As Rabbi Karo wrote in an introduction to one of his works, because of the innumerable conflicting interpretations the one Torah of Israel was threatened with becoming many Torahs. He was seeking a focal point.

In preparation for the great task, Karo took to writing *The House of Joseph,* a major work originally intended as an addendum to the *Mishneh Torah* but which he later attached to the code of Rabbi ben Asher. This took over twenty years to complete, during which time Karo moved to Palestine, there to pursue his intensive interest in mysticism.

Karo was a most colorful personality. On the one hand, he was a mystic trying to establish a direct, unmediated relationship to God. On the other hand, he was the rational rabbinic scholar attempting to find God in a mediated manner through the Law. By piecing together small clues, fragmentary perceptions, insights and foreshadowings, he hoped to broaden the Jew's vision as to what was God's will.

During this period he also completed the *Kesef Mishneh,* a commentary on Maimonides' master code. Karo's job was to clarify the text and to rectify a grave omission which Maimonides personally acknowledged later in one of his letters—his failure to record the sources for his decisions.

In classical Jewish law one accepts only God's will and revelation on faith, but a rabbi's Talmudic judgment has to be patently based on reason and precedent. Thus when Maimonides attempted to impose his conclusions upon the Jewish people, there was resistance and even revolt. Karo therefore took it upon himself to indicate that the Rambam had not acted capriciously, that his verdicts were not the results of arbitrariness or whimsical preference. They were instead determinations carefully deduced from a reasonable and compelling understanding of the Torah and Talmudic material.

By 1542, Karo had completed the magnum opus which he had started twenty years earlier; but still not satisfied, and during the next twelve years he completely revised *The House of Joseph.* This book was then summarized and published in the year 1567 as the *Shulhan Arukh,* literally the "set table." It became his best-known work.

Karo, following his mentor Maimonides, seemed to have the intention of setting, once and for all, a table so replete with all intellectual fare that a rabbi would on the basis of the digest in the *Shulhan Arukh* be able to come to a satisfying and speedy conclusion without having to go through all earlier primary source materials.

It might be valuable to point out that Jewish tradition knows, in the main, two kinds of codes. One contains within its covers the whole continuum of Jewish law: herein falls Maimonides' famous work, the *Mishneh Torah,* consisting of fourteen major divisions.

The second kind of code, like Rabbi Jacob ben Asher's *Arbaah Turim,* includes only those laws operative in the writer's day. The *Shulhan Arukh,* as an extension of the second type, deals only with those laws applicable in the contemporary Diaspora. For example, it excludes laws dealing with sacrifices, Temple worship and agriculture laws as having no relevancy outside of the Holy Land. It deals extensively, however, with all concrete problems in the purview of Jewish religious life in the post-exilic community.

Organizationally, too, the *Shulhan Arukh* was highly practical. Various topics were carefully arranged in separate divisions and then in turn subdivided for purposes of broader and deeper analysis. Each "branch" included one point which could be followed structurally and logically from a general principle down into the specifics. In this, there is little doubt that Maimonides' influence was crucial.

In style, however, Karo was no match for the "Great Eagle."

Though written in lucid rabbinic Hebrew, the *Shulhan Arukh* does not have the purity of Maimonides' language. Yet a rabbi could run his eyes over a section quickly and come to the core point which he needed. Speed and ease were the principal goals of the *Shulhan Arukh,* which it achieved superbly.

Moreover, it represented the distillation of over a thousand years of legal thought, going as far back as the Talmud and then moving swiftly forward through the channels already carved out by Maimonides. In addition, it filled the gap left open between the Code of Maimonides of the twelfth century and that of Rabbi Jacob ben Asher of the fourteenth century, and also bridged the span to the sixteenth century in which Karo was living.

But, in the final analysis, Karo did not succeed in making his work the definitive and authoritative text he intended it to be. In the first place, he had repeated the very error which he had attempted to correct in Maimonides' Code—namely, not listing his sources. He had relied, but without success, on the fact that his decisions were clearly derived from his *Bet Joseph,* where they were all carefully documented.

Moreover, as a Spanish Jew, Karo naturally followed the tradition of his great Sefardi teachers, mainly Maimonides, Rabbi Isaac Alfasi of North Africa, and Rabbi Asher ben Yaakov, or more popularly, the Rosh, a Spanish teacher who had, however, been raised in Germany and therefore partook also of North European or Ashkenazi scholarship. Karo's policy was to examine the opinions of these three rabbis, and usually to rule according to the majority decision. There were times when all three had come to an identical conclusion. On other occasions Maimonides and his Ashkenazi confrere, the Rosh, were in the majority. Most frequently, however, the latter was outvoted by the Rambam and the Alfas; the influence of Sefardi thought was therefore heavily reflected in the *Shulhan Arukh.* So central a tradition as that of Rashi and his Franco-German disciples was too little in evidence for Ashkenazi Jewry.

It was therefore no surprise that a great deal of opposition greeted the *Shulhan Arukh* on its first appearance. Unfortunately, moreover, this great scholar was not exempt from personal attack. There were those who accused him of writing a textbook for children. Some charged that he had written this book in his old age, and therefore had fallen victim to many errors. Others condemned the book as unreliable because they claimed that he had irresponsibly assigned the writing to his pupils.

The most crucial charges were on ideological grounds, that Karo had ignored the important and basic texts of the Franco-German school of interpretation, which were often in disagreement with the Sefardi ones. Moreover, Karo had also disregarded much of Franco-German custom, the modes that the people themselves had created out of their own urge for a deeper God relationship. By this omission, Ashkenazi Jewry felt alienated and entirely ignored; the sacredness of their way of life had been slighted. In addition, the fact that the *Shulhan Arukh* had no obvious sources for its decisions made it, in the words of one great teacher, a "sealed book," a "dream without interpretation."

How could one be expected to understand a decision if one did not know its source? Without original sources a rabbi would be studying Torah "standing on one leg." He would then legislate not by going back as he ought to the original constitutional principle and seeing its development through the ages, but, in referring to the latest textbook or most recent manual, uncritically accept the conclusions of the last author. This is not the way of the great. The scholar and sage must in every new question refer back to the Torah, the source of the tradition, and with the skill and perseverance of a deep sea-diver plumb the depths of Biblical and rabbinic thought in order to see the original precept representing the will of God, as it has meandered its way through life. Then only can one apply the Law to the particular experiences of one's generation.

For this very reason there were some scholars who remained opposed to all codification. Their contention was that codes inevitably tend to freeze creative original thinking. The free movement of Jewish thought becomes rigid and unbending. Let the rabbi who wants to arrive at a decision struggle through the forest of commentary and build his own road.

The demands of the day, however, gave rise to other codes written after the *Shulhan Arukh*, which even threatened to replace Karo's version. Errors were pointed out in his interpretations and decisions, and weighty authority adduced to prove that his conclusions, though based on two of the three "giants," were untenable. The fate of Karo's work was consequently at stake.

Thanks to an Ashkenazi teacher, however, the *Shulhan Arukh* was finally rescued and became the great new code of world Jewry. Rabbi Moshe Isserles, born in 1520 in Kraków, Poland, was a student and later the son-in-law of one of the greatest scholars of his day. When he was ordained and returned to his native city, he founded a yeshiva there. Before long his fame spread as the master of Jewish learning. In addition to rabbinics he was adept at philosophy, science, history, Kabbalah and mathematics. His forte, however, remained in the field of Jewish law.

In preparation for his life's work Isserles wrote commentaries on several Talmudic tracts, on the *Turim* of Rabbi Jacob ben Asher, as well as a digest of one of the earlier codes. As a recognized teacher, he exchanged many Responsa with rabbis in all parts of the Jewish world.

His major contribution, popularly called by the abbreviated initials of his name, the *R'ma,* was originally named by the author the *Mapah,* meaning "the cloth." As its title implied, it was to serve as a complement to the "Set Table" of Karo.

Rabbi Isserles felt that the *Shulhan Arukh* needed this complementary touch; like many of his contemporaries he was dissatisfied with Karo's ignoring the Ashkenazi teachers. He valued greatly, however, the virtue of its organization and its tremendous achievement in bringing Jewish law up to date. Isserles' additions were intended to fill in and round out the *Shulhan Arukh* so that it might yet become *the* code for his and perhaps succeeding generations.

To this end he recorded the basic views of the great Franco-German masters. When their decisions were in conflict, Rabbi Isserles would introduce their dissent with the words: "There are those who rule otherwise," and then proceed to state their position. He also underscored the local practices pervasive in the East European community, thereby raising custom (*minhag*) to the binding stature of Law. Furthermore, he was careful not to record a decision without providing the source. These served to give his supplement substantial strength and win for it considerable support.

To talk about the *Shulhan Arukh* means really to speak of the combination of both Karo's and Isserles' versions. With the Isserles addition, the *Shulhan Arukh* no longer ignores Franco-German teachers or disregards Ashkenazi customs; nor does it omit sources. All serious deficiencies were corrected by Rabbi Isserles.

Although the fight against the *Shulhan Arukh* continued for at least another hundred years, it was a losing one for the opponents. In the seventeenth, eighteenth and nineteenth centuries, when great scholars began to write commentaries, revisions, amendments and additions to these two supplementary codifiers, the enlarged and enriched *Shulhan Arukh* began to emerge as the authoritative text. It received the seal of approval of scholars, and henceforth all new situations or problems had to be filtered through not only the Torah, the Talmud, the Responsa, the commentaries and the early and later codes, but also through the *Shulhan Arukh.*

Jewish law has thus been continuous and unending in its development and application. Its influence, however, does not rest on forced imposition nor its vitality on artificial production. The Law, if it is to live, must be voluntarily accepted as Halakhah, "the way," and must be responsive to the religious needs of the day. To serve these goals is the basic purpose and intent of a code.

But no code claims infallibility or omniscience. The *Shulhan Arukh* characteristically emerged the victor only after years of struggle and challenge, clarification and modification. Today, it no longer stands as the sole creation of the *M'haver* (the author), as Karo was called by the initiate, in literary partnership with the *R'ma*. It represents instead a veritable storehouse of generations of scholarship, devotion and critical thinking. It is the pooled genius of the great masters and their many "weapon-bearers" who by their loving but searching study strove to keep the past contemporaneous and the will of God continuously operative as living Torah.

The Kaddish

Sidney Greenberg

THE Kaddish exercises a powerful grip. It is recited every morning and evening by bereaved Jews in every land, by the learned and the unlettered, by teen-agers and graybeards, by the richest and the humblest. The sense of obligation to recite the Kaddish is the strongest motivating factor behind the organization and perpetuation of the daily prayer service in hundreds of congregations.

Jews who know few other prayers know the Kaddish. Jews who keep few other traditions are faithful in reciting it for eleven months after the death of a parent, and every succeeding year on the *Yahrzeit,* the anniversary of the death in the Jewish calendar.

The Kaddish is the prayer which bears most eloquent testimony to filial reverence and respect. In Yiddish a man affectionately refers to his son as his *Kaddish'l,* his little Kaddish-sayer. This is a son's posthumous gift to his father, a refuge against oblivion.

In several modern prayer books, the Kaddish is the only prayer found in transliteration. Worshippers in liberal congregations may recite any other prayer in translation, but never the Kaddish, which is always recited in its original Aramaic, the vernacular of the people. Even the Reform prayer book, which has eliminated much of the Hebrew of the traditional siddur, has preserved the Kaddish in Aramaic and added a paragraph to it.

The enduring appeal of the Kaddish in the face of the most forbidding circumstances was attested to in a melancholy way by Heinrich Heine. He was among those post-Emancipation Jews who sought to obtain through baptism the fuller freedom and larger opportunities denied to members of his faith. The hoped-for benefits of this act of desertion never quite materialized. In the end, he felt excluded from both camps. Significant was Heine's way of expressing this bitter truth:

> *No Mass will be sung,*
> *No Kaddish will be said;*
> *Nothing said and nothing sung*
> *On the anniversaries of my death.*

The unspoken Kaddish, the unmarked *Yahrzeit*—these epitomized for Heine better than anything else his ultimate alienation from his people.

It is easier to describe the magnetic hold of the Kaddish than to explain it. Though it is "the mourner's prayer" it contains not a single reference to death, resurrection or immortality. The anguish of sorrow or the pain of parting are not even touched upon. The thoughts uppermost in the mourner's mind and the feelings in his heart find no expression in the Kaddish. (For this reason the Reform prayer book added a paragraph which explicitly refers to the departed.) The traditional Kaddish is instead a hymn of praise to God.

> Glorified and hallowed be His great name in the world which He has created according to His will. May He establish His kingdom during your lives and the life of all Israel. Let us say: Amen.
> Let His great name be blessed to all eternity.
> Hallowed and extolled, lauded and exalted, honored and revered, adored and worshipped, be the name of the Holy One, blessed be He; though He be beyond all blessings, hymns and praises which are uttered in the world. Let us say: Amen.
> May abundant peace and life descend from heaven upon us and upon all Israel. Let us say: Amen.
> May He who ordains the harmony in the universe bring peace to us and to all Israel. Let us say: Amen.

One of our oldest prayers, the Kaddish was not originally designed as a prayer for mourners. Some of its passages were part of the Temple services. Its two basic themes—the sanctification of God's Name and the hope for the coming of His kingdom—are echoed in the best-known Christian prayer:

> *Our Father who art in Heaven,*
> *Hallowed be Thy name.*
> *Thy kingdom come;*
> *Thy will be done . . .*

Some of the phrases and ideas of the Kaddish are suggested by Biblical phrases. Others were added with the passage of time.

In its present form (attained twelve centuries ago, in the Gaonic period), the Kaddish was recited at the conclusion of a lecture in the House of Study. In the view of our sages, one of the most effective ways of bringing God's kingdom nearer was through the study of Torah and the good deeds to which such study leads. The teacher would therefore follow his discourse by reciting the Kaddish, the sublime expression of that hope.

The link between the Kaddish and the House of Study is reflected in the *Kaddish d'Rabbanan*, "The Scholar's Kaddish," recited after the reading of a passage from the Mishnah or the Talmud. This is the basic Kaddish with a special prayer inserted on behalf of "the teachers and their disciples and all who engage in the study of Torah."

Later, the Kaddish passed from the House of Study into the House of Prayer. In the synagogue it was and is recited at the conclusion of a distinct section of the service (the half Kaddish) and also at the conclusion of the entire service (the whole Kaddish).

Still later, the custom arose for disciples to recite a special Kaddish at the end of the seven-day mourning period for a learned Torah scholar. This Kaddish followed the religious discourses delivered in his honor. Subsequently, the democratic impulse extended this honor to every Jew.

This then was the route traveled by the Kaddish—from the House of Study to the House of Prayer to the house of mourning.

The only *explicit* mention of the dead is found in the special Kaddish recited at the graveside immediately after burial. It contains this added section:

> Magnified and hallowed be His great name in the world that is to be created anew when He will revive the dead and raise them up into life eternal and when He will rebuild the city of Jerusalem and establish His Temple in the midst thereof and uproot all false worship from the earth and restore the worship of the true God.

The earliest reference to the Kaddish as a mourner's prayer is found in a thirteenth-century prayer book (*Mahzor Vitry*). There is, however, an earlier legend connecting the recitation of the Kaddish with an orphan. Rabbi Akiba once met a ghost carrying a burdensome load of wood for the fires in hell to which he had been condemned for having exploited the poor during his life as a tax collector. He had only one hope for release from his torments. If his infant son could be taught to recite the Kaddish in public so that the congregation could respond with "May God's great name be praised for ever," he would be spared further sufferings. Rabbi Akiba found the child and taught him to recite the Kaddish and thus effect his father's release from Gehenna (or hell).

This legend establishes a connection between the Kaddish and the orphan. It also introduces a thought that was to dominate many writings in the Middle Ages—that the Kaddish has the power to release the dead from suffering. So strong was this belief that it survived the determined opposition of many leading rabbis and was largely responsible for the practice of engaging someone to say the Kaddish for a man who left no sons.

Traditional authorities differ on whether a daughter may recite the

Kaddish where there is no son. Most modern Jews would agree with the position taken on this matter by Henrietta Szold. To her the Kaddish was essentially an expression of identification, a means of linking herself with her family and with her people, past and future. She had seven sisters and no brothers. When her mother died, a friend of the family offered to say the Kaddish for her. Henrietta graciously refused. She explained:

> The Kaddish means to me that the survivor publicly and mark-edly manifests his wish and intention to assume the relation to the Jewish community which his parent had so that the chain of tradition remains unbroken from generation to generation, each adding its own link. You can do that for the generations of your family. I must do that for the generation of my family.

But what of the intrinsic meaning of the Kaddish itself? Though not originally designed to be recited by the mourner, does it have nothing to say to him?

The Kaddish makes several vital affirmations addressed to the mourner's emotional and psychic needs. The very name of the prayer Kaddish means "sanctification." From beginning to end it sanctifies the name of God, thus attesting human submission to and acceptance of His will. It proclaims that in spite of our loss we are among those who add our praise to the glorification of God's name. Our belief in God is strong enough to overcome bereavement.

Sorrow often places a severe strain upon man's faith in God and in the goodness of life. "How can I believe in God if He permits such things to happen?" The structure of our faith totters in the winds of misfortune. The Kaddish is intended to steady and restore our perspective. We have returned what was lent to us and what we have enjoyed. In this spirit a father who had lost his daughter wrote: "On our books she is a net gain. She was worth so much more than she cost and she left so much more behind than she took away that we are flooded with joyous memories and cannot question either the goodness of God or the decency of man."

The Kaddish proclaims further that this is a "world which He has created according to His will." Even though sorrow may temporarily dull our vision or threaten to rob life of meaning, we affirm that there is a plan and a purpose to life.

The Kaddish also offers the reassurance that God can supply one of the mourner's most desperate needs—the need for inner peace and serenity. "May He who makes peace in His heights, bring peace unto us . . ."

Modern studies of the dynamics of grief indicate that in every situation there is present an element of guilt. No human relationship is so perfect that the survivor cannot berate himself for things done and said and for things left undone and unsaid. He needs peace from an accusing conscience. He needs the peace which comes from the faith that He who has created imperfect creatures makes allowance for their imperfections.

The mourner also needs release from the anxiety over his own death that the death of a loved one often engenders. He needs relief from the fears which thrive in the soil of sorrow. He needs surcease from the resentments and rebellions that follow in the wake of separation. The hope that such peace can come to him may help dispel the heavy overcast of grief and anxiety.

Finally, the Kaddish offers the mourner a challenge to contribute his energies to the making of a better world. Emotionally and psychologically the Kaddish is a link with the past. But the Kaddish itself looks forward, not backward. "May He establish His kingdom." This cannot remain a passive hope. It must involve the mourner actively in the creation of a better world. The Kaddish sounds a call to action on behalf of that kingdom for whose advent we pray.

By requiring that the Kaddish be recited with a quorum of worshippers, Judaism renders the mourner a profound service. A *minyan* almost invariably includes other mourners and thus brings home the realization that we alone have not been singled out.

The burning question: "Why did God do this to me?" loses much of its sting when others also rise to recite the Kaddish. We are not lonely travelers in the valley of the shadow. We thus see death for what it is—not a malevolent act of a vindictive God, but part of the incomprehensible mystery of human existence in which light and dark, joy and sadness, birth and death are interwoven and inseparable.

"The Bube-Mai'seh"

Hasye Cooperman

WHEN a prattling old woman tells a far-fetched story, a bit of lore, a superstitious notion or anything that seems extraordinary, we designate this as "an old wives' tale." Among Yiddish-speaking people this is known as a *bube-mai'seh,* or grandmother's tale, denoting a story so outlandish, so fantastic, so incredible that only one person, grandma, could have concocted it.

What is the origin of this term? Is it true to the facts? Actually grandmother had little to do with the phrase or its origin. The term is an aberration and a misnomer; and thereby hangs a tale.

It is the tale of a Renaissance Yiddish bard Elia Levita or Eliyohu Bokher, as he is better known. He was probably the most distinguished Hebrew scholar of his day, a grammarian, lexicographer, humanist, teacher, and not least of all, a Yiddish poet whose disciplined artistry is still revered. Born in 1469, near Regensburg, Germany, he lived in Venice and Padua, and for a time taught Hebrew to an eminent humanist and scholar in Rome. Eliyohu Bokher also spent much time copying and preparing extracts from the great storehouse of Hebrew and Kabbalistic lore.

When King Charles sacked Rome, our Yiddish poet and scholar took to wandering from city to city, finally settling again in Venice, where he taught the French ambassador, and the humanist Sebastian Muenster. The latter translated into Latin Levita's handbooks of the Hebrew language, from which non-Jewish scholars of the day learned Hebrew and read the original text of the Scriptures. His prestige and scholarly renown were so great that King Francis I invited him to occupy the Chair of Hebrew in the University of Paris; he refused on the ground that Jews had not been permitted to live in France since the year 1394.

His best-known Yiddish work is the *Bovo-Bukh,* written between 1507 and 1508, a passionate romance of adventure and intrigue composed in Italian verse form, *ottava rima,* and based on the adventures of Prince Bovo d'Antona (English, Sir Bevis of Hampton; old French, Bovon or Bueves; Italian, Buovo). The materials he used were part of the stock-in-trade of the medieval Renaissance poet-singers all over the continent, but, as he himself tells us, altered, condensed, and incorporating Jewish attitudes and concepts. He added his own touch of irony and an indulgent humor, as he related the intricate web of adventures and supernatural plot. But while he poked fun, he nonetheless enjoyed it; it was a tongue-in-cheek recital, which he relished. Like Cervantes, who is said to have written *Don Quixote* as a satire, a romance of chivalry to end all chivalresque fol-de-rol, Ilye Bokher wrote the *Bovo-Bukh* as a piece of adventurous nonsense to end all such nonsense.

His readers loved every bit of this book, which became the most popular, most sought-after story among Yiddish-speaking people chiefly among the women and the less learned. Published and republished in many editions, it fired the imagination of Jewish households and its story was repeated until it became part of popular lore. It was still reprinted and read until about the beginning of the nineteenth century, when many of its words and phrases had become obsolete.

Just as Chaucer has now become outdated and has had to be modernized to be understood, so Levita's romance had to be recast in modern Yiddish. *Bovo-Bukh* became *Bovo-Mai'seh*. Since readers clamored for the tale, the easiest way out was to rewrite the *mai'seh*, not in verse but in prose. And *Bovo-Mai-seh* it has remained. Early in the twentieth century, versions were still being printed in Vilna and Warsaw in chapbooks distributed by peddlers. And because the story had become household lore, a tale only ignorant folks and old women could believe, *Bovo-Bukh* became *bube-mai'seh,* or an old wives' tale.

The story itself recounts the love of Bovo and Druziana. Bovo is the son of a young woman, married to an old count; she murders her husband with the aid of a young count, whom she marries. They plot also to do away with Bovo, but, by a miracle, the boy escapes. He wanders from place to place until at the age of eighteen he reaches Flandern, where he becomes a slave of the king and eventually falls in love with Druziana, the king's daughter. After many feats of prowess, intrigues, separations and last-minute rescues, he and Druziana are united; after a year an accident separates them once again. Believing that Druziana is dead, Bovo returns to the place of his birth, kills the young count who murdered his father and married his mother, and shuts his mother up in a cloister. Just as he is about to marry the Sultan's daughter, he hears the song of a beggar-woman who has come with her twin sons. He recognizes the voice of Druziana and the song which tells of their love. They are reunited and presumably live happily ever after.

So ends this chivalresque romance, the highlight of the so-called Italian school of Yiddish poetry, first called *Bovo-Bukh,* then *Bovo-Mai'seh.* *Bube-Mai'seh,* the humorous misnomer which has stuck, has by now become part of our folkways, part of our lore. All of which proves that Jews love a good romance as well as anybody else. And thereby hangs the tale.

The Shtetl
Yudel Mark

THE *shtetl* is no more. The last two generations of young people who grew up within its confines sought with might and main to escape to the large cities, to America or to Palestine. Their one desire: get out of the *shtetl!* Yet when they trod the unfriendly pavements of distant cities or tearfully ate their hard-earned bread in some "new home"— they longed for the *shtetl,* seeing it through a romantic aura. The *shtetl* thus came to be described both as a puddle of stagnant water and as the garden spot of one's childhood, reminiscent of the cradle and a mother's tender lullaby. It was the subject for biting satire as well as romantic idyll.

The *shtetl* was more than a town—it was an historic and cultural concept reflecting a whole way of life. To understand the *shtetl* is to understand hundreds of years of Jewish life in Eastern Europe, the way of life of our grandparents and great-grandparents, their mood, outlook and everyday existence. Bialik once said that it was necessary to step over the threshold of a *bes-medresh* (house of study or worship) if one wanted to feel the spirit of the Jewish people. In order to understand the life of that people it is necessary—at least in imagination—to live in the *shtetl.*

Until the middle of the nineteenth century most East European Jews lived in thousands of *shtetlakh* strewn over the length and breadth of the territory bounded by the Black and Baltic Seas and the Vistula and Dnieper River basins. Jewish settlements were minute islands in a sea of Poles, White Russians, Ukrainians, Lithuanians and smaller nationalities. However diverse the general environment may have been ethnically, the configuration of the Jewish *shtetl* was uniform; each was a tiny, half-autonomous territory, linked by economic and family ties into a kind of great Jewish territory, made up of all the *shtetlakh* together.

Commerce and trade made for communication, and the fairs in centrally located towns attracted Jews from outlaying *shtetlakh.* Jewish ties were forged by matchmakers, itinerant cantors and preachers, and even wandering bands of beggars which Mendele Mocher Sforim divided into Jewish "cavalry" and Jewish "infantry." This led to many-branched family trees with close and distant relatives through the *shtetlakh.* The existence of a famous yeshiva or the residence of a learned and authoritative rabbi in a given *shtetl* radiated light which also illuminated all the *shtetlakh* in the region.

A *shtetl* was a unit in itself, but its separation from other *shtetlakh* in the same country or across the national borders, or from the local center of learning and trade, was only relative. A feeling of Jewish unity, of common problems and an identical way of life, bound all the towns together. Yiddish proverbs tell us that "all *shtetlakh* look alike," and "all the world is one big *shtetl*."

The truth is, however, that the *shtetlakh* varied a great deal. First, there was a considerable difference in size, ranging from a hamlet of ten families to a town of a thousand families. Second, there were degrees of poverty. In the *shtetlakh* of Rumania, Jews complained and jested about their constant diet of *mamelige* (cornmeal cereal), just as White Russian Jews lamented over their dry black bread. The *shtetlakh* of White Russia and Lithuania originated the folk song "Sunday potatoes, Monday potatoes . . . potatoes again and again"; here Jews used to jest that "if barley soup's a meal—then Khandrivke is a commonweal." Life was less prosperous there than in the *shtetlakh* of Poland which traded in grain and lumber, or in those of Volin, where Jews ate "white bread on weekdays," or in fertile Bessarabia with its wine and corn.

Quite often the *shtetl* was located near a river or a small lake. It rose at the crossroads or occupied the top of a hill, or the valley between hills. It cuddled up to a forest or presided over surrounding fields. If a town had no visible landmark, it was said to be "outside"! If a *shtetl* was in some exceptional out-of-the-way place, remaining inaccessible even in winter when the mud was frozen solid, Jews said, "Here even Adam never set foot." (According to Jewish legend, God showed Adam the whole world.)

However they differed physically, there were some general features characteristic of all *shtetlakh*. The center was always the market place, a large or small square, depending on the size and economic status of the *shtetl*, thick with stores and stands and booths of market women displaying a few fruits and vegetables. The big day was market day, once or twice a week, and differing among neighboring *shtetlakh* so as to avoid competition. Of even greater importance were the fairs, once, twice or at most three times a year, and generally arranged to coincide with major Christian holidays. Jews waited for the fairs, hoping that business would be good enough to enable them to marry off a daughter or pay off long standing debts. Each fair was either the fulfillment of hopes or the source of bitter disappointment. As the Yiddish saying goes, "After a good fair one deserves a drink and after a bad fair one needs a drink."

The *shtetl* economy was based on trade with the peasants and, to some extent, on the landowner's business. The Jew was the bearer of culture and the creator of economic demands for the peasant. If the peasants living near the *shtetl* were serfs or had little or unfertile land, the *shtetl* was very poor. When the peasants' economic status improved, the *shtetl* profited.

In spite of sporadic pogroms in the 1880's and after 1905, and annual pre-Passover fears of ritual murder accusations, the Jew-peasant realtionships were on the whole friendly. It was with the advent of the organized boycott of Jews, which developed after World War I, that things took a turn for the worse. By this time there were gentile artisans and tradesmen (or cooperatives) in the *shtetlakh* in competition with Jews.

Jewish journalists and theoreticians of the Socialist and Zionist movements bemoaned and decried the petty merchant of the *shtetl* who dominated its economy up until the twentieth century. They overlooked his positive role as the middleman between city and village, industry and agriculture, and one district and another. There were of course too many storekeepers, which created cut-throat competition. "In the *shtetl* there are stores, like mushrooms after it pours."

Some *shtetlakh* specialized in certain trades—there was a town of brushmakers who worked with bristle, a town of carpenters, tailors, shoemakers and smiths. In Lithuania, Jews were raftsmen guiding lumber down river. At the beginning of the century groups of them went to the big cities and worked at paving the streets. A proverb says, "A craft is a thing which makes one a king." But the king was often half-starved.

The *shtetl* women had a hard lot. The poorest of them were the market women, the food peddlers who sold hot beans to schoolboys, the seamstresses or the bakers (typical occupations of the working woman). Many were storekeepers. Their husbands helped out on market days or at a fair, but most of the time, they spent their days studying in the *bes-medresh*. It was the wife who operated the business, talked the language of the peasant and knew how to deal with the customers. Even if the husband wanted to help, he was clumsy and helpless in the business world.

The woman bore and nursed a houseful of children, cooked the meals, cleaned the house, worried about debts, ordered merchandise. She rarely complained or considered herself imposed on or exploited.

Birth control was unknown in the *shtetl*. "He who gives life will also sustain life," was the age-old pious expression of hope. The education of the children was very important, never a problem. As soon as the child learned to talk, he learned the blessings. At five, in some instances earlier, a boy went to heder, where he learned to read, read Bible with Rashi's commentaries, and then Talmud. A boy stayed in the heder until he had to learn a trade, help his father, study on his own, or go to yeshiva in another town. Except for boys from well-to-do families, most yeshiva students lived on the charity of the Jews in yeshiva towns, taking their meals with a different family each day, and often going hungry.

The family included not only parents and children but grandparents, uncles, aunts, cousins and even second cousins. There were often three generations under one roof. Old age homes were unknown in the *shtetl.* When a daughter married, the son-in-law was taken into the house and a little room was partitioned off for the couple.

Just before Yom Kippur, the whole family went to its eldest member for a blessing. There were circumcisions, Bar Mitzvahs and weddings. There were family holidays when a child went to heder for the first time wrapped in a prayer shawl; when a boy had his hair cut at age three, at a *pidyon-haben* ceremony, or at a betrothal with its attendant plate-breaking.

Couples married young. In normal times the ancient principle of a man getting married at eighteen was followed; the bride was even younger. There were periods when marriages took place right after Bar Mitzvah. Matches were made by parents, generally with the aid of a match-maker. The major consideration was whether the families were suitable, whether their social acceptability and their economic status in the community were comparable. Although dowry and the period of time the father of the bride would support the young couple played an important role, social acceptability was the vital factor, based on the status of the whole family for several generations, and on the bridegroom's erudition.

There were no bachelors in the *shtetl.* A spinster was a curse. The marriage of a very poor girl, or one who had been orphaned, was a community concern. Special organizations, *Hakhnoses-kaleh,* raised funds to provide such girls with dowries and trousseaus. Cripples were married and even the chronically ill were matched, particularly during epidemics, when it was thought such marriages could halt the epidemic.

Families lived in the same *shtetl* for generations; as a result an entire *shtetl* might consist of several branches of a few families. Sometimes there would be a feud between two leading families and all communal decisions were subject to heated arguments by the two groups.

Another important set of relationships was that between neighbors. As the saying went, "A close neighbor is better than a distant relative." People were always involved in their neighbor's affairs. They lent and borrowed things, helped in time of need and generally were closely bound to each other. No one was isolated or alone. The whole *shtetl* was like one chain, providing strength and endurance for its inhabitants.

Because of mutual involvement and the close-knit community, many events transformed the everyday life of the *shtetl* from its generally gray and monotonous pattern. A wedding or a circumcision ceremony would create a joyous mood, or a funeral evoke sadness or tears.

Holidays were important. On the Sabbath a change took place in what people did and in their moods and attitudes. From Sunday through Thursday the *shtetl* Jews were busy earning their livelihood. But on Friday things changed. Early in the morning the sounds of women chopping fish, in preparation of the Sabbath meal of fish, soup, fowl, wine and *hallah,* could be heard throughout the *shtetl.* All week long the people scraped and borrowed to provide the components of this festive meal.

Toward afternoon the bath attendant rushed through the streets, calling the men to come to the public bath so that they could approach the Sabbath in physical and spiritual cleanliness. The public bath was an important institution in the *shtetl's* life, the men alternating with the women in its use. On Friday afternoon the women carried their pots of *tsholent* to the bakers' oven where it could be kept warm until Saturday noon. After the Sabbath meal, the master of the house usually took a nap from which he arose to test his sons on what they had learned at heder during the week. As evening fell, the *Havdalah* candles could be seen flickering in the windows and the odor of aromatic spices filled the house.

On Rosh Hashanah the *shtetl* smelled of apples and honey. People dressed in their best clothes and went to the synagogue to pray for a good year to come. Yom Kippur was a solemn day. Tall wax candles flickered in sandboxes. Men and women in white filled the streets leading to the synagogue. And the pinched look of fasting Jews was relieved only by the *Neila* prayer which ended the long all-day service.

That very night, they began to build their *sukkot.* Great ingenuity was required to construct these booths out of doors, table tops, loose boards and even the board normally used for rolling the noodle dough. On Simhas Torah the men's synagogue was thrown open to the women and children and the procession around the platform with the Torah scrolls was a happy and joyous occasion. Since Simhas Torah was one of the few days on which it was accounted proper to take a few drinks, the whole *shtetl* was sometimes a little tipsy.

In winter, on Hanukkah, groups of children visited relatives to collect Hanukkah gelt. On Purim the town took on a different appearance. Children scurried through the streets with covered plates containing *hamentashen* and other sweets as Jews exchanged *shalach mones*. And they took a few extra drinks in honor of the escape of their fathers from annihilation.

Immediately after Purim, preparations for Passover began. Matzos had to be baked and people who rarely had work during the year now found employment as matzo bakers. Tailors, cobblers and hatmakers were very busy making new clothes. For the women this period was one of feverish activity. Houses had to be cleaned from top to bottom. Bedding had to be aired and the straw mattresses replaced. During Passover the spirit of the town was more hopeful—the long, hard winter had ended.

On Shavuot greens were brought into the home. The walls were bedecked with branches, and reeds covered the floors. Warm clothing was shed and people began to spend more time outdoors.

The intellectual center was the *bes-medresh*. It was, of course, a house of prayer, but prayers were not its basic function. It was the town hall, the meeting place for all communal gatherings, the locale for discussion and for arguments and debates. Here paupers and wandering beggars spent the night when there was no special poorhouse in the *shtetl*. Here too came those who had left home and family to immerse themselves in studying. It was a sort of free men's club.

The most important event in the *bes-medresh* was study. Hardly anyone ever studied at home. The *bes-medresh* had all the necessary books, it was warm all winter and there was help available with a difficult passage of the Talmud. Many Jews studied by themselves, or in earnest discussions with their fellows. The larger the number of scholars, the more the *bes-medresh* was respected. It was always open. Some scholars sat up all night studying, others came in the middle of night, still others came at dawn before morning prayers.

Then there were the *hevra* (societies). A *G'mara* society studied the Talmud tractate by tractate and page by page until it finished the whole Talmud, when it would hold a special celebration before beginning all over again. Another society studied only the Mishnah, a lower level of scholarship. The less educated studied the Midrash under the instruction of a teacher or a more learned householder, who sought merit by teaching the uneducated. On the eve of the Sabbath the ordinary Jews studied the weekly portion of the Torah. Even those unable to study chanted the Psalms either in groups or alone.

If the *shtetl* was large, it had several houses of study. With the development of Hasidism, little houses of study known as *shtiblekh* developed. Every group of Hasidim, which revered a given holy man or *rebbe,* had its own *shtibl*. There was also a different *bes-medresh* for the different social or occupational groups in the large *shtetl*, a tailors' *bes-medresh* or teamsters'. This was not due to divisiveness but to a desire to involve more people in the *bes-medresh* activity and make it possible for greater fellowship to develop. Also, more men could then be called up to read from the Torah during services.

In larger *shtetlakh* or in very old ones there was also a "great synagogue," often called the "cold synagogue" because it was generally unheated. It was used only for services. There, the visiting cantor and his boy choir performed. There, too, the rabbi read his sermons several times a year, or the itinerant preacher was invited to speak. Some synagogues had ornate interiors, and many *shtetlakh* prided themselves on the size, age and beauty of their houses of worship.

In the synagogue yard or the area near the *bes-medresh* the itinerant bookseller displayed his merchandise of prayer books, religious guides, special women's prayer books, little volumes in Yiddish and religious articles. These wandering booksellers brought life into the *shtetl* with news of the outside world. Even the beggar was welcome; the Yiddish word for him was *oyrakh* or "guest." Every solid citizen of the community took such a guest home over the Sabbath, and the guest sat at the table with the family, even if he were dressed in rags. The family listened to the stories he told and the children imagined that he was Elijah the prophet, come to help people in need.

Charity in the *shtetl* was provided in various forms. There was organized charity, contributed through the various societies, for the local poor, the sick, widows and orphans, wandering beggars and other needy persons. The highest form of charity was to give help anonymously to aid someone who had lost his livelihood and was in great need but too ashamed to ask for help. He would receive a gift without knowing where it came from or whom to thank. Matzos for Passover and wood for the winter were always provided those in need. Charity was especially important on the eve of Yom Kippur and Purim. The *shtetl* also had a free loan society. Sometimes there were "emergency campaigns" and the rabbi or sexton went from house to house collecting contributions to replace a teamster's horse that had died, or to help a nearby *shtetl* that had burned down.

Tradition governed every aspect of human behavior, from rising in the morning to bedtime. To this were added the forms of social organization. Everyone was a member of one or more societies. Each had its special function and all sought to serve God or man. One society was dedicated to special midnight devotion, another provided clothes for the poor. Very important was the burial society which managed the local Jewish cemetery and made funeral arrangements.

To understand the many-faceted social activity of the *shtetl*, think of it as a small state. The Jewish community organization, *kahal*, was responsible for the collection of taxes from Jews in Poland until the middle of the eighteenth century. During the reign of Czar Nicholas I, the *kahal* had to provide the quota of Jewish recruits for military service. It was also responsible for the supply of kosher meat. In almost all aspects of Jewish life, from birth to death, in matters spiritual and temporal, the community had a supervisory role. The individual was never alone, there was always someone to share his burdens and responsibilities.

The agnostic, the freethinker, had to hide his ideas. To dress "like a German"—in a short jacket instead of the long *kaftan*—was a revolutionary idea introduced by the Enlightenment in the second half of the nineteenth century (in some parts of Poland and Galicia, only at the start of the twentieth century) when modern nationalist or Socialist concepts began to penetrate the *shtetlakh*. This was followed by women wearing their own hair and by men smoking on the Sabbath. Finally an open break with *shtetl* life came during the period of the revolution of 1905, and more so during the first World War. The youth were drawn into the various political parties that had been organized; and the *shtetl* began to disintegrate—or, more accurately, to disperse.

But even during this period the *shtetl* remained the breeding ground for those who were to influence Jewish life up to the present day. The *halutzim* and David Ben Gurion came from the *shtetl*. The Yiddish and Hebrew writers came in the main from the *shtetl*. From the *shtetl* stem our social idealism and the warmth and close ties between one Jew and another. For in the *shtetl* no one lived for himself.

Torah in Slutzk

Ephraim E. Lisitzky

THEY say that the Jews of Slutzk always keep their little finger bent. Why? Ten measures of pride were given to this world, and nine of them were appropriated by the Jews of Slutzk. And when you ask a Slutzk Jew: "What is the reason that you have assumed this overweening pride?," he puts his right forefinger on his left little finger, bends it and begins to enumerate his praises: "First of all, I am a Slutzker: In the second place . . ." There is no second after his first, this is the first and the last—and his little finger remains bent.

Slutzk was renowned for its poverty, the poverty of the Jewish cities and townlets enclosed within the Pale of the Settlement of which Slutzk took the lion's share. The Jews of Slutzk were, for the most part, utter paupers who came by their livelihood only by great struggle and tribulation. They were clothed in tatters, lived in shanties, and ate dried crusts and groat soup called *krupnik*—a Slutzk dish that actually consisted of nothing but boiled water in which slices of potato and bits of groat were few and far between.

Slutzk was a poor town—but a center of Torah, and there was a host of outstanding scholars in the town who used to study at fixed hours in the synagogue, learning, and teaching the gentry and simple folk of the town. Even the empty-headed of Slutzk's Jews inhaled the fragrance of Torah, like the thorn inhaling the fragrance of the myrtle growing near it. There were yeshivot in Slutzk for child and adult, and boys and young men of poor parentage streamed to them from far and near, applying themselves assiduously to the study of Torah. The Jews of Slutzk, poor as they themselves were, shared with these students their slice of bread and bowl of soup, and in their synagogues gave them a roof over their heads and a bench to sleep on.

In Slutzk I passed the eight years of childhood and boyhood during which the human personality is formed, and Slutzk it was that molded and puts its stamp upon my spiritual personality. From the Pentateuch and the Prophets I went on to the study of the Talmud, and the noble world of the Pentateuch and the Prophets was replaced by the practical world of the Talmud.

In this world there is no exploration of matters appertaining to Genesis or the "Divine Chariot," as in the world of the Pentateuch and of the Prophets, but of banal realities of life. My imagination, however, sublimated these realities and transformed them into ethereal abstractions, and shaped the sages dealing with them in the real-life visage of the elders of the Slutzk synagogue, as I saw them grappling with each other in the elucidation of a difficult Talmudic disputed passage, angrily grimaced, frowning, their looks ablaze, debating with bristling thumb and arched back as if poised to join in a battle to the finish. But these sages approached me with grace and dealt with me with friendly countenance and sweet voice in order to disclose to me the mysteries of the Torah. And in their company, my orphanhood was sweetened.

My orphanhood was sweetened by my week-day studies, but it turned bitter again on the Sabbath. Seated in a corner of the synagogue I would regard the boys of my own age, and my heart was consumed with mortification; there they sit, those happy boys, beside fathers wrapped in prayer shawls, drawing gratification from their beaming faces that turn to them from time to time and from the faces of their mothers glowing at them from the windows of the women's gallery—both caressing. And I—wherein have I sinned that I am orphaned of mother and bereft of father?

Sometimes on my way to the Sabbath afternoon services, I would visit the home of one of my heder comrades. Sometimes upon entering the house I would see my teacher. He made it a practice every Sabbath to visit the homes of his pupils, each pupil in turn, to examine them in the presence of their parents, and that Sabbath was my comrade's turn.

I felt that I was an unwelcome guest in his house just then, and I stole outside, to await him there until his examination was over and he could join me. I stood peeking in at his window and saw the beaming faces of his parents during the examination, the satisfied look of the rabbi after he had pulled him successfully through the examination, and their general satisfaction when they finished off with some goodies—and again a deep mortification consumed my heart: Am I inferior to my comrade; why then does my teacher not visit *my* house to examine *me:* am I to be ignored because I am an orphan? I stalked off to the synagogue, disconsolate and humiliated.

When the afternoon service was over, I stayed for the recitation of the Psalms. Shadows of the gloaming filled the synagogue and their dimness absorbed the glow of twilight glimmering in the western horizon. On the Alememar stood Yeke, the tinsmith, who had a "claim" on the conducting of the Psalms recitation of this time of day, reading aloud the verses of the Psalms designated for the accompaniment of the departing Holy Sabbath. He read with aching heart and wailing tone, and the sparse congregation, immersed in shadow and sadness, responded. I also joined him, and, through these verses, bemoaned the mortification inspired in me by my orphanhood.

I began to long for an examination in my studies, if not in the presence of my parents, then at least in the presence of my grandfather, and not by my teacher—I resented him for discriminating against me out of all his pupils—but by one of the learned men whose fame I knew. At that time I was studying in heder the Talmudic section dealing with "the merchants of Lod," and I decided to memorize it for an examination. When I knew it by heart I began to press my grandfather to take me for an examination to Rabbi Heshke—a venerable scholar, former head of a yeshiva, who prayed at the yeshiva synagogue which counted my grandfather among its congregants.

At first my grandfather refused. His seat in this synagogue was on a bench behind the Alememar, with the other lowly and common folk like himself—who is *he* to dare approach Rabbi Heshke, whose place of honor is beside the Holy Ark, and at whose coming or departure everybody rises; who is *he* to presume to have words with the Rabbi? Finally, he gave in to my entreaties and took me to Rabbi Heshke one Sabbath afternoon. In fear and trembling he approached his seat of honor in the synagogue, and I tagged after him with quaking knees. The Rabbi's head was bent over the Talmud tome. My grandfather coughed several times and interrupted Rabbi Heshke's study. The latter looked up:

"What do you want, Reb Yid?"

"I want," my grandfather stammered, "I want—I mean—he wants —this is my grandson, my dead daughter's son—his father is in America—a colt drawing the yoke of Torah—he wants—he wants—I mean, he would like to be examined in his studies, Rabbi."

When Rabbi Heshke asked me, I began to recite the whole section of "the merchants of Lod" by heart, my eyes lowered out of shyness and fear at his grim countenance. When I had completed my recitation he began to ply me with questions.

"He is blessed," he praised me to my grandfather in my presence. "A precious vessel: Happy is his mother in heaven and happy is his father in America."

Tears rose in my grandfather's eyes, and, as for me, my heart constricted and a lump rose in my throat.

"My son," Rabbi Heshke addressed me, "study diligently and let your father in America rejoice in you and your mother in heaven be glad in you, as it is written: 'Let your father rejoice—.' "

Levi Yitzhak of Berditchev

Samuel H. Dresner

> *Rabbi Israel Baal Shem Tov appeared one day before his disciples, gave drink and cakes to each, and bade them be seated and rejoice. They looked at one another in surprise. How is this day different from other days? When they asked the reason for the celebration, their teacher explained:*
>
> *"A holy soul will soon descend into the world, a soul who will stand fast for our brothers, the household of Israel."*
>
> *The year was 1740.*
>
> *The man about whom he spoke was Rabbi Levi Yitzhak of Berditchev.*

IN THE resplendent chain of Hasidic masters which stretches more than seven generations through a hundred communities in Eastern Europe, there is none, excepting the Baal Shem himself, about whose life so many stories have been told. It was said by the mystics that there was within the holy one from Berditchev the soul of Rabbi Akiba. Great was his holiness and his clinging to God. Words cannot capture his fervor in prayer or his love of Israel. Perhaps there were men wiser than he, more profound and greater leaders, but none of purer heart.

Whether the stories of Levi Yitzhak are accurate or the product of fancy we do not know. But piece them together and there emerges the image of a man in whom the fire of divine glory burned so brightly that his prayers to God could shake sleeping souls awake, his compassion for the needy arouse the miser to charity, his observance of the mitzvot open to men a new path of service, his words of Torah strike fire in their hearts, his songs give them hope and his dancing bring them joy. His endless love of the children of Israel could blind him to their faults and lead him to cry out in their defense, even against heaven itself.

Rabbi Shneor Zalman of Ladi said: "The Holy One blessed-be-He is the *zaddik* in heaven. Rabbi Levi Yitzhak is the *zaddik* on earth."

Rabbi Levi Yitzhak was among the humblest of his generation. In Warsaw he met a Jew, a coarse, common fellow named Beinush.

"Beinush, my brother," said the rabbi, "pay attention to what I say, my brother Beinush. Cling with love to the Higher Source, to the Merciful One, Beinush, my brother, and you will see that there is nothing more precious than this."

Thus he would enter into conversation with the lowest of people and thereby draw them to Torah and its observance. He never raised himself above them nor looked down upon them. "Even if pride were commanded in the Torah," he said, "I still could not believe it possible, for man is but 'dust and ashes.' How then should he be proud?"

When the news became known that he had been appointed the rabbi of the city of Berditchev, Rabbi Levi Yitzhak said:

"Woe to the generation if such as the likes of me can be its leader!"

"He who causes pride to enter his heart," Rabbi Levi Yitzhak used to say, "transgresses a law of the Torah: 'Thou shalt not bring an abomination into thy house' (Deuteronomy 7:26). For there is no abomination greater than the abomination of pride. And there is a verse to indicate this: 'An abomination of the Lord is every lofty heart' (Proverbs 16:5). And if one who causes pride to enter his house sins, how much the more so one who causes it to enter his heart!"

Because God was the center of Levi Yitzhak's life, he was neither flattered by praise nor offended by scorn. Once, before he came to Berditchev, while walking in the street of one of the communities where he served as rabbi and where he was persecuted bitterly by the *Mitnagdim,* he passed the wife of one of those who disliked him. She spat upon him and cursed him. He hastened to the *Bet Hamidrash,* approached the holy ark, and said:

"Master of all worlds, do not punish this woman. She is a good woman and only does the will of her husband."

When God is truly the center of a man's life, taught the *zaddik* of Berditchev, that man is not jealous of his neighbor's success. It matters not who serves God best, only that He be served. "Whether a man really loves God," he said, "can be determined by the love he bears his fellow men, which, in turn, depends on his own selflessness." And he proceeded to relate the following:

A Parable: "A country was suffering from the ravages of war. The general who was sent against the foe was vanquished, and the king put in his place another who succeeded in driving out the invader. The first general was suspected of betraying his country. The king wondered how he might find out whether he was loyal or not. Then he realized that there was one unerring sign which would reveal the truth to him: if the man about whom he was in doubt showed friendship for his rival and expressed true joy at his success, he might be regarded as trustworthy; but if he plotted against him, this would prove his guilt.

"God created man to strive against the evil in his soul. Now there is many a man who does, indeed, love God, but is defeated in that bitter struggle. He can be recognized by his ability to share wholeheartedly and without reservation in the happiness of his victorious fellow man.

"When a Jew studies Torah or performs a mitzvah, he must do so for the sake of God. And even after he has done so, the thought must not arise in his heart, heaven forbid, that he has already fulfilled the will of the Creator. He who thinks thus, his deeds are not accepted, for he has not even reached the threshold of true service. Indeed, although he has performed a mitzvah with all his heart, he remains humble in the awareness that he has still not served God."

Another Parable: "Once there was a man who wanted to enter the palace of the king. The closer he came into the inner chambers of the palace, the more he saw of the treasures and the glory of the king, the smaller he felt.

"So it is with the mitzvot. The greater the love and fear with which one fulfills a mitzvah, the deeper he merits to penetrate into the inner recesses of the temple of the King, the more he perceives of the majesty of the King, blessed be His name, the more the awe of the King falls upon him, the more unworthy he knows himself to be.

"Thus when pride stirs a man, thinking he has brought joy to the Creator through his deeds, he is really far away, not even upon the threshold of service.

"But the *zaddik* is as nothing in his own eyes, as if he has not yet begun to serve the Lord.

"All the while that he cleaves to the holiness of the Creator, blessed-be-He, he himself believes that he is far from the holiness of the Creator, blessed-be-He.

"How then should he know when he is near to the holiness of the Creator?

"When he believes he is far, this is the sign that he is near."

Levi Yitzhak taught that man should be generous toward others, but critical of himself. "To search out transgressions and to speak words of praise," he wrote, "are two good qualities which every Jew is obliged to possess. However, it is necessary to understand in what manner they should be used.

"Transgressions, a man should search out in himself.

"Praise, he should speak in regard to others."

This good advice was sometimes forgotten, as he tells of an early period in his life:

When I saw that the people of my city did not need me, I began to examine my deeds. Soon I discovered that the members of my own household did not respect me, and so I looked further into my ways. At last, the Almighty opened my eyes so that I realized the error was in myself, in that I failed to conduct myself as I should have. I determined to improve myself. When the members of my household noticed this, they began to listen to me, and soon after, the people of the city no longer refused to accept my opinions.

The problem of pride is eternal, and the battle against it never-ending. The saint knows that love of self is always present in man and must ever and again be met and defended through self-judgment and the love of God.

Once he asked his friend, Rabbi Shneor Zalman:

"How can we prevent self-interest, with which we are occupied even against our will?"

Replied Shneor Zalman: "If it is possible, one must drive it away. And if it is not possible, then one can at least be consoled by the fact that the Almighty, of whom it is written, He made everything for His own glory, was also touched by self-interest during the creation of the world."

"But what consolation is this," said Levi Yitzhak, "for all the acts of self-interest which the Holy One, blessed-be-He, did, were done for the sake of heaven!"

While still quite young Levi Yitzhak became known as a brilliant student of the Talmud and Codes. One of the wealthiest Jews of Libertov, Yisroel Peretz, chose him as husband for his daughter and arranged for him to live with them and spend his time in the study of Torah. This good fortune was the talk of the town.

As a mark of respect for his father-in-law, Levi Yitzhak was honored on Simhat Torah, in the first year of his marriage, by being asked to recite the passage *ata horayta,* before the congregation in the House of Prayer. The *shamus* called him to the pulpit in a loud chant marked by many trills so that everyone's eyes were upon him. He went to the pulpit and for a while stood motionless. Then he put out his hand to take his tallit, but laid it down again. The *shamus* whispered to him not to delay the service. "Very well," he said and took the prayer shawl in his hand. But when he had almost covered his shoulders, he put it down again. His father-in-law was ashamed before the congregation, and sent him an angry message either to begin the prayer or leave the pulpit. But even before Levi Yitzhak heard these words, his voice rang through the hall: "If you are versed in the teachings, if you are a Hasid, then you speak the prayer!" With this he returned to his place. His father-in-law said nothing.

But when they were at home and Levi Yitzhak sat opposite him at the festive table, his face bright with the joy befitting the day, his father-in-law could contain himself no longer and shouted:

"Why did you bring this disgrace upon me?"

"When I first put out my hand to draw the prayer shawl over my head, the Evil Urge came and whispered in my ear:

" 'I want to say *ata horayta* with you!'

"I asked: 'Who are you that you regard yourself worthy to do this?'

"And he: 'Who are you that you regard yourself worthy of this?'

" 'I am versed in the teachings.'

" 'I too am versed in the teachings.'

"I thought to put an end to this idle talk and said contemptuously:

" 'Where did you study?'

" 'Where did you study?' he countered.

"I told him.

" 'But I was right there with you,' he murmured laughingly. 'I studied there in your company!'

"I pondered for a moment. 'I am a Hasid,' I informed him triumphantly.

"And he, unperturbed: 'I too am a Hasid.'

"I: 'To what *zaddik* did you travel?'

"And he, again echoing me: 'To whom did you travel?'

" 'To the holy *maggid* of Mezritch,' I replied.

"Whereupon he laughed again. 'But I tell you that I was there with you and became a Hasid just as you did. And that is why I want to say with you *ata horayta*.'

"Then I had enough of it.

" 'If you are versed in the teachings,' I said, 'if you are a Hasid, then you speak the prayer.'

"At that I left him. What else could I have done?"

It was the custom of Rabbi Levi Yitzhak of Berditchev each evening before he went to sleep to make a *heshbon hanefesh,* to examine his thoughts and deeds for that day. If he found a blemish, he said:

"Levi Yitzhak will not do that again."

Then he would chide himself:

"Levi Yitzhak, you said the same thing yesterday."

Then he would reply:

"Yesterday Levi Yitzhak did not speak the truth. Today he speaks the truth."

Study of Torah may lead to pride, and such pride was indeed characteristic of many scholars of the time; the writings of all the early Hasidic leaders protested against this danger. Rabbi Levi Yitzhak taught that the Torah requires humility. Once he was asked the question: "How is it that Moses, who in his great humility had implored God not to send him but another Pharaoh, did not for a single instant hesitate to receive the Torah?"

"He had seen the tall mountains come before God," said the rabbi, "and each asked for the privilege of being the one on which the revelation should be given. But God chose lowly Mount Sinai. That is why—when he saw that he too was chosen—Moses did not resist, but followed the call."

"If one should sin through error by doing any of the mitzvot (commandments) which the Lord has commanded not be done . . ."

"Why in its verse does the Torah use the word mitzvah in reference to a sinful act? To teach us how evil is the quality of pride before the Lord. When a man commits a sin, God forbid, but knows that he has committed a sin, he will repent. But he who does a mitzvah and takes pride in it, boasting of it in the streets and in the market place, as if he had enriched the Holy One blessed-be-He—this is sin and transgression."

Rabbi Levi Yitzhak asked:

"Why is it that the tractates of the Talmud, that massive work which occupies the central place in Jewish learning, are printed in a manner different from ordinary books? For each book of the Talmud begins on page two instead of page one."

When no one replied, he answered: "In order that one should know that no matter how much he has learned—he has still not even begun."

The Library in Jewish Life

Horace M. Kallen

JEWS are the only people of antiquity that had a people's library. The common word for the Jewish library is Bible, that collection of a great many different books with different purposes, backgrounds and origins. They range from Chronicles and Histories to Prophecy, Law and Wisdom, and even to profound philosophy as in the Book of Job. The Chinese also had a Bible, but it was not for all the people.

Heinrich Heine called the Bible of his people their "portable fatherland" because fundamentally their ideals, ways of life, rules of righteousness and justice in human relations were expressed and prescribed in this book or collection of books, and could be followed anywhere. The Bible was never the monopoly of a selected clerical class, though it has so become in the modern world; in Jewish history, it was something that all the people everywhere shared in, read and reread, repeated and studied year after year, at home and in the synagogue.

The Jewish people, as Jews, have lived by and from this library. Everything else, from the Talmud to the literature of the Zionists and anti-Zionists, is commentary—commentary upon this "portable fatherland," through the study of which the identity of the Jew as a certain type of human personality, with a creed and code of life all its own, was maintained from generation to generation. It was defined in the form of prescriptions—there is the series of admonitions in the Book of Deuteronomy especially—among which the requirement to write and rewrite the Torah, to study and elaborate on it, was the fundamental. Without this library, transmitting the past and designing the future, there would not have been any Jews or any Jewish cultural heritage.

We can think of a library in two ways: as a repository of books where specialists may come to improve their knowledge and verify their errors, a kind of bank for dead knowledge; or as living knowledge, absorbed by living people and made use of for the creation of their own futures. Too many libraries, alas, especially among us Jews, are repositories of dead knowledge.

But when a living human being does take hold of his recorded heritage, it then becomes part of his own personal history and enters into the living past without which there can be no future for anyone. The thing we have to remember always is that, as individuals, we are our past from the day we are born to the day we die; that by learning, we create our past and achieve our future; and that what we presently do with what we have learned alters that past. All learning is a transformation of the learner's past, thus a transformation of his personality. A person who forgets his past forfeits his personality; and the same is true of a society, which to be alive and not a fossil must have an historical awareness.

Both for the individual and the group, there is only one way to accumulate the past. It is the way of the written or printed word, the library. In the library exists the past of every culture, science, art and religion. As George Santayana noted a long time ago, "He who forgets his past is doomed to repeat it." The future, that is, history and growth, depends on transforming this past. Where there is only repetition there can be neither history nor growth. The arts and sciences "progress" only in the degree that they diverge from the past. Their divergence is their future, which is new and different in the degree that it has altered that past, yet becomes one with it.

In the history of the Jewish people, whether in Biblical times or in our own day, that process of alteration through study of the past is ongoing and continuous. Among Jews there still is a kind of reverence for the spoken and printed word. There is a feeling that to study, somehow, is to worship. As George Foot Moore, the renowned Christian student of Judaism, has said: "This conception of individual and collective study as a form of divine service has persisted in Judaism through all the ages and has made not only the learned by profession, but men of humble callings, assiduous students of the Talmud as the pursuit of the highest branch of religious learning and most meritorious of good works."

The late Justice Brandeis, writing in 1916, saw the modern significance of this commitment:

> Our intellectual capacity was developed by the almost continuous training of the mind through twenty-five centuries. The Torah led the people of the Book to intellectual pursuits at times when most of the Aryan peoples were illiterate.
>
> Religion imposed the use of the mind upon the Jews, indirectly as well as directly; it demanded of the Jew not merely the love, but also the understanding, of God. This necessarily involved a study of the Law. The educated descendants of a people which in its infancy cast aside the golden calf and put its faith in the invisible God cannot worthily in its maturity worship worldly distinction and things material . . . We are bound not only to use worthily our great inheritance, but to preserve, and, if possible, augment it; and then transmit it to the coming generations.

Preserving, augmenting, transmitting depends upon the library, the growing depository of the changing heritage. And what better uses can be made of it than for the survival of the Jewish people? For example, in the Genizah in Egypt, every kind of printed word, even the most banal, was preserved simply because it was printed. But it was out of that vast Genizah that Solomon Schechter, one of the founding fathers of Conservative Judaism, drew so much of the material from which he built his idea of what he called "Catholic Judaism."

But libraries are meaningless until and unless they are used. How they are used, by whom, and in how many different ways—that determines what the role of the library may be in the survival of the Jewish cultural heritage as a way of life for people who have chosen to call themselves Jews. They cannot be Jews without it, and they will not be Jews except in the degree that it comes alive within them. And it cannot come alive unless there is a definite orchestration between their Jewish heritage and the culture of the world of which that heritage is a part, and within which it must make its way as a creative and cooperative partner.

We cannot have schools or adequate instruction, whether of teachers or of pupils, without the library equipment, and the modern components of that equipment have changed the nature of the library. Today, in the great public libraries, most conspicuously in our own country, where the use of the library and the art of the librarian have become matters for professional training, the library is diversified by oral records, motion pictures, and by a variety of other collections —oral, graphic, pictorial, as well as printed—that also have to be communicated to the people.

Our libraries record the sequential changes of our existence. As living individuals, we retain our identities only as we change. We are different today from what we were yesterday, a year ago, or as children; and every day until we die, if we truly are alive we go on making ourselves different in order to stay the same. Our struggle to preserve ourselves consists in continuously changing ourselves. This is no less deeply true of groups, societies, peoples, religious denominations. If we were to compare today's way of life even of the Neturai Karta in Israel, the most rigid of the Judaist groups, with what it was twenty-five years ago, we would find much variation and change. No individual or group can live without altering; and the basis of whatever transformation we make becomes the recorded heritage of the past. Because we are alive we are changing that past at the frontier of our struggles for tomorrow. And tomorrow is indeterminate because it is not possible today to know the future. What we have to rely on at any time is only our past. The commoner word for it is tradition.

Now Jews who today want to maintain and develop the Jewish tradition must needs remember that many other interests and ways of life constantly compete for attention. Jewish children go to the public school for most of the day. What most Jewish adults earn their living by has nothing to do with their Jewish heritage. For many of us, our Jewish interests are segregated to our leisure time, to holidays, Saturdays and Sundays, and must rival for our attention with television, sports and all kinds of other alternatives.

The function of today's Jewish library should be to meet this rivalry, to provide us with and make us hunger for a Jewish extension of our intellectual horizon, and an intensification of our consciousness of what the Jewish heritage can offer in the way of ideals, enterprises and vicarious experiences. It can enable us to live vicariously from day to day, in addition to the lives of heroes about whom novelists write, the lives of all the Jews who are recorded in the Bible and other Jewish works. Through the library our Jewish world can be enormously enlarged—if only we want to seek that enlargement.

III

Views, Beliefs and Attitudes

The Meaning of Jewish Existence
Alfred Jospe

COUNTLESS attempts have been made to define the meaning of Jewish existence. To John, in the fourth Gospel, the Jews are of the devil, while to the Talmud they are as indispensable to the survival of the world as the winds. To the German historian Heinrich von Treitschke, who lived around the turn of the century, the Jews are the ferment of decomposition, an element of unrest and change in civilization, while for Judah Halevi, Israel is the heart of mankind by its special propensity for religious insight.

To Max Weber, the sociologist, the Jews, because of their lack of power and their persistent insecurity, had to be classified as a pariah group, while even so rational a thinker as Abraham Geiger claimed that Jews have a special genius for religion. And to Arnold Toynbee the Jews are merely a fossilized relic of an ancient Syriac civilization, while to the philosopher Alfred North Whitehead the Jews are very much alive and their survival is largely the result of their being in his view probably the most able people of any in existence.

A bewildering maze of contradictory definitions and claims! Perhaps the best way to arrive at an understanding of the meaning of Jewish distinctiveness is to familiarize ourselves with the historic image Jews had of themselves. What has been their vision of themselves, their view of the meaning of their existence, and their role in history?

The Jewish image of the Jew is embodied, first, in what Arthur Lelyveld has called a *value stance,* a specific attitude toward life and the world.

Man, basically, has only two possibilities of establishing a relationship to the world. He can accept it, or he can reject it. Judaism accepts and affirms life and the world. As Leo Baeck has put it in his *Essence of Judaism,* Judaism demands the moral affirmation of man's relation to the world by will and deed and declares the world to be the field of life's tasks.

Judaism is the expression of the command to work and create; it works for the kingdom of God in which all men may be included. It calls for ascent, development, growth, the long march toward the future. It seeks to reconcile the world with God. Judaism is, therefore, ultimately, the affirmation of an active, creative relationship to the world in which man's life finds meaning and fulfillment.

But there are various ways in which life and the world can be affirmed. In which way does Judaism differ from other affirmations?

The Greeks, for instance, also affirmed life and the world, but in a way that was wholly different from the value stance of the Jews. Socrates accepted death even though he was innocent by his own definition of justice. He refused to escape when his friends wanted to make it possible because he accepted and affirmed the higher authority of the state. The state cannot exist when law is set aside. Defiance would result in chaos.

Compare this attitude with that of the prophet Nathan, who castigates David's defiance of justice in his affair with Bathsheba; of Elijah, who denounces Ahab for his murder of Naboth; of Isaiah, who denounces the religious and political leaders of Jerusalem because of their corruption; of Jeremiah, fearless and flaming in his indictment of the religious hypocrisy and moral depravity of his generation and government. While Socrates was a detached thinker who gave passive assent to the existing social order even though it might have been evil, the prophets challenged the social order precisely because it was evil.

For the Greek, government embodies laws which cannot be challenged. For the Hebrew, government itself stands under the judgment of the law and can be challenged in God's name. For Socrates, the highest virtue and achievement are that man *think* correctly; for the prophets, the highest virtue and achievement are that he *act* correctly.

For this reason, the value stance of Judaism is also profoundly different from the world view of Christianity, which insists that the highest virtue is that man *believe* correctly. Though works are important, the indispensable condition of salvation is faith in Jesus as the Christ; salvation is achieved not by the merit of one's deeds but by the acceptance of the officially formulated correct form of belief. For Judaism, however, it ultimately is man's acts which matter and not his notions or thoughts, which may well be erroneous or mistaken. God's nature and thoughts are beyond our grasp. But His commandments are "neither hidden nor far off."

The Jewish value stance toward life and the world is the context, the frame of the picture, as it were. Within that frame, there emerge the details of the image the Jews had of themselves as Jews.

This image has several dominant features. One is what is usually called the concept of Israel's "election," or the "chosen people." The world is created by God, and man's place in the world is part of a divine plan. At a particular time in this cosmic drama and at a particular place, on Mount Sinai, God revealed Himself and His will in a particular document, the Torah. This document reveals not only the will of God, but the instrument through which God has chosen to make His will known to the world. This instrument is the people known as Israel; Israel is therefore God's "chosen people."

The concept of the "chosen people" permeates much of Jewish literature, folklore, prayers and liturgy. When a Jewish man is called to the Torah, he recites the traditional blessing, *"Asher bahar banu mi'kol ha-amim,"* praising God, who has chosen us from all other nations. When we recite our daily morning prayer, we say the benediction, *"She'lo assani goy,"* thanking God that He has not made us gentiles. When we pronounce the benediction over the Sabbath wine, we declare that God has chosen and sanctified us from among all other peoples, in the same way in which he has distinguished between Sabbath and weekday. When we make *Havdalah* on Saturday nights, we recite the traditional *Hamavdil,* glorifying God for setting us apart from all other peoples just as He has set apart the sacred from the profane and light from darkness.

Few of Judaism's teachings have been so misunderstood as this concept of the "chosen people." George Bernard Shaw compared it to the *Herrenvolk* concept of the Nazis; H. G. Wells considered it a hindrance to world unity; Protestant theologians persist in speaking of the God of Judaism as a tribal deity, interested only in protecting His own people and not a God who is concerned with the whole of mankind; and avowed anti-Semites cite this idea as proof for their claim that there is a Jewish conspiracy to seek to dominate the Christian world. The concept has even been rejected by Jewish thinkers, especially by Mordecai Kaplan and the Reconstructionist movement as incompatible with the dignity of man and the mandates of democracy.

What then did the Jews mean when they spoke of themselves as the "chosen people"? How did they understand the meaning of their election?

The Jewish concept of the "chosen people" does not imply a feeling of racial or political superiority. It does not represent a claim that Jews are superior to the rest of mankind by reason of birth, blood or racial endowment. Anyone can become a Jew by embracing Judaism. A person who converts to Judaism is called a *"ben Avraham,"* a son of Abraham, which he becomes by the *"b'rit Avraham,"* by entering into Abraham's covenant. Rabbi Meir said that man—Adam—had been created from dust which had been collected from all corners of the earth so that no nation could claim the distinction of being better or having cradled mankind. Some of the greatest rabbis are said to have been descended from converts to Judaism, and, according to Jewish tradition, King David, from whose house the Messiah would come, was a direct descendant of Ruth, the Moabite, a foreigner who married Boaz, a Jew.

The concept of election does not imply the rejection of the rest of mankind as inferior. In fact, Judaism clearly acknowledges that men can be blessed with salvation even though they are outside the Sinaitic covenant. Traditional Judaism proclaims that the righteous of all nations have a share in the world-to-come and that man should first lead a good life and then ask God for religious truth. As Morris Joseph put it, "Israel's election does not give him a monopoly of the divine love." For Judaism, all human beings are God's children and have an equal claim upon his care and solicitude. There is no magic passport to the divine favor either here or hereafter. The divine test of a man's worth is not his theology but his life.

In the same way, the protection of the law was extended to every inhabitant of the country, Jew and non-Jew alike. In the words of Leviticus, "Thou shalt have one manner of law for the stranger as well as for the homeborn." The Jew certainly did not need a Supreme Court to decide whether or not minority members had a right to attend the high schools and universities of southern Israel without being segregated. Jews have always been particularly sensitive to these problems for, as the Bible and Jewish observances constantly remind them, they had been strangers in Egypt themselves, and the memory of that experience had burned itself with acid into their consciousness. Because they knew what oppression of minorities meant and what it could do to the soul of the oppressed, they hated oppression and wanted to make sure they would never succumb to its practices.

What the concept of election has meant in Jewish life, in positive terms, is illustrated by a story of the Rabbis. The ancient sages once asked: Why did God choose Israel? Because all other nations refused to accept the Torah. Originally, God had offered it to all nations of the world. But the children of Esau rejected it because they could not reconcile themselves to the commandment, "Thou shalt not kill." The Moabites declined the offer because they felt they could not accept the commandment, "Thou shalt not commit adultery." The Ishmaelites refused because they could not square their habits with the commandment, "Thou shalt not steal." All of them rejected the Torah; finally only Israel was left and prepared to accept the Torah.

The story makes a crucial point. Ancient Israel was an insignificant little people in the vast spaces of the Near East. It could have been like all other peoples of the area, content to live, working, procreating, building houses, struggling with nature to wrest a living from it, and gradually fading away from the arena of history.

And yet, in this very people, there suddenly blazed forth the conviction that it is not enough just to exist, to live, but that man must live for something, and that, therefore, this people is different from the peoples in whose midst it had been living; that there is something that gives meaning to life and through which it becomes articulate about the purpose of its existence. For the first time in the history of mankind, national difference becomes transformed into moral and spiritual distinctiveness.

Here we can grasp the meaning of "election." It is in the idea of his "election" that the Jew becomes conscious and articulate about what he conceives his task and role to be. He becomes conscious that he possesses a truth which makes him different from other groups. Hence, election is the "living certainty of a religious community that it possesses a knowledge of the truth which distinguishes it from all other peoples or nations" (Baeck), which is a unique and vital possession and gives its existence a sense of purpose and direction.

That truth which distinguishes the Jew from all other people and gives his life a sense of purpose and direction is embodied in the idea of the "covenant," the second feature in the image which Jews had of themselves. The Hebrew term for covenant is *b'rit*, as in B'nai B'rith. It is an agreement between God and Israel by which Israel accepted the Torah. This acceptance implies two fundamental notions. First, the agreement between God and Israel is bilateral; if God selected Israel, Israel consented to be elected. If God chose Israel, Israel, in turn, chose God. As Israel Zangwill once put it, a chosen people is at bottom a choosing people. Secondly, if the concept of *election* means the consciousness of the fact that one possesses a truth which sets one apart from others, the concept of the *covenant* means the consciousness of what this truth is. It is Torah, the Law of Sinai, the acceptance and affirmation of God's design for man's life. It is the consciousness of what the Torah in its widest sense demands of man—of what we must do to make this truth alive regardless of the hardships or obligations it may entail. The covenant is man's response: *"Hineni"*—"Here I am"—to the voice that calls; it is the acceptance of the obligation inherent in election.

The concept of the covenant has numerous connotations in Jewish tradition and literature. After the flood, God enters into a compact with mankind through Noah, in which God pledges that He will never again engage in destructive violence against the human race, and by which man, in turn, pledges that he will abide by the fundamental moral laws in dealing with his fellow men. The term is used again when God enters into a covenant with Abraham. Abraham is called to train his children and those of his descendants after him to keep the ways of the Lord, that is, to do what is good and right, while God pledges Himself to bless Abraham and his descendants.

The prophet Hosea defined the covenant as an act of love between God and Israel, symbolizing their bond of partnership in which man is given a share in the never-ending process of creation and the redemption of mankind through love and faithfulness:

> *I shall betroth thee unto Me forever.*
> *I shall betroth thee unto Me with right and*
>   *justice, with love and mercy.*
> *I shall betroth thee unto Me in truth, and*
>   *thou shalt know the Lord. (Hosea 2:19–20)*

The most significant expression of the covenant can, however, be found in Exodus: "Now then, if ye will obey My voice and keep My covenant, then ye shall be a peculiar treasure unto Me above all other people. For all the earth is Mine. And ye shall be unto Me a kingdom of priests, and a holy nation" (19:5–6). Election is not a divine favor extended to a people, but a task imposed upon it. It is not a prerogative but an ethical charge, not a divine title for rights but a divine mandate for duties. And the duties are to live in accordance with the word and spirit of Sinai, to serve God in thought and act, to sanctify life, to diminish evil, to be the prophet and servant and, frequently, the suffering servant of the Lord. The obligation is upon Jews to be heirs and perpetuators of the spirit of the men who entered the arena of history as prophets of the ideal society, as legislators of the priestly and sanctified life, as visionaries of justice and human reconciliation, as challengers of evil and the singers of hope.

More, not less, is expected of Israel by virtue of the covenant. People who are ignorant of God and His will, men who have never been taught or told what truth and justice are, may be forgiven impieties and sin. But Jews cannot be forgiven so easily—Israel has a special commitment to God. When Israel fails, it commits a *hillul hashem,* a desecration of the divine name. Thus Amos warns the people in God's name, "Only you have I known of all the families of the earth. Therefore I will visit upon you all your iniquities" (Amos 3:2). To overcome evil and realize the good is man's never-ending task, a moral task for all.

This conception of life as a moral task and never-ending quest for perfection is the third and perhaps most characteristic feature of the Jewish image of the Jew. It finds its highest expression in the concept of the Messiah.

Messianic thinking is rooted in one of man's most profound needs and concerns, his concern with the future. While some nations of antiquity, living through eras of crisis and catastrophe, despaired of the future and turned their vision to the Golden Age when men lived happily in the past, the Jew did not evade the problem posed by the future. He never placed perfection in the past, but instead projected it into the future.

Of course, the Bible starts with perfection too. The first man, Adam, must necessarily have been happy and perfect until his fall. Yet this idea has never played a significant part in Jewish thought. What is important is not man's descent but his ascent, not his origin but his goal, not his past but his future. Jewish thinking looks for happiness, virtue and perfection not to a past Golden Age, but to the future, to "the end of days," a favorite phrase of the prophets.

This projection of perfection into the future is an integral part of Jewish thinking. It has been called the most striking and characteristic feature of the religion of Israel, originating in the Bible and best summarized in a single word—Messiah.

There are two views of the Messiah in Jewish tradition. The one has come to be called the *man*, the personal Messiah. The other is called the *time* Messiah, or the Messianic Era. The one is a man, the other an age. The one is a son of the House of David, the other an epoch in the history of Israel and the world. The one is a Jew, the other a time yet to come.

The concept of a personal Messiah has its inception in the historical experiences of the Jewish people and the political conditions in ancient Israel. The events recorded in the pages of our ancient history reveal no rosy picture. There were no glorious conquests, no triumphant victories. The patriarchs had to leave their native countries and wander in foreign lands. Then followed the Egyptian slavery with its memories of oppression. And even after the people had entered the Promised Land, they were constantly attacked by the tribes among whom they lived. They suffered the humiliation of frequent defeats and ultimately the loss of national independence.

It was only natural that a people with a past and such a present should long for a future when there would be an end to their suffering. They hoped for a political redeemer who would unite the people and establish a strong nation able to withstand the foreign enemies. It was not until after the appointment of David that the popular longing for such a redeemer was satisfied. Under David's leadership, the people grew powerful, establishing a kingdom reaching from the borders of Egypt to the gates of Damascus. The glory of this kingdom and of the man who had wrought this miracle caught the imagination of the masses. David became the ideal of the Jewish king, the great national hero and redeemer. He had inaugurated a state of national glory. People hoped it would last forever—a hope that was strengthened by Nathan's prophecy that David's throne would be established forever.

Originally, the Messiah was a national savior, a compensatory ideal conceived in times of national distress, a symbol of the indomitable will of the people to survive and to survive as a people. But at this time, a second ingredient was added to the Messianic concept. The Messiah now also began to personify the spiritual values and religious ideals to which the people should be dedicated. Gradually, the Messiah was conceived not only as the king but as the ideal king, the perfect ruler who would establish not only a stable government but a government based on righteousness and justice.

This hope runs through the fabric of all prophetic books and the Psalms. Isaiah crystallized this thought and expectation in immortal language when he spoke of a new king who, endowed with the divine spirit, would arise from the House of David and establish peace and equity in the land, who would usher in the time when tyranny and violence will no longer be practiced on God's holy mountain, and when the land will be full of the knowledge of God as the waters cover the earth.

The Messianic idea, at this stage of its development, was still particularistic, not universalistic. When the prophets spoke of the Messiah king, they did not refer to a king who would redeem the world. They meant a king who was to rule over Israel. When they spoke of the need for justice and perfection, they did not envision any utopian world based on justice and perfection. They demanded that the people of Israel practice justice in the land of Israel. The Messiah was still a national concept. He was the redeemer of Israel, not the redeemer of the world.

It is obvious that the development of the Messianic concept could not stop at this point. The prophets had proclaimed the one God who created man and the world and who demands righteousness. But if there is only one God, can He be merely the God of one people, of Israel? Is He not also the God of all peoples, of mankind? The prophets had preached that Israel had been appointed by God to practice righteousness, stamp out evil, establish the good society. But should not evil be eradicated and righteousness be practiced wherever men live? The prophets had proclaimed the moral law. But is there one moral code for one people, a different moral code for another people, and still another moral code for a third people? The moral law is universal law. Justice and righteousness are indivisible, valid for all people. God's demands are directed alike toward all men.

Driven by its own inner logic, Messianism widens from particularism into genuine universalism. It is at this point that the concept of mankind emerges in Jewish thought and, indeed, in Western thought, for the first time. If there is one God who created the world and fashioned man in His image, all men are His children. If there is one God, there must be one mankind. And if there is one mankind, there can be only one truth, one justice, one religion—to which not merely Israel but all men are called—and which cannot find its historic fulfillment until all men are united in it.

Deutero-Isaiah, Micah and other prophets no longer speak of the personal Messiah of the House of David, the individual who will become king and establish a reign of righteousness and peace for Zion. They speak of the new life which is to arise upon earth. The concept of the *one man* retreats more and more behind the concept of the *one time*. The personal Messiah gives way to the "days of the Messiah," in which universal peace and brotherhood will be established and all mankind will be united in the service of the one God.

The people of Israel, however, has a special task in helping to fashion the Messianic age. It is the people of Israel that has conceived of the one God for the one mankind. And it is the specific task of Israel to be the bearer and guardian of this truth until it will be accepted by all the nations of the earth. As Deutero-Isaiah puts it, "I, the Lord, have called thee in righteousness, and will hold thine hand and will keep thee for a covenant of the people, for a light of the nations, to open the blind eyes, to bring out the prisoners from the prisons, and them that sit in darkness out of the prison house."

Thus the prophets proclaimed the Messianic role of Israel in world history. They speak to Israel, but they speak of the world and the nations. Israel is to be the servant of the Lord. As God's servant, Israel will suffer. It will be persecuted because injustice, oppression and evil will continue to exist. But Israel's suffering will not be meaningless or in vain. By its very existence, Israel will be the symbol of the protest against oppression, injustice, idolatry, darkness and evil. Ultimately, Israel will be vindicated, and the world will know that "from the rising of the sun and from the West there is none beside Me"; men will mend their ways, evil will disappear and a new heaven and a new earth will be established—a day "when the Lord shall be king over all the earth, when the Lord shall be one and His name be one for all peoples."

Jewish Messianic thinking has a number of fundamental implications. First, the Messianic age will not come solely through the grace of God. It requires the labors of man. It does not signify an announcement of something which will ultimately descend to the earth from some other world. It will have to be earned by man.

Second, the Messianic age is of this world, not of another world, a world-to-come. It is an historic task and an historic possibility. It is to happen here on earth and not in apocalyptical times, after the end of time. It is the great goal toward which mankind must work and move here on this earth.

Third, Messianic thinking implies that man is not merely an object of history. He is also the subject of history. He is not merely driven by a blind fate. He can shape his future.

Hence the central core of the Messianic concept is the conviction that history is not blind. History has direction, it has a goal. The future is not what *will* be, but that which *should* be. It is a task entrusted to man, a command to shape his life and make the historic process the instrument of the realization of that which is good.

It is in these thoughts that the Messianic ideal reveals its deepest meaning and significance as the central feature of the image which Jews have of themselves and of the meaning of their existence. Man's life on earth is not a blind groping in darkness. It is not a succession of unrelated accidents, devoid of point and purpose, or, as Macbeth put it, "a veritable tale told by an idiot, full of sound and fury, signifying nothing."

Life has meaning. History has direction. There is a goal and purpose to man's endeavors. And this purpose can be lived by the man who learns to listen to the voice that calls him—*election;* who responds by saying *"Hineni"*—"Here I am"—*covenant;* and who, accepting his role in the Messianic drama, becomes God's partner in the never-ending task of creation.

How Shall Modern Man Think About God?

Ben Zion Bokser

How shall modern man think about God? Belief in God is essentially
an interpretation of the universe and of life within it. It is the antithesis of atheism, which is an interpretation of the world based on the
conviction that this whole vast existence—the entire cosmos and not
only our own tiny earth—is nothing more than an elaborate, precise
machine affected by the laws of cause and effect, but without any
purpose of its own.

The religious interpretation of life, on the contrary, insists that God
is the sole creator and ruler of the universe, and that everything in the
world, despite its complexity and apparent contradiction, exists according to His plan. Since it is obvious that there is ugliness in life as
well as beauty, pain as well as joy, good as well as evil, there would
seem, on the surface, to be a measure of chaos in the world. According
to the believer, however, what appears chaotic and contradictory is
nevertheless an integral part of God's plan, representing the creative
achievement of a beneficent intelligence proceeding toward some
great and noble purpose.

Various arguments and proofs are found in religious literature to
justify this conviction. A classic example, stemming back to Aristotle
and repeated by Maimonides, is the "argument from motion." We are
all familiar with the phenomenon of inertia that governs every object
in nature. We know that all matter must remain at rest in a fixed
position unless made to move by some outside force. Aristotle and
Maimonides both pointed out that since the universe is constantly in
motion there must be a force responsible for initiating and sustaining
this motion. In the religious view, this force is God.

Another approach which tries to prove the existence of a creator is
the "cosmological argument" advanced, among others, by the Jewish
sage Saadia Gaon, who lived in Babylonia in the tenth century. Simple
observation demonstrates conclusively that there is no spontaneous
creation in nature, that objects cannot form themselves. Since there is
a world, the world could not have sprung into existence by itself.
Therefore, there must have been a primal cause, a powerful generating agent—God—who fashioned the universe and brought it into being.

Still another proof that is often advanced is the "argument from
design." If one walks into a house and finds that the furnishings are
placed in good order, one knows that this cannot be the result of mere
chance, that some human being must have arranged the furniture, the

books and the pictures on the wall to reflect his own sensibilities and taste.

Similarly, a modern building is the product—good or bad—of some architect's design. Certainly, chance could not have brought together the bricks, beams, girders, pipes, and all the countless elements of construction in such a way as to form an edifice fit for human use. Much more wondrous certainly is the design revealed by the universe, and it argues for a being working with design and purpose to create and sustain the various enterprises of existence.

We may use a more striking analogy to demonstrate this point—the creation of a poem. Suppose one threw a bottle of ink into the air. Of course, it would come down with a crash, and if it fell on a sheet of paper, the ink would spatter. Here and there, it is theoretically possible that the spots of ink might accidentally form a letter, perhaps even two or three letters in combination to make a word. But to think even for one instant that these spots could arrange themselves into even a simple poem would be absurd. To imagine that these drops of ink could ever be shaped accidentally, without the assistance of a human intellect, into a masterpiece like Shakespeare's *Hamlet* would be preposterous.

If we are willing to accept the fact that an intellect, some reasoning power, must lie behind the furnishing and décor of a house, the construction and design of a building, or the dramatic artistry of a Shakespeare, it follows, as a matter of common sense, that the universe, with its design of infinite complexity, was shaped and is guided by a supreme intelligence that puts man's accomplishments into the shade. The vastness and variety of the universe—the thirty billion stars that have been so far accounted for; the fantastic number of animal, insect and microbic species; the multitude of human beings, not two of whom are exactly alike; even snow, every flake of which has a different crystal pattern—lead only to one conclusion: the universe cannot possibly be the result of chance, but obviously represents the work of an all-knowing, all-powerful intelligence.

In addition to the above "proofs" of God's existence, there is the wonder and majesty of the universe, which, to many, is a manifestation of God. A. J. Cronin in his autobiography, *Adventures in Two Worlds,* states that God cannot be proved like a mathematical equation. Nevertheless, he says, there are certain simple arguments that may help us to discover Him. If we consider the physical universe in its mystery and wonder, its order and intricacy, we cannot escape the notion of a primary cause.

Who, on a still summer night, dare gaze upward at the constellations, glittering in infinity, without the overpowering conviction that such a cosmos came into being through something more than blind, indeterminate chance? And our own world, whirling through space, is surely more than a meaningless ball of matter, thrown off by the merest accident from the sun. Although primarily a novelist in his later years, Cronin began his career as a scientist. For some years he was a practicing physician. Cronin's view of the workings of the universe is not far from that of many of the greatest scientists of our day. In reading of their lives and their intellectual growth as scientists, we are constantly struck by their sense of the mystery, majesty and wonder of the universe, and, above all, of the breathtaking intelligence which they see embodied in it, evoking in them an appreciative awe. As Maimonides said, the sense of wonder is the very heart of a truly religious spirit; religion begins with a sense of awe—not at nature as such, but at what is behind nature. And the highest reality to which nature points is God.

When we look at our children, how often do we pause to consider what is involved in their birth—the wonder of the creation of new life? In Thornton Wilder's play *Our Town,* when Emily, who has died, returns for one day to live among the living, she cries out against their blindness. They are surrounded by the wonders of life. But they are so insensitive that they take them for granted. Similarly, many of us tend to forget that there is a giver of life, who is the source of the beauty, the wonder and the very love that lives in the heart of the parent when he reaches to embrace his child.

If it is true that the universe represents the creation and materialization of a plan or purpose, supervised by a God who is all-powerful, wise and good, then why is there so much evil and suffering in the world? Why does life contain so much imperfection? Many people, without examining the matter deeply, take the fact that there is corruption and evil in the world as proof that there is no God.

The Jewish conception is that God deliberately made life imperfect in order to give the world a chance to grow toward perfection. No plan is complete at its inception; the perfection of any plan is visible only at its final development. Thus, much of the evil we see about us derives from the fact that God's plan remains unfinished. We are still living in the infancy, so to speak, not only of man but of the universe itself.

Science has shown us that even physically the universe is growing. It is in a constant state of expansion, of movement and change. To put it perhaps too simply, there is a "disturbing element" in the cosmic system that induces this change, just as there is a "disturbing element" in the world of men. The Biblical verse—often quoted but usually misinterpreted—states: "The nature of man is evil from his youth."

While some take this to mean that man's nature is corrupt from his very childhood, our interpretation is that man as a creature, a product of this cosmic growth, is still in the infancy of his development and is therefore an imperfect being.

Many Jewish thinkers are convinced that while the world is moving toward greater perfection, toward the kingdom of God, some imperfections would have to remain in it because a world without imperfection would lack the force to give incentive to life. The elimination of the so-called "disturbing element" from life would leave man with nothing to keep him moving, nothing to make him aspire toward his own improvement and a higher plane of existence.

Jewish theology has made the profound observation that man can never know the nature of God; he cannot give any positive definition of Him. In order to define an object, we must, in some respects, master it or transcend it. To define literally means to draw a boundary of words around an object so that it can be recognized. But God has been called illimitable, and is often referred to as the "boundless."

Abraham Heschel uses a term popular in Kabbalistic and Hasidic literature: "God is the ineffable," defying description. Just as words fail to convey the grandeur of most natural wonders, so too are God's attributes inexpressible, remaining greater than our power to characterize them except by resorting to indirect techniques drawn from our own limited observation and knowledge. That is why Jews say that it is daring and almost frightening to hope to encompass our praise of God in words.

There is a parable in the Talmud concerning a pious man who was overheard by a rabbi as he sang the praises of God. After he finished, the rabbi said to him: "Did you list all the praises there are? Have you exhausted the subject?" "No," the man replied. The rabbi then said: "When you kept adding adjective after adjective and finally stopped, the implication was that you had exhausted them. Isn't it better, therefore, not to use any adjectives at all?" Recognizing that silence is at times the greatest form of eloquence, our sages also sensed the hopelessness of attempting to define God's omnipotence and greatness by resorting to mere words.

When we say that God cannot be defined, we also admit that we cannot know what God is. God is a reality, a being, an intelligence. Sometimes we use the phrase, "God is a spirit." But what is spirit? In the Bible, when Moses addresses God and asks: "Tell me Your name. How will I be able to identify You?" God answers: "I am that I am." This means, simply, that God is pure existence.

Why then *do* we talk about God? How can we fill the prayer book and the Bible with so many characterizations of God?

This is not a contradiction. Although we cannot know God as an essence, there are two possible ways in which we can gain knowledge about Him. One is the negative: we know what God is not. No matter what we know in our experience concerning tangible representations of greatness and perfection, God is not like that. God is not a person; He is not a body; He has no concrete shape or form.

The second way in which we can know God is through the qualities of His work. To draw a parallel, it is true that without having met or heard anything about the personal life of a serious creative writer, it is possible to know a great deal about him by reading his books. God is the great unseen author of the universe. We cannot look into His face, but we can see what He, as author, has brought into being. From these observations, we can generalize and use certain adjectives to describe Him.

We know, for example, that in the universe there is order, beauty and a ceaseless urge to create life and perfect it. That means that order and beauty, creation and the search for perfection are apparently part of God's plan. We say that God is just, that He is merciful, compassionate and gracious. Certainly, this is applying the limited vocabulary of man to describe God. But again, knowing God's works—His incorruptibility, His concern with all of life from the highest to the lowest, the bounty of His natural treasure bestowed equally upon the good and wicked alike—it is possible to use adjectives drawn from human experience to describe Him.

It must be noted that the various human attributes used to describe God are not to be taken literally. They are figures of speech used to express God's grandeur and power. In Isaiah, for example, we find the expression: "The mouth of the Lord hath spoken." This does not mean that God has a mouth and speaks as human beings speak. When Isaiah used the phrase, he meant that the words that had come out of his own mouth were inspired by God, that he was merely the instrument of God's message to the people of Israel. What Isaiah intended to convey was that God is the source of all inspiration, the author of all wisdom. Isaiah's passionate call for moral reformation, his flowing affirmation of hope in a good world that was yet to be born out of the chaos of his time, was not a figment of his own imagination but came to him from God. Thus, graphically and vividly, he asserted: "The mouth of the Lord hath spoken." In this poetic statement he paid tribute to God's presence, which had imbued him with the strength of heart and mind to speak words that will endure for all time.

One other term applied to God merits special discussion. God is sometimes described as the judge of the universe. This implies that there is law in the world, and when that law is violated punishment is meted out. That is the essence of judgment. When a catastrophe occurs—war or famine or flood or plague—we say that it is God's judgment. Certainly a scientist can trace the catastrophe to the violation of certain principles, principles of human relations or of hygiene. But these principles are part of the structure of life, they are part of God's plan, of the law by which He wants life to be governed.

The commission of moral evil, the pursuit of vanity, of wealth or bodily pleasures as the supreme goal in life lead to an inner distress, to a sense of guilt or futility and emptiness. Thus God visits judgment upon those who live in violation of principles by which He wants man to govern his life. Man has of course the privilege to change his life and return to obedience of God's law, and God will forgive him. We, therefore, say that God is a merciful judge, who waits like a loving father for His children's return.

The Jewish conception of God is noble and exalted. It is free from the weaknesses and limitations characteristic of man, while giving us a vocabulary that enables us to speak of God in terms that are vivid and stirring to the human heart. It is a doctrine of God equal to the intellectual needs of our time—and of all time.

Two Modern Approaches to God

Eugene B. Borowitz

MORDECAI KAPLAN and Martin Buber represent two major divergent opinions in Jewish thought today. Each has set forth a clear and definite approach to God.

Before discussing Kaplan's view, it will be helpful to understand why he believes modern man has trouble believing in God. If, as Jews believe, God is everywhere, why indeed do modern men have such difficulty finding Him? If the unity of God is fundamental to our picture of the unity of both the universe and mankind, why do we have such difficulty coming to believe that He is there?

Kaplan rejects the idea that modern man neither can nor wants to be religious. In his view, religion is the human effort, organization or pattern of living which seeks to take man's latent possibilities and fulfill them. What human being does not want to be better than he is? Is there anyone who does not feel that within him there are possibilities for growth and development, for moral and spiritual accomplishment which he has only begun to achieve? Until the last day of his life man has plans, goals and purposes. He is still waiting to be fulfilled. Therefore, by his very nature man must have faith in a world which makes self-realization possible. This basic attitude toward the universe is the religion which is natural to man and the essence of all religions.

Man wants to believe in a God who makes life worth living, Kaplan says. Yet he cannot—mainly because of the way in which belief comes to him. Modern man is trained to think analytically and question carefully, but his idea of God generally comes to him in an imagery foreign to his intellectual world. In the prayer book or the Bible he reads that God is a king. But what does that mean to a modern man who does not live in a monarchy and rejects such a system as archaic? He assumes then that Judaism thinks of God as a great and extraordinary man sitting on a throne, wearing a crown, holding a sceptre. He hears of angels who make up His court, of the earth as His footstool, of the hem of His garment visible to the prophet in the Temple. He reads in the prayer book on Rosh Hashanah and Yom Kippur that God is a shepherd who exercises judgment by holding out His staff and having the people pass before Him like sheep, selecting this one for life, that one for death. Or, with a shift of metaphors, God sits before His books entering man's fate. So many of the images of the Bible and the prayer book grow out of the life of a pastoral people living in a non-technical, unscientific culture.

Modern man has difficulty accepting such an idea of God, which seems outdated and meaningless. How can he believe God is in a place called heaven? Today we send rockets up higher than any person in the Semitic world would have imagined heaven to be. We send radio beams far out into the universe and listen to their echoes. We construct giant iron saucers to pull in radio waves which the galaxies in distant space started toward the earth tens of millions of years ago.

The problem of belief today is that people connect God with the naive pictures of Bible and prayer book and do not conceive of Him in a modern way. The Jewish conception of God was never static: ways of speaking to Him, the images and symbols Jews have used changed from generation to generation. The God whom Genesis describes walking in the garden at the cool of the day is different from the God whom Isaiah sees sitting on His throne with the hem of His garment filling the Temple. This in turn differs from the God of Deutero-Isaiah, depicted as the universal creator and ruler of the universe. These variations are exceeded in later centuries when the God of the medieval Jewish philosophers is an unmoved mover and the God of the mystics not only moves and is moved but operates through ten interrelated "spheres."

If Jews in the past have had the courage to explain the idea of God in terms meaningful to them, we must do the same in our day. We too need a God who will prod us to become better and more sensitive. We have a moral responsibility and a traditional warrant to explain God in terms that make sense to contemporary man and satisfy his natural will to believe and thus fulfill himself.

We must make clear that God is not a man—that we do not consider Him really a king, a shepherd or a father with arms, eyes, ears, a voice. Our God is the God of the vast cosmos, who unifies and orders everything that man can see through radio or light wave telescope, through microscope or atom smasher. God is neither man nor person. Let us rather, in modern terms, call God a power, a force, a process like gravity or light. In line with the modern view of nature let us make God impersonal and thus rid ourselves of the old-fashioned anthropomorphic notions which keep us from believing in Him.

Yet God is more than a force. According to Kaplan, God is a power that moves in a certain way, with specific direction or tendency, a process that works to develop man's best and most significant aspects. By God he means those forces in nature which help man achieve self-fulfillment—or, more simply, God is the power that makes for salvation.

Mordecai Kaplan thus emerges as the only major Jewish philosopher who has tried to define God. While he would agree that his definition is not to be equated with what God really is, that God is somehow more than any human statement concerning Him, Kaplan feels it is important that we define what we mean by God so that we may make belief possible. Moreover, Kaplan repeats this definition to create his reconstruction of Jewish religious life. There are forces and processes in the universe upon which he believes man can rely for his development. As man reaches out to understand and incorporate them into his life, he becomes stronger and better. The religious life becomes a reality.

In projecting this clear and definite point of view, which enables the modern Jew to overcome that paramount difficulty of belief, namely, having a primitive image of God in an otherwise sophisticated mind, Kaplan performs an extraordinary service. Even the Jew who believes that science is the most important intellectual as well as practical enterprise of the twentieth century need no longer feel that Jewish belief is impossible. In Kaplan's conception he can see God as part of a developing and forward-moving universe. Through this bold and far-ranging view, many a Jew has been able to find his place today in the faith of his fathers.

Yet there are problems with Kaplan's view. Is it possible to be personally religious with an impersonal God? Religious men have always had the feeling that when they reached out into the universe there was something in the universe reaching back, that when they reacted to what they found in the world around them, whatever it was that they found somehow responded. Through the centuries religion has been characterized by its deep personal involvement and the intimacy of the believer's association with his God.

Kaplan believes that religion can be personal but only from the human point of view. Man can make it part of his very being so that it becomes as significant and valuable as life itself. As with the impersonal idea of democracy, which has created passionate concern in its followers, many Jews have accepted Kaplan's impersonal, unconscious God and have been able to feel it is an idea impinging on their own lives. Through its very impersonalness they have been able to associate it with their own growth and struggling, and discovered themselves somehow linked with a divine force in the universe. Or, to give the problem a specific focus, Kaplan and his followers have found it possible to pray in a personally felt way to a God who, by definition, does not hear prayer but does act in man as in nature.

A second problem arises from Kaplan's view of God as finite, part of the forces functioning in the universe, and limited, by definition, to those forces in nature making for human good. But what about those forces which do not make for human good, which seem neutral or damaging to man? Kaplan's answer is precise: God is only that God who is the God of the good. Evil is the part of the world which the God-force in the universe has not yet been able to overcome. Thus Kaplan enables us to give an honest and clear, if radical, answer to the problem of evil.

God cannot be blamed for the evil in the world; He is responsible only for the good. God, too, is growing and developing, and we have the faith that ultimately God will conquer those forces in the universe which are not good. We can thus find confidence in the face of evil for we know God to be supreme. In the end of days He will triumph. As for the moment, evil is a challenge, a job to be done, a task uncompleted. Man is called upon to join God in the fight to conquer cancer as we have conquered polio, to tame the rivers that flood and the atoms that threaten to explode. Evil should be a moral spur to us and not a reason for self-pity or disbelief in God.

And yet, the sureness of the solution is precisely a problem. Intellectually, how shall we understand those forces which do not make for human development in the world? Where do they come from? Can there be a world outside of God? Is there perchance another god more powerful than God?

On a personal level how shall man relate to evil? If some aspects in the world have nothing to do with God, to whom shall we turn for consolation or assuagement? Indeed, to whom shall we complain, with whom shall we argue and contest over the evil that has befallen us if God is not its master? At least, Job could strive with God and Levi Yitzhak could demand a reckoning. But with Kaplan's view the Book of Job could not have been written; Job would have been told in advance that God is not responsible for evil. Kaplan's view settles the problem of evil only by abolishing that unqualified, unified view of the world, that extraordinary enveloping Jewish religious vision that somehow everything in the world is ultimately related to one cause. And with it, for many, goes the assurance that evil not only *will* but *must* eventually be overcome.

Kaplan's point of view appeals to many Jews. Since every approach to God has its problems, some have found the advantages which this way of thinking has brought into their life far outweighing any supposed disadvantages. For them Kaplan has not only been an intellectual phenomenon but also a guide to the religious life.

A diametrically opposed point of view is that of Martin Buber. In analyzing why modern man finds it difficult to believe in God, Buber would disagree with Kaplan that it is because God cannot be explained in a scientific way. To the contrary, the problem is rather that modern man thinks he can treat *every* question in a scientific fashion, taking it apart, analyzing and putting it back together again. Thus, many individuals coming to religion demand definitions and proofs of God before they will believe in Him.

The problem is that when man takes an object apart and manipulates it in a laboratory, when he measures and tests it, he is superior to that object. The great virtue of science is that it has given man control over nature. But is God an object? When we want to treat Him as one is it not because we would really like to have control over Him? Then we could keep from being disturbed by Him and His demands, we could define Him in manageable and comfortable proportions. The great sin at the heart of modern man's quest to be religious, according to Buber, is that man, wanting to be God, does all he can to cut God down to human size. This lies behind our effort to try to understand God in so-called scientific terms.

Our difficulty in finding God, Buber says, is that we want to turn Him into an object. But this cannot be done. As the Jewish tradition long ago knew and emphasized, God is a subject. Thus the way to get to know God is not by cold observation, but by bringing all of ourselves to it—our heart as well as our mind. We have to reach out to Him with all that we are. Most of the time when we are with other people, only part of us is talking and participating. The other part is a watcher seeing what is going on. That is what we would like to do with God: to talk to Him and then watch to see if He is really there, to observe Him, to check on Him, to control our relation to Him. One does not make real friends this way. One cannot fall in love and remain an onlooker.

Immediately after declaring that the Lord our God is One, Jews affirm, "you must love the Lord your God with all your heart and with all your soul." The Hebrew goes on to say, "and with all your *m'od,*" which means "very." We must love God with all our "very," with all that extra, that special, that self that is left over after we think we have given our all.

In commenting on this, the Rabbis said that "thou shalt love the Lord thy God with all thy heart" means indeed that we should love God. "You shall love the Lord your God with all your soul" means that even if He takes your soul from you, as He will, you should still love God. As for loving God with all your might, the Rabbis said that means "with all your money." Why? Because there are some people to whom money is more important than either love or life. Thus, whatever is left over, whatever you might want to hold back, that too you should love God with. Objects we prove, define, observe, but with God we must relate personally. We must engage, reach out to and meet Him.

Buber says that we do not have to be any special place or do anything special to find God. Nor are we seeking any mystic experience, such as is depicted in the movies with violins sobbing in the background while the clouds open up and the sun comes out. Nothing more happens than when we truly get to know another person. He is talking to you and you are talking to him: and then you understand him, not just his words, and he understands you.

That is the way it is with God, Buber says. We know God as simply and directly as we truly know another person. Whenever we really know another person, whenever we reach out to another individual for what he is in his own very specific and personal way, whenever we, with our limitations and talents, our abilities and frustrations, reach out to another human being and have that encounter, we know something more than just the other person. We know this is a world in which it is somehow more real to know persons as subjects than as objects. We know that it is possible for us, even though we are isolated single human beings, to find others. We are not objects, and can reach out one man to another and, in the process, find God, who is the context, the occasion, the basis of all man-to-man meeting.

Human efforts to describe this are futile, Buber points out. Descriptions make such a meeting an object, not a lived event. Words always fail to express the fullness and reality we have found.

Thus Buber helps us rediscover what lies at the heart of Jewish tradition. We cannot take its language literally: it is not the words which are important but the relationship which the words enable us to recapture. Thus, when the tradition called God a king it was not because God was thought to be a man on a throne; rather, a man who had known God wondered how he could describe what he had just lived through. Since this relationship had given him a sense that there was One greater, superior, wiser, deeper and more sensitive than himself, he called Him king. Others called Him father. When the prophets talked about God in ordinary human terms they did so because they knew that what lies at the heart of real human relations is what lies at the heart of the relationship between man and God.

Buber also helps explain the phenomenon that even when a modern man believes half the time, half the time he does not. If we take love as the closest analogy to this kind of relationship, we realize that no two lovers, friends, parents and children, husbands and wives, can always be on the level of full communication. Most of the time we are not on a person-to-person level but live with one another almost as objects. Therefore, though we say we love we admit that some of the time we do not have the experience which ties and binds us to one another. But we say we are in love because we have had those moments of understanding and we know they will return. The Jewish tradition permits divorce because there are times when these moments of understanding do not return and the relationship is destroyed. True love is based on faith.

Having faith in God is similar: not always to have God with one, not always to be able to hold on to God as if He were a possession or object, but to know Him from time to time. When God is not with us we have faith that other such moments will return. For a modern man to have faith, says Buber, is both to believe and to have moments of disbelief, but to understand the moments of doubt within the context of those deeper moments of understanding.

Buber says we must try to understand everything we meet in the world as somehow related to God. The greatest evil we can know is the absence of God's presence, when at any given moment we turn to God with all our heart and soul and might and find Him absent.

The Bible describes this in a peculiar way: "God hides His face," He takes away His presence. Though we do not know or understand, though we are left utterly bereft and despairing, one thing remains: we remember that it was not always so. At that moment, in faith, we wait for Him to return. He is not always here but ours may be the grace in the next moment or the moment after or the moment after that to find Him again. Because we have found Him in the past, it is possible for us to live and wait for Him now.

Other than that which man himself creates, Buber does not explain the existence of evil. But he does give us a way of living with it, understanding it and, hopefully, even enduring it.

To be sure, there are problems with Buber's point of view. How explain this concept to a man who has never had such an experience? Buber uses short, emotional, poetic sentences, hoping less to inform than to evoke. He knows he cannot describe "person to person" meeting as if IT were an object. The best thing to do would be to live and work with such a man until the event occurred. Until then most of the discussion might be fruitless. It can only open one to the encounter.

A second problem with Buber is how one can understand that such a God is the God of the vast cosmos. We can understand that we have intimate relations with people, but it is difficult to believe that we can meet that God who fills the entire universe. Persons, at least, have bodies. With God there is no objective basis to the relation.

Buber's answer would be a warning to stop trying to reduce this to conceptual terms. We are not to turn God into an object; we are not to think about Him but to relate to Him.

In the efforts of these two great Jewish philosophers we see modern man's searching, probing efforts to use all his capacities to understand the meaning of the world.

What is extraordinary is that in the one religion of Judaism, two men can take such different approaches to God. Each knows that God is more than any system, that God is somehow beyond our efforts to explain Him. Each has sufficient humility to say this is the best he has been able to discover, but God is obviously more than that. Both, therefore, say that Jewish tradition is right in urging man to think, search, look, reason and work it out for himself. God is so great that we must continue in every generation to extend our ideas of Him, to make them ever more comprehensive and more adequate.

Spokesmen of God

Arthur J. Lelyveld

THE Hebrew prophets who lived and taught in the land of Israel more than 2500 years ago created but one small segment of the Jewish tradition, but a segment of overwhelming importance. Fully a century before Aeschylus, Confucius and Buddha, these great moral teachers brought into the consciousness of men the insight that right living and moral conduct are the only reliable tests of conviction—an insight radical in their time but fundamental to religion today.

When we speak of the prophets we mean Isaiah, Jeremiah, Ezekiel and the so-called minor prophets. In this company we include not only the sixteen "writing" prophets and their predecessors, whose work has come down to us only in the Books of Kings and Samuel, but also the entire prophetic tradition, whose influence is found in the Torah and throughout Scripture. These great teachers, through the power and moral grandeur of their utterances, influenced the thinking of the entire Western world.

With all of their influence on the West, the prophets have been largely misunderstood. The word "prophet" itself, used to translate the Hebrew word *navi,* is the source of some of our misconceptions. Christian scholars searched Scripture for clues to insights which the people of Israel might have had regarding a future coming of a Messiah. Wanting to prove their contention that Jesus had come to redeem mankind, they hoped to find in the Bible words that would confirm their conviction that his life fulfilled Biblical promise. As a result, the word "prophet" and the verb "to prophesy" came to be connected with looking into the future; we are inclined to think of a prophet as a seer, a man able to foretell tomorrow, a gazer into the crystal ball. But the prophets of Israel were forthtellers, rather than foretellers.

In Hebrew, the word *navi,* usually translated as "prophet," does not in any way contain the concept of foretelling. Amos, the first of the writing prophets, particularly in his great speech at Beth-el eight centuries before the Christian era, actually disclaimed the role of "prophet" in the familiar verse, "I am not a prophet, neither am I a prophet's son." He had gone up to the northern temple and sanctuary of Beth-el during the period of the great fall festival. He delivered an address of great dramatic power and incisiveness, shocking the defenders of the *status quo* in ancient Palestine who had fallen prey to practices which Amos found reprehensible and which he condemned in the name of God. His oration was filled with statements which were heretical to the ruling powers.

At the conclusion of his address, Amos is contemptuously called *hozeh,* "seer" or "soothsayer." He is reprimanded: "You seer, what are you doing here in Israel? If you don't like this country, go back where you came from. You are a professional *navi.* Go back to Judea, and earn your bread there, and don't come again to the king's sanctuary." According to linguists, *navi* is related to a similar word which means "to bubble over." Amos responds: "You misunderstand me. I am not a *navi* and I am not a *ben navi.* I am not a wandering ecstatic nor a member of a professional guild of soothsayers. I am a simple shepherd, a herdsman. I was tending my flock, and God took me from behind the flock, and said 'Go speak unto My people Israel.' "

In the Book of Kings, the term *navi* in its earlier meaning referred to bands of wandering ecstatics, *neviim,* or guilds of people dedicated to this order of service. They went about the land in groups, playing instruments and working themselves up to high pitches of enthusiasm. Like Balaam in the Book of Numbers, they "fell down with their eyes open" and spoke oracles from which truth was presumably derived. During the eighth century these wandering bands were looked upon by the upper classes and intellectuals with a measure of contempt. When Saul, the first king of Israel, joined such a company of prophets, stripping himself naked and going into a frenzy, the scornful question was asked, "Is Saul too among the *neviim?*"

By Amos' time a great change had taken place in the word "prophet." In the Book of Kings when Jehoshaphat, king of Judea, and Ahab, king of Israel, are attempting to decide whether or not to embark on a war on Syria, they call in four hundred *neviim* who dutifully agree with the monarchs' warlike intentions. But Jehoshaphat, not satisfied, asks Ahab: "Is there not here somewhere in the court a *navi l'Adonai,* a 'prophet' of God?" Micaiah is brought forward, though Ahab warns: "I hate him; for he doth not prophesy good concerning me but evil." Unlike the band of "yes men" who always told the king what was pleasing to him, Micaiah tells Ahab that in the four hundred prophets there is a lying spirit—they are not telling the truth. With Micaiah a new type of *navi* emerges; he refuses to tell Ahab what he wants to hear. "As the Lord liveth, what the Lord saith unto me, that will I speak," he proclaims.

Nathan plays the same role when King David takes Bathsheba for himself and arranges to have Uriah, her husband, killed in battle. Though this kind of brutality was the common practice of Oriental monarchs, Nathan tells David a story of a great landowner with huge flocks of sheep, who takes from a poor man his one little ewe lamb. The king, indignant about the injustice, says, "Who is that man? He shall feel the full weight of Israel's justice." Nathan with his ringing response, "Thou art the man," challenges David's immorality on the basis of standards of justice and morality above the state, higher than himself, and on the basis of his memory of standards of desert democracy and equality.

A similar story is told of Elijah, who is known in Jewish tradition as *the* prophet, *Eliahu Hanavi.* King Ahab had been egged on by his wife, Jezebel, to take over Naboth's vineyards. Elijah comes before him and denounces him, "Hast thou killed and also taken possession?"

Kings themselves are challenged by these new *neviim,* for they speak for something higher than the king. *Ko amar Adonai,* "thus saith the Lord," is the compelling refrain that runs through the words of the prophets. In the new context, a *navi* is a man who speaks on behalf of God; because he feels that he has learned the moral law, he can speak with authority on the basis of the standards of right and wrong which it demands. Speaking in the name of the God who gave that moral law, he feels compelled to bring God's message to mankind.

This conception of the role of the prophet is confirmed in the familiar passage in Exodus, in which God speaks to Moses and tells him what his relationship to Pharaoh will be: "Thou shalt be as God unto Pharaoh, and Aaron thy brother shall be thy *navi.*" God speaks to Moses, and Moses must have an intermediary in approaching Pharaoh. Aaron is the spokesman of Moses, standing in the same relationship to Moses as that in which the prophet stands in relation to God. The *navi* is regarded as the channel through which God may speak.

The same concept of the *navi* occurs when Jeremiah, the great sorrowing prophet, wants to throw off the yoke of prophesy that at times is burdensome to him. He would rather not suffer all the disabilities of being God's spokesman. "I will not speak in God's name any more." But God's word was "in my heart as a burning fire shut up in my bones," and speak he must.

The new prophets were champions of God who deemed it their obligation to speak out forthrightly at whatever cost to themselves for what they believed to be true and just. They were men who spoke with a blessed stubbornness, with a burning zeal for righteousness as they saw it. They believed that justice was more important than creature comforts, truth more important than security, and divine discontent more important than peace of mind.

The range of the prophets was over three hundred years in time, beginning with Amos in the eighth century B.C.E., a period of great social turmoil. Though idolatry had been largely eliminated, a narrow tribal view of God still prevailed. God was related by covenant to the people of Israel; they were His people, whom no evil could befall. Along with this reliance upon God for special favor went much debauchery and complete forgetfulness of moral obligations.

The opening chapters of Amos speak scathingly of this social setting. In the development of what we now call the prophetic ideal, the henotheism of the eighth century gave way inevitably to the universalism of Deutero-Isaiah, the great unknown poet of the Exile, who comforted his people and tried to teach them their new role as servants of a just and universal God who loved all mankind. Clearly, the prophetic tradition is not static but is rather a set of ideals and principles that evolved over a period of years.

The first of those ideals is the prophetic emphasis on the good life as being of greater importance than mere ceremonial observance. Whereas the priestly tendency had stressed practices and rituals, ceremonies and sacrifice, the prophetic tradition emphasized asceticism, cleanness of living and purity of ideas in an attempt to strip off externals and arrive at the central moral problem. Harking back to the simplicity of desert life the prophets protested against the emptiness of ceremonial form and valued instead goodness, decency, justice.

The good life receives its major emphasis in the opening chapter of the Book of Isaiah. After comparing the people of Israel to the wicked inhabitants of the legendary cities of Sodom and Gomorrah, Isaiah asks: "To what purpose is the multitude of your sacrifices unto Me? I am full of the burnt-offerings of rams, and the fat of fed beasts; and I delight not in the blood of bullocks, or of lambs, or of he-goats." Like all the prophets, Isaiah speaks in the name of God.

The people were gathering for the fall festival at the courts of the great sanctuary of Israel and Judah. "Who hath required this at your hand, to trample My courts?" God asks. Did God ask the people to come to the festival? Does He require going through the ritual practices? "Bring no more vain oblations; it is an offering of abomination unto Me; new moon and Sabbath, the holding of convocations."

God continues: "I cannot endure iniquity along with the solemn assembly . . . Yea, when you make many prayers, I will not hear. Your hands are full of blood. Wash you, make you clean. Put away the evil of your goings from before Mine eyes, cease to do evil, learn to do well; seek justice, relieve the oppressed, judge the fatherless, plead for the widow."

Amos speaks in almost the same terms, saying: "I hate, I despise your feasts." These are radical words. The prophet hates festivals and holiday observances because of their emptiness. "Let justice well up as waters, and righteousness as a mighty stream." "Trust not in lying words," Jeremiah warned. The people who are always parading about the temple of the Lord are not concerned with its major purposes.

Micah makes the same point: "Wherewith shall I come before the Lord? Shall I come before Him with burnt-offerings, with calves of a year old? Will the Lord be pleased with thousands of rams, with ten thousands of rivers of oil? Shall I give my first-born for my transgression? The fruit of my body for the sin of my soul?" The answer is simple: "It hath been told thee, O man, what is good, and what the Lord doth require of thee: only to do justly, and to love mercy, and to walk humbly with thy God."

While the prophets were not necessarily speaking against ritual, they were opposing empty and meaningless forms unaccompanied by righteous action. In the nineteenth chapter of the Book of Leviticus, or what scholars have come to call the Holiness Code, the patterns of human relationships that should exist between man and his neighbor are outlined. The keynote is "Ye shall be holy." Why? "For I thy God am holy." The role of the religious individual in Israel, the role of the Jews as the covenant people, was to be holy because God set a pattern of holiness.

A second idea to be found in the writing prophets is that of God as a universal, just and loving Father. At first the people of Israel and Judah felt that God was the God of Israel and dedicated exclusively to the preservation of Jews. They believed that Amos, at Beth-el, was uttering heresy when he said that doom would fall upon Israel. After Israel was destroyed and the Israelites became exiles, weeping by the waters of Babylon and remembering Jerusalem, however, their belief about their own indestructibility was ripe for change. Experts who have studied the development of the Bible have come to believe that the great creation story which conceived of God as a universal God, the God of creation, the God who brought into being Adam, or man, and not just Israel, was written under prophetic influence.

In Isaiah the idea of God as the Creator of heaven and earth is developed and repeatedly alluded to: "I am the Lord, and there is none else. Beside Me there is no God." Here is a frontal attack on the earlier idea that God is exclusively the God of Israel. "From the rising of the sun, and from the west, there is none beside Me. I form the light, and create darkness. I make peace, and create evil. I am the Lord, that doeth all these things." In another significant passage in Isaiah God proclaims His universality: "Blessed be Egypt My people and Assyria the work of My hands, and Israel Mine inheritance."

This quality of universality leads inevitably to the area of human brotherhood. Amos challenges the people of Israel: Do you think that you are so important, that you are a special people? "Are ye not as the

children of the Ethiopians unto Me? . . . Have I not brought the
Philistines from Caphtor, and Aram from Kir?"

"Thou shalt love the stranger, for ye were strangers in the land of
Egypt," says the Holiness Code. We have the obligation to love the
stranger. This concept of human brotherhood is enunciated repeatedly
in prophetic tradition.

Along with the concept of the universal God goes also an emphasis
upon the responsibility of every individual for his own actions, an idea
that was first stressed by the prophets. The eighteenth chapter of the
Book of Ezekiel records a prophetic protest against an earlier concept
that the sins of the fathers are visited upon the children. The popular
proverb—"The fathers have eaten sour grapes, and the children's
teeth are set on edge"—is not true, Ezekiel says. Every man bears the
weight of his own action and must fulfill his responsibility before God.
"The soul that sinneth, it shall die." The same emphasis upon the
individual's role is found in Jeremiah, who affirms the covenant but at
the same time says that it must be written in the hearts of men.

What are man's responsibilities? The prophets did not speak in
vague, general terms but were concerned with the social and political
problems which they confronted. The God of the moral law imposed
definite social commitments upon men. In the first place, there was to be
a just and equitable distribution of the world's goods. "The earth is
Mine, and all the fullness thereof." Since the earth belongs to God, no
individual has the right to accumulate for himself more than his just
share of the world's goods. Alluding to the increasing power of the few
who were taking over the land, Isaiah cries out: "Woe unto them that
join house to house and lay field to field until there be no room and ye
be made to dwell alone in the midst of the land." In our own time, the
Jewish National Fund was conceived as an implementation of the prophetic idea that the land belongs to God. Man is only a tenant and has
no right to take in perpetuity the bounty of the earth and exclude
others from its use.

In the codes in Exodus one finds a concern for a just distribution of
goods and for proper relationships between employer and employee.
Mention is made of the rights of employees to cease work, the importance of not keeping a hireling's wages overnight, and of assuming the
responsibility that goes with managing the labor of others. Other
social commitments include respect for the personality of the individual human being, created in the image of God, and concern with
the underprivileged. Despite their concept of God as the loving Father of all men, the prophets saw a special role for Israel as a people.
Indeed, the prophetic tradition harmonizes the idea of a special role
for Israel with the concern for the rights and needs of all nations. The

Messianic dream of the Second Isaiah of "the end of days" reflects the concept of living together harmoniously, worshipping together, but each people preserving its own identity as one of God's special creations. In the development of the "suffering servant" idea in the Second Isaiah, Israel becomes the instrument by which the concept of the universal God will be preached to all mankind.

Of course, the love of Israel brought with it the hope that Israel would be restored in a more ideal state after the Exile. The Haftorah on the very Sabbath of the declaration of the State of Israel, in May 1948, was the passage in the ninth chapter of Amos in which the prophet predicts that God will raise up again "the tabernacle of David that is fallen. . . . And they shall build the waste cities and inhabit them. And I will plant them upon their land, and they shall no more be plucked out of their land which I have given them."

It has been well said that the function of prophetic religion was not so much to comfort the afflicted as to afflict the comfortable. The most important role of the prophets was that of gadfly who pricks the consciences of those who are too smug by reminding them of their responsibilities to their fellow men.

The prophets were realists, in the best sense of the word. They looked at the events of their day and they attempted to say what they believed to be true. "As the Lord liveth, that which God speaketh unto me, that will I speak." While they could look at the world of evil and darkness and see the forebodings of doom, the later prophets were also able to comfort their people in the midst of destruction. They were able to look through the darkness of the moment to a fulfillment of God's will in the "end of days." The night might be dark, but morning was sure to come. As Micah writes:

But in the end of days it shall come to pass,
That the mountain of the Lord's house shall be established as the top
*   of the mountains . . .*
Nation shall not lift up sword against nation,
Neither shall they learn war any more,
But they shall sit every man under his vine and under his fig-tree;
And none shall make them afraid;
For the mouth of the Lord of hosts hath spoken.

The prophets were titans of the spirit. Their message of faith, enunciated two millennia ago, speaks meaningfully to modern man.

Man and God: The Moral Partnership

Harold M. Schulweis

JEWISH religious literature contains every argument used by the traditional faiths to justify the ways of God to man. In addition, Judaism contains a unique—indeed revolutionary—element: a cry of resistance, never completely stifled, by which man openly revolts against being pushed downwards in the balancing between him and his God. In the earliest Biblical documents, the Jew asserts his moral equality with his Father.

> And Abraham drew near, and said: "Wilt Thou indeed sweep away the righteous with the wicked? Peradventure there are fifty righteous within the city; wilt Thou indeed sweep away and not forgive the place for the fifty righteous that are therein? That be far from Thee to do after this manner, to slay the righteous with the wicked, that so the righteous should be as the wicked; that be far from Thee; shall not the Judge of all the earth do justly?"
>
> (Genesis 18:23–25)

> *Right wouldest Thou be, O Lord,*
> *Were I to contend with Thee,*
> *Yet will I reason with Thee:*
> *Wherefore doth the way of the wicked prosper?*
> *Wherefore are all they secure that deal very treacherously?*
> *Thou hast planted them, yea, they have taken root;*
> *They grow, yea, they bring forth fruit;*
> *Thou art near in their mouth,*
> *And far from their reins.*
>
> (Jeremiah 12:1–2)

> *How long, O Lord, shall I cry,*
> *And Thou wilt not hear?*
> *I cry out unto Thee of violence,*
> *And Thou wilt not save.*
> *Why dost Thou show me iniquity,*
> *And beholdest mischief?*
> *And why are spoiling and violence before me?*
> *So that there is strife, and contention ariseth?*
>
> (Habakkuk 1:2–3)

Awake, why sleepest Thou, O Lord?
Arouse Thyself, cast not off for ever.
Wherefore hidest Thou Thy face,
And forgettest our affliction and our oppression?
For our soul is bowed down to the dust;
Our belly cleaveth unto the earth.
Arise for our help,
And redeem us for Thy mercy's sake.

(Psalms 44:24–27)

Thou that art of eyes too pure to behold evil,
And that canst not look on mischief,
Wherefore lookest Thou, when they deal treacherously,
And holdest Thy peace, when the wicked swalloweth up
The man that is more righteous than he?

(Habakkuk 1:13)

As God liveth, who hath taken away my right;
And the Almighty, who hath dealt bitterly with me;
All the while my breath is in me,
And the spirit of God is in my nostrils,
Surely my lips shall not speak unrighteousness,
Neither shall my tongue utter deceit;
Far be it from me that I shall justify you;
Till I die I will not put away mine integrity from me,
My righteousness I hold fast, and will not let it go;
My heart shall not reproach me so long as I live.

(Job 27:2–6)

Similar protests echo throughout Jewish writings, from the Midrash and Talmud, medieval poetry, the parables of the Hasidim, intimate conversations between God and Levi Yitzhak of Berditchev, to the literature created out of the flames of the Warsaw ghetto. "I believe in the God of Israel even though He has done everything to destroy my belief in Him. I believe in His laws even though I cannot justify His ways . . . I bow before His majesty, but I will not kiss the rod with which He chastises me" ("Yossel Rackover Speaks to God"—Zvi Kolitz in *The Bridge*, Vol. III).

Such religious audacity may come as a shock to those who conceive of the believer as one who always submits to the will of God. Traditionally, the man of faith may be depicted as once-born or twice-born; he may be subject to doubt or conflict; but once in the presence of God, kneeling is his posture.

Nonetheless, the tone of rebellion in Jewish literature is authentic. It is not considered blasphemous; indeed, it is canonized. The indignation rises from *within* the religious framework, not from without. Expressions of its tensions are not debates but internal conflicts. Out of personal anguish, the sufferer questions, cries out, defies but does not deny.

What is the origin of the moral courage of the Jew? The right to resent is predicated upon an arrangement between God and Israel, in which both parties agree to a unique and unusual set of terms. The everlasting covenant, entered into with God by Abraham and his seed, unites the two in a moral partnership. While man is to keep the commandments of the Lord, it is also understood that the pact is undertaken with a God of "righteousness and justice" (Genesis 17:10 ff.).

Since both sides are mutually responsible, it follows that a miscarriage can call forth sanctions against either transgressor. This special covenant, setting forth the moral responsibilities expected of both partners, gives Abraham and his descendants courage to dissent, even against so awesome a co-signatory as God. Clearly, so long as man is a partner with God in sustaining the moral universe, accusations can be hurled from below as well as from above.

Elevated by this, man receives status as a competent moral agent. His capacity to distinguish good from bad, happiness from adversity, saint from sinner, is fully asserted. Both man and God are released from the amoral decrees of fate, the *moira* of the pagan world.

Even God is free to change His decrees, to repent of His decisions, to alter the course of events because He is a moral being. And man too is freed from passive silence, through his moral agency. He may appeal from God to God. "I will flee from Thee to Thyself, and I will shelter myself from Thy wrath in Thy shadow; and to the skirts of Thy mercies I will lay hold until Thou has had mercy on me. I will not let Thee go until Thou hast blessed me" (Ibn Gabirol, *The Royal Crown*).

The God of Israel can be addressed thus because there resides in Him not only the metaphysical attributes of power and wisdom, but also the moral attributes of justice and mercy. The religious rebel in his anger does not turn *from* God but *to* God; even as God Himself says, "May it be My will that My mercy may suppress My anger, and that My mercy may prevail over My other attributes" (*B'rakhot* 7a).

The defiance found in the Bible is perpetuated in the post-Biblical tradition. Noah, who accepts the decree of the deluge and hides his impotence in a shelter for himself, is not admired by the Rabbis. Their praise is for men like Abraham and Moses who draw near to God and contend with Him on the grounds of justice. The rabbinic tradition sees the Biblical hero as one who chastises his people for transgression and yet rises up in their defense even against God's judgment. Abraham challenges the justice of God's exile of his people, demands confrontation with those who have accused Israel of sin and successfully silences the Torah from testifying against them (*Midrash Rabbah:* Lamentations: introductory proems).

Moses rebukes God for keeping silent before the slaughter of mothers and children. And Rachel dares contrast her compassion and forbearance with God's zealousness, so as to move God toward charity. Even Elijah "speaks insolently towards heaven."

In another interesting interpretation, the Rabbis see Moses as seizing hold of God's cloak and refusing to let go until God forgives His errant people (from a Midrash based upon Exodus 32:9–14). "And the Lord repented of the evil which He said He would do unto His errant people" (Exodus 32:14). Another time, Moses "hurls words against the heavens" and "remits God's vow for Him," for, while the Lord cannot break His word, the righteous may break it on His behalf (*B'rakhot* 32a; also *T. Taanit* 23a and *T. Moed Katan* 16b).

The extraordinary intimacy and audacity allowable within this relationship between Israel and the deity are totally incomprehensible without a clear perception of their unique covenant. That explains not only the Jew's profound respect for man's moral dignity but his more revolutionary faith in God's responsiveness to the call of justice. This is exemplified in the following rabbinic commentary:

> While Moses in prayer attributed to God greatness, might, and awesomeness, the prophet Jeremiah rebels: "Aliens are destroying His Temple; where then are His awesome deeds?" Jeremiah thereby deletes the attribute of awesomeness from God. Daniel, observing the captivity of his people, similarly reduces the attribute of might from God. The Rabbis are perplexed. How could Jeremiah and Daniel abolish the attribute established by Moses? Rabbi Eliezer offers an explanation: "Since they knew that the Holy One insists on truth, they would not ascribe false attributes to Him." (*Yoma* 69b)

What is more, in the *Din Torah,* the tribunal of justice to which the Holy One is summoned by man, God cannot lose. Whenever justice triumphs, God is the victor. Even in what may appear as defeat, when the voice of law and righteousness is heeded and the Heavenly Echo is ignored, God rejoices: "*Nitzhuni Banai:* My children have defeated Me" (*Baba Metziah* 59b).

In Israel, the man of God does not acquiesce. Like Jacob-Israel, he girds his loins to wrestle with God and is allowed to prevail.

God the Accused

Elie Wiesel

ONE day when we came back from work, we saw three gallows rearing up in the assembly place, three black crows. Roll call. SS all round us, machine guns trained: the traditional ceremony. Three victims in chains—and one of them, the little servant, the sad-eyed angel.

The SS seemed more preoccupied, more disturbed than usual. To hang a young boy in front of thousands of spectators was no light matter. The head of the camp read the verdict. All eyes were on the child. He was lividly pale, almost calm, biting his lips. The gallows threw its shadow over him.

This time the Lagerkapo refused to act as executioner. Three SS replaced him.

The three victims mounted together onto the chairs.

The three necks were placed at the same moment within the nooses.

"Long live liberty!" cried the two adults.

But the child was silent.

"Where is God? Where is He?" someone behind me asked.

At a sign from the head of the camp, the three chairs tipped over.

Total silence throughout the camp. On the horizon, the sun was setting.

"Bare your heads!" yelled the head of the camp. His voice was raucous. We were weeping.

"Cover your heads!"

Then the march past began. The two adults were no longer alive. Their tongues hung swollen, blue-tinged. But the third rope was still moving; being so light, the child was still alive . . .

For more than half an hour he stayed there, struggling between life and death, dying in slow agony under our eyes. And we had to look him in the face. He was still alive when I passed in front of him. His tongue was still red, his eyes were not yet glazed.

Behind me, I heard the same man asking:

"Where is God now?"

And I heard a voice within me answer him:

"Where is He? Here He is—hanging here on this gallows . . ."

On the eve of Rosh Hashanah, the last day of that accursed year, the whole camp (Buna) was electric with tension which was in all our hearts.

. . . At the place of assembly, surrounded by the electrified barbed wire, thousands of silent Jews gathered, their faces stricken.

Night was falling. Other prisoners continued to crowd in, from every block, able suddenly to conquer time and space and submit both to their will.

"What are You, my God," I thought angrily, "compared to this afflicted crowd, proclaiming to You their faith, their anger, their revolt? What does Your greatness mean, Lord of the Universe, in the face of all this weakness, this decomposition, and this decay? Why do You still trouble their sick minds, their crippled bodies?"

Ten thousand men had come to attend the solemn service, heads of the blocks, Kapos, functionaries of death.

"Bless the Eternal . . ."

The voice of the officiant had just made itself heard. I thought at first it was the wind.

"Blessed be the Name of the Eternal!"

Thousands of voices repeated the benediction; thousands of men prostrated themselves like trees before a tempest.

"Blessed be the Name of the Eternal!"

Why, but why should I bless Him? In every fiber I rebelled. Because He had had thousands of children burned in His pits? Because He kept six crematories working night and day, on Sundays and feast days? Because in His great might He had created Auschwitz, Birkenau, Buna, and so many factories of death? How could I say to Him: "Blessed are Thou, Eternal, Master of the Universe, who chose us from among the races to be tortured day and night, to see our fathers, our mothers, our brothers, end in the crematory? Praised be Thy Holy Name, Thou who has chosen us to be butchered on Thine altar?"

I heard the voice of the officiant raising up, powerful yet at the same time broken, amid the tears, sobs, the sighs of the whole congregation:

"All the earth and the Universe are God's!"

He kept stopping every moment, as though he did not have the strength to find the meaning beneath the words. The melody choked in his throat.

And I, mystic that I had been, I thought:

"Yes, man is very strong, greater than God. When You were deceived by Adam and Eve, You drove them out of paradise. When Noah's generation displeased You, You brought down the Flood. When Sodom no longer found favor in Your eyes, You made the sky rain down fire and sulphur. But these men here, whom You have betrayed, whom You have allowed to be tortured, butchered, gassed, burned, what do they do? They pray before You! They praise Your Name!"

"All creation bears witness to the greatness of God!"

Once, New Year's Day had dominated my life. I knew that my sins grieved the Eternal; I implored His forgiveness. Once, I had believed profoundly that upon one solitary deed of mine, one solitary prayer, depends the salvation of the world.

This day I had ceased to plead. I was no longer capable of lamentation. On the contrary, I felt very strong. I was the accuser, God the accused. My eyes were open and I was alone—terribly alone in a world without God and without man. Without love or mercy. I had ceased to be anything but ashes, yet I felt myself to be stronger than the Almighty, to whom my life had been tied for so long. I stood amid that praying congregation, observing it like a stranger.

The Problem of Evil

Israel H. Levinthal

JUDAISM is unique in that it is a way of life. Its stress is on this world of here and now, and on morality and conduct rather than on dogma or creed. Unlike other religions, it offers no fixed set of beliefs or authoritarian theology through which man can win salvation. It is not surprising, therefore, that Judaism offers no single answer to one of humanity's most difficult problems—that of evil and suffering.

Indeed, the concept of evil is one of the most difficult subjects in Jewish thought. As Kaufmann Kohler, the great Jewish scholar and leader of Reform Judaism, has put it, "a leading objection to the belief in divine providence is the existence in this world of physical and moral evil." Isaac Husik, in his classic work *Medieval Jewish Philosophy,* places the problem in historic perspective: "The presence of evil in this world, physical and moral, was a stumbling block to all religious thinkers in the Middle Ages." Today also the existence of evil makes it hard for many to believe in a divine power.

There are various aspects to the subject. First is the problem of evil in the mind and nature of man. Why was man created with a desire to do evil? Why should God, the God of goodness, have created within man the temptation to do evil?

To the Rabbis this question did not pose a problem at all because in their conception of human nature man was not supposed to be an angel. While man was given an evil inclination, the *yetzer hara,* he was also given a counterforce, the *yetzer tov,* a good impulse. And God challenges man as to which inclination will prevail, the evil or the good.

One of the basic teachings of Judaism is that man has free will, the power to choose between evil and good. In the Bible God says to man, "Behold, I have given thee life and good, death and evil. Choose the good." We are placed here on earth to have this battle within ourselves and to try to conquer our evil inclination. The Rabbis even advise man that if the impulse to do evil is so strong and so overpowering that it is leading us to commit a sin or crime, we are to seize the *yetzer hara* and take it to the synagogue, to the House of Study, where—by immersion in prayer and study—we can conquer it.

This conflict is illustrated in the Biblical passage where Jacob, sleeping on a bed of rocks, dreams of the ladder that touches the earth and reaches to the heavens. The Bible says that he saw angels "ascending and descending *on it,*" but, as the Rabbis suggest, the Hebrew *bo* really means "in him"—in Jacob. In other words, the Rabbis interpret the story to emphasize the thought that there were two forces struggling within Jacob, one leading him heavenward, and the other pulling him downward. Jacob had this struggle, as it comes at times to all of us, within himself. The answer of the Rabbis to the basic question, "Why do we have the possibility to do evil?," is that this is a challenge to man over which he *can* be victorious. "Unto thee shall be his desire," says the Bible, "but thou shalt rule over him."

But there is a more difficult aspect to the problem of evil than that a man has to struggle with himself as to whether he should do good or evil. That is the general problem of the existence of evil and human suffering in the world. Why should there be suffering? Why do we sometimes see righteous, saintly people who suffer, who are diseased, poverty-stricken? Why must innocent children, just born, suffer? And conversely, why do the wicked often prosper? This aspect of the problem is one that has baffled philosophers through the ages. Many have echoed the sentiment of Job, "The world has been turned over into the hands of the wicked."

Malachi, one of the Hebrew prophets, also refers to the problem, and the same question reverberates throughout Jewish literature. In the Yom Kippur liturgy we read of the martyrdom of the great rabbis who were put to death by the Romans. And the question is put to God: "Is this the reward for upholding the Torah?" Here are saintly men who gave all of their lives to the Torah and yet they suffer such tragic deaths. "Does God *avid dina b'lo dina,* pass sentence without justice?"—this was the plaintive query of many who were baffled by the problem.

While there is no single answer to the problem of evil in Jewish thought, many of the sages speculated on this subject and have formulated views which are worthy of consideration.

The first answer that appears in the Talmud is that punishment is the result of sin. Pain is God's way of chastising man. The Talmud says, "There is no suffering without sin." Sometimes we may not even be conscious of what our sin is, and we are made to suffer in order to expiate that sin. The suffering that God thus imposes upon us is to make us search and amend our ways, and so do penitence and avoid further wrongdoing.

Job is the symbol of the righteous man who suffers. When his friends visit him, they argue: "You must have sinned because there is no suffering without sin." But Job keeps repeating that he has not sinned. George Foot Moore, the eminent Christian authority on Judaism, in discussing this scene in Job, says, "It may be uncharitable when applied by others, but it did have merits when man was led to examine himself and was led to repentance and amendment." It had its purpose in making man search his ways; in many cases he discovered that he did commit some sin, and perhaps atoned for it through suffering.

This is the answer that the Rabbis gave not only for an individual's suffering, but also for the suffering of exile visited upon the Jewish people. In all religious services Jews repeat: "It is because of our sins that we have been driven from our land." No other answer could be found.

But that answer did not always satisfy people, particularly when they saw that little children or the completely innocent were often afflicted. The Rabbis therefore evolved a new theory, that the righteous man and the innocent child suffer for the "sins of the generation." If many people sin at a given time, as it is said in the Talmud, "the righteous are seized and made to suffer for the sinners." And when there are no righteous, little children are taken from school and are made to suffer because of the sins of others.

When the Rabbis saw that this reply did not fully satisfy everyone, they evolved another theory—that "these sufferings and pains are the sufferings of love." They are not really punishment but "the chastisement because God loves you so." And one of the great rabbis, Israel ben Yaacov, said, "Whom the Lord loveth, He chastiseth. This is like the father who chastises a child whom he loves because he wants to encourage him to be better than he is."

But this answer also failed to convince many. It only led some people to say, "I hope God does not love me so much."

Another answer offered was that of *olam haba,* "the future world." This concept of the "future world," which was not at all popular in the early days of Jewish life, took hold of the Jewish mind and heart and became a great influence because Jews had no other answer.

The prophets had railed against the sins of nations and had promised the children of Israel rewards and great glory here on earth. But after the destruction of the Temple and the capture of Jerusalem, it seemed as if the very foundation of Jewish life had been broken asunder. The whole problem of reward for suffering and punishment for evil now begged for a new and more satisfactory answer. Their dream of national glory shattered, Jews had to believe that somewhere, some time, justice would be done. The heathens would then be punished and the Jews find the reward that was justly theirs. In times of sorrow and stress, the human heart wants to feel that somehow, somewhere, and at some time, justice will bring redress for the misery endured. And sorrow and stress were the lot of those generations. They were under the severest political and social oppression.

Jews were reassured by the thought that if man suffers here, he is going to be rewarded in the other world, and if the wicked person enjoys life here, he is going to suffer in the other world. This provided an answer that sounded plausible, and it gave justice to "God's justice." In this way, the theory of future reward and punishment evolved and became popular in Jewish thought. The more the Jew suffered, the stronger became his belief in *olam haba*—that was the only recompense he had.

It is true that the medieval Jewish philosophers—Maimonides and others—tried to give philosophic, metaphysical reasons to explain the existence of evil, but their reasons never took hold among the people. Maimonides identifies God, as Philo of Alexandria did before him, only with the good. If He is the good, evil cannot come from Him. How then account for it? Evil, Maimonides tells us, is the absence of the good, just as darkness is the absence of light. The theory is a very intricate one, too involved to interpret here, and one which, as the historian of Jewish philosophy, Isaac Husik, says, "was extremely unsatisfactory." In fact, after sumarizing the theory, Husik concludes: "Maimonides has nothing essentially new to contribute to the problem." This was hardly a theory that could sustain the ordinary human being, and when the later philosopher Crescas appeared, he taunted Maimonides for the latter's philosophic answers. Crescas repeated what others had said earlier: "There is only one answer and that is *olam haba*—the future world—because you will never sustain a human being by telling him to think that evil is not evil, that it is the absence of good, and that God is not responsible for it."

But even *olam haba* did not answer the problem for many. The final answer that the Rabbis offered was that that is God's way—"it is so decreed before Me." What is decreed before God is futile for man to question. "God so decrees it." Why? We do not know. We must have faith in God and His justice.

In this spirit, the prophet Malachi answers the question, "Where is the God of justice?," by saying, "You have wearied the Eternal with your talk. 'How have we wearied Him?' you ask. In that you say . . . Where is the God of justice?" You should not even ask the question! That is Malachi's answer. Man has to accept God's judgment, and the Jew has been taught to say, "The Rock, His work is perfect and all His ways are just."

There is a beautiful passage in the *Mekilta,* one of the classic works of the Rabbis, which states: "There is a great difference between the gentiles and the Jews. The gentiles rebel and curse their gods when they are punished, but Israel becomes humble and prays: 'I found trouble and sorrow but then I called upon the name of the Lord.' "

The Jew does not rebel; he accepts his judgment and prays to his God.

Solomon Schechter, in his work *Aspects of Rabbinic Theology*, after discussing many of these theories, concludes that "there is really no general view on suffering. All of the views offered are simply meant to pacify the mind of the afflicted person so that he should not become despondent and that it may help him to bear his lot courageously."

Schechter is correct. None of the theories provides an absolute answer to the problem. They were offered simply as a means to help the sufferers, to ease their suffering so that they should be able to bear their lot courageously. There is no answer to the problem of evil. It is God's way. "His work is perfect, and all His doings are just." That was the Jewish answer.

There is one further phase to the problem. While certain evils come from God and we must have faith in God's doing, there are other evils and sufferings that come from man, and which man himself can and must conquer. The solution of the first type of evil, we must leave to God; the solution of the second type—man-made evil—must come from man himself. The evils of war, crime, poverty, ignorance—these are man-made, not God-made; and they offer a challenge to man to eradicate them.

There is a passage in the Bible which beautifully interprets this thought—the battle that the Israelites had to wage against Amalek, one of the great enemies of the Jew. In the Bible tale, God urges the Jews: "Remember what Amalek did unto thee." This admonition ends, "*I* will blot out the memory of Amalek." The same story is repeated in another passage in the Bible, but with the concluding note, "*You* should wipe out the memory of Amalek." Amalek is the symbol of wickedness and evil. It has two aspects: the eradication of one type of evil we have to leave to God, who in His own time will wipe out that evil; the other type of evil "thou must eradicate"—man himself has to blot out.

In commenting on the same problem, Abraham Heschel says: "We do not know how to solve the problem of evil, but we are not exempt from dealing with evils in the world which we can eradicate. At the end of days, evil will be conquered by the Holy One. In historic times, now, evils must be conquered one by one."

In a striking passage in Deuteronomy, God speaks about economic justice and how we should grapple with the problem of the poor. One passage states: "The poor man will never cease to be in the land." There will always be some who are poor, and therefore we must always open our hand to the needy in the land. A few sentences earlier, a contrary statement appears: "However, there should be no poor among you." The Hebrew text makes clear the apparent contradiction. "There shall not be *in you* any cause for your fellow man's poverty."

Even in the ideal state, there will always be people who cannot or do not want to work. But each man must see to it that no poverty should result because of his doings or his wrong or immoral economic way of life. When we are responsible for the existing poverty, we are guilty of the evil.

In summary, there are aspects of evil which man has the potentiality to remedy. But there are other aspects of evil which he cannot eradicate and which must be left to God. That is the Jewish answer to the problem.

In a beautiful passage in one of the Midrashim, the Rabbis compare evil to a huge rock, placed on the crossways, over which men stumble as they walk. The king issued a decree to his servants: "Chip it off little by little until the hour comes when I will remove it altogether." Similarly, there are evils which we cannot explain, which God, in His own time, will remove altogether. But there are also evils—part of that "rock"—which man can and must chip little by little so that the road to life's happiness may become easier for all mankind to traverse.

On Jewish Chosenness

Arthur Hertzberg

 EITHER of two sets of assertions is true as description of Judaism, but neither is true without the other.

The first: God made covenant with a particular people that it should be His priesthood. To this people, the seed of Abraham, the slaves He had just redeemed from Egypt, He revealed the Torah, the Law which they were to obey, as the particular burden of the Jews and as the sign of their unique destiny in the world. He chose the land of Canaan as His inheritance and that of His people, the Holy Land which would forever remain the place in which He would most clearly be manifest.

The second: God exists in the world and cares for all men, for are not the children of Israel, as Amos said, no more to Him than the Ethiopians? It was out of His love for mankind as a whole that He taught all men His way of redemption, the Torah, which He revealed in the desert of Sinai, to show that, like the desert, the Law belongs to anyone who would dare to claim it. God does not speak to man only in the Holy Land, for He addressed Noah in the land between the rivers, Abraham in Ur, Moses in Midian, and He spoke even to Balaam, who came to curse the Jews in the desert of Sinai. The Talmud contains a vision of the end of days in which the holiness that is particular to the land of Israel will "spread out" to encompass all the lands.

It would be easy to say that these two versions of Judaism, the so-called *universal* and *particular* aspects, are in uneasy tension; this has indeed been said by non-Jewish commentators and polemicists for many centuries. From the perspective of one who stands inside the Jewish tradition, in the faith and experience of the Jewish believer, such a distinction does not exist. Jewish faith addresses itself not only to the Jews; it prescribes the Law and the way of salvation for all mankind.

The Jewish ideas of God, Torah and the people of Israel, as well as the lesser but quite important doctrine of the Holy Land, do not represent a catechism or a theology, for there is none such in Judaism. They are rather the lasting values, areas of concern, foci or problems around which the mass of Jewish spiritual devotion and thought through the ages has organized itself.

Men of simple faith, scholars, mystics and philosophers have differed from one another in their understanding and interpretation of these values. Nonetheless Judaism has remained recognizably one faith through all these permutations because, at least until the last century or so, the contemporary age of doubt, the normative tradition has been believed, and obeyed, by all Jews who intended to remain within the fold.

Jews have regarded it as self-evident that the God of all the world had made them His priest-people, His "suffering servant," to live by the Law and to bear the burden of woes that might come to them in order to achieve redemption for themselves and to lead mankind to the day when, in the words of the liturgy, "the Lord will be One and His name One."

The truest key to understanding Judaism in its own terms is to be found in its concept of the "chosen people." This doctrine of *chosenness* is a mystery—and a scandal. It was already a mystery to the Bible itself, which ascribed the divine choice not to any inborn merits of the Jews but to the unknowable will of God. It soon became, and has remained, a scandal to the gentiles—and even to some Jews. There have been many attempts through the ages to defend and explain this doctrine. It has been attacked in our day by Mordecai Kaplan, a theologian whose version of Judaism is naturalist and religio-cultural. Certainly the secularist versions of Jewish experience, like some forms of Zionism, have tended to abandon this doctrine.

It is nonetheless my view that Judaism is inconceivable without the idea of *chosenness*. Obviously there can be no chosen people unless there is a God who does the choosing. History, especially modern history, knows too many examples of self-chosen peoples. No matter how high and humanitarian a "civilizing mission" such a people may assign to itself, self-chosenness has invariably degenerated into some form of the notion of a master race.

Nor can we attempt to rationalize the classical Jewish concept of the chosen people, as some nineteenth-century Jewish theologians did, by arguing that various peoples have particular talents innate within them—the Greeks for art and philosophy, the Germans for order, the English and Americans for liberty, the Jews for religion.

Quite apart from the massive evidence from sociology and allied disciplines that such thinking is untrue, it has about it an air of arrogance which is morally repugnant. A "chosen people" has a right to exist and so think of itself only if there is a God in the world who is more than a First Cause or the order of the cosmos. He has to be conceived as the Creator who has not washed His hands of creation, who cares for and speaks to man, and to whom man's doing is not a matter of indifference. Such a God can be imagined as choosing a particular people for the task of strictest obedience to His will, as an instrument in His hand for the redemption of mankind, and as a teacher whom God Himself keeps from pride by applying to His chosen people the severest of judgments.

Stripped here of all argument, there are two possible approaches to religion: either God created man to achieve His purposes, which is the traditional Jewish view; or man invented God, for man's own purposes—a favorite belief of the last several centuries.

Some have approved of this inventiveness on man's part, and others have denounced it as an unnecessary and even harmful illusion. Especially since Voltaire, the idea of God has been explained as the antidote that man has devised to the menace of the world and to death. It is a crutch that man can, indeed ought to discard—so this argument goes.

There is no real comfort for the traditionalist in the classical philosophical and theological attempts to prove that God exists. Each of the well-known "proofs"—that creation implies a Creator, that the design of the world implies a designer—has been refuted in the realm of philosophical argument, and a verdict of *not proved* has been returned by the jury of reason.

I say *not proved* rather than *disproved* deliberately. Philosophical argument can indeed produce no undeniable proof of God's existence, but neither can it make it certain beyond argument that there is no God. The choice can only be made by faith. Man surveys the world and it can appear to him as an uncaring universe, indifferent and perhaps chaotic, to which he gives some passing meaning. Or he can view it as purposeful, though, like Job, he may not comprehend its purposes. Here we are confronted by an ultimate choice and we cannot argue ourselves into one or the other position.

Judaism, the religion of the Bible, on the other hand, is the classical example of a God-made religion for God's own purposes. It is the assertion—not the philosophical proof—that God exists and that He has spoken and speaks to man, giving man clues to the road that he must follow. A God who cares about men is likely to have revealed Himself to His favorite creation, though this is not an absolute necessity, for He could have so created the world that men's destiny would work itself out without immediate contact with the divine; but a God who has chosen a people for a role of transcendent importance in the scheme of redemption must have informed it of His choice, though here too it is just possible that the choice can exist without its knowledge. Classical Judaism believes that this people is conscious of its appointment, for God has spoken to it.

Classical Judaism is, therefore, a *revealed* religion. The very notion of revelation is in itself of the utmost difficulty, not only to the unbeliever but especially to the believer. What need does God have of man at all? Why should He have wished to speak to men? Even if one's faith in His revelation is of the most orthodox kind, there still remains the question: what does the divine command require of me, of my individual life in the context of my immediate situation?

The Jewish faith has from the earliest time, even in the Bible itself, confronted the question of what is true and what is false revelation. Every man can experience the divine revelation, but he can also imagine that he is experiencing it while really engaged in self-delusion.

Revelation must therefore be *personal* but not *personalist*. For the Jew, the form into which the revelation is cast is the Law. Judaism throughout all the ages is a tension between true and false prophets, between religious enthusiasts who come to recharge the experience of the obedient believer with refreshed devotion to the Law and those enthusiasts who come to break it in the name of some higher experience.

> If a prophet should arise among you or a dreamer of dreams, even one who gives you a sign or a miracle, and these signs and miracles of which he speaks to you come to pass, and he says, "Let us follow after other gods which you have not known and let us serve them," do not listen to the words of that prophet or that dreamer of dreams; for the Lord your God is testing you to know whether you love the Lord your God with all your heart and with all your soul. You shall follow after the Lord your God with all your heart and with all your soul. You shall follow after the Lord your God and fear Him, keeping His commandments and obeying His voice; you shall serve Him and cleave unto Him.
>
> (Deuteronomy 13:2–5)

In every age, Jewish religious expression is rich in mystical fervor. Such fervor is regarded as valid so long as it remains the handmaiden of obedience to the original revelation, so long as it is judged by it and does not presume to become its judge.

What the divine revelation contains has of course been at issue between Judaism and both Christianity and Islam for many centuries. In the realm of history, in the actual living experience of an all too often persecuted minority, this debate has had large and tragic consequences.

Though many Jews have lost their lives as a result of this difference, it has had relatively little effect on the Jewish faith. Occasionally a philosophical theologian within Jewry, such as Maimonides, has posited a missionary role among the gentiles for the daughter religions which have sprung from the Bible. But throughout the ages all Israel has stood fast in the faith that the Torah is the inheritance of the congregation of Jacob. It is only in the modern age that the meaning of revelation, which implies, most crucially, the binding character of the Torah, has become a most serious and severe problem for Jewish religious thought.

Biblical criticism of the modern kind has tended to undermine the Talmudic notions that every word in the Torah was dictated by the Lawgiver to Moses on Sinai and that the further tradition of interpretation in the Talmud and the later writings has been guided by divine inspiration. Religious anthropology has called into question the idea that the ritual prescriptions of the Bible are unique and God-given, for many parallels to them have been found, especially in ancient Near Eastern religions. Above all, the political and intellectual emancipation of modern Jewry, the entry of large segments of the Jewish community into the general life of Western man, has been regarded by most Jews as a primary practical objective. Since the life of obedience to the inherited Law required of the Jew a considerable conscious apartness, it has inevitably been regarded as a bar on the road to complete social integration.

The attacks from Biblical criticism and the anthropology of religion were not directed against Judaism alone. They were part of a major current which has dominated Western thought in the last several centuries, the criticism of revealed religion in the name of reason and science. The story of the defense of Judaism against such attack is not essentially different from that of Western religious thought as a whole. It is by now commonly agreed that scholarly investigation into the composition of the text of the Bible, no matter what the results of such study may be, cannot by its very nature pass final judgment on the faith in revelation. As for the argument from anthropology, man is obviously more than the chemical elements that make up his body. By the same token, a religious system is quite another thing than the sum of its individual practices.

For Judaism, however, the theological problem in modern times has been made more acute by the historic implications of the changing political and social history of the Jews. From the beginning of the Exile in the year 70 until the eighteenth century all Jews lived as a separate enclave, both in Christian Europe and in Moslem North Africa and the Near East. With the beginning of the social and political emancipation of Jewry, the overarching theme of Jewish experience in the nineteenth century became the finding of ways to cease being outside society.

Jewish thought devoted itself to definitions of Jewish faith and identity which would make it possible for the Jews to think about themselves as very much like everybody else, as a religion among religions, a group among groups, a nation among nations. Hence Jewish religious thought was more radically Westernized than it had ever been before, even by the most philosophical of medieval Jewish theologians. It was defined, especially by liberal theologians, as a religious denomination among the several which dominated West European culture.

The Law therefore became increasingly a social inconvenience. It was even more fundamentally in question because, of all the key values of Judaism, it was the most foreign, the hardest to explain, within an outlook that proceeded in the form and mode of Western philosophical theology.

But authentic Judaism is inconceivable without the Law. To be sure, there is a difference between moral principle and ceremonial observance. The Talmudic tradition rules that on the Day of Atonement man can find forgiveness from God for his sins in the realm of ritual, but no ceremony can absolve him of his sins against other men. He can atone only by redressing the wrong. Many other proofs of this distinction could be added. It is nonetheless an essential of the faith that the regiment that has been ordained for the religious practice of the Jew is God-given. This people was chosen to be a corporate priesthood, to live within the world and yet apart from it. Its way of life is the appointed sign of its difference. At the end of time, in a completely redeemed world, this unique way will perhaps disappear. But the world is not yet redeemed and the Messiah has not yet come.

The force of what I am saying is, perhaps, a bit obscured by the analytical language in which it has been put so far. Let us therefore state the position in historical and existential terms: there are only two possible alternatives for long-range Jewish survival. We can either be a religious community obedient to its inherited Law or we can attempt to become a secular nation in Israel, "like all the nations."

Those who reject the second alternative must, however, explore the full implications of the first. The plain truth is that we cannot affirm Judaism as morality, Messianic ideal, liberalism, group feeling, or anything else for more than one generation or so. Pretty soon some among the young start asking unanswerable questions: Is the Jewish morality really so different from decency in general? Is it necessary to be a Jew in order to be a good liberal and democrat? Why is it treasonable for some one born a Jew freely to choose some other culture than that of his parents?

The failure of Jewish modernity for two centuries has been written large in the fact that it has nowhere perpetuated itself effectively into the third and fourth generation. By its very nature it cannot do so outside of Israel. No amount of theorizing can substitute for the lack of faith in and commitment to the Law as God-given. Without it we can either choose radical Zionism, or wait to vanish.

Judaism is a religion not of nature but of history. There are many passages in the Bible which sing the praises of God in nature, but the characteristic Jewish experience of God is the awareness of His presence in human events. Every aspect of the Jewish tradition is pervaded by the memory of His redemptive act in the Exodus from Egypt. Almost the whole of the religious calendar is an act of recalling the past experience of the Jewish people as the record of God's relationship to it. The emphasis of Jewish faith is therefore neither on metaphysical speculation nor on dogma, but on human action. Life is the arena of moral choice, and man can choose the good. He can make himself worse than the beast or he can ascend to but little lower than the angels. Every man plays his role, for good or ill, in the redemptive history of mankind, for man is God's partner in the work of creation.

Judaism constructs its present out of a memory reaching back to Abraham and looking forward to the Messianic age for humanity as a whole. It is the way which began with the breaking of the idols and with risking all for the sake of God. To lead is often to suffer, and throughout all the centuries Judaism has found in the tragedy which is so much of Jewish history, in its role as the "suffering servant" of God, the surest sign of its ordained task.

Jews have often been restless under their burden. Even before the modern age some longed for peace and ease; the quest for a *normal* identity and destiny is human, all too human. But Jewish experience has not been like that of all the nations. The generation which has witnessed both Hitler and the third return to Zion engages in great self-delusion if it imagines that the place of the Jew in the world is as yet "normalized." Like Jonah, some Jews may attempt to cease prophesying against Nineveh, but Nineveh is always there. Jonah's knowledge that God wants something special from him is the inescapable and continuing groove of Jewish experience.

Meaning of the Sabbath

Erich Fromm

To the modern mind the Sabbath is a familiar, acceptable institution. We have no quarrel with the idea that we should rest from our work one day every week. This sounds to us like a self-evident, social, hygienic measure intended to give us the physical and spiritual rest and relaxation we need in order not to be swallowed up by our daily work. No doubt this explanation is true—but the Sabbath law of the Bible and the Sabbath ritual as it developed in the post-Biblical tradition go much deeper and require interpretation. Many questions come to mind.

Why is the Sabbath law so important that it is placed among the Ten Commandments, which otherwise stipulate only the fundamental religious and ethical principles?

> Remember the sabbath day, to keep it holy. Six days shalt thou labor, and do all thy work; but the seventh day is a sabbath unto the Lord, thy God; in it thou shalt not do any work, thou, nor thy son, nor thy daughter, thy man-servant, nor thy maid-servant, nor thy cattle, nor thy stranger that is within thy gates; for in six days the Lord made heaven and earth, the sea, and all that in them is, and rested on the seventh day; wherefore the Lord blessed the sabbath day, and hallowed it (Exodus 20:8–11).

Why is the Sabbath compared with God's rest on the seventh day and what does this "rest" mean? Is God pictured in such anthropomorphic terms as to need a rest after six days of hard work?

In the second version of the Ten Commandments (Deuteronomy 5:12–15) the observance of the Sabbath is commanded again, although here reference is made not to God's rest on the seventh day but to the Exodus from Egypt:

> And remember that thou wast a servant in the land of Egypt, and that the Lord thy God brought thee out of thence through a mighty hand and by a stretched out arm; therefore the Lord thy God commanded thee to keep the sabbath day.

Why this shift from God's rest to freedom in the explanation of the Sabbath? What is the common denominator of the two explanations? Moreover—and this is perhaps the most important question—how can we understand the intricacies of the Sabbath ritual in the light of the modern social-hygienic interpretation of rest? In the Bible, a man who "gathers sticks" (Numbers 4:32 ff.) is considered a violator of the

Sabbath law and is punished by death. In later post-Biblical and Talmudic development not only work in our modern sense is forbidden but activities like the following: making any kind of fire, even if it is for convenience's sake and does not require any physical effort; pulling a single grass blade or flower from the soil; carrying anything, even something as light as a handkerchief, on one's person. All this is not work in the sense of physical effort; its avoidance is often more of an inconvenience and discomfort than the doing of it would be. Are we dealing here with extravagant and compulsive exaggerations of an original "sensible" ritual, and with obsessional overstrictness, or is our understanding of the ritual perhaps faulty and in need of revision?

Essentially, the concept of work underlying the Biblical and the later Talmudic concept is not simply that of physical effort. Work is better defined as man's interference, constructive or destructive, with the physical world. The opposite of "work" is "rest"—a state of peace between man and nature. And the Sabbath is the day of the realization of that peace. On that day, man must leave nature untouched; he must not change it in any way, either by building or by destroying anything.

Even the smallest change made by man in the natural process becomes a violation of "rest" and of the Sabbath. In this sense, even lighting a match and pulling up a grass blade, while not requiring effort, are symbols of human interference with the natural processes, a breach of peace between man and nature. The same is true of carrying something of even little weight on one's person, which is prohibited in the Talmud. It is not the actual carrying as such which is forbidden. One can carry a heavy load within his house or his property without violating the Sabbath ritual. What one cannot do is carry even a handkerchief from one domain to the other, for instance, from the private house to the public street, because just as man must not interfere with or change the natural equilibrium, so too he must refrain from changing the social order. That means not only not to do business but also the avoidance of that most primitive form of transferring property by carrying it from one domain to the other.

The Sabbath thus symbolizes a state of complete harmony between man and nature and between man and man. By not working—that is to say, by not participating in the process of natural and social change —man is free from the chains of nature and from the chains of time, although only for one day a week.

The full significance of this idea can be understood only in the context of the Biblical philosophy of the relationship between man and nature. Before Adam's "fall"—that is, before man had reason and self-awareness—he lived in complete harmony with nature. His first act of disobedience—eating of the tree of knowledge—was the beginning of human freedom. He "opens his eyes," he knows how to judge good and evil, he becomes aware of himself and his fellows. He is tied to other individuals by bonds of love and yet he remains alone.

What is God's "curse" for his disobedience? Enmity and struggle are proclaimed between man and animals: "And I will put enmity between thee (the serpent) and the woman, and between thy seed and her seed; it shall bruise thy head, and thou shalt bruise his heel"; between man and the soil: "cursed is the ground for thy sake; in sorrow shalt thou eat of it all the days of thy life; thorns also and thistles shall it bring forth to thee; and thou shalt eat the herb of the field; in the sweat of thy face shalt thou eat bread, till thou return unto the ground"; between man and woman: "And thy desire shall be to thy husband, and he shall rule over thee"; between woman and her own natural function: "in sorrow thou shalt bring forth children." Conflict and struggle are now part of human history, replacing the prehistorical, pre-individual harmony of the Garden of Eden when men lived at peace with nature.

In the prophetic view of the Bible, the goal of man is to live again in peace and harmony with his fellow men, with animals, with the soil. But this new harmony is different from that in paradise. It can now be obtained only if man develops fully in order to become truly human, exhorted by the prophets: by knowing the truth and doing justly, by developing his power of reason to a point which frees him from the bondage of man and of irrational passions. The prophets repeatedly express in various symbols this idea.

And it shall come to pass in the end of days,
That the mountain of the Lord's house shall be established as the top
    of the mountains . . .
And many peoples shall go and say:
"Come ye, and let us go up to the mountain of the Lord . . .
And He will teach us of His ways . . .
For out of Zion shall go forth the law,
And the word of the Lord from Jerusalem.
And He shall judge between the nations . . .
And they shall beat their swords into plowshares,
And their spears into pruning-hooks;
Nation shall not lift up sword against nation,
Neither shall they learn war any more.

(Isaiah 2:1–4)

This new harmony, the achievement of which is the goal of the historical process, reaches its fullest expression in the figure of the

Messiah. And the Sabbath is the anticipation of the Messianic time, just as the Messianic period is called the time of "continuous Sabbath." The Sabbath is not only the symbolic anticipation of the Messianic time but is its real precursor. "If all of Israel observed the Sabbath fully only once, the Messiah would be here," the Talmud promises.

Resting, not working, then, has a meaning different from the modern meaning of relaxation. On the Sabbath, in the state of rest, man anticipates the state of human freedom that will be fulfilled eventually, when the Messiah will come. The relationship of man and nature and of man and man is one of harmony, peace, non-interference. Where work is a symbol of conflict and disharmony, rest is an expression of dignity, peace and freedom.

For this reason, the Sabbath ritual has a central place in the Biblical religion and in the further development of the Jewish tradition. It is more than a "day of rest" in the modern sense; it is a symbol of the overcoming of separateness and a symbol of freedom. Similarly, God's rest is not necessary because He is tired, but it expresses the idea that great as creation is, harmony is the greater and crowning creation. God must "rest" because He is free and fully God only when He has ceased to work. So is man fully man only when he does not work, when he is one with nature and his fellow men. That is why the Sabbath commandment is at one time motivated by God's rest and at the other by the liberation from Egypt. Both mean the same and interpret each other: rest is synonymous with freedom.

For the past two thousand years, the Jewish Sabbath, in contrast to the Babylonian day of rest, has been a day of joy and pleasure, a day of eating, drinking, singing, sexual intercourse, in addition to studying the Scriptures and other religious writings. Symbolically, it is a day celebrating man's victory over conflict and strife, over time and death itself. The Sabbath ritual is the acting out of a central metaphysical idea: that of man's development from prehistorical oneness, through the separateness and alienation which occurs in the historical process, to the achievement of a new harmony and oneness on the level of the full unfolding of man's reason and consciousness. In the Sabbath ritual this Messianic end is anticipated and acted out symbolically each week.

Aging—The Biblical View

Raphael Patai

MODERN American culture is characterized by a great preoccupation with aging and its concomitant problems. In trying to solve these problems we Americans focus our attention largely on the physical changes that accompany the aging process, and consequently our main avenue of approach consists of attempts to eliminate, alleviate and postpone the symptoms of physiological deterioration.

We tend to emphasize and overemphasize the desirability of youth and youthful traits; aging is invested with a horror from which we feel we must escape at all costs. In our preoccupation with physiological deterioration, we tend to overlook the psychological aspect of aging— the fact that advancing age means greater understanding, a better grasp of essentials, a clearer outlook on life and the world, and an accumulation of experience and wisdom.

Since the only alternative to becoming old is to die young, the whole emphasis on youth is futile, and man feels himself doomed to the fate of growing old which he cannot avoid in spite of all his frantic efforts. There is thus a deep tragedy beneath all our institutionalized insistence on youth and fear of age; the culture forces us to value that of which we have less and less every day, and to abhor that which inevitably envelops us more and more.

Youth is consequently placed by modern American culture on so high a pedestal as to amount to idolization. Indeed, thoughtful students of the contemporary American scene describe our society as "child dominated." Extreme permissiveness on the part of the parents often makes the child or the teenager the dominant personality in the family whose wishes and whims must be fulfilled and whose behavioral excesses must be silently suffered.

The accent on youth and the corresponding fear of age are so strong that people desperately try to preserve at least an appearance of youthfulness when advancing age begins to show its alarming signs. They dye their hair; they stew themselves in steam baths and engage in all sorts of strenuous exercises in order to keep slim (not so much because they believe that it is healthful but because it is youthful); "face-lifting" operations become more and more popular; and youthful mannerisms and postures, gestures and speech patterns are purposely maintained or adopted. All this is practiced by both men and women, although among women it is more emphatic because it is reinforced by a craving for beauty, defined strictly in terms of youthful attractiveness.

Fear of old age is so strong that the very term "old" is carefully avoided. People in their forties are still called "young men" and "young women." In their fifties they are referred to as "middle-aged." In their sixties they are called "mature." In their seventies they are still not "old" but merely "aging." These semantic euphemisms help us close our eyes to old age; we attempt to deny or ignore its encroachment, and to live our lives as if aging did not exist.

The ancient Hebrews, some of whose thoughts and feelings are preserved in the Bible, were also preoccupied with the problems of aging. They too recognized that old age is a life period in which physical strength declines. The classical expression of this feeling is found in the Book of Psalms in the outcry to God:

> Cast me not off in the time of old age,
> When my strength faileth, forsake me not!
>
> (Psalms 71:9)

But the general attitude to old age was diametrically opposed to the one prevalent in our society today. Attention was focused on the psychological and mental traits which become dominant in old age, and consequently the evaluation of age and the aging process was positive, cheerful, optimistic. In fact, the occasional comparisons made by Biblical authors between youth and old age invariably stress the advantages of the latter over the former. Childhood was regarded as a period of ignorance and folly, a time when all the faculties of the mind are not yet developed (Proverbs 7:7). "Foolishness is bound up in the heart of a child" (Proverbs 22:15). The older a person gets, the more understanding and wisdom he acquires; and the more honor and, indeed, veneration is due him.

Since years meant accumulation of wisdom, the aged in Biblical society ranked with the princes and persons of high office as leaders of the people. "The elder and the man of rank, he is the head" (Isaiah 9:14).

In accordance with this high valuation of old age, one of the basic educational aims (there were, of course, several others as well) among the Biblical Hebrews was to instill, into the hearts of the young, respect for the aged in general, and for parents in particular. As an emphatic Biblical commandment has it: "Thou shalt rise up before the hoary head and honor the face of the old man" (Leviticus 19:32). Incidentally, the first half of this Biblical verse could well be used today on posters in subways and buses where the respectful practice of offering one's seat to old people has completely disappeared among our children and teenagers.

Another Biblical expression of the respect for age that undoubtedly would be welcome in many a modern family was the custom for the young to keep silent while the elders spoke. There is no express commandment requiring this, but it was the accepted practice, as can be seen from the scene in which the stricken Job is surrounded by his four friends who try to comfort him. Three of them are old, and the fourth, Elihu, is young. While the three old men spoke, Elihu kept silent: "Now Elihu had waited to speak unto Job, because they were older than he" (Job 32:4). And only when he saw that the older men had nothing more to say did he start speaking, prefacing his utterance with the following words:

> I am young, and ye are very old; Wherefore I held back, and durst not declare you mine opinion. I said: "Days should speak, and multitude of years teach wisdom." (Job 32:6–7)

After stating the traditional attitude inculcated into the young with regard to age, young Elihu, however, goes on to state that wisdom is not a natural property of the aged, but is given to man by God. This being so, he, the youth, "also will declare mine opinion."

Within the group of elder people, the father and mother had to be paid special respect. The Fifth Commandment enjoins upon everyone to honor his father and mother; and, as a reward for fulfilling this precept, it promises the greatest of all gifts: long and prosperous life (Exodus 20:12; Deuteronomy 5:16). More specifically, honoring one's parents meant to "hear the instruction of thy father, And forsake not the teaching of thy mother" (Proverbs 1:8). "A wise son is instructed of his father" (Proverbs 13:1), while "a fool despiseth his father's conviction" (Proverbs 15:5). In fact, children were expected to fear and obey their parents (Leviticus 19:3). "Hearken unto thy father that begot thee, and despise not thy mother when she is old" (Proverbs 23:22).

To filial respect and the general regard on the part of society as a whole which equated age with wisdom, an additional factor that contributed to making old age an enjoyable period in life was the institution of the extended family. Under this pattern a man and his wife (or wives) and all his male descendants and their female dependents constituted one integral family group, living, in most cases, under one roof as members of one and the same household and tied together by bonds of intense loyalty. The grave problems of old and lonely parents, and of the old and lonely single widowed parent, which in our own society have to be faced by so many of us as the inevitable, sad and desolate last part of life, simply did not exist in a society where the extended family was the rule.

On the contrary, within the framework of the Biblical extended family, the older the parents grew, the more descendants lived under their actual or nominal tutelage, the more respect they commanded in the society as a whole, and, consequently, the more satisfaction they derived in the concluding period of their lives. An old age spent thus in semi-retirement, but as counselor and adviser whose words are respectfully listened to in the circle of one's children and grandchildren, was indeed a time to look forward to. It was the crowning achievement after an active manhood or womanhood, rich in values that could more than compensate for physical weakness and failing health.

In fact, old age with its honor and prestige was regarded as such a desirable period in life that people would often exaggerate their age. And by the time a chronicler came to record the life-span of the first fathers and leaders of the Hebrew nation, these exaggerated figures were accepted as historical facts. This is one of the explanations of the great ages appearing in the brief Biblical death notices: Sarah lived to be 127 (a traditional "round" figure, like the 127 provinces of Ahasuerus); Abraham 175; Isaac 180; Jacob 147; Moses 120.

Nor was it regarded as bad manners to ask a person how old he was. Thus, when Joseph introduced his father Jacob to Pharaoh, the king of Egypt politely inquired of the visiting chieftain: "How many are the days of the years of thy life?" (Genesis 47:8). And Jacob answered with a modesty barely hiding his pride in the age he and his fathers achieved: "The days of the years of my sojournings (i.e., on this earth) are a hundred and thirty years; few and evil have been the days of the years of my life, and they have not attained unto the days of the years of the life of my fathers in the days of their sojournings" (Genesis 47:9). The prophet Isaiah depicts the days to come as a period when even "the youngest shall die a hundred years old" (Isaiah 65:20).

In the tradition-bound Middle East, where Biblical concepts and values have survived down to our own day, it has remained customary to exaggerate one's age in order thereby to gain added prestige. As an example, one day in Palestine in 1933, an Arab friend took me to visit the Khalidiya Library in the Old City of Jerusalem. We were received in a friendly and hospitable way by Sheikh Amin al-Ansari, keeper of the library, an aristocratic old man with finely chiseled features, a dark olive complexion and a beautiful, flowing white beard. He climbed up ladders with great agility to show me rare manuscripts kept on top shelves, and when I asked him not to exert himself he answered: "Allah be thanked, although I am eighty years old, I am still in good health." I complimented him on this, and after we left, my friend said to me with a smile: "Did you really believe that he was eighty years old? He is only in his early sixties."

Thus the entire life-line had a radically different aspect in Biblical society from the one it has in modern Western civilization. In our own world the line curves rapidly and sharply upward, reaching its peak soon after the full development of the body. Early youth is this peak, the period regarded as the best, the most desirable phase in life. We try to hold on to it, at least to its attributes, as long as possible.

To the Biblical Hebrews the vital curve took on a very different shape. In childhood and youth it rose slowly and gradually. In middle age it continued to rise, and in old age every year added to its height. Ideally death came at a very old age, without a diminishing of the physical or mental powers, as in the case of Moses, who "was a hundred and twenty years old when he died: his eye was not dim, nor his natural force abated" (Deuteronomy 34:7). Abraham's end came when he was sated with all that life could give, "in a good old age . . . full of years" (Genesis 25:8), while David looked to his imminent death when he "was old and full of days" (I Chronicles 23:1). The vital curve did not decline; it was cut off by death somewhere near its zenith to be continued, in a different form, in another world.

It would not be easy to apply the Biblical valuation of old age to our lives, which are so different. But we can begin by using wisdom of the Bible as an example when faced with difficult decisions, including everyday problems that confront each of us in dealing with the aging and the aged within our own family circles. Again, we can also keep before our eyes the Biblical attitude of respect for parents and grandparents when training our own children. Above all, the Bible has much to teach about the inherent worth of every human being, which increases—not diminishes—with his years.

Sex in Jewish Tradition

Henry Raphael Gold

JEWISH tradition regarded sex as a great river of life rendering fruitful untold acres of precious soil and capable of carrying the shipping and wealth of a nation. It was felt, however, that this very river might go on a rampage devastating fields and forests and leaving in its wake miasmic swamps. Judaism therefore set itself the goal of humanizing sex—to curb its destructiveness and enhance its capacity for the enrichment of life.

In the Bible a clear motive for the creation of two human beings of opposite sexes is stated at the beginning: "And the Lord said, 'It is not good that man should be alone.'" The emphasis is on loneliness and the need for communication. The urge for communication takes for granted a fundamental common denominator, the striving for unity. Freud was later to emphasize that such going out to another human being, the libidinal tie, is the basis for altruism and the first limitation upon the primary selfishness or narcissism with which the human being is endowed at birth. The Talmud with characteristic poetic imagery summarizes this process of sex humanization by praising the Divine Creator for His wisdom and mercy in placing the breast of the human mother near the heart rather near the organs of elimination as in the case of animals (Babylonian Talmud, *B'rakhot* 10, 31).

The Talmud also stresses the common denominator of man and woman by saying that Adam was originally created bi-sexual, of two aspects or façades (*B'rakhot* 61 and *Eruvin* 18). This remarkable statement is based upon the Biblical passage that "He created them male and female and He called their name *Adam*," Hebrew for "man." The famous "rib" story describing Eve's creation is actually a mistranslation of the original Hebrew.

The Biblical expression in Genesis "And He built the *tzelah*" was erroneously interpreted in early translations to mean "And He built the rib." Originally, however, *tzelah* had an architectural significance, as in the "façade" of a building. In the building of the Temple, for example, *tzelah* is used to refer to the side or aspect of the tabernacle facing eastward toward the sea.

Instead of Eve's being fashioned out of Adam's rib, therefore, the creation of the two sexes was regarded as a splintering of two façades or original aspects of primal man, who was both male and female. The Biblical writers seemed to understand what students of medicine know today as a fact—that there are feminine remains in the male body and masculine "rests" in the female. Because of this insight, though the sages of the Bible and Talmud did not believe in the *equality* of man and woman, Judaism strongly championed their *equivalence* before the law and society. In a sense, this was a part of the Jewish attitude toward the equal value of the individual, regardless of difference in status and position. Whereas the Fifth Commandment ordered the individual to "honor his father and his mother," the Book of Holiness (Leviticus 19) commands that one "revere his mother and his father." The Talmud arrives at the conclusion that the purpose of this transposition which sometimes puts the father first and then the mother, and vice versa, is to emphasize the equivalence of man and woman before the law (*Kiddushin* 31).

Judaism differs markedly from certain forms of Christianity in its attitude toward the existence and function of sex. Judaism has never regarded sex as carnal contamination of the soul or as a concession to the depravity of man. Though Judaism was definitely intolerant of sex perversions, it accepted the idea of the existence of a variety of individual sex expressions (*Nedarim* 20).

Judaism struggled particularly against incest, in full awareness of the dangers of an ingrown society, but it never allowed itself to be paralyzed by the horror of that perversion, of which Freud speaks in the first chapter of *Totem and Taboo*. Indeed, the Biblical passage on incest is read at the afternoon service on Yom Kippur, the holiest day of the year. The battle against incest was based first of all on the fear of biological attrition—a danger threatening all small cohesive societies; but there was also a deep concern that it might inevitably undermine the security and affection of family relations and bring jealousy and rancor in their place. The same concern governs Jewish law in the case of divorce, where the husband is not permitted to marry the sister of his divorced wife although he would be permitted to marry the sister of his deceased wife. The principle here, as in so many aspects of Jewish law, is to protect and strengthen tender family emotions.

In general, the subject of sexuality was approached in Jewish tradition with frankness, candor and sincerity. Completely absent is that hysterical "mechanism of denial" which regards the unseen and the unfelt as non-existent. In the tract called *Yomah* describing the preparation of the high priest for the exalted ritual of the Day of Atonement, it is clearly stipulated that he should be married. Here was a man, spiritually speaking, who was the most exalted personality in the nation, who on the most solemn day of the year was about to enter the Holy of Holies, and yet the Talmudists were concerned about his being mated. Clearly, mating is more than physical or carnal relationship in the Jewish realm of ideas, but is rather the link between the generations and a mainspring of emotional security.

Fear of sexual desire and shame and guilt about its very existence are alien to classic Jewish tradition, as expressed in the Bible and the Talmud. Centuries later, Maimonides, in *The Guide for the Perplexed* (2nd chapter, 6th subdivision), speaks of an angel whose function is sexual passion.

Instead of fearing or camouflaging sexuality, Judaism found a way to channelize it for the benefit of society. If Judaism has made a specific contribution to the understanding of sex, it is largely through its passion for justice, which is an outgrowth of religious ideals and the historic experience of a people who have been dogged and hounded, and for whom justice became the condition of living and surviving. The Jewish emphasis is on the holiness of *justice* rather than on the holiness of *abstinence*. Here it is in marked contrast to some early forms of monastic Christianity. Under the influence of the Hindu idea of the renunciation of desire, emphasis on the ideals of poverty and abstinence crept into some forms of Christianity. Holiness came to be epitomized as withdrawal from life and carnal contamination.

In great contrast, the Talmud reveals a far more realistic understanding of human life. It speaks (*Sanhedrin* 108) of the extreme degradation of the generation of the flood, which even practiced zoophilia or animal love. However, their doom (to be washed off the face of the earth) was not sealed until they began to practice murder and robbery. Sexual immorality was a major sin, but it was still secondary to the practice of injustice.

In the story of Joseph and Potiphar's wife there was a dispute between two great Talmudic sages as to whether or not Joseph was on the point of yielding to Zulikha's advances (*Sotah* 36). In substance he says to her, "Do you realize that you are asking me to betray the trust of the man who saved me, who gave me a position in life?" He is actuated by a sense of justice and fair play rather than by the mere idea of abstinence.

In the opening of the historical book of Joshua, the spies who are sent forth to explore Canaan learn the secret of the defense of Jericho from a lady of ill repute called Rahab, who lives in the wall on the outskirts of the town. In return for the information which she provides, Rahab exacts from them the promise that she and her family will be saved when Jericho falls. That promise was kept with meticulous exactness so that not one member of the woman's family was touched despite the general devastation that ensued when Jericho's walls did come tumbling down.

The central theme of the Book of Holiness is "Love thy neighbor as thyself." Therein one also finds the accent on justice and mercy. The Talmud also links the Golden Rule to the impropriety of bringing bright lights into the privacy of the marital chamber lest there be a sudden exposing of bodily blemishes (*Niddah* 17). These are refinements of considerateness and justice which have penetrated many aspects of Jewish law and life.

Finally, by the separation period during and following the menstrual cycle and by the ritual immersion symbolizing purification and rebirth, woman was guarded against man's brutality, and man himself was spared the extremes of sexual surfeit and frigidity. Sex as a biological appetite has thus been both distinguished from and related to love as a profound need of the human spirit. The presentation of these two aspects of sexuality is found in one of the ancient Midrashim. The poetic story relates that when Adam awakened from the divine surgery and beheld the beautiful Eve at his side, he asked, "What is going to be the plan of our life together?" She responded, "We shall have a common table, you will seek to provide it with bread, and I shall cover it with fresh flowers."

Study or Action?
Torah in Jewish Life

Raphael Zvi Werblowsky

STUDY, or Talmud Torah, has always been held to be one of the central and most essential activities of Jewish life, whatever our other professional, intellectual and cultural interests. We cease from Talmud Torah only at our death, and rabbinic legend, in its love of learning, does not recognize even that end. After dying, the old texts say, we do not merely go to paradise, but—if lucky—we graduate to the *yeshivah shel ma'alah* (Academy on High). The Hebrew school, the yeshiva, the Talmud Torah train us for one of the main pursuits of the genuine Jewish life: continuous study of the Torah in the sense of a permanent cultivation of the classical sources and expressions of Jewish thought, learning, piety, serious self-awareness and searching.

Study came so much to be considered as an ultimate value in its own right that the ancient rabbis seriously discussed the respective claims to priority of study (*talmud*) on the one hand, and action (*ma'aseh*) on the other. Is *talmud* merely the preparation for the good life of *mitzvot u-ma'asim tovim,* or is the good life itself nothing but a life devoted to a maximum of study? Some of the ancient rabbis were extreme in their views, and adopted an attitude which, to our minds, would seem inimical to the values of active life and cultural creativity.

The story is told of R. Simeon b. Yohai, who, as he emerged from the cave where he and his son had lived (and evidently studied) for many years, beheld people at work in the fields. He angrily said: "If people plow in the plowing season, and sow in the sowing season, and thresh in the threshing season . . . what is to become of the Torah?" God, so the Rabbis tell us, disapproved of this exclusive emphasis on the studious as against the practical life, and a voice was heard from heaven, saying, "Didst thou come out to destroy My world? Get thee back to thy cave."

The case for the active life was stated by R. Ishmael in his comment on the words of Deuteronomy, "and thou shalt gather in thy corn." R. Ishmael explained:

> Since it says (Joshua 1:8), "This book of the Law shall not depart out of thy mouth, and thou shalt meditate therein day and night," I might think that this injunction is to be taken literally. Therefore it says, "and thou shalt gather in thy corn," which implies that you are to combine the study of Torah with a worldly occupa-

tion . . . Said Abaye: Many have followed the advice of R. Ishmael and it has worked well; others have followed R. Simon b.
Yohai and it has not been successful.

One suspects that many scholars with whom, in the words of Abaye,
"it has worked out well," have, in fact, shown remarkable capacities
for combining the necessary amount of worldliness with their devotion
to study. But if we examine more closely R. Simeon b. Yoshai's somewhat uncompromising and forbidding views, we find that he did not
reject the active life because he objected, on principle, to worldly
occupations. R. Simon merely felt that with the limited time and
energy at our disposal, we should concentrate on what is more valuable and important—that is, Talmud Torah. There is nothing
intrinsically wrong with our various interesting and useful activities;
but they do take away time from that most important of all pursuits
—the Law, on which we should meditate day and night.
One of the reasons why moneylending came to be considered an
honorable business by many pious men in the Middle Ages was their
devotion to Talmud Torah. If a man could find a way of having his
capital work for him, then his own days and nights would be free for
meditation on the Torah. Whatever R. Simeon b. Yohai and other
Rabbis had to say in deprecation of work and the professions was due
to the high value they placed on study. For how can you prevent "this
book of the Law" from "departing out of thy mouth" if your mouth is
busy most of the time with business talk, conversations, professional
discussions and committee meetings? R. Simeon b. Yohai once remarked: "If I had been present at Mount Sinai when the Torah was
given to Israel, I would have asked God to give men two mouths, one
wherewith to study the Torah (without interruption), and one for his
other needs."
This utopian dream was repudiated by an opposing tendency in
Judaism. "When thou eatest the labour of thy hands, happy shalt thou
be and it shall be well with thee." R. Simeon b. Yohai had to admit:

> Only to those who have manna to eat is it given to study the
> Torah. For behold, how can a man be sitting and studying when
> he does not know where his food and drink will come from . . .
> Hence, only to those who have manna to eat is it given to study
> the Torah.

And R. Joshua said: "If a man studies two halakhot in the morning
and two in the evening, and the whole day he occupies himself with
his trade, it is accounted to him as if he had fulfilled the whole
Torah." But note the words "it is accounted to him as if"—it is only
second best.

What do these rabbinic sayings tell us? They suggest two ways of looking at Talmud Torah. We may consider study as the process by which we acquire the necessary knowledge of certain things, e.g., Jewish law, Halakhah (if we take Talmud Torah in the narrow sense), ethical teachings, religious ideas and values. In that case study is not life itself, but a means to enable us to live properly and perform the Torah. To quote the ancient rabbis again, *talmud* is great because it leads to *ma'aseh*.

The second view holds study to be life itself, or at least the ideal life, and the supreme and all but exclusive contents of our minds and aspirations. It is the highest value, the one activity really worthy of man, in comparison with which all other activities—even prayer—are sheer waste of time. When R. Simeon b. Yohai beheld the farmers laboring in the fields instead of studying the Torah, he said, "they forsake eternal life and occupy themselves with temporal life."

But these same words were also spoken by another rabbi in a very different situation.

> Raba saw R. Hamnuna prolonging his prayers. Said he: These people forsake eternal life (i.e., Talmud Torah) and occupy themselves with temporal life.

Just imagine: prayer is classed as a worldly activity! Only study brings us contact with things eternal and leads to communion with God.

This is the scholar's scale of values. And indeed, as we read our sources carefully, we soon discover a third tendency in Judaism. In addition to the proponents of the active life—two halakhot in the morning and two in the evening, and for the rest an active and creative life—and the ideologists of the exclusively studious life such as R. Simeon b. Yohai, there were a third group, the contemplatives and mystics. Among the early representatives of this group were the *hasidim ha-rishonim,* the pious men of old of whom the Mishnah tells us that they used to wait one hour before praying, and one afterwards, in order to concentrate their minds on God.

Clearly, for these *hasidim rishonim* prayer was no "worldly activity" but rather something akin to "life eternal," the converse of the soul with God. They held that too much active life, like too much study, was an unpardonable waste of time for the soul that should be immersed in the contemplation of things divine. Raba had felt that prayer was part of the active practical life because, after all, what was prayer but petition for prosperity and success in active life or, as Rashi put it, for *baney, hayyey u-mezoney* (children, long life and sustenance)? Hence prayer, like the practical activities to which it is related, should be reduced to a decent minimum.

The *hasidim ha-rishonim* took a similar view of study. What is study, they seem to have thought, but part of and preparation for the practical active life? In order to live rightly and honestly, we must know what to do and what not to do on a Sabbath day, what to eat and what not to eat, and so on. But why should we meditate day and night on Reuben's ox that has gored Simon's cow, or on the egg which a hen has laid on a festival day, or on the laws of evidence in criminal cases, when our mind should contemplate God?

The Talmud seems to have been slightly worried by the inordinately long time which these pious men of old spent in prayer. If we calculate three prayers per day, plus one hour before and one after each prayer, then they spent nine hours in prayer. The Talmud asks: "How did they remember the Torah and how did they do their work (i.e., how did they earn their bread)?" and replies "Because they were saintly men they easily remembered their Torah, and their work was blessed." In other words, they did not need constant repetition and memorizing of the Law, and little work produced sufficient for their few and frugal needs.

This little passage gives us, in a nutshell, the mystical as against the purely scholarly scale of values: contemplative prayer is the supreme spiritual value, and one's time should be devoted to it above all else. Other activities are merely means to keep one alive, and Torah is something one should know and remember in order to live righteously and correctly, but it is not something to be meditated on all the time. There is *instrumental* value in knowing the Law, but no *intrinsic* value in the activity of studying it.

It was inevitable that tensions should develop between this "mystical-contemplative" scale of values and the powerful tradition of Talmud Torah which considered the study of Halakhah and the intellectual effort focused on the Torah as the supreme value of Jewish life and, in fact, as a kind of sacramental activity in which one communed with God and shared in eternal life.

This is not the occasion for reviewing the history of these tensions in ancient Jewish piety, in medieval pietism and Kabbalism, and again in eighteenth-century Hasidism. One thing, however, is certain. We cannot complain that Jewish tradition is too narrow, too one-sided, giving scope to one kind of temperament only. Alongside the major rabbinic tradition which sees in Talmud Torah the greatest of the commandments and the highest type of Jewish life, we have the practical ideal of active realization of values and aspirations in life, and the mystical ideal of contemplation.

What all three forms of life have in common is that they are unthinkable without Talmud Torah. Study as the absorbing pursuit and overriding value of life, or as the guide to and companion of our practical endeavors, or as the foundation and safe compass of mystical meditation, whether as a full-time occupation or as two halakhot in the morning and in the evening, or as the foundation of a spiritual life soaring to greater heights, Jewish learning has always been the root and fountainhead of Jewish life. The exact connotations, methods and even the contents of Jewish learning may undergo change as part of the changes of history. But without Jewish learning we cannot be Jews.

IV

Encounter and Dialogue

The Parting of the Ways: Two Articles

Ellis Rivkin

I. WHO CRUCIFIED JESUS?

THE question of who crucified Jesus is one of the oldest and most stubborn problems that historians and theologians, both Christian and Jewish, have ever faced. Bias and preconceived opinions have unfortunately served to becloud and obscure the entire issue.

This, of course, is easily understandable. If one is already committed to Christianity, it is difficult to look at the Christian record as though it were just another document in the history of mankind. Similarly, Jews, who have suffered so grievously from the charge of having crucified Jesus, can scarcely view the documents in the New Testament with the kind of ease, indifference and scientific objectivity with which they would view the history of India, China, Rome or Greece.

As a consequence, whether the approach has been by Christians, on the one hand, or by Jews, on the other, the accounts in the New Testament have been made to yield not what was there, but that which was assumed must be present. This does not mean that scholars intentionally distorted the documents, but rather that they were incapable, in matters relating to something basic to their own contemporary lives, of conceiving them objectively. Some Christian scholars, for example, who have wanted to set the records straight, frequently, in their very aim at liberalizing their approach to the problem, failed to see the truth. Such scholars, in their anxiety over the pain that Jews have suffered because of the crucifixion, have sometimes gone so far as to indicate that there is practically no difference between Judaism and Christianity. Or they will say that the sources of the New Testament are confused, and perhaps Jesus was not even crucified.

Similarly, liberal Jews at times tend to oversimplify the problem. After all, they say, did not Jesus get his teachings from the Jews? And do not Jews and Christians have the same ethics? the same God? the same basic beliefs?

Unfortunately, all of this is a sad misunderstanding; none of these approaches is adequate as background for understanding the truth about the crucifixion.

Normally, the professional historian, with no particular bias for or against Judaism or Christianity, would be the scholar best qualified to ferret out the truth; for this question is basically an historical problem. After all, Jesus did live at a point in time. The Jews had been in existence long before Christianity came on the scene. In time, the latter movement arose, developed, expanded and unfolded into a whole variety of different beliefs, opinions, sects and denominations, and separated itself from the Judaism out of which it had evolved. Yet though the problem is clearly an historical one, most scholars who have dealt with it have been theologians or have been interested because of their prime interest in either Judaism or Christianity. The doctrinal issue has frequently been crucial.

The historian's major concern, however, is not with the truth of a doctrine. The question is not whether Jews or Christians have the true religion, but how we can best understand how and why new doctrines emerged. It is all too easy to lose sight of the central issue. For example, in the New Testament, bitter struggles go on between Jesus and his followers and the Pharisees. These Pharisees are called hypocrites by those who wrote the Gospels, and, to this day, the word "pharisee" is synonymous with "hypocrite." The Pharisees, presumably, were law-minded, and therefore had no pity or mercy. Jesus, on the other hand, is pictured as being above the Law, a spiritual figure. He is shown as being something good, while the Pharisees are depicted as bad.

One can approach the problem by asking which group had the true doctrine: Christianity in its opposition to the Law, or the Jews or Pharisees in their insistence upon its significance. As long as the problem is viewed in this way, there can be no solution. But suppose one accepts the fact that there was controversy and difference. Instead of passing judgment as to whether these differences were good or bad, we can try to understand why the controversies arose at the time that they did, and not earlier, and why some did love Jesus while others hated or were indifferent to him. Why, for example, did Jesus' message win so few supporters in his own lifetime? Yet, why were Jewish doctrines unsuccessful when they came into competition with Christian doctrines for the loyalty of the pagan masses?

It is thus more important to understand the circumstances under which the controversy took place than to pass judgment on its doctrinal merits. The historian must attempt to reconstruct the world in which Jesus lived and recognize its dynamic and revolutionary character. This is all the more necessary in view of the fact that no written evidence contemporary with Jesus refers to him or his ministry. Indeed, some scholars actually argued that Jesus did not exist. After all, the accounts are garbled: the Gospels of Mark, Matthew and Luke do not agree, and where they are in agreement, John, in the Fourth Gospel, presents an entirely different version. After all, no witnesses wrote down what occurred at either the time of Jesus' ministry or his crucifixion. For a considerable period after his death the story of his life, message and crucifixion was handed down by word of mouth. The Gospels naturally reflect this general uncertainty.

After the destruction of the First Temple and the period of the Babylonian captivity, some of the Jews returned and restored the Second Temple, creating once more a settlement within Palestine. Around 445 B.C.E. a firm theocratic structure based on the Pentateuch was established. At this time Palestine was a very small country with most people making their living in agriculture, and with no large cities in existence. It was backward and primitive in comparison with what the country had been before the First Exile.

The new settlement was important because it marked the acceptance by all the people of the Five Books of Moses. Though the Pentateuch had had a long history of development before this time, it was only now that it became the constitution of all the Jewish people. Indeed, with Ezra, in about 445 B.C.E., the Five Books of Moses came to be the Law which ruled the people. The Jews in Palestine at that time were peasants. Leviticus, probably the most important book in the Pentateuch, gave them specific instructions about sacrifices and support of the priests, and they were promised agricultural abundance if they obeyed its laws. The system prescribed here is an hereditary theocracy, in which the authority came from God through the priests who, in turn, controlled the people. There was no democracy, and the people had no voice in the government. The priesthood was very firmly established.

Because of the geographical location of Palestine, at the juncture point between Egypt and Syria, Persia and Asia Minor, and all the connecting routes to Greece and Rome, the Jews were always being conquered by other peoples. While the theocracy was still flourishing, the Greeks came in with Alexander the Great and brought Palestine under their control. They brought Hellenistic civilization into Palestine; a new kind of Greek city, dynamic, affected and changed the countryside and disrupted the even tenor of the agricultural life—the mainstay of the theocratic system.

The structure of society underwent a radical change. Whereas before the emergence of cities the vast majority of Jews had been peasants, now shopkeepers, artisans, craftsmen, businessmen, merchants emerged. A complex economic and social structure replaced a simple agricultural structure. The Pentateuch had been primarily concerned with the tiller of the soil; it was no longer adequate to a society big with change, that knitted Jews together in novel ways, that churned up problems for which the *literal* words of the Pentateuch had no answer.

The new elements in society, struggling with the problems of life in a new world, could not be content with a fixed and permanent law which foreclosed change, nor with a religious orientation that blocked new ventures of the spirit. The outcome was nothing less than a new orientation toward God, man, religion and destiny—an orientation which in its way was as significant as the Bible itself—for it emphasized the worth and significance of each single individual human being in the eyes of God. It declared the revolutionary doctrine of personal salvation in the world-to-come. This new orientation is to be found at the heart of every single monotheistic religion that subsequently was to evolve out of Judaism. This personal concern of God with each of his creatures is still the core of the monotheistic religions of our own day. The men who so daringly formulated this crucial doctrine were the Pharisees.

The Pharisaic movement that give birth to these revolutionary ideas has been not only maligned but thoroughly misunderstood.* Although both Jewish and gentile scholars are generally in agreement that they were an elevated group of superior religionists, they have been described in a wide variety of ways, from unctuous to sincere pietists, depending on the personal biases of their evaluators. The word "pharisee" means "to separate," and, according to most scholars, it designates an elite that separated itself from the mass of people, who were not sufficiently religious. Most scholars agree that the Pharisees, for good or ill, were particular about laws of ritual cleanliness and uncleanliness, which were an inheritance from Leviticus. It is even said that these Pharisees were more concerned about laws of cleanliness and uncleanliness than were the priests themselves. They are depicted as vaunting their ritual purity as they looked down with contempt at those who wallowed in ritual uncleanliness.

And yet, this picture, which is spread over pages of the most learned works, is far from the truth. In reality, the Pharisees virtually abrogated the laws of cleanliness and uncleanliness as they affected non-priests. Never once did Jesus accuse them of being primarily concerned with these laws. In the only passages in which Jesus refers to them (Mark 7:1–8, Matthew 15:1–11, Luke 11:37), he implies that the Pharisees did not go far enough in doing away with these laws, for they still insisted on the washing of the hands before eating. It is thus clear that Jesus recognized that that ritual washing was virtually all that remained, for the non-priest, of the elaborate system of ritual purity.

Similarly, the charge that the Pharisees were aloof and elevated themselves above the people is starkly contradicted by the sources. Josephus, himself a Pharisee and an historian at the time of the destruction of the Temple, said that the Pharisees were so popular that

* See article on "The Pharisees" by Jacob B. Agus, pp. 28 ff.

the priests carried out all of the Pharisaic laws with respect to sacrifices lest the people rise up in revolt. Not once, in any of the passages in which Jesus refers to the Pharisees, does he indicate that they were unpopular.

In actuality, the Pharisees got their name "separatists" because they opposed the theocracy. They were denounced by the theocratic priests, the Sadducees, as having separated themselves from official Judaism. The name, as frequently in history (cf. Dissenters, Protestants, Roundheads, Sansculottes, *Mitnagdim*), became the permanent designation, even though the Pharisees themselves did not coin the word, nor did they refer to themselves by that name. They called themselves *soferim*, or *hakhamim*, or *zekenim*, i.e., scholars.

Pharisaism was a movement which sought individual salvation not through the Temple but through a personal religious life, concentrated in the synagogue. In opposition to the theocracy, this Pharisaic movement modified the laws of the Pentateuch and made them bearable for people living in a new type of society. For example, although previously it had not been permissible to walk out of one's house on the Sabbath, the Pharisees, *i.e.,* the sages, permitted people to walk anywhere in the city on the Sabbath day. When the law was unyielding and unbending, the Pharisees made it pliable and subject to change. They also modified the laws of ritual purity for non-priests.

They recognized, however, that if the Law was to change, it had to change through regularized channels. Here is where they came in conflict with Jesus, who seemed to be asserting: "I will make the Law when I want to make the Law because I am the son of man. I am the Messiah." As the Gospel of Mark (I:22) so succinctly states: "And they were astonished at his teaching, for he taught them as one who had authority, *and not as the scribes*" (italics mine).

The Pharisees opposed Jesus because they did not believe that any individual should change the Law merely on the basis of his own personal authority. Jesus' basic difference with the Pharisees was over the acceptance of his role. Since the Pharisees refused to recognize Jesus as the Messiah, he looked upon them as having rejected him and his message. Normally, he lived a Pharisaic life and urged his fellow disciples to do likewise. But when the Pharisaic laws were broken, he refused to consider such violations as important as the rejection by the Pharisees of his message.

The Roman conquest of Palestine brought much suffering to the Jews. Large numbers of independent farmers, unable to meet the heavy taxes that were imposed, lost their land. The notorious policy of "divide and conquer" was put into effect. At the time of Jesus, the Roman procurator was responsible for law and order in Palestine, and he in turn appointed the high priest who was held responsible for the good behavior of the populace. His position was dependent on his unswerving loyalty to Rome, his ability to keep the people calm.

At the time of Jesus the high priest was Caiaphas, who had been appointed by Pontius Pilate and who successfully held on to his office longer than most high priests. If he managed to achieve this under Pontius Pilate, we must conclude that he must have been an extraordinarily crafty, cruel and ambitious person who was especially sensitive to the slightest stirring against Roman rule. For Pontius Pilate was one of the most vicious of the procurators, as Josephus, a friend and admirer of Rome, starkly affirms. He repeatedly provoked revolts so that they might cruelly be put down.

That Roman rule was very harsh and cruel at this time is amply proved by the fact that it was not long after the death of Jesus that a bitter revolt broke out against that rule (65–70). Long before the war against Rome, large numbers of Jews were desperate. In response to the troubles of the time, two different solutions were offered by groups that broke off from Pharisaism.

One of these groups, referred to by Josephus as the Fourth Philosophy, called for revolutionary violence against Rome and against Jews who collaborated with Rome. The goal of this group was the equality of all men under God.

The second group consisted of apocalyptic visionaries, who foreswore violence, but who preached that the kingdom of God was at hand. Its coming would bring to an end domination, suffering and inequality. Jesus was one of those who preached the imminent coming of the kingdom of God and who called upon his listeners to live the kind of life that would hasten the kingdom and assure them of membership in it. Such preachment, though eschewing violence, was revolutionary in character, for it most definitely implied the sweeping away by God of Roman rule.

The high priest was always on watch for any signs of rebellion. When Jesus came to Jerusalem on the eve of Passover, he was greeted, as he went through the streets, as the king of the Jews, the son of David. It was festival time and tens of thousands of people were milling around. Pontius Pilate, the procurator, had come with troops from his headquarters to live in Jerusalem in case of trouble.

And Jesus was causing trouble in that he claimed to be, or people said in his name, that he was the Messiah. People were referring to him as the descendant of David, which to High Priest Caiaphas and the procurator suggested a dynasty, the replacement of Roman rule. What could the kingdom of God mean except the end of the Roman kingdom? Jesus was arrested, not because he was preaching violence but because he was identified with the Davidic dynasty, the Messiah, the kingdom of God, and, as such, threatened the whole Roman system.

Jesus was brought to the high priest, and was tried before a *sanhedrin*—a Greek word which merely means "council" and not the official *Bet Din* or *sanhedrin* of the Pharisees. Jesus was brought before the council of the high priest made up of Jewish collaborators with Rome. As members of the wealthy classes, they were dependent on Rome for protection of their wealth from the threatening masses. Their decision was rendered not in terms of a law court, but in terms of whether Jesus was politically dangerous or not.

According to various statements in the Gospel, Pontius Pilate would have saved Jesus. But a closer reading of the account discloses that Pontius Pilate kept repeating over and over again to Jesus, "Are you the king of the Jews?" Or he asked, "Shall I save the king of the Jews?" The word "king" was used provocatively to trap the people. To have asked for Jesus' release would have been equivalent to rebellion.

The emblem on the cross which read "King of the Jews" is stark and conclusive evidence that Jesus was crucified because he was viewed as a threat to Roman sovereignty. He was believed to have had Messianic pretensions and therefore deserved, from the Roman point of view, the death of all rebels—crucifixion. The high priest, far from being the representative of the Jewish people, was the representative of Pontius Pilate, the instrument of Roman domination. If he agreed to Jesus' death, it was to indicate that the Jews were loyal to Pontius Pilate and to Caesar, and were not considering any kind of revolt. They owed no allegiance to any other king.

Thus the drama of the interplay between oppressors and oppressed becomes clear. The whole Roman system was geared to preventing anyone from emerging who might disrupt its rule. The Roman authorities appointed people like High Priest Caiaphas to make sure that their rule and regime would remain. They sought the collaboration of the wealthy. They used every means to see that the people did not give loyalty to anyone but Caesar.

In crucifying Jesus, the Romans were using a mode of punishment commonly used for those who in any way indicated that they had any other loyalty or recognized the sovereignty of any other kingdom than that of Caesar. Crucifixion was a daily occurrence in Palestine at that time. It was meant to be a frightful warning to the discontented.

From the historical point of view, therefore, the question of "who crucified Jesus?" should be replaced by the question "what crucified Jesus?" What crucified Jesus was exploitation, the destruction of human rights, Roman imperialism, selfish collaboration. What crucified Jesus was a type of regime which, throughout history, is constantly and forever crucifying those who would bring human freedom, insight or a new way of looking at man's relationship to man. Domination, tyranny, dictatorship, power and disregard for the life of others were what crucified Jesus. If there were among them Jews who abetted such a regime, then they too bear that same guilt.

The mass of Jews, however, who were so bitterly struggling under Roman domination that they were to revolt in but a few years against this very regime of tyranny, can hardly be said to have crucified Jesus. In the crucifixion of Jesus, their own plight of helplessness, humiliation and subjection was clearly written on the cross itself. By nailing to the cross one who claimed to be the Messiah to free human beings, Rome and its collaborators indicated their attitude toward human freedom.

II. PAUL AND EARLY CHRISTIANITY

How did Jesus who came as a Messiah for the Jews become Christ? How did an apocalyptic visionary with a message for the poor, the humble, the downtrodden and rejected of his people become the risen Lord? How did a helpless crucified victim of Roman power become the son of God whose death brought eternal life? How did a simple teacher from Galilee become the heir of the Roman Empire and redemptive God for much of mankind?

How did it come about that the redeeming Christ was irresistible in the pagan world and yet made little headway among the Jews? What was there about Judaism that enabled it to give birth to a religion that won a world, without itself being overwhelmed by its own creation? Yet why was Judaism no match for Christianity in the struggle for the souls of the decaying, pagan world?

These questions are indeed crucial and require answers that clarify the phenomena rather than underwrite our preconceptions. A depreciation of the Christian doctrine of the redemptive Christ makes its victory over paganism incomprehensible. Christianity must have been more adequate than Judaism for the needs of gentiles suffering in the disintegrating societies of the ancient world. Otherwise Judaism not Christianity would have triumphed. Christianity therefore must have possessed certain crucial elements that were not present in Judaism. On the other hand, the Judaism that flourished in the Roman Empire must have been adequate to the needs of those who lived it, for there is no question that it maintained its integrity against the powerful doctrines of Christianity. The problem is therefore not to determine which is the truer religion but rather to comprehend the historical processes that brought about the separation of Christianity from Judaism, that enabled Christianity to be so successful, and that preserved Judaism as an independent and viable religion.

The historical Jesus belongs to Jews and Judaism even though most Jews rejected his claims, and even though his Judaism was a deviant form of Pharisaism. He came for Jews, he ministered to Jews, he sought to usher in the kingdom of God for Jews, his message was expressed in the language of Judaism, and his immediate disciples were Jews. The historical Jesus survives in the Gospels as a human being. The immediate disciples of Jesus had known him as a Jewish teacher who had come to his fellow Jews with the message of the imminent coming of the kingdom of God; and since they themselves were Jews, they were unable to dissociate their belief in the resurrected Jesus from their intimate knowledge of the Jesus who had healed the sick, driven out the demons, quarreled with the Pharisees, and who had been arrested and crucified. Such a Jesus might have an appeal to some Jews, but little at all to gentiles, especially if circumcision and the observance of the Law were as essential for salvation as was the belief in Jesus as the resurrected Messiah.

Paul was the true founder of Christianity. He concentrated on the crucifixion of Jesus and its redemptive meaning, while he ignored the actual life and teachings of Jesus. What Jesus had said was of little consequence; but what had happened to him, for him and by him was the turning point in human history. God the Father had given His son to mankind so that through his death sin itself might be crucified and the believing who had taken on Christ would be resurrected to life eternal. Faith in the redemptive power of Christ was absolutely necessary for salvation; the mitzvah (act of the Law) system of salvation of Pharisaic Judaism was rejected as a hindrance; all who believed in the Christ were the true members of Israel.

How did Paul come to such radical conclusions? Why did he reject so totally the Judaism of his earlier years? Paul had been a Pharisee (Philippians 3:4–6; cf. Galatians 1:13–14); he considered himself to have been more advanced in his Judaism than most of his fellow Jews (Galatians 1:14), he had been a rabid persecutor of the early Christians (Galatians 1:13; Philippians 3:6). Suddenly he had been transfigured, and he was totally transformed. The rest of his life was dedicated to fervent and agitated spread of the gospel of the Christ crucified and resurrected, and this gospel he preached primarily to the gentiles.

Paul's transformation from persecutor to persecuted, from a zealous devotee of the Law to its annihilator, from a Hebrew of the Hebrews to apostle to the gentiles is closely bound up with the character of Pharisaism. The Pharisees were the intellectual and religious leaders of the vast majority of the Jews in the days of Jesus and Paul. They were the *hakhamim* and the *soferim,* i.e., the sages and scholars. Hillel had been one of the great Pharisaic teachers, Gamaliel another.

These Pharisaic teachers had developed Judaism into a mitzvah system of salvation, one that insists that personal salvation in the world-to-come is dependent on performing the mitzvot, i.e., the authoritative religious acts. These mitzvot were assumed to have divine authority, whether they were specifically commanded in the Pentateuch or by the Oral Law of the Pharisaic legislators. This was the only way an individual could achieve salvation or find favor in the sight of God. It was a system that placed full responsibility on the individual. No intermediary stood between the individual and God, who had commanded the mitzvot.

The mitzvah system is thus dependent on internalized authority. The young child incorporated into himself the teaching of his parents as to which acts (mitzvot) please God and which acts (*averot,* sins) displease Him. Failure to keep the mitzvot creates feelings of guilt; the fulfillment of the mitzvot gives comfort and reassurance. For most Jews this was highly satisfying precisely because it offered salvation to its faithful adherents.

But what of an individual whose early life experiences were such that he had great difficulty in the process of internalizing the religious demands taught by his parents? What if in such a person the wish to overthrow and to defy first parental authority and then God's authority was so powerful that the demands of the mitzvot became a relentless source of guilt and pain? Such an individual might fight his rebellious impulses by being over-zealous in the performance of the mitzvot and by becoming an arch-persecutor of those who deviated in any way from the mitzvah system.

This very over-zealousness which aimed at stilling the impulses to rebel might actually make those impulses more powerful, even though they had been dissociated successfully from the rest of the personality. Under certain conditions, a complete reversal might occur if the dissociated impulses burst through the restraining defense. The persecutor might then seek persecution; the zealot for mitzvot might become the arch enemy of the mitzvah system; the champion of the "chosen people" might turn into an apostle to the gentiles.

It would seem that something of this sort must have happened to Paul. He felt that the Law itself had stirred up within him the wish to sin and violate it. He says that if the Law had not commanded "thou shalt not covet," he would not have felt covetousness. Behind the Law lurked sin. The Law did not destroy the sinful impulses; it evoked them. Only when he had experienced Christ crucified and had freed himself from the Law—only then were the demands of the flesh crucified. Christ had redeemed him from the internal struggle with the demands of the mitzvah system and had given him the feeling that he was indeed a new creation. So thorough had been his transformation that he dedicated all his energies to the spread of his gospel (*cf.* Romans 7; Galatians 2:15–21).

And Paul's gospel touched many an agonized soul in the Mediterranean world. Not that the gentiles to whom he preached had undergone his own experience. Indeed, Paul had the least influence over those who lived the mitzvah system of salvation. The gentiles who were drawn to Paul's teaching benefitted by the emancipation from the Law only in the sense that it was no longer a hindrance to becoming a believer in Christ.

The doctrine of Paul that had deep meaning for them was the emphasis on the redemption from sin that was made possible by God's grace through His son who was crucified so that eternal life would be assured all those who believed. Paul's inner struggle with the mitzvah system was the means whereby he came to those beliefs which were to have such a vast influence, but in itself it was not the crucial message. Those converted to his gospel had never lived under the Law.

Paul's gospel promised triumph over death through identification with the crucified and resurrected Christ. But other religions offered equivalent promises. The mystery cults that flourished at this time promised immortality through participation in the rites of the living, dying and resurrected gods of the cults. These cults were extremely popular.

Pharisaic Judaism likewise offered immortality through the mitzvah system. It taught that there was one God and Father who had revealed His will in the Written and the Oral Torah. This will involved the carrying out of mitzvot which affected all aspects of life. Among the mitzvot were those which provided for visiting the sick, burying the dead, ransoming of captives and dowering of brides. Thus though Pharisaic Judaism lacked a dying and resurrected god, it offered that which the mystery cults did not have: a single cosmic God, yet a Father vitally concerned with the salvation of every individual, a system of mitzvot which was internalized and not limited to the cultic moments, and a religion which was very much concerned with social responsibility to the suffering and less fortunate.

Pauline Christianity uniquely combined certain features that were characteristic of Judaism with certain other features that had affinities to the mystery cults, and added that which was qualitatively different. The one cosmic yet fatherly God who had revealed His will in Scriptures is preserved by Paul. True, the Law of Scriptures is abolished, but its promises are used to justify faith in the Christ. So too, the internalized character of Pharisaic Judaism is preserved even though the mitzvot are no longer internalized. When one truly accepted Christ, one's whole life was transformed by the Holy Spirit. Salvation was dependent on continually being in Christ. No true Christian was a Christian on a part-time basis. In this sense, Christianity maintained Pharisaism's emphasis on the total character of God's demands.

Similarly, Pauline Christianity preserved the tightly knit social character of Judaism. Every Jew who accepted the mitzvah system felt a closeness and responsibility for every other Jew who accepted the binding character of the mitzvot. So too every true Christian considered every other Christian as his brother in Christ, and he felt a responsibility for his welfare. Like the Jew under the mitzvah system, so the Christian who was in Christ visited the sick, clothed the naked, ransomed the captive, buried the dead and aided the poor. Just as the synagogue of Israel expressed the unity of those who sought salvation through mitzvot, so the church of God bound together those who sought salvation through faith in the Christ.

But the Pauline doctrine of the Christ also had close affinities to the mystery cults. Although Christianity was not a mystery cult, some of its doctrines and practices had the appeal of the latter. Jesus could certainly be viewed as a savior God who had lived, died and been resurrected. Like the savior gods of the mystery cult, he could bestow eternal life on those who, through baptism, died with him and who thereby gained immortality through his resurrection. The communal meal of the true Christian believers likewise resembled cultic practices. In eating the bread, the Christian ate the body of Christ; in drinking the wine, they drank his blood. In this way Christ entered their bodies and transformed them.

An additional link between Pauline Christianity and the mystery cults was the appeal to an ancient god whose power to save was attested by ancient revelations and a devoted priesthood. Too much was at stake for the individual to trust his immortality to an untried savior God. Paul pointed to the ancient God of Israel and to his revealed Scriptures as proof that Jesus was the very son of this renowned God and therefore no upstart or usurper. The Christ was the fulfillment of the promise made by God to Abraham, and he was therefore prior even to the giving of the Law (*cf.* Galatians 3). Thus Jesus was the very embodiment of the eternal God and Father of the Scriptures and of the traditions of the Pharisees.

Links and affinities unquestionably exist which bind Pauline Christianity to both Judaism and the mystery cults. These, however, were not elements that Paul mechanically combined into a composite. Paul's teachings contain these elements, but they are transmuted by the formative principle of the redemptive Christ. It was this principle that ultimately was responsible for Christianity's great success. The appeal of the mystery cults with their savior gods and the appeal of Judaism with its one God and Father, its revealed Scriptures, its ethical, moral and social concern, its emphasis on religion as permeating all of life and its promise of salvation in the future life—these were experienced through the Christ who had died to free man from sin.

The actual identification of the true believer with a man-God who had so recently lived and suffered as a human being and yet was the son of the Father God of ancient Judaism was the crucial feature that made Paul's doctrines virtually irresistible. Here were the promises of Judaism without the mitzvah system; here was the mystery cultic experience without its polytheism, amorality and social disinterestedness; here too was the overcoming of sin, death and suffering through a human God who had personally experienced agony and death for *each* individual—such a vital and intense formulation that structured both experience and the meaning of experience for the thousands who suffered and hoped in the Greco-Roman world. When the Roman world itself began to collapse in the third century, the message of Christianity more and more seemed the only adequate answer to decay, misery and death.

Yet one other religion was adequate to the problems of a collapsing world, and that was the mitzvah system of Judaism. The pagan mystery cults were found wanting; Christianity was more than a match for them. But Judaism did not succumb to Christianity. What did Judaism possess that made it virtually immune to the powerful doctrines of the redemptive Christ?

Judaism did not have a savior God, that is, a God that lived and died and was resurrected. The mystery cults did, and yet they were unable to withstand Christianity. It is therefore clear that a savior God was not in itself sufficient to guarantee survival, nor was it in itself essential for survival—Judaism survived without such a god.

The answer must therefore be sought elsewhere, in the monotheism of Judaism and its mitzvah system of salvation. Through Christianity monotheism triumphed over paganism; but Judaism had been the source of Christian monotheism. Judaism was therefore not only adequate to a world organized around monotheistic concepts; it had itself provided the organizing principle.

In itself the monotheistic principle is not a sufficient explanation;

for the Sadducean rendition of Judaism was likewise monotheistic, yet it did not survive. Monotheism had to be linked to the daily experience of the individual, and the one God also had to be the loving Father who granted salvation to those who followed His will. This will was incorporated in the mitzvah system which was the path of individual salvation. This integration of monotheism and individual salvation through mitzvot was not capable of winning the souls of the pagan world—Judaism did not have a savior God—but it did organize the complex experiences of life in the Greco-Roman world adequately. Its religious system not only withstood the disintegrating forces of the Roman world but also the integrating powers of triumphant Christianity.

Thus from an historical point of view both Judaism and Christianity were necessarily interlinked in the processes that ultimately dissolved the polytheistic interpretations of human experience. Judaism generated the idea of monotheism welded to individual salvation. Christianity secured the triumph of this idea in the pagan world through its doctrine of the one God and Father who through the Christ crucified and the Christ resurrected promised eternal life to every individual soul that believed. Both Judaism and Christianity proved adequate to the demands of the historical process.

Philo of Alexandria

Erwin Goodenough

AT THE beginning of the Christian era the Egyptian city of Alexandria dominated the cultural and philosophical life of the Roman Empire. Though some Romans went to study at Athens, the great new movements no longer began in Athens but in Alexandria, where a new world was being created. Founded three centuries earlier by Alexander, who had collected settlers from all the eastern Mediterranean, especially Greeks and Jews, along with his own dominating Macedonians, the city boasted the greatest library and the greatest science of the ancient world.

At the height of Alexandria's glory there lived in it a great interpreter of both Greek Hellenism and the Bible, Philo Judaeus as he was called, Philo the Jew (c. 20 B.C.E.–50 C.E.). He is distinguished for having made perhaps the greatest single attempt to "modernize" Judaism by squaring it with the best in the gentile thinking of his day. That day is long gone, and its ideas are now far from modern. But his refusal to abandon Judaism because the gentiles had much he also admired came from a spirit that has often re-emerged, especially among modern Jews.

Philo came from a Jewish family of culture and distinction. His brother Alexander, according to the historian Josephus, was "foremost among his contemporaries at Alexandria both for his family and his wealth," and actually served as head of the Jewish community in Egypt.

Neither Philo nor his brother ever faltered in devotion to the Jewish people, who lived in Alexandria by the hundreds of thousands. In the year 40 C.E., when Emperor Gaius punished with paranoiac cruelty anyone who showed reluctance in paying him homage as a divinity, the Alexandrian mob, jealous of the prosperity and political favor the Jews were enjoying, made a pogrom against them for their refusal to set up cult statues of the emperor in their synagogues. Philo was selected by the Jewish community to lead a delegation to Rome, where, eventually, after unceasing abuse and insult, Philo won from Gaius a niggardly toleration for the Jews.

This belies the usual image of Philo as a metaphysician with no practical sense or interest. Actually, Philo was intimately in touch with all aspects of the teeming life of Alexandria, in spite of the philosophical and religious concern of his extensive writings. He was a critical observer of the athletics of the day, and speaks with almost an expert's insight about boxing contests he had seen. He tells of being at chariot races where excitement ran so high that some of the spectators rushed into the course and were killed. He describes the enthusiasm of the crowd at a now lost play of Euripides when some brilliant lines in praise of freedom were recited.

Philo's writings tell us much more elaborately, though not directly, that he had had the best education available in Alexandria. He wrote in Greek, chiefly in the form of Biblical commentary, a form long known in Jewish tradition as Midrash and now familiar also in the Dead Sea Scrolls. His treatises could have come only from one steeped in the text of the Bible, especially the Five Books of Moses, for his sentences are studded with Biblical quotations and phrases.

Thoroughly familiar with the Greek translation made from the Hebrew two centuries before his day, he comments upon the nuances of Greek phrases in a way to show that he considered the Greek text verbally inspired and correct. He apparently had a guide to the meaning of the strange Hebrew proper names, but never questioned a line of the Greek translation as compared with the original. Most scholars see no evidence that he knew Hebrew. He was, however, well trained in Greek literature and civilization. He quoted the classical poets and dramatists freely, seems to have known Greek history well, and had at least a good working knowledge of the classical philosophers.

The two traditions of thought, the Jewish and the Greek, so completely blended in his mind that the favorite dispute as to whether he was more Greek or more Jewish had little meaning. Out of the two strands he had woven himself as a single cloth, warp and woof. He read Plato in terms of Moses, and Moses in terms of Plato, to the point that he was convinced that each had said essentially the same thing. Indeed, he used to say that Plato had cribbed his ideas from Moses. Philo, an open-minded Jew, no more rejected the best of the gentile world than the modern Jew should be expected to reject modern science and Shakespeare. He not only remained loyal to Jewish people and customs, but he made a herculean effort to see meaning in the Jewish traditions in such terms of "meaning" as the deepest and most valuable knowledge of his day had taught.

What then did Philo retain from his Jewish tradition, and what in the Greek background did he unconsciously identify with his Judaism? And what was the blend that resulted?

The Jewish people, at least since the time of Ezra, have been the People of the Book. If Jews had not believed in the unique quality of both the people and the Book there would have been no surviving Judaism. In Philo's eyes each created and strengthened the other, and he had not the least thought of discarding either. His loyalty to the people involved him in his political activities on their behalf, and his immense literary production was dedicated to their defense and advancement. Membership among the people he regarded as a function of the Book itself. In this Bible (which for Philo, as for the Rabbis, usually meant the Pentateuch) the Jews had a revelation of God's nature and will that was utterly unique among sacred writings. A Jew was one who accepted this revelation. If Philo got ideas from other sources, as he patently did, he felt uneasy until he could find some way to read them into the Bible. However differently from the Rabbis he often interpreted the text, no rabbi ever revered the text more than did Philo.

Many of his books were written to point out to gentiles the supreme value of the Hebrew Bible, but even more important are those of his writings addressed to an inner group of Jews. For them he wrote like a preacher, assuming that his readers already knew his way of thinking. The writings of Philo were not especially original in the sense that he was creating a new thought world or solving new problems. As an "initiate" in a tradition he speaks to those already "initiated" into a Judaism made of his own warp and woof, which interpreted the Pentateuch as a revelation of the metaphysic of Platonism.

In this tradition, as Philo's writings reveal, God was still the one God of the Bible, with special relation to the Jews. But He was no longer the tribal God of the Book of Judges, or the mythological figure that could walk and talk with Adam. He now was the remote principle. He contained the world, was its space, but Himself was not spatial and the world did not contain Him. Eternal, He included time, but was Himself timeless. All objects and qualities emerged from, manifested His nature, though He Himself was beyond qualities. He was the fixed, unmoved, unchanging being, in whom no emotions, no events occurred.

Philo seems sometimes to accept literally the Biblical stories of God's relations with man and the universe, but at other times protests against the impropriety of such stories. "It is quite foolish to think that the world was created in six days, or in general in any measure of time." As for God's "planting and tilling" the Garden of Eden, he says, "let no such myth ever enter our mind."

Jewish tradition made Philo still want a God who was in relation with man and the universe, a God of anger and love, justice and mercy, law and forgiveness, the God of His people and His Book. For Philo the Bible supremely revealed the metaphysical as well as the personal God. On some occasions, he finds the personal God of the prophets, Jewish ethics and Law; on other occasions, the abstract God of the budding neo-Platonism.

Philo declared, accordingly, that in the Bible Jews had a uniquely inspired revelation of God's nature and Law, which were not two but one. Pagans (and Jews influenced by pagan thought) considered any verbal code of laws such as the Torah inferior to the true law of the universe; but the only way to recover that law would still be to study the implications of a divinely inspired codification. Such a codification the Jews supremely, indeed uniquely, had in the Books of Moses. Ordinary Jews who followed its literal commands had an ethical guidance superior to that of any other code of people, a guidance literally formulated by God. But for people of spiritual sensitivity the greater value of the code was that, by allegorizing its words, one could see the supernal law of God itself.

The Torah, then, offered itself as the way to God's utterance, rulership and light. It is to be doubted that the psalmist had meant all this when he said: "The Law is my light"; but this is what such texts meant to Philo, as they have to Jewish mystics ever since.

Philo (and the little group to whom he addressed his most intensive writings) clearly had learned from pagans that the best way of coming to the divine Light-Law was not through a code, not even the code of Moses, but through the true nature of God as revealed in specially endowed persons or "wise men." With a sweep of his hand Philo had dismissed and ignored the mythological heroes and stories of the Greeks; for him the great patriarchs of the Bible represented the "living laws" which all people were seeking.

Those early heroes of Judaism, as Philo describes them, had done all that the pagans had dreamed for their "philosopher kings," "wise men" or "divine men." Before Jewish law had been revealed on Sinai at all, Abraham, Isaac, Jacob and Moses had lived by it, for they were just or righteous, which in both Judaism and Greek thinking meant that they conformed to the Law. The patriarchs fulfilled the ideals expressed in terms any pagan would know. Philo was saying what Paul is later reputed as saying to Athenians: "What you worship in ignorance, I reveal unto you."

In effect, Philo and his group invited all men of the world to find in Judaism the solution of their problems. The archeological remains have convinced me that Jews continued to do this in Egypt for many years. How long some Jews thus explained their Torah we have no way of deciding, since we have no books at all from the following centuries of Greco-Latin Judaism. All that we have are writings from rabbinical centers and the decorations on synagogues and tombs.

In the decade after Philo presumably died, a Jewish group left Judaism altogether, carrying the Torah with them, and proclaiming a "new" and "true" Israel in the followers of Jesus. The Roman world finally came to hear and accept their message, while sooner or later those who remained Jews went back to the Hebrew language and more Hebraic conceptions. They rejected Hellenized Judaism, and we should never have heard of Philo had Christians not preserved his writings.

Philo has thus come into an anomalous situation, and has been studied relatively little by either Jews or Christians. Particularly has he had little standing in Jewish historical writings. Yet I am confident that Philo would indignantly have repudiated Christianity had he ever heard of it.

Christians broke from Judaism primarily because most Jews refused to accept three major claims: that in Jesus a new living law had appeared to reveal God's nature in the flesh, to reveal it so fully, indeed, that he completely eclipsed the patriarchs and Moses; that following Jesus meant an annulment of the Law of Moses; and that succession to Abraham had nothing to do with lineage—the "true" Israel consisted in those who followed Jesus. Everything I have read in Philo assures me that such a perversion of Jewish tradition would have seemed to him utterly blasphemous.

However much his ideas may later have been what he would have considered misused by Christians, he himself never faltered in his devotion to the people and the Book. He should always be recognized as the outstanding leader in one of the most interesting developments of Judaism, one of the truly great Jews of history. He may also serve as a model or suggest possibilities for contemporary Jews who face a similar problem—that of being Jews in a world of ideas of which Moses, the prophets or the ancient rabbis never dreamed.

Medieval Folklore and Jewish Fate

Salo W. Baron

MUCH of what is decided in history in one particular period remains alive for centuries thereafter. That heritage embraces much that happened by mere accident or decisions completely defying human reason, since behind the rational behavior of men there is a great deal of irrationality. Medieval folklore and legends about Jews are a dramatic and often tragic example.

In the Christian Middle Ages a dichotomy existed between popular concepts and the official teachings of Church and State concerning Jews. Although the official doctrines dominated legislation, the popular attitudes played an equally portentous role in the destinies of the Jewish people.

For example, the Church frequently used the term "the perfidy of Jews." In the Latin parlance of canon law "perfidy" did not necessarily refer to treacherous behavior; often it simply meant unbelief or lack of belief in Christian doctrines. Though Jews were unbelievers, the Church taught, they ought to be preserved to the end of days for they were necessary to the Christian world as witnesses to the truth of Christianity. But they should be maintained only on a very low social level.

The popular mind, however, did not make such fine distinctions. It did not follow the doctrine of the Church, which combined toleration with discrimination and segregation. The ordinary citizen took the line that the Jews were both treacherous and unbelievers, and hence undesirable. If on Good Friday for centuries past Christian congregations were praying for the salvation of the "perfidious" Jew and expressing the hope that some day the latter would see the light and become Christian, the ordinary man reciting or hearing such a prayer only inferred that Jews were double-faced and should be removed. (Incidentally, the late Pope John XXIII eliminated the phrase "the perfidious Jews" from the Good Friday prayer in 1963.)

Similarly, the Gospel story of the crucifixion of Christ, recited in all schools and churches, especially on Good Friday, has played a tremendous role in the history of anti-Semitism. This tradition still persists in the Christian world.

Here again, the popular mind cast off all distinctions and nuances implicit in the ecclesiastical tradition, and presented the Jews as the Christ-killers, exclusively responsible for the crucifixion. In the New Testament there is somewhat more of a balance. Although essentially polemical and directed against the then established order, it also tells the other side of the story, in part, at least, placing the blame on Pilate as the actual executioner of Christ. But in the medieval passion plays, which are still performed in many parts of Europe today, the Jew alone is responsible for the crucifixion. Time and again Jews are depicted as offering money to the Roman soldiers accompanying Jesus, encouraging them to beat him harder.

The passion plays also presented the Jewish contemporaries of Jesus in medieval garb, with "Jew" hats and badges; they often gave them Jewish names known in the particular locality where the plays were being performed. Through such tricks the authors succeeded in identifying, in the minds of their audiences, the contemporary Jews with what they considered the greatest crime in history.

With particular relish the passion plays frequently depicted Judas in his role as betrayer of Jesus. For example, in many theatrical performances the Rabbis of the ancient Sanhedrin, resembling in their dress and speech certain contemporary rabbis known to the onlookers, bargain with Judas. They begin by offering him thirty pieces of silver, in accordance with the New Testament version, and then reduce their offer to twenty-nine, twenty-eight, and finally to a single piece. Judas is also depicted as a shrewd bargainer. All this has nothing to do with the New Testament story; its intent is to warn the onlookers against the hard bargaining and ever perfidious Jew who behaves treacherously even when dealing with his own people.

Judas was supposed to have committed suicide, and through the ages many Christian pilgrims have sought to visit his alleged tomb in Palestine. Even this theme of Judas' suicide lent itself to anti-Jewish presentation on the medieval and early modern stage. It showed no understanding whatsoever of the fact that most Jews in the Middle Ages were prepared to suffer martyrdom for their faith. Hence, when attacked by Crusaders, entire congregations, afraid that they might be tempted at the last moment to accept conversion, sometimes committed mass suicide.

Suicide has always been sharply condemned by Jews. Even today, an individual taking his own life is looked upon as having committed a religious sin, and often will not be buried by an Orthodox congregation in a regular cemetery plot. Despite this great appreciation of life by traditional Judaism, those communities of martyrs who had sacrificed their lives for the sanctity of the Name of the Lord were glorified by rabbis and poets and remembered by worshipful congregations for many generations.

The medieval presentation of Judas' death, often performed in public squares with great fanfare and with the whole city participating during the Easter season, was but a travesty of that incomprehensible Jew who committed suicide for his religion.

The idea of the Jew as the perfidious enemy of Christianity also penetrated the graphic arts. In a book written some thirty years ago, the French scholar Marcel Bulard disclosed that many church paintings in Italy, France and Northern Spain include somewhere in a corner or in the garment of a person the figure of a scorpion prepared to bite and insert venom. That scorpion had become the symbol for perfidious medieval Jewry. Though most tourists looking at these paintings today may not even notice the scorpion, the medieval worshiper was fully conscious of that figure symbolizing the Jew as the alleged perennial antagonist and treacherous enemy of his own people.

This explains why certain popular accusations like that of Jews' poisoning wells were accepted at face value. During the Black Death (1348–1349) pestilence, Central and Western Europe lost more than a third of their populations. In many communities, more than half and sometimes three-quarters of the people were wiped out. The masses were terror-stricken, and even scholars of the time could not explain the phenomenon. A ready scapegoat was poison in the wells, allegedly placed there by Jews seeking vengeance for their persecutions.

Of course, reasonable contemporaries knew that that was impossible: how could large rivers like the Danube or the Rhine, which purify themselves after a short time, be poisoned? Nevertheless, Jews in Germany and in parts of southern France, Spain and Italy were almost totally eliminated as a result of massacres brought on by that accusation.

Other crimes were also attributed to Jews. One such accusation concerns the host or the wafer celebrated at Mass, in which, according to the Eucharistic doctrine, is symbolically hidden the blood and flesh of Christ. In the Middle Ages it was firmly believed (and is still believed today by certain unsophisticated Catholics and Greek Orthodox) that Jews desecrated the host.

One story has it that in 1285 a certain Jew acquired the wafer from his Christian maid at a very high price for the sole purpose of calling in other Jews and showing them that no blood or flesh existed in this wafer. But a miracle happened, one of the standard miracles in the desecration of the host legends: blood came out. Some modern scientists have tried to explain that oft-asserted phenomenon biologically by demonstrating that bread or flour kept in damp or dark places over a long time is likely to develop a fungus which gives it a hue resembling blood. Because this sometimes happened to wafers, medieval men attributed it to miracles attesting to the presence of Christ's blood in the wafer in order to repudiate the doubts of Jewish unbelievers. Churches where such "miracles" occurred usually became centers of pilgrimages and miraculous healings.

For example, such a miracle, which allegedly happened in Paris in 1285, was examined and re-examined by several Church commissions. The house where this Jewish crime was supposed to have been committed was converted into a large church, and down to the present day annual processions commemorate that great miracle of the host in the French capital.

A similar event took place in Brussels in 1370, where Jews were accused and imprisoned. Under torture some of them confessed. Not only were the "culprits" executed but also Jews of neighboring communities who had had nothing to do with that "miracle" suffered bloody retribution. There the local church commemorated the miracle in panels which graphically depict each stage of desecration and redemption. Prior to 1870, an international jubilee celebration was staged in Brussels every fifty years; it was finally abandoned because of the protests of Belgian socialists and liberals. Despite this, the jubilee continued to be observed locally all through the nineteenth and twentieth centuries; annual processions are held to the present day.

The same is true in the Bavarian city Degendorf, which is also a center of attraction for pilgrims and sick persons in search of miraculous healing. In certain years this small town has attracted as many as a hundred thousand visitors. A French journalist visiting Degendorf in 1961 was told by several natives that they themselves doubted the authenticity of the "miracle" of the host but could not publicly denounce it because the town's economy depended on it.

A second equally persistent crime alleged to Jews is the Blood Accusation, an example of folklore dominating the mass mind even in defiance of State or Church. There had been blood accusations against Christians by pagan Romans in the ancient world, but not against Jews. In the twelfth century, when such rumors related to Jews were first spread in England, they were given no official credence. The sources do not even mention any prosecutions on this score, but the populace believed them.

In the very first Blood Accusation in Norwich, the theme of the international Jewish conspiracy came to the fore. As told by a convert from Judaism, every year representative Jews from all European countries gathered in one or another locality and designated the exact country and city where the following year a young Christian boy would be seized and crucified at Easter time in commemoration of the crucifixion of Jesus. First it was Norwich. Later it was Lincoln—little Hugh of Lincoln, so well known from Chaucer. No less a man than

Charles Lamb, the nineteenth-century English essayist, could write in a letter: "I have no nerve to enter a synagogue. The spirit of little Hugh of Lincoln perseveres with me."

A similar story in LaGuardia, Spain, not far from Madrid, was so patently an invention that no body of any victim was ever found. Since this alleged ritual murder happened in 1491, it became a contributory cause to the expulsion of the Jews from Spain in the following year. Subsequently it inspired Lope de Vega, the Shakespeare of Spain, to write a drama entitled *The Little Boy from LaGuardia,* which is still performed in Spanish-speaking countries. One need but remember the impact of Shylock on modern readers and audiences to imagine what role Lope de Vega's dramatic depiction of a boy crucified and killed by Jews for the purpose of using his blood has played in the persistence of anti-Semitism in Argentina and other Spanish-speaking countries.

Other great Spanish dramatists of the fifteenth and sixteenth centuries wrote passion plays on the sacrament and the crucifixion. It is small wonder, then, that in the 1930's, when Nazism was rampant, its world-wide anti-Semitic propaganda evoked a responsive echo in Spain and Latin America. Some Catholic priests and laymen began preaching the doctrine of the redemptive quality of violence. This doctrine harkened back to the Inquisition and the idea of Torquemada that he was doing a favor to the Marranos burned at the stake because he thereby made it possible for the victims to escape eternal damnation and to participate in the life of bliss in the hereafter. Even Nazi atrocities could now be classed by some persons in Spain and Latin America as the type of violence leading to redemption.

Obviously this folklore heritage is not merely a matter of the past; it still is very much alive today. From the thirteenth century on, one pope after another condemned the Blood Accusations. In 1540, Pope Paul III wrote to the Bishops of Poland, Bohemia and Hungary: "We have heard with displeasure from the complaints of the Jews of those countries how for some years past certain magistrates and other officials, bitter and mortal enemies of the Jews, blinded by hate and envy, or as is more probable by stupidity, pretend, in order to despoil them of their goods, that the Jews kill little children and drink their blood."

In the thirteenth century, too, Frederick II, Holy Roman Emperor and King of Sicily, a great and enlightened monarch, called together an international congress. He asked the kings of France, England and other countries to send him experts in Jewish law, particularly converts from Judaism, well-versed in Jewish religious practices. That congress unanimously decided that there was not a shred of truth in the Blood Accusation. The Emperor then issued a decree prohibiting all such libels in the future. Nevertheless the ritual murder libel has persisted. As recently as 1928, in Massena, New York, a boy disappeared; the mayor was ready to imprison some Jews because they supposedly had slain the boy for their Passover blood ritual.

Of a different order is the legend of the eternal Jew, the wandering Jew. According to one of its early versions, a certain man who later became Bishop of Schleswig saw in a Hamburg church, in 1542, a stranger approximately fifty years of age. He learned that the new arrival was a Jew named Ahasverus, born in Jerusalem and a shoemaker by trade. (Incidentally, in the museums of Berne and other cities a large shoe is exhibited which had supposedly been worn by the wandering Jew centuries ago.) Ahasverus had personally participated in the crucifixion of Christ, had remained alive over the centuries and had traveled through many lands. He described many details of Christ's encounter with Pilate and subsequently with Herod as well as his behavior during the crucifixion. None of these details had been reported by either the evangelists or the Church historians. He similarly told many stories about changes in government which had taken place in Oriental countries several centuries after Christ. He also gave a perfectly good account of the apostles.

That story of the wandering Jew, symbolizing the whole Jewish people, migrating from place to place, having no permanent abode, rejected and contemptuously treated by their neighbors, has become one of the remarkable stories in world literature. The booklet containing the original story appeared in German in 1602. In the following two centuries it reappeared in 188 different editions in various languages. The story inspired Shelley, Goethe and other great poets. Professor Minor, who studied the fragment of Goethe's *Eternal Jew*, discovered that between Goethe's work and 1930, no fewer than 480 books in various European languages had dealt with the theme of the wandering Jew.

Behind this relatively modern tale looms an old medieval legend which in turn had its inception in the days of the North African jurist, Tertullian, in the second century. Elaborated by Tertullian's successors, the story seeks to explain the Biblical narrative of Cain and Abel, of an older and a younger brother bringing sacrifices to God. When the sacrifice of the younger brother was accepted by God and that of the older brother was rejected, Cain killed Abel. To Christian homilists every story in the Bible had some deeper meaning. In the Cain and Abel story they saw, therefore, an adumbration of the Old and New dispensations. The older brother Israel-Cain slew, or rather crucified, the younger brother Christ-Abel because the latter's sacrifice had been accepted by God.

The Bible next states that Cain not be killed; if he were slain he would be avenged sevenfold. The homilists interpreted that statement to mean that the Jewish people must not be eliminated or otherwise disappear. Israel must live, like Cain, an eternal migrant on the soil of the world, carrying with him his Cain sign. In the Middle Ages Christians interpreted circumcision as the mark distinguishing Jew from gentile. Yet, despite their permanent estrangement from their environment and their perpetual sufferings, the Jewish people must remain alive until the second coming of Christ, until the Messianic age when all peoples would be united under the aegis of Christendom.

All these abstruse, often irrational legends have exerted a great influence on history, which has often been shaped by such irrational forces. Nazism, for example, has in many respects been but another elongation of some such medieval irrationalities. The Jewish badge was a direct adaptation of the medieval idea that the Jew, being different, must be thus marked outwardly. The whole Nazi ideology, even the doctrine of race, however modern it sounds with its pseudo-biological and pseudo-anthropological rationalizations, had its mainsprings in popular mythology and folklore.

Present-day Soviet anti-Semitism is similarly rooted. Russia had no Jews to speak of until the first partition of Poland in 1772. She refused to tolerate Jews at all because of her medieval image of the Jew. Even when the largest Jewish community in the world came to be concentrated in Czarist Russia during the nineteenth century, as a result of the partitions of Poland, her interior beyond the so-called Pale of Settlement was still closed to Jews. The ordinary Russian peasant in the interior or the Russian burgher in the large cities along the Volga had never seen a Jew. Yet he had before him the image of the Jew as the permanent implacable enemy, one ready to betray him without provocation. It is that image which still operates in the Soviet Union today, explaining more than anything else the popular anti-Semitism of a people which up to two centuries ago had practically no Jews.

We in America are fortunate in that our history began at a time when that medieval folkloristic heritage had begun to weaken. We started afresh. While our immigrants, coming from various countries, brought with them some medieval traditions and while some of these and other folkloristic elements have penetrated our consciousness via literature, there is always a difference between experiences acquired through hearsay and reading, and those acquired directly from life.

One cannot be too optimistic that this heritage will completely vanish in the space age. All we can do is hope that at least in all crucial moments human reason will reassert itself.

Christianity and Judaism: Two Articles

I. A CHRISTIAN VIEW
W. D. Davies

THE Talmud reports how the great and gentle Hillel was once asked to explain the whole of Judaism while standing on one leg, and how he succeeded in doing so in one short phrase.* Here I attempt to do something even more difficult: to explain in a few words the meaning of Christianity and its relation to Judaism and their common relevance to the modern world.

I take it that if one sought to define Judaism one would have to do so on the basis of its foundation documents of the Law. In the same way, it seems to me possible to understand the meaning of Christianity only by examining the foundation document of the Christian faith, the New Testament.

It is in the New Testament that we are at the fountainhead of Christian truth, and it is with Christianity as the New Testament reveals it that I shall concern myself here.

One verse seems to me to summarize the essential content of the Christian faith: called "the Gospel within the Gospels," it is from John 3:16: "For God so loved the world that He gave His only begotten son that whosoever believeth in Him should not perish but have everlasting life."

The Christian Gospel is concerned from first to last with the reality, nature and purpose of God. There are in the Gospel no arguments for belief in God; as in the Hebrew Bible, the existence of God is not treated as a quandary for the intellect but as a self-evident axiom, without question. The Gospel is good news about God. While it supplies us with no formulated proofs of the fact of God's existence, it drives us back to the living God who created, sustains and governs the universe, and apart from whose fellowship we can never be truly at rest.

But the assumption or declaration of God's existence does not constitute the Gospel. We must be acquainted with His nature; and this our text reveals. It lays bare God's attitude toward us—"God so loved the world."

The Greek term for "love" in the New Testament is *agape:* in pre-Christian times this word was pale and insipid, and little-used. But in

* "Do not do unto others what you do not wish them to do unto you. All the rest is commentary."

the New Testament it is given new life; it becomes almost a new creation of the Gospel to denote the pure, unmerited, persistent, ever-flowing, creative and redemptive will of God.

God is no blind force or cosmic energy, no mere personification of the values of goodness, beauty and truth. He is the living God, all-knowing and all-powerful but also all-loving. The verb "loved" used here is in a timeless form: God always has loved and always will love the world. The Greek term for "world" here—*cosmos*—signifies not merely the created universe of nature and man, but the universe as it is misdirected, as it is organized against God, in its brokenness, sorrow and sin: it is this world that God loves.

But how can we believe this? The New Testament asserts that it is only because the love of God has been active that we know it. God is only known for what He is by what He does: God so loved the world that He *gave;* it is through one particular act, the gift of His son, that we have come to know Him fully as the loving Father. God is largely the hidden God until this happens—the gift is given, and it is in the life, death and resurrection of Jesus that the loving attitude of God is illuminated and made credible to us.

In the verse from John, the verb "gave" is in a tense which denotes the magnitude and completeness of a recorded act: once and for all God has acted in the life of Jesus, at a particular time and in a particular place. Not even a declaration of a loving attitude on the part of God constitutes the Gospel: such an attitude might merely be one of benevolent neutrality. The Gospel declares that this attitude has become action—is indeed known only through an act. It is not by a revelation of the nature of God that we are redeemed: rather the act whereby God has redeemed us has revealed the nature of God. It is in the coming of Jesus that the power and wisdom, the kingdom of God have come upon us.

The Christian faith, therefore, ties us down to a particular history —that of Jesus of Nazareth. God would have us know Him and meet Him in Jesus, in a real person who lived, loved and suffered, who is now alive in the unseen world and very near to all who seek to know God. To the question "show us the Father," the Gospel always returns the answer "he that hath seen Christ hath seen the Father." The whole life of Christians, as such, is molded and controlled under the authority of the historical revelation of God in the life, words, death and resurrection of Jesus.

John 3:16 also reveals the purpose which God has in giving us Christ: that we may have eternal life. The Christ who walked the ways of Galilee both shows the meaning of eternal life and gives it to us.

By eternal life John means the life of that age when God's will is perfectly fulfilled, in which the rule of God is made effective: or, to use a Platonic metaphor that John himself used, it is the real life that God gives to us in Christ, in this world as well as in the world-to-come. To know Christ is, here and now, to have eternal life, to enter into that life which God purposes for us.

The knowledge of God in a personal sense—a deep, inward, spiritual awareness of Him—leads to the real life; it involves that surrender to the lordship of Christ which Paul meant by faith. It is not something which we can struggle to attain by ourselves: it is His gift. He gives sight to the blind, the bread of life to the hungry and life to the dead.

The marks of the new life, the gift of Christ, are joy, peace, boldness to draw near to God and enjoy His communion. The Christian ethic is based on gratitude: we give ourselves in obedience because Christ gave himself for us, so that there is a discipline, an effort, a striving in the Gospel as a result of God's gift. Moreover, since the demand that Christ lays upon men is that of love—the new commandment—those who accept Christ must love their brethren. They are inevitably caught up into a community—the church—a society which is part and parcel of the Gospel.

Essential Christianity, then, is the good news of God's permanent attitude of love toward us, of God's active intervention on our behalf in the gift of Christ, and of God's purpose to give us eternal life.

This leads to a new demand—the demand of love—which in turn creates a new community in Christ through which the entire world is to be saved. God, Christ, eternal life in obedience and community—these are the marks of the Christian Gospel.

For Christians, if one may say so without presumption or arrogance, Judaism is neither a false religion nor a religion in which the true God is worshipped in ignorance. Along with Islam and Christianity, Judaism forms a group of religions which claim to reveal the one true God.

Its relation to the Christian faith is at the same time simple and intricate, and above all very intimate. There are three things, in particular, that account for this intimacy:

Their identity of origin: the God who chooses. I have already stated that both Judaism and Christianity belong to the category of revealed religions; both claim to be revelations of the same one and true God. The God who speaks to Christians in Jesus Christ is the God of Abraham, Isaac and Jacob. The God who, Christians believe, wrought their redemption in Christ, is also the God who brought Jews forth out of the land of Egypt, who led Jews through the wilderness, spoke to them at Sinai, gave them the prophets and brought them safely out of Babylon.

Christianity has never doubted that it is the God who spoke to Israel in diverse ways and manners who also speaks in His son. It is true that there have arisen in the church those who have often tried to deny this. In the second century there were the Marcionites, and in the twentieth there are those who have tried to oust the Hebrew Bible from the services of the church as an outmoded volume which can only be read seriously as good literature, touched perhaps with good morality.

But such people have failed to move Christians from the conviction that the God of the Old Covenant is also the God of the New Covenant; that the voice heard at Sinai and at Calvary is the voice of the same God.

As a result, the Old Testament is still part of the Christian Canon of Scripture, and has thus become, we hope, bone of our bone. Through it Christians, to some extent at least, breathe the same air as Jewry. As a recent Pope has expressed it, "spiritually we are all Semites."

This identity of origin then—the fact that both Judaism and Christianity purport to have their origin in a revelation of the same God, the one God—naturally gives them a peculiar intimacy.

Their identity of aim: the yoke He imposes. In a real sense, Judaism and Christianity also have a large identity of aim. Just as the aim of Christianity is to give its adherents what the New Testament terms eternal life both in this world and the world-to-come, so too the Torah has been given to Israel that men might live by its precepts. Life in conformity to the will of God is the aim of both religions. Both church and synagogue pray that the rule or kingdom of God may come, and His will be done so that the Lord may be one and His people one.

In other words, the ethical tradition of Judaism has passed over into Christianity. Here again, there is no need to knock at doors that have long been opened. Jesus was in some sense a rabbi no less than a prophet. Both the method and, very largely, the substance and form of his ethical and religious teaching were rabbinical. Nourished in the synagogue, Jesus gave his followers much of the ethic of the synagogue—modified in many ways, it is true, and some ways fundamentally—but nevertheless intact in its chief content.

Both Judaistic and Christian ethics are intimately connected: for both, gratitude to God is the dynamic of the good life and obedience to the will of God its content. It is thus possible and correct to speak of a Judeo-Christian ethic which Judaism and Christianity share.

Their identity of the means they employ in achieving their aim: the people God uses. Judaism and Christianity reveal an identity of conception as to the means whereby the purpose of God is to be achieved.

James Parkes has constantly reminded Christians that for Judaism the community of God's people, the Israel of God, is the agent of God in the world. It was a *people* that God chose at the Exodus to be His messengers in the world, and in a real sense the Old Testament is the record of God's attempts to prepare for Himself a peculiar people that should make known His ways.

But what is true of Judaism is also true of Christianity. In the New as in the Old Testament God's purposes are to be achieved through a community—the New Israel of God, the church.

It is probably true to say that historically Christianity, especially in some of its Protestant forms, has not always paid sufficient attention to this truth, and that herein Christians have much to learn from the synagogue. Nevertheless, that God's purpose is to be fulfilled, not only and not chiefly by isolated individuals but by the life of a witnessing community, is as true of Christianity as of Judaism.

I have claimed what is an obvious truth: in origin, aim and method Judaism and Christianity are largely identical. But in the last point, their method, if we may so term the matter, they also reveal a fundamental difference.

Both Judaism and Christianity aim at achieving their purpose, we have claimed, through a community. But for Judaism that witnessing community is centered in and governed by the Law, i.e., the revelation on Sinai and subsequent interpretation are determinative of the nature of the community which is to be God's agent of salvation. And as a matter of history, although at various periods Judaism has welcomed proselytes, that community has been conceived largely as the community of Israel—the nation that came into being at Sinai.

So it is that in Judaism nationalism and religion are inextricably bound: to accept Judaism is not only to be initiated into a religion but also to be incorporated in a nation which is the agent of God's purpose. Thus Marmorstein could define Judaism as "a fortunate blend of history, a people and a religion."

Now Christianity too, as we see, proclaims the community as the instrument of God's salvation, but this community is rooted in Christ. It is constituted not by obedience to the Law but by allegiance to Christ. As a matter of history, it is a community that almost from the first transcended national distinctions: it has, in fact, been the means whereby the national treasures of Jewry have become the common property of countless peoples.

For Christianity it is those who are "in Christ," not those who are "in Israel after the flesh," who constitute the people of God; in short, Christianity gives to Christ the place which Judaism gave to the Law.

This, I believe, is the essential difference between Judaism and Christianity: for the one salvation is by the Torah, for the other by Christ, to whom the functions and attributes of Torah are applied.

This means that the point at which Judaism and Christianity part company is the person of Jesus of Nazareth. It was the valuation of Jesus as the Messiah of Jewish expectation, with all that this involved, which gave birth to Christianity. In the rejection of this valuation, Judaism continued as a separate religion—separate, that is, from what the New Testament regards as the true and final form of Judaism, which is the meaning of Christianity.

But what do Christians mean by the valuation of Jesus of Nazareth as the Messiah? To understand this we have to recall another well-known element common to Judaism and Christianity: Messianism.

Judaism in the first century had come generally to divide history into two main divisions. In the present age the powers of evil might be triumphant, and there are sorrow and sighing, pain and death. But this would ultimately give place to the "age-to-come." This "age-to-come" would be the fulfillment of all Israel's desiring, and it was commonly, though not universally, assumed that this would be introduced by the Messiah, the anointed of God.

The New Testament accepts this concept of history but asserts that in Jesus Christ the "age-to-come" has already begun to invade this world: in his ministry, death and resurrection, the powers of the age-to-come are already active—the present evil age is passing—and those who are in fellowship with or solidarity in Christ already taste the powers of the other age that is now come. In other words, "in Christ" we already have eternal life.

This means that in the coming of Jesus Christ the long historic process whereby God was seeking to reveal Himself to men has reached its culmination. That process which began when God called Abraham out of Ur of the Chaldees, or when He led His people forth out of the land of Egypt, has reached its climax in Jesus. The result is that Christianity, so Christians believe, stands in relation to Judaism as the final event does to the preparatory, as the complete to the incomplete.

Judaism is for us, as I have already asserted, not a false religion or one in which God is ignorantly worshipped. To us as Christians it is rather a partial or unfulfilled religion whose completion is found in Christianity. Thus, the Old Covenant wrought at Sinai finds its fulfillment in the New Covenant wrought by Christ in his death; the Old Israel its fulfillment in the New Israel, the church; the old Law its fulfillment in the life and words of Jesus—in his life of obedience and his uttered words recorded in the Sermon on the Mount.

Christianity is not so much the annulling of Judaism as its completion. Christ is the end of Judaism, not in an iconoclastic sense, but in a teleological or Aristotelian one; in the sense that it is the outcome and full flowering of Judaism, so that for us Christianity is essentially Judaism "come of age."

II. A JEWISH REPLY
Samuel Sandmel

Passages dealing with Jews in New Testament writings have come to be an embarrassment to noble-minded Christian scholars of our day. Affirmative impulses in the Christian tradition necessarily lead to a repudiation of hatred and animosity as un-Christian; and historical perspective discloses that rise of new movements within established religions almost inevitably produces transient, partisan and unfair formulations intended to justify the separation of the new movement.

What Christians said and wrote about Jews in the second century does not differ too greatly in tone and "charity" from what Protestants said about Roman Catholics in the sixteenth century—or from similar contexts, Jewish, Mohammedan, as well as Christian.

Normally, the passing of time brings appropriate oblivion to the unfair formulation. In the case of the early Christian attitudes toward Jews, however, these attitudes were recorded in literature which was in turn incorporated in Christian Scripture. Instead of oblivion, the transient attitudes were not only preserved, but for many generations of Christians have had a divine sanction. As a result, the earnest Christian is today confronted by a dilemma: how to establish an equilibrium between the affirmative in his tradition and the anti-Jewish sentiments within Christian Scripture.

Modern Christians have dealt with this dilemma in differing ways. Some, like Frederick C. Grant in his *Ancient Judaism and the New Testament,* forthrightly reject the anti-Jewish passages as transient and lamentable. Others, like the authors of a number of articles in *The Catholic Encyclopedia,* suggest that in early New Testament times Judaism had sunk to such a disreputable state as to merit the denunciation found in New Testament literature.

The inference is that the attitudes were once justified, but are now not necessarily so. In sum, modern responsible Christianity, with rare exceptions, has deviated from the anti-Jewish sentiments in the New Testament or has totally rejected them.

Yet Christianity was born in Judaism, and left it. Even those Christians who deplore the anti-Jewish sentiments of the New Testament must come to grips with the fact that Christianity is a rejection of at least significant motifs in Judaism.

The New Testament writings differ considerably in tone and manner in expressing this rejection and its implication. The Gospel according to Mark paints the blindness of Jesus' Jewish opponents—the Pharisees, Sadducees and "chief priests"—and the opaqueness of Jesus' Jewish disciples. The Gospel according to John is shot through with aspersions against Jews and Judaism. Paul's Epistles deplore the Law of Moses as an inadequate means for attaining righteousness, and, indeed, an obstruction to its attainment.

The modern Christian who is a serious student of Judaism can scarcely remain within the orbit of the nineteenth-century New Testament scholarship which denigrated Judaism. George Foot Moore's *Judaism* and other publications have made that approach impossible for serious scholars.

As an alternative, a modern Christian may lean toward the manner of the Epistle to the Hebrews. The late Clarence Tucker Craig used to summarize that New Testament book by saying that the Epistle sets forth the view that Christianity is the best religion because it is even better than the second best, Judaism.

"Hebrews" lacks the vicious tones found in the Gospels, in Acts and in other New Testament writings. It consists of an admiring comparison of the Jewish sacrificial system ascribed to the Tabernacle in the Wilderness, wherein annual atonement offerings were made by the high priest, with Christianity, wherein Jesus, the high priest after the order of Melchizedek, made one single sacrifice—himself—for all time and all men. Though it underscores a supposed lack of perfection in Judaism, "Hebrews" nevertheless treats the Jewish faith with respect.

Dr. Davies' article is in the tradition of the Epistle to the Hebrews. He writes with some authority on rabbinic literature of which he has made a deep study. I have met Dr. Davies all too seldom, but always most pleasantly; our last meeting included some conversation about how he, a Welshman trained in Britain and a newcomer to these shores, might further increase the competency he had already attained in rabbinics.

His article does not fully reflect the genuine profundity of his scholarship in Judaism. A man of good will, his silence on the ugly passages about Jews in the New Testament unquestionably reflects his rejection of their tone and content.

His article, however, calls for certain comments. Nor is this the first time that I feel impelled to take issue with his views and ideas. His book on Paul (*Paul and Rabbinic Judaism*) I described in my own work *The Genius of Paul as* "an admirable book, indeed, a great one—and one with which I disagree about one hundred per cent."

Dr. Davies sets forth in the first part of his article certain motifs distinctive of Christianity. Herein he is responsibly epitomizing basic Christian elements; since he is necessarily condensing and omitting, one need not quarrel with his formulation.

In the second part, Dr. Davies insists that Judaism must not be classified with false or "ignorant" religions. Dr. Davies then takes his stand with the dominant Christian view which stresses the continuity from Abraham into the Christian community.

Next, he speaks of the identity of aim of Judaism and Christianity, and it is here that my quarrel with him begins.

Dr. Davies moves from his first paragraph on "identity of role" to that of "identity of ethics." It is gratifying to note that he correctly abstains from a contrast drawn by some commentators between the ethics of Judaism and those of Christianity; yet it seems to me to be quite a leap, and a misleading one, to the matter of ethics at all. Moreover, one of the great divides between Judaism and Christianity has been the manner in which the ethical was conceived of as attainable.

Judaism prescribed the mitzvot, while Christianity, following the lead of Paul, rejected the mitzvot as being, on one level, an ineffective way, and, on another level, a wrong and an obstructed way. Dr. Davies knows this, and it is strange that he omits even mentioning it.

Furthermore, it was not ethical theory which separated Judaism and Christianity; rather, it was *theology*. It is quite irrelevant whether the Jesus of history was a prophet or a rabbi. New Testament Christianity regarded Jesus as a divine being, not as a gifted man. The adulation, since the Age of Enlightenment at the end of the eighteenth century, of Jesus as a fine man is a repudiation of New Testament Christianity. It was the specific claim that Jesus was more than man which Jews rejected. Jews and those Christians—if such they may be called—who do not attribute divinity to Jesus can in our day arrive at certain broad or even specific areas of agreement (the documents provide ample room for minor disagreements); but this agreement would be strictly on Jesus the man, not Jesus the Christ.

In his thesis on the people whom God uses, Dr. Davies concedes a difference, and here again certain comments seem in order. First, Dr. Davies overdoes the contrast, for he is attributing to Judaism a particularism which ignores its universalistic aspects, and to Christianity a universalism which ignores Christian particularism.

One hesitates to revive the quarrels among Jews prior to the re-establishment of the State of Israel as to whether Jews are a nation, nationality or religious community.

Dr. Davies states that "to accept Judaism is . . . to be incorporated in a *nation*" (my italics); let me only state that my nation is the United States, not the State of Israel. It is not correct to use a particular term such as nation to describe the nature of the Jewish community.

In his succeeding paragraph, Dr. Davies has been betrayed by his own condensation. It is not the whole story to say that Christianity "gives to Christ the place which Judaism gave to the Law." It could be better phrased as follows: "*there is a sense in which* Christianity gives to Christ, etc."

If one can peer through the condensation, Dr. Davies is oversimplifying to the point of distortion when he states that "the point at which Judaism and Christianity part company is the person of Jesus of Nazareth." If he means "a principal point," yes; if he means *the* point, then he should at least phrase it that the person of Jesus is the theorem from which countless corollaries were derived.

Perhaps this is his real intention. If that is so, perhaps he is saying what might be put in a different way, that Jews rejected not Jesus but the views on Jesus, *as the Christ,* held by the followers of Jesus, and the subsequent inferences, such as the abrogation of the laws of Moses, which the followers made.

As Dr. Davies continues, he spells out some aspects of Jewish Messianism as these are refracted in Christianity. He gives an eloquent view of Christendom as beginning with Abraham and culminating in Christianity, so that Christianity "stands in relation to Judaism as the final event does to the preparatory, as the complete to the incomplete." In his context, he is asserting that since Christendom regards itself as the completion, not the annulment of Judaism, one can discern an essential unity in Christianity and Judaism.

All this Dr. Davies says in a genteel and conciliatory way. I wonder, though, if he realizes the implication of what he is saying. Am I to take it as a compliment that his religion is complete and mine incomplete? That his is perfect and mine imperfect?

He has the right to believe this and to say it.

My own subjective approach to Christianity is, I trust, free of condescension of any kind. I disagree with a frequent Jewish view which holds that Christianity represents a blend of Judaism with pagan elements, and that Christianity has served well in bringing the message of Judaism to the world in diluted form but if one wants a pure version he must turn to Judaism.

Similarly, it does not seem to me to be a compliment to Judaism to say, or imply, that it is an imperfect or incomplete version of Christianity.

It is possible to describe the relationship of Judaism and Christianity free from unconscious condescension. In the long history of Judaism, and in the shorter but still long history of Christianity, neither was able to remain monolithic.

From the standpoint of Judaism, Christianity is neither the first nor the last schismatic movement; the Samaritan schism predated it by several centuries. Moreover, in the time of Jesus different versions of Judaism existed side by side—Pharisaism, Sadduceeism, Qumran and Christianity. These varieties had in common, at one stage, that they were all contained within Judaism, even though great tensions existed among them, and acute differences marked them off from each other, within the common Judaism.

Pharisaism developed into rabbinic Judaism, and of the varieties of Judaism in the time of Jesus, two alone survived to our day, Christianity and rabbinic Judaism. (If the theory of an unbroken but underground connection ties the eighth-century Karaites to the Sadducees, we might, in view of the handfuls of Karaites still to be found, stretch the number from two to three.)

Judaism—here is a fact which many Christian interpreters overlook —did not come to an end when and because Christianity appeared on the scene. Rather, it continued its creative development. Indeed, rabbinic Judaism and Christianity in a sense represent a somewhat parallel growth—the Mishnah was "canonized" about 200 C.E., and the New Testament was canonized at about the same time. For the first six or seven centuries they lived in quite different worlds, Judaism in Palestine and Babylonia, and Christianity in Asia Minor, North Africa and Europe. Not one European religion survived in Europe after the ascendancy of Christianity, for Christianity extirpated all of them, including the Greek and Roman religions and Hellenistic Judaism.

Jews migrated to Western Europe in the wake of the Mohammedan conquests, and by this time it was matured rabbinic Judaism and matured Christianity which encountered each other. Where events permitted, the two witnessed somewhat similar developments, such as the scholasticism and philosophizing of both medieval Jews and Christians.

The point here is that Judaism and Christianity can be viewed as parallel developments from a common source. A diverse theology, a diverse history and diversity of folk-ways contributed to the differences in the tone and textures of the religions. The student can have his personal loyalties—but these need not lead him to assessing a tradition not his own with faint praise.

As Jews, we have never felt an incompleteness in our religion because it lacks a place for Jesus. Indeed, our religion would not be the same were we to try to make some place for him, or for any man. Our prayer book is replete with Scriptural passages, from Moses, Isaiah, Micah—from virtually all the books in the Hebrew Bible. In certain editions notes to the prayer book identify the source; the prayers themselves seldom include the person to whom the statement is attributed. Indeed, only when an entire pericope is quoted, and it chances to contain the name, does the prayer mention the author.

In Judaism it is the sentiment, the idea, the thought which have sanctity, and not the man. Since in Judaism there is no special place for Moses, Hillel or Maimonides, there could scarcely be a place for Jesus.

This latter may well be the key to the most important point: religion comes to have a tone, a character, a texture. Two examples from Judaism must suffice in the mere mention: one, our disposition toward charity through the identification in our tradition of philanthropy and righteousness; second, the traditional universality of our education and the consequent intellectual tradition, as a consequence of our view that ignorance and piety are mutually exclusive.

The Jewish and the Christian tones are different in ways far beyond theology and opinions about Jesus.

Does this mean that I must regard Christianity as superior or inferior? I do not think so. For me, an ardent Jew, it is sufficient to say not that Christianity is complete or incomplete, better or worse, but that, despite overlappings with Judaism, it is quite different.

Conversion: The Jewish Approach
Arthur Hertzberg

CONVERSION and missionary activity among the major faiths are once again a subject of considerable public interest. There is now a group in Jerusalem organized to convert non-Jews, and another such project has been announced in Chicago.

On the other side, in Christian circles, the subject of missionary activity is very much debated. Distinguished Christian theologians are beginning to wonder whether the missionary traditions of the church should be continued, at least among Jews. The mainstream of Christianity does not doubt but the church must continue to spread the gospel and that those who would put limits on this activity are guilty of misstating the Christian message. It would, therefore, seem useful to define what appears to be the Jewish attitude on missionary activities.

It has been said many times that Judaism and Christianity do not encounter each other on the same level. For Christianity its relationship to Judaism is of fundamental doctrinal concern. The very name of its sacred scripture, the New Testament, forthwith implies the need to answer such questions as: what is the Old Testament? what of that scripture is old and what remains a true testament? and what is the relationship of the new Israel of the spirit, the bearer of the new dispensation, to Israel in the flesh? It has been debated throughout the modern age whether anti-Semitism is merely the most pervasive and devastating form of the hatred of the unlike, or whether its ultimate roots, at least in the West, are in religion. Whatever one's opinion may be on this question, there can be no doubt that both Judaism and the Jew are an inescapable and central concern in Christianity, from its very beginning, and not merely the most persistent minority with which Christendom has had to deal.

Left to itself Judaism, as faith, is under no such essential compulsion to define an attitude toward Christianity. To be sure, the successes of Christianity and, for that matter, of Islam have evoked some occasional reflection through the centuries among Jewish philosophers. Obviously the religion which succeeded in dominating Europe in a few centuries could not quite be treated by philosophers of Judaism with as little attention as all the sectarian and splinter groups which left the main body of Jewry and soon disappeared from sight. Nonetheless the initial breach between Judaism and the early Church was not a crisis of the faith which required the older religion to redefine itself in antithesis to the new.

Such definitions are to be found in profusion in Jewish literature from the early Middle Ages to the present day. These many volumes of apologetics were, however, evoked by the fact that the Jews were a minority within Christendom. Had historical accident carried the Jewish Diaspora to Asia, there would, no doubt, have arisen, in due course, a comparable apologetics explaining, in terms comprehensible to the majority, the Jewish attitude to Buddhism.

Jewish tradition does demand, through rabbinic commentary and the Law itself, certain attitudes and behavior on the part of Jews to non-Jews. It must be remembered that the Judaism that we know today was really crystallized in the Talmud. The Mishnah, the core of the Talmud, was edited in Palestine in the second century, when Christianity was still far less powerful than Judaism in the Roman Empire, and the *G'mara,* the elaborate commentary on the Mishnah which makes up the rest of the Talmud, was composed in its accepted form in the next several centuries outside the borders of the Christianized Roman Empire among the Zoroastrians of the Parthian realm.

For the Rabbis of the Talmud, just as for the Biblical writers, the societies that they knew were multi-national; they were marked by an intermingling of religions. The Jews who lived within them were inevitably aware that the God of their tradition, who had "chosen" their people, had clearly not guaranteed it either power or even security. Especially in Talmudic times, the Rabbis were ever more conscious that both knowledge and moral uprightness were to be found outside the boundaries of their own community. To use Toynbee's term, the Talmud was created by a millet living in the midst of other millets. It is therefore natural and understandable that it defined further the Biblical doctrine of God's universality and its specific applications in the commandments relating to hospitality to the stranger.

The basic rabbinic doctrine concerning non-Jews is expressed in sayings such as these: "Ben Azzai teaches: Highly valued as is the commandment, 'Thou shalt love thy neighbor as thyself' (Leviticus 19:18), the sentence, 'This is the book of the children of Adam' (Genesis 5:1) is, in the last resort, of superior weight, because it teaches the doctrine of common parentage of the family unity of the human race" (*Jerushalmi Nedarim* 9:4). "R. Nehemiah says: A single human being outweighs the whole creation. If a man saves a human life, it is as if he has saved the entire world, and if he destroys a human life, it is as if he has destroyed the entire world (*Avot de Rabbi Nathan* 31)."

In the time of Bar Kokhba's rebellion, in the second century, against the tyranny of Rome, the question as to whether non-Jews have a share in the life to come was seriously discussed, and even at that desperate time the accepted decision was that of Rabbi Joshua that "the righteous ones among the nations have a share in the life to come" (*Tosefta Sanhedrin* 13:2).

One could go on quoting copiously from many such sayings in Talmudic literature, but, as is well known, in the rabbinic tradition Halakhah (Law), and not *Aggadah* (various moral reflections of individual Rabbis), is of paramount authority. We must, therefore, turn to the legal literature for an absolute definition of normative Judaism's attitude to other faiths.

All men are the children of Noah. To one group among his descendants, the seed of Abraham, God gave particular responsibilities through his revelation to them of the Torah, with all its various laws which are incumbent upon them as a "kingdom of priests, a holy nation." All the rest must obey the following: "Our masters taught: Seven commandments were given to the children of Noah—to practice justice, to avoid blasphemy, idol-worship, lust, blood-shed, robbery and eating flesh cut from an animal while alive" (*Sanhedrin* 56).

Thus, while Jews regard themselves as the bearers of special responsibilities, they claim no monopoly on salvation. All people are under certain obligations, and the righteous among them "have a share in the life to come."

There are, of course, both in the Talmud and in the Bible, less generous comments about the out-group, just as there are in Christian writings. Jewish educators, like Christians, must assess the basic attitudes toward "others" demanded by the essential message of their faith, and stress those lessons and passages which will reinforce such attitudes—not "censoring" the others, but placing them in appropriate historical perspective. This kind of evaluation is incumbent upon all who wish their children to grow in religious faith and knowledge, and yet to live without religiously-nurtured hatred. To live together, with mutual regard for the other's faith, but not to engage in active efforts at conversion—this is the attitude of Judaism.

But what of Christianity? It is only among the Protestants that the question can arise of missionary activity among Jews, for Catholics of course are firmly committed to the doctrine that theirs is the only true church. Such debate has recently begun among the Protestants.

Jews cannot but prefer Reinhold Niebuhr's proposal of several years ago (which represents a position not far different from that which Paul Tillich is known to hold) that there be theological coexistence between Judaism and Christianity till the end of time. Nonetheless, one must agree with Niebuhr's most recent critic, George E. Sweazey ("Are Jews Intended To Be Christians?" in *The Christian Century* for April 29, 1959), that coexistence would represent a theological revolution. Sweazey's assertion that, since New Testament times, the Jews have always been a, if not *the*, prime target of Christian proselytism seems undeniable.

Nor can it be gainsaid that, on Sweazey's premises, proselytism is an integral element of that evangelism which is the "Great Commission" of the church, and that to excise it by making theological peace with Judaism would call all Christian evangelism into question. Sweazey thus appears as the defender of classical Christian theology against a radical new proposal. In his approach to the Jews he seems to walk consciously and resolutely on the highroad marked out by his Christian ancestors through the centuries: he believes that he brings them the higher truth which has come to replace and indeed fulfill what he considers the partial truth of Judaism.

Such a classicist no doubt expects the Jew also to react in the ancient way: to debate about all the Biblical texts that have often been a Jewish-Christian battleground and to argue against the truth and divinity of the Christian revelation. In the medieval age, a Christian classicist would agree, the discussion could never reach its fullest stature on either side; for Christians too often vitiated the spiritual power of their case and mission by involving force, and Jews, even if they might have wished to proselytize for their faith, were debarred from doing so.

Hence a twentieth-century Christian like Sweazey is, to his credit, very insistent on the responsibility of the missionary today to recognize the equal rights of Jews in our democratic society, and to labor, in Christian love, for their complete religious liberty. By the inherent logic of this acceptance of freedom, such a Christian undoubtedly would welcome free competition with a Jewish missionary movement, which is possible in the democratic world today. This indeed is the "answer" of some Jews to Christian evangelism: they are proposing a new departure for Jewry, something which has been foreign to it for at least as long as Christianity has dominated the West; i.e., campaigns are being announced for conversions to Judaism.

A Jew does not have the right to suggest to Christianity how it shall solve its own basic dilemmas on the contemporary scene. He does, however, have both the right and the duty to speak about the meaning of Christian evangelism for the future of America in its life-and-death struggle for the minds of men in the non-Christian world. America as a whole and all that it stands for will go down to defeat and disaster if our age is made into a new seventeenth century, a time of "wars of religion." The peoples of Asia and Africa will respond to our American leadership only if what we offer as a counterfaith to Communism is not Christianity or even Judeo-Christianity, but rather the greatest of all American values: the vision of a world order in which all men serve side by side and help each other to be true to themselves, to their own hopes and aspirations.

Let me add that in the next century American society and indeed the whole Western world will inevitably tend to become pluralist in a much more complex way than ever before. A few years ago America took the first step toward opening the door of immigration to Asiatics and Africans by assigning modest quotas to that part of the world. And now it has admitted Hawaii to statehood. That means that more and more Buddhists, Hindus and Moslems will come to our shores, because America cannot be true either to itself or to its responsibilities if it refuses them entry.

The pluralism of our society will therefore have to take on a differ-ent cast. No longer will it be merely Jewish-Christian or religious-secular. Our society will have to devise a framework in which religions essentially foreign to each other will be able to meet in the common market place of an America which is steadily becoming a microcosm of all humanity. A revived Christian evangelism reasserting its "Great Commission" to convert, and hence to dissolve, all other faiths will not only embarrass America before the world; it will undercut our foreign policy and lend new fuel to the appeal of Communism in the East.

But what of the "Great Commission"? A classicizing Christian like Sweazey might share every one of my fears and yet declare, "God helping me, I can do no other." Assuredly the social consequence of a faith cannot always be allowed to determine its expression. But, on the other hand, it is obvious that American society and the world need theologies that are at once true to themselves and yet make possible a reasonable peace among religions.

No one who believes in a divine revelation can possibly be satisfied with the easy answer that every one of the great religions has some good in it and that all are therefore equally valid. If this be true, then idolatry and paganism have had some uses, for they certainly produced great esthetic values, at very least in ancient Greece. I for one am not much happier over the Niebuhr-Tillich idea (which Franz Rosenzweig prefigured) that Judaism and Christianity are both aspects of a larger revelation and that they exist to correct and supplement each other.

Being a classicizing Jew, I stand with classicizing Christians like George Sweazey in insisting that these two faiths cannot both be ulti-mately right. If Christianity is God's true revelation of Himself, then clearly I, the Jew, am living in the greatest error, for I continue to reject the "highest light" that God has vouchsafed. But the converse is also possible: if Judaism is true, then the Christian has arrogated to himself the claim of being the true Israel, made a man into God, and falsely proclaimed the Law to be abrogated. For classicists like Sweazey and myself there is no escape from living in the gravest danger, for we have bet our life and our salvation on one of these two possibilities.

How then can we refrain from trying to convert each other? How can we seriously propose to live in peace?

It seems to me that the clue to an answer is to be found in the very worldwide movement within which Sweazey is laboring. The Eastern Orthodox Church is part of the World Council of Churches, though it is known not to have surrendered one iota of its conviction that other bodies with which it is sitting are not true churches. Each church remains free, and indeed commissioned by its own light to convert members of other denominations. It is nonetheless clear that there is a largely unspoken acceptance of the premise that the church is likely to remain divided on matters of faith and to live with this division; that the historic denominations will, despite some normal traffic across the various lines, not engage in an all-out attempt to destroy each other; and that the question of which of the many churches is the true church will be left for the judgment of God at the end of time. If this be not the inherent meaning of ecumenicity, then the Protestant response to Pope John's recent call for a council of churches makes no sense. What Protestantism asks as the price for attending such a meeting is acceptance by the Roman Catholic communion of the idea that Protestants have a right to the danger of living outside the authority of Peter's successor, until God shall judge between them.

I can only propose to Christianity as a whole and to Protestantism in particular that this premise on which it is refounding modern Christianity, and this demand that it is making of the Roman Catholics, be applied in the relationship of all religions in the modern world, both East and West. Let us stand separately for our various truths. Let us stand together for the peace of society. Let us not do to one another that which is hateful to any of us. And let us await the judgment of God.

V

Creative Jews of Our Time

Three Modern Yiddish Writers

Hasye Cooperman

I. MENDELE MOCHER SFORIM

MENDELE Mocher Sforim, born Sholem Yankev Abramovitsch, is the least known of the three great modern Yiddish classics: Mendele, I. L. Peretz, and Sholom Aleichem. Yet it was he who set the mold in Yiddish literature for a modern style of writing, who enriched and standardized the language and made it the vehicle of so many memories and records of a people.

Born in Kopyl, Lithuania, in 1836, Mendele was a teacher most of his life until his death in Odessa in 1917. He started as a Hebrew author, an adherent of the *Haskalah* or Enlightenment. Like all *maskilim* (those engaged in the *Haskalah,* who sought to educate themselves in Western culture) he shunned Yiddish, the language of the masses rather than the scholars, until he became convinced that he was thus defeating his own purpose. If he meant to address himself to his people, then it would have to be in the very medium in which they lived and breathed. Calling himself a *moicher sforimnik* or "bookseller," this itinerant peddler was welcomed in the homes of eager readers. He knew the people intimately, he could spin a yarn, give advice, bring tidings from far and wide.

Mendele is known as the *zeyde* (grandfather) of modern Yiddish literature, a term of endearment and reverence by which Sholom Aleichem addressed him in a famous letter. Mendele's first Yiddish novel was *Dos Kleine Mentshele* (The Little Man), published in 1864. It was the story of a respectable member of the Jewish community who had climbed to a position of honor by wheedling his way up, by oppressing the weak and flattering the powerful. This acid social satire was so effective that the original prototype for Mendele's "little man" was pointed out and ostracised.

Die Takse (The Tax) repeated the theme of the "city benefactors" who robbed the poor through an excessive meat tax. This five-act play described the workers who sporadically protested against exploitation but were too ignorant to sustain their struggle and organize properly. It introduced a young *maskil*, Veker by name, who leaves town to study at the university, and who never loses hope that a liberal and enlightened government will come to the aid of his people.

Fishke der Krumer (Fishel the Lame) is a love idyll between the lame Fishel and the hunchbacked Beile. It is based in part on an episode in Mendele's own life, when at the age of seventeen, by a ruse, he became part of a band of schnorrers (beggars) whose leader mistreated and threatened him. Wandering with them he was able to see various Jewish communities in the Pale; he also observed the caste system operating among these dregs of society—the physically handicapped, the lame, the tormented. Those who seemed maimed and insignificant were beautiful people at heart. They yearned for something lofty, beyond themselves; they lived with truth, not deceit. Mendele the bookseller, the warm, understanding but never obtrusive observer (and busybody), was introduced in this novel. His moods are mirrored in nature; whatever surrounds him becomes an extension of the self, bewildered, compassionate, melancholy.

> All is hushed and quiet, *slichos*-time in the woods, as in the *shtetl* on the Sabbath when the folks sleep during the day; the quiet of the woods makes one melancholy. The trees stand lost in thought, worried—not at all the same as they were before, not the same countenances and not the same demeanor. When they rustle their branches, that is their way of wringing their hands; their sound is now a bitter lament, a sigh, the complaint of a devoted mother who remains alone after her children have been scattered far and wide.

Nature is permeated with his own thoughts and feelings. Every dog, cat, goat is reflected upon with human kindness by Mendele the bookseller. Even his horse knows his master's thoughts, and when the bookseller is tempted to sin by breaking his fast, his eye has only to meet that of his horse to be reminded of what is right.

After this romantic interlude, Mendele returned to his favorite vehicle: satire. *Die Kliatche* (The Nag), appearing in 1873, became his most popular work. An allegory of Jewish persecution, it described a nag who had once been a prince, stoned by ruffians, shunned by friends, hungry, miserable, alone. By now Mendele had come to realize that the exploitation from within was but a pale reflection of a greater denial, that of fundamental human rights. To see the Enlightenment or assimilation as a way out was to perceive a half-truth; even liberalism, which he bitterly called *Tsar Baali Khaimnikes,* or the society for protection of animals, he regarded with skepticism. While listening to a letter from this society, the nag interposes, "Will this twaddle, this rigmarole, ever have done?"

Mendele's satire had by now taken the long-range view; he was less impatient and more compassionate. And significantly, the mellowness was to be observed in his lyrical descriptions of nature. Addressing himself to the nightingale, he says:

> Dearly beloved nightingale, what makes you so sad and mournful? Why, even when you chant something cheerful, do you seem to tug at the heartstrings to inject a note of melancholy? Why do billows of bitter tears heave and surge across your symphonic ocean? After all, you are going to be in your glory now, you will be the host of the entertainment. Your little spouse has renovated your abode, the air is charged with the scent of summer, the forest is draped with green tapestry, and the earth, in her resplendent green bridal dress, is longing for the impassioned kisses of the groom. And yet, on this momentous occasion you choose to blend melancholy with delight!

There is ecstasy, insight, wisdom, a feeling of transcendental powerlessness and powerfulness as man (the student Yisroelik) beholds nature.

One might almost say that Mendele the rationalist, the *maskil,* had by now come closer to Hasidic transports. But not quite. For he was to write another satire, his most powerful and subtle.

Masoes Binyomin Hashlishi (The Adventures of Benjamin the Third) was a Jewish version of Don Quixote with his Sancho Panza, going forth to right the wrongs of the world, to challenge the outer world. Of all Mendele's works this one is best known on the European continent, winning him the name of the Jewish Cervantes.

The work possesses a bitter sweetness, exhibiting the disparity between the real and the ideal, the chasm between dire necessities and sweet romanticism. Benjamin, who is so afraid of the dark, who trembles when a dog barks, becomes Benjamin the intrepid when he is lured by the great world beyond, when he is buoyed up by the dream of freeing his people, of bringing the Messiah. His companion is Senderl, an almost selfless creature, hen-pecked, obedient, naive, who nevertheless is able from time to time to give Benjamin some sound advice. While Senderl (townfolk call him *die Yidene*) provides the food—bits of white bread and rye, salt, cucumbers, radishes, onions, garlic—Benjamin provides the abounding faith, the vision and the goal.

Though both lack knowledge and worldly wisdom, these befuddled creatures have a strength all their own, invisible, impenetrable. Not the phylacteries, not the prayer shawl, but *bitokhen,* faith, fortitude. Benjamin and Senderl are to all intents and purposes two pathetic "flops," they must return to the fold, but somehow they remain undaunted.

"Are you the two charged with leaving the barracks at night without official leave?" the general asked them in a stern voice. "Are you aware of the penalty for such an act?" . . .

"Your honor!" Benjamin vociferated. "Trapping people in broad daylight and then selling them like chickens in the market place—that's permissible? But when these same people try to escape, you call it a crime? If that's the case, the world must be coming to an end and I fail to understand what you call 'permissible' or 'not permissible'!"

In their mock heroism there is wistfulness. The tale remains unfinished as the two march off after being released from military conscription as total nitwits. But one puts the book down with the feeling that such resoluteness is a shield, an invisible bulwark against a threatening world.

Mendele's next work, *Dos Vintshfingerl* (The Wishing Ring), was a study of this invisible bulwark of the Jewish people. Written in 1888–9, it explored the traditions, folkways, stamina, faith and spiritual values which brightened the otherwise dreary lives of so many Jews. This novel of stark realism reads like a story from Dickens. It tells how the orphaned Hershele, loved and protected by Reb Avrohom der Mekubal (the mystic), who falls into the hands of *khappers* (snatchers, or kidnappers, paid for conscripting children into the Russian army). He is rescued, becomes Heinrich Kahan, an assimilated merchant in Germany. After the pogroms of the 1880's, he returns to the town of his childhood, visits the grave of his childhood sweetheart and is overcome by sorrow.

Mendele's most ambitious work, *Dos Vintshfingerl,* described the impoverished life of the adults and children, their barren and austere world. It portrayed many types, as if the town were a microcosm of humanity. Avrohom the mystic, a father surrogate to Hershele and his friend Moishele, speaks of the *Zohar* and the hidden beauties of the world; dry rationalism is not for him. Indeed, one wonders whether Peretz's Hasidic heroes may not have found a source in this lofty person.

This work was in many ways a song of praise for the Jewish people. Observing its religious life, Sabbath, holidays, mores, family relationships, Mendele esteemed what he now held to be the internalized and spiritual values by which Jews breathed. Theirs was a completely integrated way of life that could transcend much hardship. The nag which he had seen before, lean, harrowed and unkempt, could transform itself into a Sabbath prince. Was not this the wishing ring, the magic of awe and reverence and beauty, when the Sabbath, or any other holiday, might by its soft radiance and quiet glow make life so sweet? Shmulik, the second-hand dealer, lives in a hovel.

> Six days in the week Shmulik lived like a dog. But on the eve of the Sabbath all changed in his house. The walls whitewashed, the house cleaned; a new cloth shines on the table, and the rich and yellow bread, a joy to the eyes, rests thereon. The candles burn in their copper candlesticks, burnished for the Sabbath.
>
> His wife's face is resplendent, the children joyous and "the invisible angels" come into every Jewish house when the father returns from the house of prayer on the eve of the Sabbath . . . today he has a new soul. It is the Shabbos and Shmulik is a prince . . .

Mendele has come full circle. The irony is gone and a gentleness permeates his writing. His next book, *Shloime Reb Khaime,* an undisguised autobiography, is an authentic record of Jewish childhood and youth. Its charm lies in its introspective quality, its insights into childish fears and imagination, a child's ability to create his own intensive inner realities. God's *veltl* (little world) is so full of busy creatures, storks, whippoorwills, insects, frogs, trees, boys; and nature and God belong intimately to youth and its secret world. There is majesty and serenity in Mendele's pantheistic descriptions of the trees and fields, and lyricism in the youth's wandering through the woods, contemplating the world and yearning to become a writer. The wishing ring is his.

Mendele the bookseller was wont to say that in him there dwelled two creatures, one a talkative, sometimes meandering busybody, the other observant, critical, contemplative, laconic. Mendele's style of writing exploited both, leaving an indelible record of Jewish life in nineteenth-century Eastern Europe. Forging the various dialects and colloquial expressions into a superior literary medium, he erected a monument to the traditional Jewish spirit and portrayed a wide range of Jewish characters. His prose poetry is gentle and human in its feeling for nature, and transcendental in its sweep.

> Up above, on a branch, a whippoorwill is swinging, seeming from afar to be wearing a white prayer shawl with pale blue stripes in front. It is praying, swaying to and fro. It makes a bow, then returns to its praying as it shakes its head. Then it hops a bit, croaks a wee bit now and then, and remains standing without a sound as it stretches its neck and gazes at nowhere in particular with sleepy eyes [the Yiddish is *eigelekh,* the diminutive] . . .
>
> It is hot and quiet and so wonderfully beautiful. Hush! God's creatures are at rest.

II. SHOLOM ALEICHEM

Sholom Aleichem (in Hebrew, "greetings" or "peace unto you") is the pseudonym of Sholom Rabinowitz, born in Pereyaslav in the Ukraine, in 1859. When he died in New York City in 1916, *The New York Times* recorded that "over 150,000 persons turned out to do him honor." In his last will and testament he asked to be buried among "the common, honest people who in his lifetime honored their folk-writer." His tombstone bears an inscription he wrote himself: "Here lies a simple Jew." In 1959 UNESCO decided to "stimulate and participate" in celebrations of the one hundreth anniversary of his birth throughout the world.

No Yiddish writer so intensively identified himself with his readers, their racy language, their picturesque and rich idioms, the very rhythm of their speech and its images. He sensed their genius for turning misery into humor, for making merry over their own short-comings. The unbearable pathos became humor, wit, a sparkling play of the imagination, poetic, lyrical, surrealistic. Basically Sholom Aleichem was writing of a very real world, complete with characters and types of all descriptions, whose central figures became universal symbols: the *kasril* or *kasrilik;* Menachem Mendel, the dreamer; Tevye, the searching folk philosopher; Motl, the orphan, both pensive and ebullient.

While Mendele Mocher Sforim immortalized the *shtetlakh* of Tuniyadevke, Glubsk and Kabtzansk, Sholom Aleichem did the same for Kasrielevky, Mazepovke and Yehupetz. But while Mendele's mood was caustic satire, Sholom Aleichem's was humor filled with loving-kindness.

> The town of the tiny folk which I am leading you into, dear reader, is situated in the very heart of the blessed Pale of Settlement, where Jews have been huddled together, packed like herring in a barrel, and told to be fruitful and multiply. The name of that town is Kasrielevky . . .
>
> In our town, as everybody knows, a poor man is called by a variety of descriptions, depending upon the degree of his poverty: he may be hard-up, or needy, or in straits, or in dire need; he may be impoverished; a receiver of gifts, an indigent; he may be destitute, poverty-stricken, a pauper, or a dyed-in-the-wool pauper. Each of these epithets is uttered in a different tone of voice. There

is still another name for a poor man: a *kasril* or *kasrilik*. Now this name is pronounced in a very different note, for example, "My, my, am I a *kasrilik*."

And Kasrielevky sets great store by its witticisms. As it laughs at itself, it also laughs at the incredibly rich world outside, as in the tale of the *kasrilik* who went to see Rothschild in Paris, to sell him, of all things, eternal life.

> Our man first pocketed the cash, then he addressed Rothschild, saying, "If you want to live forever, I advise you to get away from this noisy city of Paris and come and settle in our quiet town of Kasrielevky. There you'll never die, for as long as Kasrielevky has been in existence, no rich man has ever died there."

Kasrielevky is proud of her two fine cemeteries, an old one and a new one; the little people are especially proud of the old cemetery which is overgrown, and with scarcely a tombstone intact. They regard it "as their ornament, a precious thing, a treasure, and they guard it as the apple of their eye." Aside from the fact that it is the resting place of their forebears, saints, rabbis, scholars and others of distinction, the very flower of Israel—added to all this, there is reason to believe that it contains quite a number of martyrs of the massacres of the days of Khmelnitzki. "This 'sacred place,' as they are wont to call the cemetery, is the only possession in the world of which they are the sole owners; this is their only piece of ground, their only bit of field where a blade of grass sprouts and a shrub grows and where the air is fresh and one can breathe freely."

Thus these people are merry and inventive; life is confined to one's immediate environs and to the sad and noble past. These are the little people in their own little world.

It is quite otherwise with Menachem Mendel who does try his fortune in the world, that is, in Yehupetz, Boiberik and Odessa. He, too, like Mendele's Benjamin, is a Jewish Don Quixote, restless, imaginative, daring. As we read the letters which he writes to Shayne Shayndl, his wife, and her answers to him, the trips, the finagling, the stocks and "papers" become symbols of an unsure world, even a frightening world. This "speculator" with his unrealized hopes represents the dichotomy between Don Quixote's "enchantment" and Sancho Panza's (Shayne Shayndl's) "disenchantment," between the poet and the realist.

The emotional accords and subtle perceptions that underlie all of the goings-on make this a classic applicable to all humanity. As Shayne Shayndl says, "I think there is more to witchcraft than there is to all of your Yehupetz portfolios." But Menachem Mendel is not disheartened:

> You seem to think, my dear wife, that I am the only one that's trading in papers. Brodski, the millionaire, he trades in them, too . . .
> I'll go a bear, sell out and so make money both going and coming. After that I shall return to bull and make a pretty penny again . . . How else, little goose, do you suppose you can become a millionaire, a Brodski? And who do you think Brodski is? Just a human being; he eats and drinks and sleeps like the rest of us.

Mendele is also a modern Everyman. He tells himself that there are three things needed in this world: brains, luck and money. Brains he knows he has; as for "luck, that's in God's hand. And money—that's in Brodski's hands." The *kasrilik* has become a *luftmentsh,* an adventurer.

Not so with Tevye; he is productive, brooding, rooted. Tevye only seems simple; but as he relies upon the old roots, the Scriptures which he often misquotes, the human values which mean everything to him, he probes into the meaning of man, he unfolds, he gains insight. He becomes a Job seeking an answer, coming back upon himself, at last comprehending the ways of the complex world and the rift between the generations.

Tevye's greatest treasure are his seven beautiful daughters, whom he must marry off; ironically, they are also his greatest burden. Menachem Mendel, with all of his dashing about, scheming and dreaming, never has time to think about himself or his children; he leaves that to his wife and his mother-in-law. But Tevye's pace is slower:

> Well, there I was, driving home, deep in melancholy thoughts, asking the Creator all kinds of questions and answering them myself. It isn't the acts of God that worry me so; somehow, I've become reconciled with Him after a fashion. It's the acts of men that hurt me. Why should men be so vicious when they can be good? . . . Is it conceivable that God created man only that he should suffer on earth? What good is that to Him?

What Tevye cannot define, he cannot completely accept. The ways of the Lord, the ways of the world, the ways of the younger generation *are there* and he stands stalwart in their midst. It vexes him to think that he is not as well versed as other men so that he might find a sound answer to his own perplexing questions. But do they?

> Man is a fool. If he were wise he would never let anything touch him too deeply. He would know that if things are a certain way

that's the way they were intended to be. For if things were intended to be different, they wouldn't have been as they are. Don't we say in the Psalms: *"Put your trust in God?"*—Have faith in Him and He will see to it that you stagger under a load of trouble and keep on reciting: *"This too is for the best."*

Motl Peyse, the cantor's son, presents a synthesis between the restlessness of Menachem Mendel and the steadfastness of Tevye. Firmly rooted in the traditional past, he belongs also to the future and to the new land (America). Motl states gleefully and ironically, "See what I mean? Everybody sides with me. They all take my part. I'm lucky, I'm an orphan."

But he also asks, "What will become of me?"

His brother Elye has bought a book full of schemes for getting-rich-quick. Motl admires his older brother (another Menachem Mendel) and he works as his assistant. No matter that their schemes are complete flops (ink that blackens all the river, exterminating powder that makes the whole street sneeze, a beverage that is putrid); it's so much fun to be planning and trying things out! And then they're off to America, where Motl's mother finds the Kasrielevky synagogue. All of Kasrielevky seems to have moved to America ("try not to love such a country!").

The last chapter is headed *We Move,* and these are the last words which the author wrote before death overtook him. Motl's story remained unfinished.

Motl is only one of many children about whom Sholom Aleichem wrote. The unsophisticated and natural world of the child fascinated him. If life could be perplexing to a Tevye, if a Menachem Mendel could be caught up in its turmoil, how much more the child?

The Jewish holidays and children were almost synonymous for Sholom Aleichem. Shavuos, La'ag Ba'omer, Hanukkah, Simhas Torah, Pesakh, Purim, Sukkos—there are countless tales. Yiddish anthologies are never complete without them and in no Yiddish school in the world is a Jewish holiday celebrated without a Sholom Aleichem story.

The story of the grievous Passover is perhaps best loved. It tells of a little boy whose mother had clothes made for him to grow into. The other children surround him and jeer, saying, "That's no jacket, it's a lounging robe!" Even here we have the inside-out of comedy, as it were. What seems so funny to the reader is anguishing to the child.

Sholom Aleichem once wrote: " 'Through laughter which the world sees flow tears that the world does not see,' said Gogol. I say: 'The world only sees the laughter because it does not want to see the tears, which often flow through the laughter and can move stones.' "

This might be the secret: Sholom Aleichem *was able to move stones*. His extravaganzas and fantasies emerge from the imagination of a poet for whom reality is often tragic. To make it bearable it has to be sublimated, distorted, or even expanded. It has to be translated into the whirl of a spinning-top.

> My eyes closed. The wind howled, and the cricket chirped, "Tchireree! Tchireree! Tchireree! Tchireree!" And there spun around before my eyes a man like a top—a man I seemed to know. I could have sworn it was the teacher in his pointed cap. He was spinning on one foot, round, and round, and round. His cap sparkled, his eyes glistened, and his earlocks flew about. No, it was not the teacher. It was a spinning-top—a curious, living top with a pointed cap and earlocks. By degrees the teacher-top, or the top-teacher ceased from spinning round. And in its place stood Pharaoh, the king of Egypt, whose story we had learnt a week ago. Pharaoh, king of Egypt, stood naked before me. He had only just come out of the river. He had my little prayer book in his hand.

"Laughter is good. Doctors tell us to laugh." Laughter defines the excesses, peculiarities, shortcomings. Laughter points out the logical by showing up the illogical.

Sholom Aleichem often said that this was a topsy-turvy world. And laughter set things right.

"Let winds blow," he wrote. "Let storms rage. Let the world turn upside down. The old oak, which has been standing since the creation of the world, and whose roots reach to God-knows-where—what does he care for winds? What are storms to him?

"That old tree is not a symbol; it is a living being, a man . . ."

III. ISAAC LOEB PERETZ

Of all three writers in the golden era of modern Yiddish literature, Peretz presented the most facets and the widest horizon. He was the most dynamic and most intellectual, his style changing feverishly as he experimented and was influenced by other European cultures and modes of writing. He moved from the realism and rationalism of the *Haskalah* to a philosophic idealism or the wonder and awe of romanticism, and from there to a symbolism synthesizing the Jewish folk tradition with ultra-modern forms, sometimes impressionistic, sometimes expressionistic, abstruse or even deceptively simple.

Itzhak Leibush Peretz, of Sefardi descent, was born in Zamosc, Poland, in 1852; he died in Warsaw in 1915. He received a traditional religious education. At the age of fourteen he was given a key to the library of a scholar in his native town; there he found the answer to his unsatisfied hunger.

There were scientific books, philosophic tracts, histories, and a miscellany of literary masterpieces in foreign tongues. Sedulously, he taught himself Russian, Polish, German, French. Secular learning intrigued him. After studying for the Russian bar in Warsaw, he became a prosperous barrister for eleven years.

During the last twenty-five years of his life Peretz was an official of the Warsaw Jewish community. His home in Warsaw was the center of Jewish cultural and literary renaissance. Writers like S. Ansky (author of *The Dybbuk*), Sholem Asch and David Pinski were inspired by Peretz. *Die Yiddish Bibliothek,* of which he was editor, attracted a wide range of talented young authors who looked upon Peretz as their mentor. He was active in the newly organized Yiddish schools and wrote poems for children's textbooks. He helped found the first orphanage for Jewish children who were made homeless by World War I.

Peretz the intellectual, who thought of himself as a working man's author, was never removed from the people or their immediate problems. It is estimated that more than a hundred thousand Jews came to his funeral. Many Polish towns have, or have had, streets bearing his name, and in downtown New York City Peretz Square was named at the close of World War II.

Peretz began as a Hebrew poet, later became a Yiddish poet. In *Monish,* a long narrative poem which evoked much consternation and criticism, he introduced—in addition to irony and satire—romantic love, a theme hitherto unknown in Yiddish poetry. Social themes underlie many of his poetic dramas, the best known of these being *Beim Fremdn Khupe Kleid* (The Wedding Gown). The characters are the owner of a dressmaking establishment, her two modistes and a chorus of seamstresses. The first modiste tells the story of the "Two Brothers," a tale of exploitation, which is now often recited at workers' meetings and has been much anthologized.

Peretz's poetic dramas, such as *Die Goldene Keit* (The Golden Chain) and *Beinacht Oifn Altn Mark* (The Old Market Place at Night), produced in Warsaw in 1906 and 1907, were experiments in impressionism and symbolism. They glorified the old traditions, the holy Sabbath, spiritual beauty; they exalted the past, but their form and skills were ultra-modern.

Modern Yiddish poetry owes a great deal to Peretz's innovations and experiments with images, symbols, mood and tempo.

I want to soar the boundless blue
Where winds and tempests have their birth,
And let the clouds conceal from me
Not heaven, but the earth.

But Peretz's greatest popularity derives from his tales. His earliest novellas and short stories were steeped in social realism. His style was unaffected, tender and graceful; his protagonists humble people, rich in spiritual beauty, even elegant and refined. A happy accord between husband and wife was often delicately described, as in his story *Sholem Bayis* (Domestic Bliss). And he emphasized the superior position of the woman, her understanding, her sense of purpose and her reverence for the man of learning, and above all, her intuitive grasp and her own definition of happiness.

In his sketch *The Widow* he tells us that "the little house stands just under the hill. The low, thatched roof is full of holes—there is no one to mend it." The husband has died after a year's illness and the young widow contemplates the dark and dismantled room where her child lies asleep.

> And yet one thought revolves ceaselessly in her mind; no other seems able to drive it away—it is not to be dislodged.
>
> "Hannah," he had once said to her, "hand me the scissors."
>
> He had no use for them just then, and he had given a little artful smile. What had he really wanted?
>
> Did he wish me to go near to him? I was peeling potatoes. Did I give him the scissors? No. Just then someone came in—but who? She cannot recollect, and goes puzzling herself—who?
>
> The child sleeps on, and smiles; it is dreaming.

Some of Peretz's simplest tales about poor people appeared in *Travel Pictures,* which he wrote when he joined Yan Bloch's statistical expedition whose purpose was to explore Jewish life in Poland, and some were part of his *Folk Tales,* which he gathered throughout his life. Peretz described the writing down of these folk stories as a process of peeling the literary rind off the original spoken version. Too many writers polish the story. The people, he was often wont to say, have an uncanny gift for matching the content to the form; the tale was meant to be told, mouthed. If there was a delicacy in his own stories it was because he saw that quality in his people. One of his earliest pieces, *What Is the Soul?*, ends:

> "They all say, Gitele, that you are so wise. Tell me, what is the soul?"

She smiled and answered, "I'm sure I don't know."

Then she grew suddenly sad and tears came into her eyes: "I just remember," she said, "that when my mother was alive (may she rest in peace), my father always said she was his soul—they loved one another so dearly."

I don't know what came over me, but that same instant I took her hand and said trembling:

"Gitele, will you be my soul?" and she answered me quite softly: "Yes."

Peretz leaned toward socialism. Many of his stories depicted working people as important characters, ignorant but honest and beautiful, waiting to be taught, eager for so much. *Bontshe the Silent,* the original of which was probably a parable told by the Baal Shem Tov, is Peretz's most celebrated tale of humility and grandeur. By contrast, the writer described the *batlen* (beggar-student) as one withdrawn from life, lost, miserable, asking, "Who am I?" In *Mad Talmudist,* the young man appeases his anxiety by telling himself that whatever they call him he's still human.

As you read this recital of an anguished soul, you cannot but wonder whether this and similar psychologically oriented stories by Peretz might not have had a tremendous effect upon Kafka, who so greatly admired Yiddish literature.

When I pinch my cheek it burns—that means I have a cheek. I have hands and feet, a head, a heart, and maybe even a soul—everything. But I myself, what am I? Not the cheek, not the feet, the head, or the soul. What then? Nothing.

If I could kill myself and see what happened to me—to see what would remain of me when there were no longer a head, hands, feet, cheeks, torn boots—then I might know something! It might be good to try.

This mad student suffers the pangs of hunger, but the torments deriving from his loss of contact with reality are greater than his physical deprivations. The pursuit of learning has drained him dry.

In his Hasidic tales Peretz described truth and beauty among the lowly who knew reality, but who were capable of sublimation, joy, ecstasy, release—in a simple deed, a melody, a parable. The Hasidic movement turned man outward toward a contemplation of nature and inward toward self-realization and harmony. It was his intuitive imagination, not his rationalism, that lifted man. The uneducated artisan who performed his task well was equal to the scholar who prayed fervently. Each in his own way was articulate.

In such stories as *Between Two Mountains* and *The Migrations of a Melody*, Peretz demonstrated the magnetic powers of man's spirit. Individualism was revered as it blended with the whole, with that which is beyond man, in the over-all (what Emerson called the *over-soul*).

> And every company sang to its tune, but all the different tunes and voices blended in the air, and there floated up to the Rebbe's balcony *one* strain, *one* melody—as though all were singing one song. And everything sang—the sky, the celestial bodies, the earth beneath, the soul of the world—everything was singing!
>
> Lord of the world! I thought I should dissolve away for sheer delight. (*Between Two Mountains*)

> The melody was again transformed. It had the essence of the Torah, the fragrance of the holy Sabbath, the substance of a pious scholar's remorse. As he sang, he sensed the soul of the melody, and with each moment he sang better, with greater ease and with more freedom.
>
> Reb Dovidl, according to his usual custom, joined in, humming quietly. The others noticed this and also picked up the tune. The scholar, inspired by the crowd's participation, abandoned all restraint and now he really sang.
>
> The melody soon began to flow like a lava stream . . . The melody thus attained salvation, and so did the scholar. (*Migrations of a Melody*)

Peretz's best-known Hasidic tale is *If Not Higher*. The skeptic is eager to know where the Rabbi of Nemerov vanishes and what he does during the Penitential Prayers. Stealthily he follows him, only to behold that the rabbi dons peasant clothes, goes into the forest, fells logs, makes up a bundle of wood, brings this to a sick Jewish woman who cannot pay him, lights the fire for her and then leaves.

> As the rabbi put the wood into the stove, he said the first part of the Penitential Prayers, with a groan.
>
> And when he lit the fire and the wood burned brightly, he sang the second part of the prayers in a somewhat happier tone.
>
> He finished the third portion of his prayers as the fire glowed and as he put the lid on the stove.

After that, the story goes, the skeptic became an adherent. Whenever he was asked whether it were true that the rabbi rose up from the earth and flew to heaven every *Slichos* morning, he answered, "If not higher."

For the heights to which man might soar were unlimited, in Peretz's mind. He wrote his essays with great vigor and optimism, foreseeing a future when all humanity would walk in dignity. Then the Jews and their cultural contributions would be truly esteemed.

To live, wrote Peretz, "is to have divine conceptions and, in some degree, a divine will, to change the world about us in accordance with this conception, idea and will; to bring forth ever new forms; to be partner in the act of creation.

"I live, ergo I possess a divine spark. All who live possess it, and I feel that everything lives."

Peretz wanted "the Jew to feel like a man, to take part in all that is human, to live and strive humanly, and if he is offended, to be offended like a man!"

Again:

"Now, I am not advocating that we shut ourselves up in a spiritual ghetto. Let us go out of the ghetto, but as Jews, with our own spiritual treasures. Let us interchange, give and take, but not beg.

"Ghetto is impotence. Cultural interchange is the only basis for human development. Humanity must be the synthesis, the sum, the quintessence of all national cultures and philosophies."

Peretz's theories of cultural cross-fertilization and cultural pluralism are pertinent and alive today. His influence upon the younger writers has been far-reaching. But it is as one of the most modern of the Yiddish writers that we remember him.

His stories remain with us—full of symbolic meanings and eternally refreshing. Satya, the fisherman, encounters a miracle at sea:

"There!" shouts Satya excitedly, "there is my fish!" Surely God had answered him out of his anguish of heart, out of his longing, that he might fulfill his holy duty. And he is off, after that fish! The sea grows agitated and enraged; the waves rise higher and higher. The sun is now almost hidden by clouds, but its rays force themselves through, and beat down upon Satya. The fish is breasting the waves, and Satya's boat flies after it, quickly. Suddenly the fish is lost to sight; a wave has rolled up between them, and the boat is being tossed high upon the crest of a huge wave, whipped up and swollen by the storm. "I am fooled; my eyes are deceiving me," Satya mutters to himself; and he is about to turn the boat towards home, when suddenly the wave subsides as if it had been sucked into the sea, the fish comes up, and looks at him imploringly with its great eyes, as if appealing to be taken . . . so that Satya might fulfill in him his holy duty. Satya turns, and immediately the fish has vanished; a huge wave rolls once more between them, and the sea begins its song again. It is no soft, pleasing melody the sea is singing, it is an angry outburst against the rash human who has dared it in its wrath. As if afraid of its anger, the sun hides behind a mass of cloud, and the wind breaks loose with a savage roar. It rages wildly, and it swirls and beats upon the sea, but the sea becomes more angry, and it shouts and thunders as if a thousand drums were being beaten within its bosom.

And he hears a cry, "Sing, Satya, sing. Your song will calm the fury of the seas."

In the end the golden fish is in the net and Satya observes the only holiday he knows. The miracle is man!

Sigmund Freud

Theodor Reik

SIGMUND FREUD was not a religious Jew. He called himself a disbeliever and had no use whatsoever for ritual. Religion was to him an illusion which ought best to be removed from our culture. Nor was he able to share the nationalistic ideals of Zionism; in his view, chauvinism or superiority feelings on the part of any group were pernicious and unjust.

And yet, Freud was deeply aware of himself as a Jew. For one thing, he had a strong sense of belonging to the Jewish people. He had warm family ties and spoke a Viennese-Yiddish dialect to his mother, who had come to Austria from Poland via Czechoslovakia. All his life some of his most intimate friends, colleagues and disciples were Jews.

In the preface to the Hebrew edition of *Totem and Taboo*, Freud describes himself as "ignorant of the language of holy writ . . . completely estranged from the religion of (my) fathers . . . unable to take a share in nationalistic ideals." But he is also one who "feels that he is in his essential nature a Jew and who has no desire to alter that nature." To the question, "Since you have abandoned all these common characteristics of your fellow men, what is there left to you that is Jewish?," he replies: "A very great deal, and probably the most essential part of my personality."

What this Jewishness was Freud never clearly expressed nor attempted to explore or define. He hoped, however, that one day it might become "accessible to scientific research." It was his conviction that "unprejudiced science cannot remain a stranger to the new Jewry." His concept of Jewishness seemed to be of an emotional and intellectual identity—the result of a common past preserved mainly in unconscious memory traces. "A man who is not interested in his past is a ne'er-do-well," he once said to me. He pointed out again and again that we cannot break with our past without emotionally damaging ourselves because what we run away from runs after us.

One of the clearest statements of his feeling of closeness to the Jewish people Freud made almost at the end of his life, on the occasion of his seventieth birthday celebration by his B'nai B'rith Lodge in Vienna. In a message read to the gathering, he explained how years before, when, as a result of his first psychoanalytical discoveries he had been ostracized by many of his former friends, who were shocked by his revelations about the sex drive, he joined the B'nai B'rith. He was happy to become part of "a circle of select, lofty-minded men who could accept me in a friendly way notwithstanding my audacity," because, despite his rejection of religious faith and national pride, he was bound to Judaism. "There remains enough that made the attraction of Judaism and of the Jews irresistible, many mighty emotional forces, the more powerful, the less able to be caught with words, as well as the clear awareness of an inner identity, the secret of the same inner construction."

Further, Freud gratefully acknowledged in the same B'nai B'rith speech, he owed to his Jewishness two qualities that became indispensable on his difficult road. As a Jew he felt free from many prejudices which restricted other people in the use of their intellect. As a Jew too he was prepared to go into opposition and to renounce a conformity with the "compact majority." Posterity has recognized that it was that very intellectual freedom from convention and that independence of thought that enabled him to write the twelve volumes that "shook the world."

As Ernest Jones, his biographer, puts it, "the inherited capacity of Jews to stand their ground and maintain their position in life in the face of surrounding opposition or hostility was very evidently highly pronounced in Freud, and he was doubtless right in attributing to it the firmness with which he maintained his convictions undeterred by the prevailing opposition to them." It was that readiness to remain in splendid isolation and to stand alone against an army of antagonists —which Freud ascribed to his Jewishness—which made it possible to carry his research forward, unperturbed and unafraid.

As far as the outside world was concerned, however, Freud revealed his Jewishness most overtly by his fondness for Jewish jokes and anecdotes. This was more than just a personal sense of humor and the love of a good story on his part—Jewish wit was an integral part of his universe of discourse, woven into the warp and woof of much of his thinking, a reservoir from which he drew at all times to illuminate and explain the most complex and profound of his psychological observations. As he put it in his *Wit and Its Relation to the Unconscious,* the qualifications he required for such illustrations—that they should make us laugh and serve our theoretical interest—"are satisfied best by Jewish jokes."

Freud inherited his taste for Jewish wit from his father Jakob Freud, a wool merchant, who had the habit of pointing a moral by quoting a Jewish proverb or anecdote. His son likewise became a raconteur of Jewish stories long before he became interested in the psychoanalytic exploration of wit and its relation to the unconscious. As early as 1897, Freud wrote a friend that he had begun to collect "profound Jewish stories."

In other letters in which Freud spoke freely of his personal and professional life as well as of his recent research, Jewish jokes are again and again quoted or alluded to. For example, on one occasion, in expressing the hope that he might arrive at basic insights into the psychology of the neurosis, if his constitution could stand it, he referred to a well-known anecdote. It seems that a destitute Jew sneaks into the express train to Karlsbad without a ticket, is caught, thrown out at each station, and each time more and more brutally treated. At one of the stations, an acquaintance sees him and asks where he is journeying. The answer is: "To Karlsbad, if my constitution can bear it." Allusions to the same joke also occurred later when Freud interpreted one of his dreams.

A year later Freud sent the same friend part of his self-analysis, the first in the history of science, and remarked that it was entirely directed to the unconscious in accordance with the principle of Itzig, the inexperienced horseman. When the latter is asked, "Where do you go?" he answers, "How should I know? Ask the horse!"

When Freud in 1900 sent the first sheets of his monumental work on the *Interpretation of Dreams* to the printer, he expressed his dissatisfaction with the book by telling the following joke. Uncle Jonas is congratulated by his nephew, who has heard that he is engaged to be married. "And what is your bride like, Uncle?" "That's a matter of taste," the uncle replied. "I don't fancy her."

Freud uses many Jewish jokes as illustrative material for his analytic exploration of the comic. We find there stories about schnorrers, rabbis and unlearned people, poor and rich Jews; cynical, sophistical and skeptical jokes. The *shadkhen* story is a particular favorite. For example: On being introduced to his prospective bride, the suitor was rather unpleasantly surprised, and drawing aside the marriage agent, he reproachfully whispered to him: "Why have you brought me here? She is ugly and old. She squints, has bad teeth and bleary eyes." "You can talk louder," interrupted the agent. "She is deaf, too."

There is another: A prospective bridegroom made his first call on his future bride in company with the agent, and while in the parlor waiting for the appearance of the family, the agent drew the young man's attention to a glass closet containing a handsome silver set. "Just look at these things," he said. "You can see how wealthy these people are." "But is it not possible that these articles were just borrowed for the occasion?" inquired the suspicious young man. "What an idea," answered the agent protestingly, "who in the world would lend them anything?"

Jewish "bath" stories also occur frequently: Two Jews meet in front of the bathing establishment. "Another year has passed by already," says one with a sigh. So too, stories of the socially pretentious: The doctor who had been summoned to help the baroness in her confinement declared that the critical moment had not yet arrived, and proposed to the baron that they play a game of cards in the adjoining room in the meantime. After a while, the doleful cry in French of the baroness reached the ears of the men. "Ah, mon Dieu, que je souffre!" The husband jumped up, but the physician stopped him saying, "That's nothing; let us play on." A little later, the woman was heard again: "My God, my God, what pains!" "Don't you want to go in, Doctor?" asked the baron. "By no means, it is not yet time," answered the doctor. At last, there rang from the adjacent room the unmistakable cry, "A-aa-ai-e-e-e-e-e-E-E-E!" The physician quickly threw down the cards and said, "Now it's time."

In my thirty years of friendship with Freud I frequently heard him tell Jewish anecdotes or quote witticisms, but never for their own end, never for mere amusement. In most cases, the comical story was used as illustration of a point he had made, a comparison of a certain situation or behavior pattern, or as an instance of the human experiences we all share. It was as if he brought the joke forward as an example of how wisdom is expressed in wit. Some of his stories compared actual situations with various aspects of the troubled life of the Jews. The need to make something clear let him call up some funny Jewish anecdote from the treasures of his almost photographically faithful memory. On rare occasions such illustrative or comparative purpose was replaced by some whimsical or satirical trend in which he made fun of the stupidity or hypocrisy of some antagonist.

While Freud was still alive, I published several articles on Jewish humor in which I resumed his research and tried to discover new characteristics of Jewish wit. In a conversation on that subject, Freud acknowledged that I had succeeded in pointing out two features he had not emphasized. He confirmed my impression that we laugh at those stories, but Jewish wit is not merry in its character. It is a kind of humor that leaves sadness in its wake. One of these profound proverbs proclaims: "Suffering makes one laugh too." Another characteristic feature of a Jewish joke is its emotional intimacy, a special atmosphere in which it is born and bred.

On one occasion, in discussing with me the secondary gains and advantages which a patient can derive from the established fact that he is mentally ill, Freud told the following anecdote: A man in an insane asylum rejects the food there and insists on having kosher dishes. His demand is fulfilled and he is served food prepared according to the Jewish dietary law. On the next Saturday the patient is seen comfortably smoking a cigar. His physician indignantly points out to him that a religious man who observes the dietary laws should not smoke on Saturday. The patient replies: "Then what am I *meshuge* (crazy) for?" I have sometimes quoted this story to patients, illustrating that they often manage to wangle various secondary compensations in the form of attention, love and even financial support from others as a result of their neurosis.

On another occasion, Freud told of a patient in whom a grossly selfish tendency, which was conscious, was put into the foreground disguising an intense unconscious need for atonement and punishment. "Do you remember the anecdote of Jacob at the synagogue on Yom Kippur?" Freud asked me. The premise of that story is based on the fact that seats for the service on the High Holidays have to be paid for, and poor Jews often cannot afford the price. Jacob pleads with the sexton at the door of the synagogue to let him enter because he has to convey an important business message to a Mr. Eisenstein who is attending the service. But the sexton is adamant in his refusal, saying, "I know you, you *gonnif* (scoundrel)! You only want to get in to *daven* (pray)!"

It is obvious that Freud loved Jewish anecdotes which were familiar to him since boyhood. He included examples of subtle and coarse, pessimistic and hopeful Jewish wit, of genuine Jewish humor, and of wit whose essence is generally human and of which only the accessories are Jewish.

In sharp contrast to so many previous attempts at evaluating and interpreting the character of Jewish humor, Freud's point of view is pervasively psychological. In penetrating the façade of those precious stories, in demonstrating their technique and in revealing their dynamics as well as their means and methods, he shows their emotional meaning. In their psychoanalytic interpretation he arrives at the recesses of the heart that beats in them. Cautiously removing layer after layer, he demonstrates their secret tendencies, their social and individual skepticism, their knowledge of the quintessence of life, and the profundity of their views.

Freud comments on the self-irony of Jewish humor: "I do not know whether one often finds a people that makes so unreservedly merry over its own shortcomings." He contrasts stories invented by Jews and directed against Jewish social and religious manners and mannerisms with jokes made by anti-Semites making fun of the same foibles and failures. Those jokes, made by gentiles who ridicule Jews, "are nearly all brutal buffooneries in which the wit is spoiled by the fact that the Jew appears as a comic figure to a stranger." The Jewish jokes which originate with Jews know and acknowledge the weaknesses of their people, "but they know their merits as well as their shortcomings."

In Freud's view, the self-ironical and sometimes even self-degrading character of Jewish humor was psychologically possible only under the premise of an unconscious or preconscious awareness of the high value and worth of one's own people, of a concealed national pride. Only a person who stands on an elevated place can jump down. Only a proud man can stoop to ridiculing himself. What emerges clearly is that Freud, in his handling of Jewish material, reveals a deep sympathy for the unbroken spirit and dignity of the Jewish people.

Franz Kafka

Harry Zohn

SOME years ago Professor Sol Liptzin undertook to trace the Jewishness of German writers in his book *Germany's Stepchildren*, and more recently, during the second "Dialogue in Israel," he stated that "Jewish books may be defined as books which embody Jewish wisdom of the past, Jewish insight of the present, and Jewish Messianism directed toward the future, books which communicate values, visions, attitudes and aspirations of the Jewish religious, cultural, and historic community, regardless in what language these books are written."

Earlier Ludwig Lewisohn had given an equally serviceable, albeit controversial definition: "A Jewish book is a book by a Jew who knows that his ultimate self is Jewish and that his creativity and that deepest self are one . . . Jewish literature consists of those books, written in whatever age or tongue, whose authors knew that they were *jüdische mentshen*."

Consonant with these definitions, substantial evidence can be marshalled to justify the thesis that Franz Kafka was—to the extent that he could be anything—a *homo judaicus*, that there *is* Jewish significance in his books, that in Kafka we find not only Jewishness but something even rarer in a writer: *Yiddishkeit*.

Franz Kafka was a Jew living in Czechoslovakia who wrote in German. The ancient Jewish community of Prague has been called "the mother of Jewry." Its origin was in Eastern Europe, and the legacy of Slavic traditions in language and culture is evident in the Hebrew writings of the twelfth and thirteenth centuries. Later, the influx of Jews into Prague was mainly from Germany. Throughout the Middle Ages Prague Jewry maintained a vital connection with the Czech language and culture; the first Czech grammarian was a Talmudist from the Prague ghetto.

But there was a dual cultural stream. It is well to remember that the first German university was founded not in Germany, but in Prague —in 1348, by Charles IV; it was where Franz Kafka took his doctorate of laws in 1906. Because of pressure from the Hapsburg emperors, the Germanization of Prague Jewry gradually came about, particularly in the eighteenth century, at the time of Maria Theresa and the "enlightened despot" Joseph II, whose Edict of Tolerance in 1781 for all practical purposes abolished the ghetto (although the Jews did not obtain full civil rights until 1860).

The Jews now shared in German culture to an ever increasing extent. But this coincided with the spiritual and cultural revival of the Czech people. Thus the German-Jewish population of Prague became again what it had once been: a small minority, more and more cut off from the homogeneous Czech population, oriented toward Germany, yet very different from the uncongenial Sudeten Germans whose outlook and aspirations were not those of the Jews.

In Kafka's time, thirty-four thousand of the four hundred and fifteen thousand inhabitants of Prague were German-speaking, and the Jews formed but one segment of these. Like most of his fellow Jews in Prague, Kafka was a *Bildungsdeutscher* only. Lacking the vitalizing influence of a local dialect, Prague German was a curiously disembodied and sterile instrument. One detects in Kafka a yearning to transcend the limitations of this language and attain a closer communion with his Jewish roots, as witness this diary entry of October, 1911:

> Yesterday it occurred to me that I did not always love my mother as she deserved and as I could, only because the German language prevented it. The Jewish mother is no *Mutter,* to call her *Mutter* makes her a little comic; we give a Jewish woman the name of a German mother, but forget the contradiction that sinks into the emotions so much the more heavily; *Mutter* is peculiarly German for the Jew, it unconsciously contains, together with the Christian splendor, Christian coldness also; the Jewish woman who is called *Mutter* therefore becomes not only comic but strange. *Mama* would be a better name if only one didn't imagine *Mutter* behind it. I believe that it is only the memories of the ghetto that still preserve the Jewish family, for the word *Vater* too is far from meaning the Jewish father.

Still, in more ways than one, Kafka was an inhabitant of a ghetto—no longer a religious or political ghetto, but a linguistic, cultural, social one. (Walking through the streets of Prague with uncertain steps, Kafka felt like a spook of bygone times—so he said—for the unhealthy old ghetto was much more real within him than the hygienic new city around him; within him the dark corners, mysterious hallways, dirty courtyards and noisy taverns were still alive.)

When Kafka was growing up, the German Jew in Prague was, typically, an industrialist, a prosperous businessman, a leading bank official, a doctor or a lawyer with a large practice, or a university professor. The Jews almost monopolized wholesale merchandising, the import and export trade. Their workers and domestic servants were Czechs, and, in many cases, so were their lovers. In German-Jewish circles, Czech was spoken only to these workers, domestics and paramours.

Next to Viennese Jewry, the Prague Jews were the cultural élite of the Hapsburg monarchy. Remaining aloof from everything Czech, only marginally Jewish in a religious and cultural sense, but also repelled by German patriotism of the Sudeten variety, the German-speaking Jew of Prague (and no one felt this more starkly than Kafka) was a stranger in three senses: as a Jew, by blood and creed; as a prosperous citizen, in the midst of petty bourgeois and proletarians; and as a "German," but not one who was surrounded and backed up by a German nation. These people were almost exiles in their own country, and while many were never even quite conscious of their strange situation, some intellectuals did realize it and tried to escape from the Prague ghetto, out into the world.

In his book *Franz Kafka and Prague,* Pavel Eisner makes the point that Jewish men of letters fled this spiritual ghetto in various ways.

> Franz Werfel escaped through his connections with Vienna, through his cult of the Southern Baroque, through his praise of Verdi in programmatic contrast with the traditional Wagner cult of the Prague German Jews, and above all (a notable instance of sublimated erotic symbiosis) through his exaltation of the Czech nurse to the position of a saint, of a refuge from the world and epitome of all purity and meekness . . . Max Brod escaped through his fervent Zionism, but also through immersion in the most authentically Czech music of a man like Leoš Janáček . . . Egon Erwin Kisch freed himself through his world traveling and his radical socialism . . . Willy Haas did so by migrating to Berlin.

And so, particularly in the early part of this century, there was a veritable outpouring of Jewish genius from Prague, Bohemia and Moravia.

Franz Kafka was neither strong nor lucky enough to effect an escape except through his writing. He was a compulsive writer; he once called writing a form of prayer. He had certain things in common with the Expressionist writers of his generation, notably their rebellion against the father generation. "My writing was all about you," Franz once wrote his father Hermann Kafka. "All I did there, after all, was to bemoan what I could not bemoan upon your breast." Kafka's entire work may thus be viewed as one great attempt to escape from the overt and covert tyranny of his father.

The letter to his father which Kafka wrote in 1919 and which never reached its addressee is a literary and personal document of great importance, Kafka's fullest attempt at an autobiography, an *apologia pro vita sua.* It is Kafka's sincere and presumably agonizing attempt at justifying himself to his father, a patriarchal, strong-willed, self-

satisfied, healthy extrovert, basically a well-meaning person proud of
his business acumen, a man whose failure to understand the genius,
aspirations and problems of his gifted son had produced a serious
estrangement between the two. (It should be noted that a number of
Jewish writers of Kafka's generation—natives of Prague or Vienna or
Berlin—encountered similar apathy and even active opposition on the
part of their successful industrialist fathers; Stefan Zweig, Siegfried
Trebitsch and Franz Werfel are cases in point.)

When he wrote his letter, Kafka was aware of the things his father
held against him: his writings, few of which had been published and
which, moreover, his father did not understand; his failure to marry,
establish a home and found a family (the subject of countless, ever-
recurring, excruciating self-reproaches on Kafka's part); his timidity
and obstinacy; and his seeming indifference to Judaism. This last
point is a crucial one. Kafka berates his father for having passed on to
him but a meaningless scrap of Judaism and for pretending that these
superficial trappings of Jewishness were the genuine article, for believing "in the absolute rightness of the opinions of a certain class of
Jewish businessmen." Since the father disliked and distrusted all his
son's occupations, he apparently resented the writer's attempts to
deepen his Jewish heritage and approach Judaism on a more spiritual
and meaningful plane.

Kafka had occasion to come close to the *Ostjudentum,* the Eastern
European brand of Jewishness, which fascinated him with its vitality.
Our best documentation of this encounter is found in Kafka's
voluminous *Diaries* (1910–23). In 1910 and 1911 a troupe of Yiddish
actors was installed in a Prague coffee-house, and viewing these plays
and becoming acquainted with some of the players constituted a Jewish education for Kafka. His diary chronicles many evenings *"bei den
Juden."* Kafka thoughtfully comments on the plays of Abraham Gold-
faden (*Schulamis, Bar Kokhba*) and Jacob Gordin (*Shechite Gott,
Mentsh und Teufel*—the Jewish *Faust*); he discusses Talmudic lore
and Jewish customs like the *mikveh* and the baking of matzos; he
reflects on the Hasidic tales that a man named Langer told him (the
same man who in Marienbad took him to visit a "wonder rabbi").

The same mind is at work here that later re-examined and boldly
recast some basic mythological tales of ancient Israel, Hellas, the Far
East and the West. Of interest also are Kafka's impressions of his
nephew's circumcision which he attended in 1911.

> Today, when I heard the *mohel's* assistant say the grace after
> meals and those present, aside from the two grandfathers, spent
> the time in dreams or boredom with a complete lack of under-

standing of the prayer, I saw Western European Judaism before
me in a transition whose end is clearly unpredictable and about
which those most closely affected are not concerned, but, like all
people truly in transition, bear what is imposed upon them. It is
so indisputable that these religious forms which have reached
their final end have merely a historical character, even as they are
practiced today, that only a short time was needed this very morning to interest the people present in the obsolete custom of circumcision and its half-sung prayers by describing it to them as
something out of history.

On the first of November, 1911, Kafka "eagerly and happily" began
to read the *History of the Jews* by Graetz. "Because my desire for it had
far outrun the reading, it was at first stranger to me than I thought,
and I had to stop here and there in order, by resting, to allow my
Jewishness to collect itself." There is a touch of Kafkaesque humor in
the *Diaries* when he records the favorite saying of the wife of the
philosopher Moses Mendelssohn (which may be taken as a valid Jewish reaction to the mainstream of European culture at a time when
Jews could be part of it but found that it only brought them new
problems and unhappiness): *"Wie mies ist mir vor tout l'univers!"*
(How sick and tired I am of the whole universe!) Later Kafka read
and took notes on Pines' *Histoire de la Littérature Judéo-Allemande,*
published in Paris in 1911, commenting on the *Haskalah* movement,
the Baal Shem, and the giants of Yiddish literature: Mendele, Peretz,
Sholom Aleichem.

Through his attendance of plays *"bei den Juden,"* Kafka got close
to some of the actors. One of his rare public appearances took
place in February, 1912, when he introduced an evening of Yiddish
recitations by Isak Lowy in the auditorium of the Prague City Hall
with a perceptive little speech on the Yiddish language (which Kafka,
to be sure, called *"jargon"*): "I would have you realize, ladies and
gentlemen, how much more Yiddish you understand than you
think . . ." In one of his conversations with Gustav Janouch, Kafka
said: "I should like to run to those poor Jews of the ghetto, kiss the
hem of their coats, and say not a word. I should be completely happy
if only they would endure my presence in silence."

It must not be inferred from the above, however, that Eastern European *Yiddishkeit* was a fountain of life and hope, the solution for
Kafka. He never quite found the bridge between Western Jewishness
as he knew it and Eastern Jewishness as he yearned for it. In 1913, for
example, he chronicled a meeting with the physician-writer Ernst
Weiss, whom he called "a Jew of the kind that is closest to the type of

the Western Jew and to whom one therefore immediately feels close. The tremendous advantage of Christians who always have and enjoy such feelings of closeness in general intercourse, for instance a Christian Czech among Christian Czechs." The same kind of ambivalence is reflected in this anguished question: "What do I have in common with the Jews when I don't have anything in common with myself?" In later years Kafka carried on a notable correspondence with his Czech translator Milena Jesenska, whom he regarded as his soul-mate. Milena, a non-Jew, was married to Ernst Pollak, a Jew, and this inspired Kafka to many musings and expressions on Judaism and Jewishness.

It has been alleged that Kafka in later life turned Zionist and that Zionism filled the spiritual void in his life; and there appears to be some truth in this—although almost any statement one makes about Kafka is bound to be fraught with ambivalence. Kafka's friends Hugo Bergmann, Felix Weltsch and Max Brod (all of whom eventually settled in Palestine) shared their own Zionist fervor with Kafka, who avidly studied Hebrew and seems to have had a practical rather than a merely theoretical interest in Zionism. When Janouch once asked him: "Are you convinced that Zionism is the right path?," Kafka is said to have replied: "The rightness or wrongness of the path is never recognized until one has reached one's goal. In any case, we are on our way."

Kafka's last great friend, Dora Dymant, was a pious Jewish girl from Poland whom he met in 1923 at a Jewish vacation colony near a Baltic resort and with whom he lived until the end of his brief life, enjoying a modicum of happiness and hope for the future. He and Dora, whose Orthodox background stood in the way of a possible marriage, toyed with the idea of emigrating to Palestine, although by then Kafka's progressive consumption of the larynx made such plans little but morbid fancies. Kafka once said that he had refused to grasp the last fringes of the vanishing Jewish prayer shawl, as the Zionists had done, but Felix Weltsch believes to this day that Kafka was a Zionist and that the Zionist ideal was in keeping with Kafka's striving for an uncompromisingly pure life.

The story of Max Brod's editorship of Kafka's works is by now a thrice-told tale, and Kafka's request to his friend, whom he had met at the university in Prague, that all of his unpublished writings and diaries be destroyed after his death, is as well known as Brod's well-premeditated failure to do so. One cannot help but wonder why Kafka entrusted Brod, of all people, with this melancholy mission, when he had ample reason to believe that Brod would be the least likely man to carry it out. The Freudians may well have a field day with this, as they have had with all of Kafka's enigmatic writings. They constitute one major school within the vast canon of Kafka criticism. Another is the generally social-cultural school of interpretation and the third is the metaphysical-religious-mystical school.

It is this last to which Max Brod himself belongs, and for many years he has tried, with varying success, to superimpose his own vibrant Judaism and Zionism upon the interpretation of Kafka. Brod views the three fragmentary novels *Amerika, The Trial* and *The Castle* as one great allegorical trilogy concerned with Jewish fate in the Diaspora. "The word 'Jew' hardly appears in *The Castle*," Brod points out, "yet K., in the novel, straight from his Jewish soul, in a simple story, has said more about the situation of Jewry as a whole today than can be read in a hundred learned treatises."

Brod is not alone in his view that *The Trial* highlights the kind of guiltless guilt a Jew incurs in the modern world. Pavel Eisner points out that Josef K. in *The Trial* is arrested by a German (Rabensteiner), a Czech (Kullich) and a Jew (Kaminer); they may well represent the population of Prague. And if Josef K. is a Jew and has certain autobiographical features (although there is no evidence in the novel that he is Jewish; in fact, his mother goes to church), he is thrice guilty and fit to be arrested: as a Jew vis-à-vis the German population; as an assimilated Jew in the face of Orthodox Jewishness; and as a German vis-à-vis his Czech surroundings. And in an essay entitled "Anti-Semitism as an Issue in the Trial of Kafka's Joseph K.," Josef Waldmeier, while conceding that all allegory is ambiguous, believes that Josef K. is doomed by an anti-Semitic judgment, with all the irrationality and finality that this implies.

Another Kafka work that lends itself to a Jewish interpretation is the story "Josephine the Singer, or the Mice Nation." This may be regarded as Kafka's picture of the Jewish people in the Diaspora, and his community feeling for it. In Josephine the artist we have the ambivalent figure of the prophet within the Jewish people, which appears here in humorous ironical form as one that has but a dim memory of its religious mission but proves most durable in the face of hardship and persecution. The mice nation displays a curious mixture of shrewdness and guilelessness, an attachment to freedom despite a long history of bondage, to dreams despite a long history of harsh reality. The presence of Josephine teaches the people the existence of something higher, but they do not quite surrender to it, remaining realists, believing and doubting at the same time—the Jewish people's attitude toward its spiritual heritage. Josephine's singing is presumably God's Word, but it is only a pale carbon copy of the songs heard long ago, and there is doubt as to the genuineness of her singing. The final disappearance of the singer may symbolize the end of the attempt to actualize the Jewish spiritual heritage in a forceful and forcible manner.

The search for Jewish elements in Kafka must ultimately be viewed as but one of many valid approaches to his work and his legend. As the British Germanist H. M. Waidson has put it, "The study of Kafka is something like the building of the Great Wall of China. It may be an incommensurable task to complete the work and make it impregnable, the building operations may give rise to unprovable legends, but the task is one of undeniable fascination, even if it makes unprecedented demands upon the builder's sense of responsibility."

In one of his cryptic, elliptic statements Kafka said: "Sometimes I believe that I understand the Fall as no one else." His work in its totality, after patient study, teaches Jews and non-Jews alike to understand it a little better as well.

Mordecai M. Kaplan

Trude Weiss-Rosmarin

MORDECAI M. KAPLAN was born in Swenziany, a small Lithuanian town, on June 11, 1881. Three months earlier Czar Alexander III had ascended the throne of Russia and pledged fullest support to Pobyedonostzev's policy of solving "the Jewish problem" by killing one third of Russia's Jews, baptizing another third and forcing the rest to emigrate.

Mordecai's father, Rabbi Israel Kaplan, was among those who emigrated. He arrived in New York in 1888 and a year later, after he had established a modest home, his wife and their two children joined him in the New World.

Mordecai Kaplan was eight years old when he first set foot on American soil. At that time, American Jewry numbered about four hundred thousand. Today, over seventy years later, an American Jewish community of close to six million is the concern of Professor Kaplan as he enters "the age of strength"—as Jewish tradition knows the ninth decade of life. Looking younger than his age, he continues to astound his associates and friends with his boundless energy and unlimited zest.

In 1956, at a testimonial in honor of his seventy-fifth birthday, Professor Kaplan volunteered his formula of adding life to years while adding years to life. He ascribed his vigor to his paying daily "insurance premiums" to good health in the form of long naps and long walks. Among the dividends of this policy in the ensuing five years are his four books (*A New Zionism, Questions Jews Ask: Reconstructionist Answers, Judaism Without Supernaturalism* and *The Greater Judaism in the Making*), scores of important essays and policy-setting addresses, hundreds of lectures, teaching at the University of Judaism in Los Angeles and at The Hebrew University of Jerusalem and, last but not least, keeping a father's watchful eye on the destinies of the Reconstructionist movement and the Society for the Advancement of Judaism.

Mordecai Kaplan's more than seventy years in this country, of which sixty were spent in active service as rabbi and teacher of rabbis, and in developing a Jewish philosophy for Jews in the modern world, coincided with the period of American Jewry's emergence as the largest and most important Diaspora community. To the molding of the spiritual-religious complexion of American Jewry, Kaplan has made the largest single contribution, one which will still grow in importance.

Harold M. Schulweis aptly states that "every Conservative congregation has something of Reconstructionism in it." In point of fact, *every* American Jewish congregation with an English speaking rabbi "has something of Reconstructionism in it." The Orthodox synagogue centers which are proliferating, and the hundreds of Reform temples which stress "Jewish peoplehood" and "Jewish art and music" are no less under the sway of Reconstructionist principles than are the Conservative congregations whose rabbis—with the exception of the latest crop of graduates—were taught by Professor Kaplan at the Jewish Theological Seminary for half a century. He taught homiletics, the course most important for the rabbi in his primary function as preacher.

When Kaplan came to the Seminary, the sermon in general vogue was a display exercise in Talmudic scholarship for the benefit of a learned handful. Kaplan proscribed such display and demanded instead that his students learn to apply the traditional texts to the problems agitating their people. This was not easy. Frequently Kaplan's "monumental temper," as Ira Eisenstein terms it, would flare up "when he encountered stupidity or fuzzy thinking." However, his students "were ever thankful to him because he made them think."

A thinker himself, Kaplan has made *all* thoughtful American Jews *think*. Like the students in his classes at the Seminary, some have gone through "traumatic experiences on first exposure to his relentless logic." While the number of "orthodox" Reconstructionists is not large, it can be said that "every American Jew who positively identifies as a Jew has something of Reconstructionism in him."

Although Reconstructionism has been most vigorously opposed by the Orthodox, it is not altogether out of tune with the traditional spirit of the Torah. As the term Reconstructionism indicates, Kaplan holds that Judaism *today* is *again* in need of "reconstruction" if it is to survive and remain meaningful in a world which is totally different from that of our grandparents. Very much in the spirit of the Rabbis of the Talmud and some of their medieval successors who reinterpreted the Biblical laws in keeping with the needs of their time, Kaplan always gives tradition the first *vote,* while denying it, however, the right to *veto* the legitimate claims of life. Reasserting the Talmudic principle that the Law was given to man, Kaplan presents in *Judaism as a Civilization* a modern interpretation of the Jewish tradition in its entirety.

Kaplan's thesis that reconstruction is imperative for Jewish survival was arrived at while serving as the rabbi of an Orthodox congregation. Raised in a strictly Orthodox home—his father had been associated with Rabbi Jacob Joseph—it was only upon entering the rabbinate

that young Kaplan became alert to the need of making Jewish tradition meaningful for the new generation. Much to the chagrin of his
congregation, the young rabbi preached sermons in which he critically
examined the American Jewish scene, suggesting new policies and new
programs. The result was, as Kaplan recalls, "I got myself into
trouble."

Fortunately, this "trouble" coincided with Solomon Schechter's arrival to become president of the reorganized Jewish Theological Seminary. Schechter appointed Kaplan dean of the newly established
Teachers' Institute and, soon after, asked him to serve also as Professor
of Homiletics at the Seminary.

Kaplan's *Judaism as a Civilization* was published in 1934 after its
author, in his fifty-third year, had lived and preached Reconstructionism for more than a quarter of a century. The Society for the Advancement of Judaism, the first and only Reconstructionist congregation at
that time, had been in existence since 1922. A small and struggling
group, it provided its leader with a platform for expounding his views
and a laboratory for testing his theories.

Reconstructionism is not à philosophy developed in an ivory tower
or a cloistered study. It is a three-dimensional portrait of Jewishness
set in the framework of a purposive program of how to apply these
dimensions to the Jewish present and future. While the book's
descriptive chapters set forth the many-faceted aspects and implications of the tradition, its programmatic sections delineate how the
tradition can be fused with the environment of contemporary Jews.

Basically, Kaplan addresses himself to the identical problem which
agitated the great medieval Jewish philosophers. Like Saadia,
Maimonides, Halevi, Gabirol, he is profoundly concerned over those
who, as Saadia put it, "were drowning in the seas of doubt and there
was none to save them." To be sure, "the seas of doubt" of Saadia's
time (882–942) were quite different from those of the first third of our
century. But the cause of the increase in the number of "perplexed"
was the same: the impact upon Jews of a culture-and-philosophy which
seemed to negate Jewish tradition.

The medieval Jewish philosophers vindicated Judaism by demonstrating that it could hold its own with Aristotle and Plato. Moreover,
they stressed that while being no less "philosophical" than philosophy,
Judaism has the advantage of being in possession of the illumination of
revelation.

Logically formulated rationalism, the virtually exclusive concern of
medieval philosophy, had to give way to "the century of Darwin."
Although Darwin's theory of evolution was concerned only with bi-
ology, submitting that the species *developed* in an ascending line from

primitive to advanced organisms, instead of having been *created,* the implications of Darwinism led to complete reorientation in the humanities as well. Historians and sociologists adduced data proving the "evolution" of cultures and societies, and the psychologists, Freud in particular, showed how the psyche "evolved" from primitive consciousness to its advanced and complex organization.

In another area, while Einstein's theory of relativity dealt with the electrodynamics of moving bodies and the relationship of mass and mechanical energy, the term "relativity" soon became a slogan of both the humanities and philosophy. The result was that absolutes were consigned to limbo, as Bergson's individualism of the *élan vital* became the *popular* philosophy of the day.

Kaplan's *Judaism as a Civilization* must be viewed against the background and within the context of Darwin, Einstein, Bergson and Freud. It is as surely a duel (or dialogue) between Judaism and the spirit of the twentieth century as was Maimonides' *Guide for the Perplexed* a duel (or dialogue) with the ruling philosophy of the twelfth century.

In accord with the evolutionary orientation of our time, Kaplan defined Judaism as an *"evolving* civilization." All and everything in Judaism are the result of evolution—attained by a step-by-step advance. Nothing was "given" or "revealed." There was no revelation and no giving of the Torah. God is not an Absolute but the projection of man's need to transcend himself. It is not God who created man but rather man who postulates God as a functional necessity. Kaplan writes, "We can no longer believe that God is a mighty sovereign, or that the universe is the work of His hands." He defines the God-idea "not as an idea but the reaction of the entire organism to life, the reaction by which man's will-to-live overcomes the fears and the miseries that only a being of his mental capacity can know." It is thus that Kaplan arrives at his definition of God as "the power that makes for salvation because we believe in the power that makes for salvation."

This is naturalism, of course. In recent years, the "religion without naturalism" tone of Reconstructionism has become more articulate. While in *Judaism as a Civilization,* Kaplan's accentuation of naturalism was not overly strong, *The Greater Judaism in the Making* (published thirty-six years later, in 1960) is almost militantly naturalistic, insisting that religion is not God-given but created (or rather "developed") by man driven by his "intrinsic need of salvation and self-fulfillment."

Those whom Kaplan terms "traditionalists" will of course ask what is the sense of praying and observing rituals when neither the prayer nor the rituals have absolute validity as the commandments of God. In *Questions Jews Ask,* Kaplan insists that we can and must conceive of God as "personal" so as to be able to pray—as pray we must to express ourselves religiously—yet without detracting from the majestic maturity of the concept of God as a process, that is to say, as the power that makes for salvation. He writes:

> Modern scientific and philosophic thought regards all reality not as something static but as energy in action. When we say that God is Process, we select, out of the infinity of processes in the universe, that complex of forces and relationships which makes for the highest fulfillment of man as a human being, and identify it by the term *God.* In exactly the same way, we select, among all the forces and relationships that enter into the life of the individual, those which make for his highest fulfillment and identify them by the term *person. God* and *person* are thus correlative terms, the meaning of each being relative to and dependent on that of the other, like *parent* and *child, teacher* and *pupil, citizen* and *state. God is the Process by which the universe produces persons, and persons are the processes by which God is manifest in the individual.*

"Prayer," Kaplan continues, "aims at deriving from the Process that constitutes God the power that would strengthen the forces and relationships by which we fulfill ourselves as persons." As for the "personal God" whom we address as "Thou" in prayer, Kaplan explains, in keeping with Jewish tradition, that "God is personal to us" without yet being a person or possessing personal-corporeal attributes. "He can not even be viewed as thinking, feeling or willing in any manner comparable to the way man does."

In their criticism of Maimonides' God concept, various medieval rabbis pointed out—as do contemporary opponents of Reconstructionism—that the God concept which is purged of all anthropomorphism is too abstract to be comforting. In the final analysis, the God of the philosophers is too remote to be addressed as "Thou" in earnest. Faith, like love, thrives on irrational illusions. Absolute logic demolishes faith and no amount of post-logical rationalizing can restore the naive trust with which the unsophisticated pietist turns to God. This is the crux of all rationalistic theologies—they satisfy the mind in direct proportion to the extent they impoverish the religious emotion which wants to reach out to the Father in Heaven.

Obviously, we cannot turn back the clock and retreat to the unsophisticated world into which Kaplan was born. By the same token, however, we cannot delude ourselves into believing that prayer by rationalization is what the makers of Jewish tradition considered to be God's command.

Maimonides' impact on Judaism was least enduring in the realm of theology and philosophy. Similarly, Kaplan's theology and philosophy have barely caused a ripple outside the small circle of philosophically oriented sophisticates. Despite the fact that for many decades he was the only faculty member of the Jewish Theological Seminary who represented a school of thought to which most of his students pledged at least a partial loyalty, Reconstructionism as a movement has remained small. Somehow, American Jewry has not taken to the Reconstructionist philosophy, and Kaplan's God concept of the Process is no more appealing to our contemporaries than was Maimonides' God concept of the One who is altogether beyond definition-and-description. If men feel like praying and want to pray, they turn to the God who is "the scandal" of the philosophers.

Kaplan's impact on modern Jewish thought has been greater in the non-theological areas. His accentuation of the evolutionary nature of Judaism in its totality has been virtually universally adopted. Except among a small group of ultra-Orthodox, his definition of "Judaism as an evolving religious civilization" is almost standard. If the greatness of a thinker is measured by the extent of the *unacknowledged* victory of the popular aspects of his philosophy, Kaplan qualifies as the greatest, most influential Jewish philosopher of our time.

Thus we speak of "living in two civilizations—the American civilization and the Jewish civilization"—within the context of "the organic Jewish community" where "the centrality of the synagogue" is firmly entrenched, while acknowledging that "religion must cease to be the sole pre-occupation" of Jews. We stress the "social values" of the Jewish center, particularly the synagogue center, without remembering that the first synagogue center was patterned on Kaplan's blueprint and that all Jewish centers (like all synagogues) "have something of Reconstructionism in them."

Similarly, the vocabulary of American Zionist ideologists is the vocabulary which Kaplan developed for recasting Ahad Ha-am's thesis of "the Spiritual Center" (Israel) and "the Spiritual Periphery" (Diaspora) into a mold adapted for American Jewry.

An innovator and a "non-conformist," Kaplan has many opponents and critics. Even in the ranks of the Reconstructionist movement, there are many who part company with him. There are Reconstructionists who do not accept Kaplan's rejection of the idea of Jewish chosenness, which he regards as a manifestation of exclusivism and chauvinism. Others are unhappy with the Reconstructionist Prayer Book and the Reconstructionist Haggadah for Passover and their changed wordings of the prayers.

The most apt description of the American Jewish community's attitude toward Kaplan comes from his son-in-law and closest associate, Ira Eisenstein:

> Among Zionist leaders he is regarded as unrealistic for believing that Jewish life can possibly thrive in the Diaspora; among the non-Zionists and anti-Zionists he is accused of setting up Israel as the authoritative center of a theocratic realm. Among social workers he is considered too much of a theologian; among theologians he is charged with being nothing more than a sociologist. Among those who call for the integration of Jews into American life, his blueprint for the organic community seems like a plan for a new ghetto; while those who worry about assimilation cannot reconcile themselves to his insistence that Jews live in two civilizations. Those who are acquainted with his personal habits of Jewish observance confuse him with the Orthodox; while the Orthodox rail at his suggestion that ritual should be removed from the category of Halakkah. Finally, he himself reports that he has been taken "for a thinker among men of action, and for a man of action among thinkers." But all agree that, right or wrong, Mordecai M. Kaplan must be recognized as one of the foremost philosophers of Judaism in the twentieth century.

Isaac Bashevis Singer

Milton Hindus

THERE is increasing recognition among English-speaking audiences of
the distinction of Yiddish storyteller and novelist Isaac Bashevis
Singer. His popularity is not likely ever to rival that of Sholem Asch;
Singer is too sensitive and intellectual to attract masses of readers. His
style in Yiddish is spare and understated, lean and direct. He writes
about the supernatural, the world of spirits, possessed people, students
of Spinoza and other unpopular philosophers. His characters live in
bygone Warsaw, where he was born and where his imagination continues to live, although he has made his home in New York for more
than a quarter of a century.

Isaac Bashevis Singer was born in Radzymin, Poland, in 1904. He
was eleven years younger than his brother I. J. Singer, author of the
novel *The Brothers Ashkenazi* and the famous Yiddish play *Yoshe
Kalb,* which has had a long run. I. B. Singer, since his arrival in this
country in 1935, has been a prolific writer for the Yiddish press, his
material appearing each week in the *Jewish Daily Forward* under
three different names. Many of his excellent articles could be creditable
additions to literature.

His reputation in English is grounded solidly on seven books which
have been translated in recent years—four novels and three collections
of stories.*

In addition to the Yiddish Lamed Prize, Singer has won a grant
from the National Institute of Arts and Letters. His story *Gimpel, the
Fool,* called by the London *Times* Literary Supplement, "the greatest
schlemiel story in literature," has been widely anthologized in short
story collections.

First in the order of appearance in English (though not in Yiddish)
was *The Family Moskat,* published in 1950. The English edition of
over six hundred pages is a somewhat abbreviated version of the two-
volume Yiddish text. Concerned with the decline of a wealthy Jewish
family in the time between the early years of the twentieth century
(before World War I) and the attack of Hitler upon Poland, the novel
is the largest and most realistic of Singer's works. It contains halluci-
natory passages (dealing with dreams) that invite comparison with the
art of his better known countryman, Marc Chagall.

Dozens of characters, major and minor, move through its pages,

* This includes his latest novel *The Slave* (1962) and a new collection of short
stories *Short Friday* (1964), both published after this article was written and therefore not discussed herein.

sharply and individually etched. The panoramic plot includes many subsidiary stories managed by the author with the expertness of a juggler who keeps a dozen balls in motion at once. The imagery is vivid, colorful, and occasionally has an obsessive, illuminating quality revealing in a flash the essence of a situation.

Take, for example, Singer's description of peddlers in a Warsaw market place:

> "Gold, gold, gold!" a beshawled woman shouted from beside a crate of squashed oranges. "Sugar-sweet, sugar-sweet!" sang out a plump girl guarding a basket of moldy plums. "Wine, wine, wine!" shrieked a red-faced, red-headed peddler, displaying a basket of spoiled grapes.

Principal character of the book is Asa Heshel Bannet, but the true protagonist is the city of Warsaw, particularly Jewish Warsaw, described romantically in the diary of the heroine.

Singer is interested in picturing the decline of the house of Moskat rather than in explaining it. "Who can explain?" Walt Whitman once asked.

Singer deals in this book with the foundering of an entire civilization. The most terrible shipwrecks dwindle into puniness beside the catastrophe that overwhelmed the Jewish community of Poland during World War II. The holocaust itself is not pictured, but the coming events clearly cast their shadow. The worst happens not before our eyes but off-stage, as in Greek tragedy, heightening the pathos of the story and making it a more powerful, because more restrained, rendition of the destruction of European Jewry, the theme of the better-known André Schwarz-Bart's *The Last of the Just,* which sought to bring us in imagination to the very door of the gas chambers.

The English translation of *The Family Moskat* gains a macabre effect by truncating the conclusion of Singer's original Yiddish text, ending with a conversation between two of the doomed intellectuals as Warsaw is being bombed. Hertz Yanovar says to Asa Heshel Bannet: "I've got no more strength. . . . The Messiah will come soon." To which Asa replies in astonishment: "What do you mean?" And the last line of the book, leaving all sorts of ironic echoes in its wake, is Yanovar's reply: "Death is the Messiah. That's the real truth."

In Singer's Yiddish text the story does not end here. There are a dozen more pages, in which intellectuals press the question as to whether their lifelong orientation toward modern thought and ideas rather than traditional Jewish values is not the source of their present tragic situation.

There is also a group of Zionists starting out in search of a new life.

In fact, each of the characters has chosen one of four different possibilities: some have gone to America; at least one, the daughter of a Jew converted to Christianity and herself a passionate Communist, has left for Russia (or at least the Russian zone of partitioned Poland); some set out for Palestine; but most are either compelled or choose to go down with the wreck.

The heroine Hadassah is killed by a bomb at the very beginning of the carnage, and Asa Heshel is resigned and passive before his impending fate.

The end toward which Singer's Jewish Warsaw was heading was unbelievably tragic and violent, but the community had long been disintegrating. In the last scenes of the story (in the Yiddish version; the English has unaccountably cut this), the house of Meshulam Moskat is left a heap of rubble by Nazi bombs; but it had begun to crumble much earlier.

One of the symptoms of its decline is the marriage of Meshulam Moskat's daughter Leah to the thieving overseer Koppel Berman and their migration to America, where Koppel promptly becomes a bootlegger. Leah's first husband had been the saintly Hasid Moshe Gabriel, as different from her second brutish husband as day from night. One of her children by her first marriage had been called Meyerl in Europe but was renamed Mendy in America. When the boy is fifteen, he is taken for a trip to Poland where he meets his real father.

> Mendy had been eager for this trip to Europe, but now he was fed up. He was tired of everything—the family, the hotels, the filth, the monotonous food, this constant talking and listening to Yiddish. He longed to be back in New York or in Saratoga Springs, where his mother took him during the summers. Mendy's mind was full of thoughts of baseball, football, horse races. He had been in the middle of a serial about Buffalo Bill. He and a friend of his, Jack, would sneak into a burlesque show once in a while. It was fun to sit in the balcony, a cigarette between your lips, chewing gum, and watch the strip-teasers take off one piece of clothing after another and finally stand there naked. He was bored by all of them—those queer uncles and aunts, who, even though he stood a head taller than any of them, kept on pinching his cheeks as though he were a baby. He made up his mind that when he got back to New York he'd never look at these greenhorns again. He'd never come to Europe again, except maybe to England.

Mendy is portentous of the spiritual attrition which is almost as much cause for alarm as the threat of physical and material destruction. Modern civilization is threatened not at one point but at many points. How are we to escape, Singer pointedly asks.

In a political and sociological sense the turning point had come in the calamitous year of 1905 (the year after Singer's birth):

> What has not happened in Warsaw since the Revolution of 1905! Hasidic youth cast off their gabardines, shaved their faces, became strikers, Zionists. Daughters of respectable homes had fallen in love with university students and had run off with them to New York, Buenos Aires, or Palestine. Mothers of children had discarded their matron's wigs and let the wide world see their own hair. It was these worldly books, printed in Yiddish, so that anyone could understand, that had poisoned decent people's minds. And these "reformed" schools, where parents were sending their daughters lately, were nothing but nests of paganism and wantonness . . .

Asa Heshel, the hero, after having experienced war and the October Revolution in 1917, returns firmly convinced that the capitalist system is the best of all economic systems. He is under no illusions as to its cruelty but attributes it to human nature and laws. Wars and revolutions, as he has seen them, have produced nothing but "hunger and a flood of silly speeches." According to his private, subjective view of the world, the Malthusian problem of overpopulation can be solved by mankind in only one way which he calls "sex-control," and which he defines as "more sex and fewer children."

When Asa Heshel's wife Adele advises him to go to a psychiatrist, his answer is that every Jew in the modern world probably needs a psychiatrist. As he watches Polish soldiers departing for the front where they are to be slaughtered like animals, he wonders at their faith. Is it religious faith? Is it Polish patriotism? "No, just healthy nerves. His father and grandfather had not spent their days sitting in the study house, bent over the Talmud." Asa Heshel's view is completely naturalistic and pagan, though he is more sensitive in expressing it than the coarse Abram Shapiro, who comments on seeing men marching off to war to be killed: "Ah, Father in heaven, You've got the heart of a bandit . . . Ah, dear Lord, what a mess You've made of things! A fine world You've managed to turn out."

The author does not necessarily identify himself with any of these views. He pictures; he does not rationalize or justify. The old-fashioned believers among his Hasidic characters are presented to us no more and no less sympathetically than the apostates and the alienated. He holds the scales evenly; he is above all passion though not above compassion. But his compassion is not of the selective, partisan kind which makes the good polemicist and propagandist but is the ruin of the artist.

His Warsaw Jews may be indiscriminately objects of persecution to the Poles, Russians and Nazis, but their wrongs and sufferings do not make them automatically or uniformly attractive, sympathetic people. Singer's Jews are human—and human nature is not presented in a roseate or optimistic light. The book of the Bible which is referred to more than any other in the thoughts of his characters is Ecclesiastes.

Aside from its distinguished esthetic qualities of rhythm, balance and proportion, the book is the most thought-provoking rendition of the experience of European Jewry in the past half century. The defects of the English version of *The Family Moskat* are due to abridgments made in the text and the occasional awkwardness of the translation, in spite of the heroic efforts of translator A. H. Gross, who died before completing his work.

But it is only fair to Singer to note that we can see his work in English only through a clouded glass. Though the translation succeeds in giving the reader a sense of the liveliness and color of the original, many Yiddish expressions have been carried over too literally, e.g., "What the black year goes on here!"

Translation is a difficult art, one with which Singer himself is familiar since he has rendered works from Hebrew, Polish and German into Yiddish. *Gimpel, the Fool,* the title story of a collection of stories, is the work of Singer's which has enjoyed the greatest popularity in English. Translated by Saul Bellow, the vigorous and lively author of *The Adventures of Augie March,* it creates the illusion of an English original so successfully that some readers and critics have attributed its triumph more to the talents of the translator than to Singer.

No reader of Singer in the original could agree; it is only that here Singer has gotten his due as a stylist. His spare and distinguished idiom has found its match in the verve of Bellow's English. Singer's present publisher has put teams at work on different stories of Singer's —one expert in English and a second expert in Yiddish. The results are not unmixed, but promise well for the future.

After *The Family Moskat,* Singer's stories seem surprisingly free from realism. The characters are an odd assortment—often sprites, demons, possessed or unborn souls; the refuse of human society, thieves, prostitutes and beggars, as well as the more familiar Spinozist intellectuals or preternaturally saintly or wise Hasidic rabbis. The author never lets his readers forget that, in the words of Gimpel, "the world is entirely an imaginary world, but it is only once removed from the true world." He makes us aware both of the difference between the daytime world of reality and the world of imagination, their similarity and interaction.

Imagination appears to him sometimes as the world of reality turned inside out. To quote Gimpel again: "Whatever doesn't really happen is dreamed at night." This conception of the imaginative realm bathes his pages with mysterious poetic light and an air of symbolic suggestiveness. In the most humble characters and most commonplace situations, Singer deciphers the message that the world is much more mysterious and wonderful than appears to our unaided sight. The people in his pages seem to be emissaries of unseen powers, either diabolical or divine. Like Herman Melville, Singer aims to penetrate the mask of deceptively simple-looking phenomena to discover the unfathomable depths below depths.

Singer's *Satan in Goray*, which first appeared in Jacob Sloan's English translation in 1955, is a short novel written many years before *The Family Moskat*. An excellent example of the historical novel, its subject is the Messianic Sabbatai Z'vi movement which afflicted seventeenth-century Jewish Poland in the wake of the Cossack chieftain Chmielnicki's pogroms of 1648. These massacres were so terrible that a Jewish chronicler of the period refused to describe them on the ground that to do so should bring shame upon the whole race of man. "They slaughtered on every hand," writes Singer matter-of-factly, "flayed men alive, murdered small children, violated women and afterwards ripped open their bellies and sewed cats inside."

The worst effects were yet to come, however, for excess of suffering unhinged the communal Jewish mind. Some of Singer's descriptions are reminiscent of Daniel Defoe's *Journal of the Plague Year*. As disease and death filled London in 1665 with impromptu preachers calling upon the people to repent, so in Singer's stricken Poland people "ran about testifying that the Jews would soon be redeemed. Some declared that they could hear the great ram's horn being blown, signifying the end of days; others aroused the people to return to God, reckoning up their own as well as the sins of others; still others danced in the street for joy, and beat drums."

In these circumstances, reason retreats and the famous scholarship of Polish Jewry is abandoned in favor of a morbid mysticism. Rabbi Benish of Goray, a devout Jew alarmed by the spread of hysterical, formless emotionalism all around him, tries to stem the encroaching tide of unreason by putting the tempting mystical volumes beyond the reach of his students. He forces them to master the traditional writings.

Mordecai Joseph, the rabbi's opponent in Goray, a Kabbalist with a desire for notoriety, cries out: "The world's aflame! Jews! Save your-selves! Jew-ws!" and the wild stampede is on. Pouring oil on the fires of hysteria until they rage out of control are the frantic followers of Sabbatai Z'vi, the false Messiah. Rabbi Benish is injured, and finally harried into leaving town.

Thereafter, the town of Goray is given over to the antics of Sabbatai Z'vi's disciples who, by their fruits, reveal themselves as the true emissaries of Satan. Their leader is a certain Reb Gedaliya, the ritual slaughterer from Zamosc, a smooth-tongued demagogue who soon makes himself virtual dictator over prostrate Goray. He introduces novel and terrible judgments of his own in complete opposition to the traditional law, and the few learned men who remain in town can do nothing to stop him.

Under the new dispensation the boundaries between good and evil are completely broken down and confused. Reb Gedaliya

> explained to young matrons ways to inflame their husbands, and whispered in their ears that, ever since Sabbatai Z'vi had been revealed, the commandment against adultery was void. It was ru-mored that young men were exchanging wives, and everyone knew that Nechele, the wife of Levi, received men in her house and sat up past midnight with them, singing prurient songs . . . The young men who studied together in the study house were up to all sorts of evil. Evenings they went to the bathhouse and, through a hole they had bored in the wall, watched the women purifying themselves.

The tyrant himself sets the example for the immoral conduct of his followers. He lives openly with Rechele, the wife of Itche Mates, who has been sent off on some fool's errand in connection with the fraudu-lent Messianic movement. Rechele is an epileptic whose seizures led her to acceptance as a prophetess in the new movement. An innocent tool of wicked schemers like Gedaliya, she dies in the process of hav-ing the evil spirit that possessed her exorcised in a terrifying ritual which recalls scenes from *The Dybbuk*.

The movement eventually collapses with the apostasy of Sabbatai Z'vi himself. Faced by the Sultan of Turkey with the choice of death or conversion to Mohammedanism, Sabbatai Z'vi forsook Judaism and died in obscurity in Albania some years later. But before this hap-pened, he had succeeded in completely splitting the Jewish commu-nity. His stubborn followers confidently expected him to come for them on a cloud and bear them in glory to Jerusalem. The demorali-zation spread by the false Messiah vied with the physical destruction inflicted by the Chmielnicki pogroms. When the spell was broken, sober-minded men like Rabbi Benish returned to work, together with repentant and misguided enthusiasts like Mordecai Joseph. It was most difficult to restore order to the community.

The grim story is a preachment on the ills to which religions are exposed. The comforts brought to believers seem on occasion to be cancelled out by the intentional frauds, self-deceivers and parasites who prey upon them. Superstition is the dark side of the medal of religion: religious ages have also been concomitantly superstitious ages, while more "enlightened" times, in ridding themselves of the evils of superstition, have not been able to retain the good of religion. This dilemma plagues each generation.

Here, too, as in the later *The Family Moskat,* Singer writes with dispassionate objectivity, lack of sentimentalism, and the sure artistic instinct, as defined by Emily Dickinson: "Tell all the truth but tell it slant." He finds the correct angle of indirection from which the story should be told. He does not bring the false Messiah, Sabbatai Z'vi, on stage but brings instead the echoes and reflections of his movement in the small town of Goray.

This same historic episode has engaged the imaginations of other talented Jewish men of letters—Israel Zangwill in *Dreamers of the Ghetto,* and Sholem Asch in a play *Sabbatai Z'vi.* But Singer's treatment seems the most perceptive.

The Magician of Lublin is probably the least satisfactory of Singer's works offered so far in English, though far from uninteresting or unimportant. It is a picturesque tale dealing with repentance of a rogue.

Yasha Mazur, "the magician of Lublin," was born into observant Jewry but had become alienated from its traditions only to return at the end to the religious and ethical truths discovered by his ancestors. The fable is ingeniously shaped. The hero is an "escape artist" of extraordinary virtuosity, a very talented though unfortunately provincial Houdini who dreams of conquering Paris and the great world while performing in Warsaw and the smaller towns of Poland. His social limitations are harder for him to overcome than any physical obstacles.

But by the end of the story, this adventurer and romantic, who has long evaded his moral responsibilities and who at last yielded to the temptation to commit a crime, immures himself in a construction of his own making from which he would not escape even if he could.

He finally escaped into a prison, a self-imposed penance of remorse and mortification of the flesh, which some East European Jews practiced but which has a morbidly masochistic quality, more usually associated in our minds with certain Christian sects.

In this story the lively escapades of the hero are much more credible than his penitence. The idea is clever, but the execution is not convincing. And yet there are sensitive strong passages which suggest the bitterness of Yasha's disillusion, the reflections which brought about his revulsion from a life in which suffering is the rule rather than the exception:

> Yasha bent his head; he belched and tasted an unfamiliar bitterness. I know, it's the world. Every second or third house contained a corpse. Throngs of people roamed about the streets, slept on benches, lay on the banks of the Vistula in the midst of filth. The city was surrounded by cemeteries, prisons, hospitals, insane asylums. In every street and alley lurked murderers, thieves, degenerates. Policemen were everywhere in sight.

With Singer's collection of stories entitled *The Spinoza of Market Street,* he returns to surer ground. There are some who believe that the genius of Yiddish literature in general and of Singer in particular lies in the field of the short story rather than in that of the longer fictional forms. Yet while it is true that the most distinguished efforts of Sholom Aleichem and Peretz were in the realm of sketch and story, Linetski's long autobiographical *Polish Boy* (unfortunately never translated fully into English), some of Mendele Mocher Sforim's work, that of Sholem Asch, to say nothing of Singer's own *The Family Moskat,* are all there to prove the generalization debatable.

In addition to the familiar sprites, demons and possessed people of Singer's other stories, the character who recurs in *The Spinoza of Market Street* more often than any other is the philosophic intellectual, whether his name is Dr. Fischelson, the commentator on Spinoza in the title story, or Dr. Margolis and Dr. Yaretsky, the disciples of Schopenhauer who are the protagonists of two other stories. These characters all live on a rarefied intellectual plane, but Singer's aim, like that of other romantic writers, is to expose the vanity of barren intellectualism.

Dr. Fischelson, confronted with human feeling in the raw, recognizes himself in the end to be no better than a fool. Black Dobbe, the unlikely heroine of this story, is described as "tall and lean and black as a baker's shovel" with a broken nose, a mustache on her upper lip and the hoarse voice of a man. The manner in which this scarecrow prevails in bringing the reluctant philosopher down to earth is told with charm, pathos and humor.

There is a serious idea here too. For is it not a confirmation of the foolish Dr. Fischelson's pantheistic philosophy that the God with whom his master Spinoza was intoxicated manifests Himself even in the form of this ugly, unwanted woman when a properly sympathetic eye is there to transfigure her?

More to the point than any intellectual philosophy perhaps is the humane wisdom of the Hasidic rabbi in *A Piece of Advice* who is able to cure a skeptical opponent of his irascible temper. The narrator of the story learns the valuable lesson from the rabbi that "if you are not happy, act the happy man. Happiness will come after. So also with faith. If you are in despair, act as though you believed. Faith will come after."

Many of these stories were first published in popular American magazines like *Esquire* and *Mademoiselle,* which indicates Singer's increasing recognition and acceptance on the part of a larger public. A natural born storyteller, his style is direct enough to reach a fairly wide range of American readers.

In his newer work, Singer is moving closer toward the frontier between imagination and fact, and it is the precise line of demarcation between these two realms that many of the experimental forays in contemporary letters seem designed to determine. A memoir, published in *Commentary, A Gruesome Question,* concerns itself with a poverty-stricken Polish Jew who wants the rabbi to tell him if Mosaic law permits him to take his rest on the same bed with the corpse of his wife. He explains that he cannot leave the body upon the floor to await burial nor can he sleep upon the floor himself because, in their basement room, the rats would eat him alive.

A second memoir, *Strange Merchandise,* which also appeared in *Commentary,* has to do with the Jew as a confidence man—an extraordinarily brilliant and learned man who has lost his faith and proposes to sell to the rabbi the share in the world-to-come due him as a reward for the vast learning he has acquired. He proves to the rabbi by citing book, chapter and verse, that, however unheard-of this procedure may be, he has the same right to dispose of his own immortal soul as of any other personal property.

These episodes reveal more about the depths of poverty suffered by Jews of pre-Hitler Poland and the crisis of faith undergone by some of the most promising young men of the community than hundreds of pages of sociological realism. And they are entertaining as realism rarely is. They constitute Singer's answer to those who have criticized his exclusive concern with "his world of grotesqueries" (to quote a phrase from a review of Singer by Irving Howe in *The New Republic*). As Singer puts it, "Things happen in life so fantastic that the imagination could not have invented them."

Singer never lets us forget his conviction (clearly expressed in

Gimpel and implied throughout his work) that imagination is the proper bridge between the lower world of reality (illusion) and the true world which lies above us. He is critical of literary realism, referring to the "naturalistic" novel as a "cinematographic parade." The superficiality of this parade fails to convey the quality of life as we know it from experience. Every hour of our lives, he states, is "a vase filled with perfumes, sounds and colors," a truth that escapes the "naturalists" who produce drab, objective, colorless representations ("slices of life").

Howe seems to have missed this crucial point in calling *The Family Moskat* an unsuccessful novel because "Singer is as alien to the world of realism as most writers to his world of grotesqueries." The implication is that Singer would be a better writer if he were more realistic, when exactly the opposite is true. It is the quality of imagination transfiguring even the seemingly realistic world of *Moskat* which will cause his work to survive.

To be sure, Howe, who was so enthusiastic about Singer in his *Treasury of Yiddish Stories,* admits even now that "within his narrow limits Singer is a genius. He has total command of his imagined world." But this feeling is more than counteracted by his statement: "I . . . fail to see any principle of growth in his work. Singer seems almost perfect within his stringent limits, but . . . he plays the same tune over and over again, and with a self-confidence that is awesome he keeps modelling his work largely on . . . his own work."

But what Howe calls Singer's "narrow," "stringent" limitations are precisely the source of his power, his "genius." Singer never loses sight of the fact that his forte is the imaginative transmutation of reality, and if this is a limitation it is one only in Goethe's sense when he said that it is "only by conscious self-limitation that mastery reveals itself."

It is something of the same sort that Fitzgerald may have had in mind when in *The Great Gatsby* he says, "life is much more successful looked at from a single window after all," and coins the paradox that the "well-rounded man" is the most limited of all specialists. A good writer must find the vein of ore which is uniquely his own and mine it conscientiously. Singer has long ago found his vein.

If Singer does not succumb to the temptations of realism, neither is he lured into the vagaries of doctrinaire or fashionable surrealism. Instead, he has made himself at home in an imaginative construct between earth and heaven. His sensitivity, lack of coarseness, shy and elusive charm may well militate against an overwhelming triumph in this country with a large popular audience. But he has made a secure and comfortable place for himself in literature.

Marc Chagall

Alfred Werner

MARC CHAGALL belongs to that relatively small number of epoch-making painters who have dared expand the traditional boundaries of art. In addition to being an outstanding artist, he has managed to translate an Eastern philosophy of life, inherited from his ancestors, into pictorial signs and symbols comprehensible to Western man.

Art historians are likely to be unfair to an artist like Chagall who defies being pigeon-holed. From the moment he arrived in Paris with a few "crazy" canvasses produced in Russia, Chagall baffled critics and scholars. Was he going to be absorbed by Cubism? He could not help being influenced by the Cubists. But his poetical pseudo-Cubism, with easily recognizable subject matter, was not to the liking of the ortho-dox Cubists who whittled down life and emotion to geometric pat-terns. A forerunner of Surrealism? It is true that the magic word "surreal" was coined by Guillaume Apollinaire, spellbound at the first sight of Chagall's paintings. It is also true that the high priest of Surrealism, the poet André Breton, paid Chagall the compliment of saying that with him "the metaphor made its triumphant return into modern painting."

To this day Chagall protests attempts to fasten the label "Surrealist" upon him. He admits that his works are "pictorial arrangements that obsess me." But he cares little for those Surrealists who claim that their works are spontaneous outpourings of the unconscious, and even less for those who crowd their canvasses with Freudian symbols. Answering the more sincere among the Surrealists, he declares: "Fantastic or illogical as the construction of my pictures may seem, I would be alarmed to think that I had conceived them through the admixture of automatism." He is determined to remain the master of his actions:

> Even if by automatism one has succeeded in composing some good pictures or in writing some good poems, that does not justify us in setting it up as a method . . . I am afraid that as a conscious method, automatism engenders automatism.

Chagall builds his world out of seemingly disparate elements: the recollections, hopes, fears and frustrations bubbling up to conscious-ness in his mind. He can be classified neither as a Surrealist, an ex-pressionist, a folk-artist nor a primitive. Unable to circumscribe Chagall's individuality by comparing him to others, one French critic coined the term "la Chagallité" to express the unique quality of his work. As early as 1910, when Chagall, then a young Russian firebrand, first arrived in Paris, a colleague who had come to Paris about the same time expressed his own desperation: "Poor us! What can we do, what can we accomplish here? Everything has been said and said again! Let's buy a ticket and go back!" But Chagall thought differently: "Why take anything from anyone else?" he asked.

He refused to be browbeaten by Cubists, with their sterile "cylinder, sphere, cone" theory. Boldly, he reintroduced poetry into painting; he felt that it was "necessary to change nature not only materially and from the outside, but also from within, ideologically."

It would seem that Chagall was able to preserve his peculiar treasure, "la Chagallité," because he was able to retain his childish naïveté and its concomitant fantasy, even in the sophisticated salons of the great cities in which he moved. But though he sees the world with the half-frightened, half-amused eyes of a brilliant child, his hands are definitely not those of a child. In a blasé world he is able to retain his childhood memories and conjure them up at will. As one prominent psychoanalyst sees it, "To a striking degree, perhaps paralleled only by James Joyce in the field of language, he has heightened the capacity to transport his symbolic imagery, unalloyed by rational contrivances, from the unconscious to his canvas."

While Chagall's art has been imitated many times, he has founded no school as Picasso and other artists have done. Whether or not he is a trail-blazer, liberating future artists from the fear of "literature," remains to be seen. Perhaps Chagall will always remain a special case in modern art, a case of the pure and simple of heart.

No other artist has as strongly and successfully resisted being absorbed by Paris. Picasso, Modigliani, Soutine and many others became French in domicile as well as by artistic adoption; even Foujita, though he used the brush of a Japanese, chose themes of the West.

But Chagall has always remained a child of the ghetto. Many art historians have incorrectly dubbed him a Russian, unaware of the unbridgeable gulf that separated the Chagalls from the Ivanovs. There is no affinity between the only genuine Russian art, the icons, and "la Chagallité." In a lecture delivered some years ago, Chagall recognized the quality of the icon tradition, but found it "essentially a religious (i.e., Christian) . . . art; and, as such, it remained strange" to him. Equally misleading are attempts to link Chagall to Russian literature. While it is true that he brilliantly illustrated Gogol's Dead Souls, he is hardly "a brother" of that writer, as André Salmon suggests. Gogol, the initiator of Russian realistic prose, had a warped pathological soul and a tragic inner conflict which almost drove him to madness. His work is filled with devils, spooks, evil spirits, sorcery and witchcraft.

Moreover, Chagall is not unaware of the plight of the masses, but social satire is absent from his work. Nor is his humor the biting irony of an Anatole France. His home is still the ghetto of Vitebsk as it existed before it was destroyed by the Nazis. Significantly, when the artist wanted to express his love of Paris, he fondly called it his "second Vitebsk." Though the Eiffel Tower and Notre Dame appear on some of his canvasses, they merely help accentuate the contrast between the Western world and the East which permeates most of his paintings.

Yet "la Chagallité" is more than a matter of geography. It is a concern of the spirit. And if the artist has a brother in spirit, it is not the grimly pessimistic Gogol, but the Baal Shem Tov, the saintly Hasidic leader of East European Jewry. Few critics have paid sufficient attention to Chagall's background of Hasidism, that most amiable of living faiths, the mystic religious movement within Judaism.

In his autobiography Chagall refers to some members of his family who were followers of the Baal Shem Tov, the founder of Hasidism. It was he who taught his followers how to live in beauty and happiness, in joy and nearness to God. He established new relationships between man and reality, and between man and God, asserting that a "holy spark" was concealed everywhere and in everything; that to live meant to rise from the lowest to the highest existence.

We have to inquire into Hasidism to understand the man who has painted the roosters crowing for joy. It is a philosophy of love—and Chagall is the painter of love. He adores the folklore and scenery of his native country, despite the blows he suffered and the pogroms he witnessed there. He loves flowers and animals, he loves love. There is sadness in his paintings—but rarely the agony of boundless despair. There is always a metaphysical hope deeper than the platitude about the cloud and the silver lining. If he paints a beggar in the snow, he puts a fiddle in his hands, and if he sets a mournful rabbi on the canvas, he adds an innocent white cow, a symbol of the peace of the universe.

Or take the painting called *The Revolution:* one side of the picture is crammed with peasants at war, the other with peasants at peace. In the center sits a moody rabbi, a samovar is boiling in the snow, a man is standing on one hand so that he may hold a flag aloft with his feet. Does all this make sense? People who seek more than photographic fidelity in paintings will read a message in that canvas: the world has gone topsy-turvy, but it is still a good world, for man is essentially good, man is a grown child, preferring the boisterous carnival atmosphere, come what may.

This metaphysical optimism is also evident in the religious paint-

ings produced around a benign suffering Jesus whom the artist loves
with all the humility of his good soul. In *The Descent from the Cross*
one of the persons taking Jesus from the cross is, significantly, painted
with the head of a rooster: even the simple animals love the Prince of
Peace. Or take *The Martyr,* which he finished in France after the
catastrophe of 1940: it shows the Jew Jesus on a cross surrounded by
figures and animals of the burning Russian village; yet even in this
portrayal of today's cataclysm the fiddler is not absent.

Chagall holds the view of the Judengasse of yore: a living dog is
better than a dead lion, and sorrow clouds communication with God.

Anyone somewhat familiar with the artist's milieu will marvel at his
faithful rendering of the atmosphere of Eastern European Jewry,
Hasidic or otherwise, with the lighting of the candles; the men moan-
ing and sighing in their white prayer shawls; the merry-makers of the
Purim festival, the religious dances of the men. The Baal Shem called
for prayer accompanied by physical ecstasy, that dancing and singing
might bring about union with God. The craftsmanship of Chagall is
most closely related to the dance in a shul, which begins slowly with a
sadness, and gradually assumes faster rhythms, until it reaches a
climax in a state of veritable ecstasy. It is no coincidence that the
ballet plays a role in Chagall's work. Is the Hasidic dance he watched
as a boy, or even participated in, still "in his blood"? One recalls the
rapture with which a *New York Times* critic referred to the scenery
and costumes by Chagall for the American Ballet Theater years ago:

> They (the designs) are overwhelming, and in front of them the
> conventional human being looks insignificant and the traditional
> dance d'école faintly foolish. He (Chagall) created a naïve and
> irresponsible world without gravity or functions, in which the sub-
> conscious (the writer means: the unconscious) reigns with such
> unquestioning authority as to achieve . . . sweet reasonableness.

Has the world benefited by "la Chagallité"? It seems so. This artist
has opened new vistas, rich and joyful, not only for his colleagues, but
for all mankind, regardless of origin or creed. It is not only the privilege of a few sophisticated ones to "understand" his works. Perhaps the
"explanations," proffered by some critics, have spoiled the fun for the
many to whom the merrymaker of Vitebsk and Paris has addressed himself. For his work can be understood with the heart; it is within the
grasp of all who can understand that a man can fly without an air-
plane, of all who can enjoy Charlie Chaplin's movies, or a circus.
Chagall's world is closed permanently only to those who stubbornly
insist that two and two always make four.

Saul Bellow

Irving Malin

SAUL BELLOW is, in my view, the most important contemporary Jewish-American novelist. In some biographical notes issued by the Viking Press, he states that at the age of four he had already been exposed to the Bible in Hebrew—"he fully accepted the reality of God—but what bothered him was *where* God was . . ." He is still trying to locate Him.

By studying his five works—*Dangling Man* (1944), *The Victim* (1947), *The Adventures of Augie March* (1953), *Seize the Day* (1956) and *Henderson the Rain King* (1959) *—we can learn much about the ways in which he and other contemporary Jewish-American writers have come to terms with their heritage—or have escaped from it.

Many critics have commented on Saul Bellow's Jewishness. Leslie Fiedler insists that we must see it in the larger context: "the Jews for the first time have moved into the center of American culture." Bellow's work combines the new and the old, the American and the Jewish. Augie March, "a Chicago kid making his way among small-time Jewish Machiavellians," is for Fiedler the "most satisfactory character ever projected by a Jewish writer in America." Maxwell Geismar, on the other hand, thinks that Bellow has not faced his heritage: "Judaism in his work is a source of nostalgia, but also of guilt and anxiety rather than an enlarging or emancipating force." Other critics also stress Bellow's ambivalence toward his heritage.

Bellow himself says little about Jewishness. He applauds Philip Roth's view of the "swamp of prosperity" American Jews inhabit. In a review of Sholom Aleichem's *The Adventures of Mottel the Cantor's Son*, Bellow notes about Jews of the ghetto: "They were divinely designated to be great and yet they were like mice. History was something that *happened* to them; they did not make it." The Jews, he continues, decline to suffer "the penalties the world imposes" on them. Bellow seems less interested in religion (he does not mention laws or rituals) than in vision. He finds Jewish vision ironic. The Jews learn to value jokes, absurdities. Their own humor seems to reflect the "immense joke of their existence": they are "chosen" and yet "rejected" —chosen by God, rejected by their society. In *The Victim*, for example, Asa hears a Jewish joke which exemplifies the sad absurdity of things. In a little town the Jews, afraid that the Messiah would come

---

* This article was written before the appearance of Bellow's latest novel *Herzog* (1964).

and miss them, build a tower and hire one of the town beggars to sit in it the whole day. A friend meets the beggar and asks, "How do you like your job, Baruch?" To which the reply is: "It doesn't pay much, but I think it's steady work."

Bellow's view of his heritage is as ambivalent as he claims the heritage itself is. In his fiction he may use Jewish vision—or irony—but he never confronts it, except by indirection. Often he avoids it, by masquerading it as something else.

Dangling Man, Bellow's first novel, is written in the form of a journal by Joseph, who waits impatiently for the Army to induct him. The time is the early forties; the setting is Chicago. Joseph's predicament is treated as a "personal" situation. We are never really told that he is Jewish or that he has old-world vision. But it is possible to view him as an archetypal Jew who, like Sholom Aleichem's characters, considers existence in ambivalent ways.

Joseph, in effect, thinks of American society as hardboiled, whereas *he* suffers. It rejects him because he is "different." (Or is it the other way around?) His journal becomes his sole occupation—it is his Talmud; he is a scholar who studies himself rather than divine laws. Joseph tells us little about his appearance, but whatever description there is indicates that he looks Jewish—dark eyes, black hair, straightnosed. When Joseph broods about existence, he is typically Jewish. He wants the Messiah to come in the guise of a "colony of the spirit"—this colony will have "covenants" forbidding "spite, bloodiness, cruelty." It will be a blessed country—perhaps like the Israel of his ancestors. But like Sholom Aleichem's characters, Joseph is trapped.

Joseph's sense of family is Jewish. Family closeness has always been important in Jewish literature—especially the father-son relationship. Joseph tries at all times to be close to his family, but he cannot achieve this colony of the spirit. He says very little about his own parents— "they are missing"—but he does describe the pomposity and false guidance of his brother Amos, who instructs him in the ways of the world. Amos is the Jew who has succumbed to the materialistic world; Joseph remains true "to the craters of the spirit," but with skepticism.

Unlike the ghetto inhabitants, Joseph has lost faith in God. He says at one point: "No, not God, not any divinity. That was anterior, not of my own deriving. I was not so full of pride that I could not accept the existence of something greater than myself . . ." Joseph wants to believe in divinity, but he is so trapped that he can only see it dimly —as in a Hayden divertimento. What would his grandfather think of this? Joseph looks for messages not in the Bible but in Goethe, Thoreau's *Walden,* Jacob Boehme, Marx, and his own journal.

The hints of Joseph's Jewishness—his "alienation," his "Messianic

vision," the almost-suffocating family ties, his physical appearance—
are less significant than the Jewish humor pervading the novel. For
example, Joseph thinks of his grandfather's photograph, which shows
an old man of faith—"his eyes staring and his clothing shroudlike."
He remembers that at fourteen he suddenly saw that *he* would resemble his grandfather: "I was upright on my grandfather's bones and
the bones of those before him in a temporary loan." Joseph longs for
the old faith—the "real Jew"—at the same time that he fears it. When
he grows up he meets the "others" who, like Mr. Harscha, the German,
stare at him. They also chart resemblances. Thus the grandfather's
head—"his streaming beard, yellow sulphurous"—hangs over Joseph,
threatening to "devour" him. The example not only holds the Jewish
themes—it gives us a clue to Bellow's tensions about his heritage.

The Victim brings these tensions to the surface. It is a tight narrative which deals with the "crazy" adventures of Asa Leventhal after he
meets the gentile Kirby Allbee. The plot is, again, less significant than
the conversations between the two about Jewishness, destiny and ethical choice. Is Albee justified in his accusations about Asa's responsibility for the evil in his life? Here Bellow emphasizes the various
problems he avoided in *Dangling Man*. In the first few pages Asa
knows that no matter what his beliefs are (is he a believer in God?) he
is a Jew for the others. Mr. Beard claims that he is "like the rest of his
brethren." Whether he likes it or not, Asa joins his fellow "victims."
The facts that his wife is named Mary and his sister-in-law is Italian
no longer matter. There is no real assimilation, as Joseph knows too.
Asa is trapped in his heritage.

Allbee constantly reminds him of his doom. He knows that Asa will
be more upset by guilt—by betrayal—than by anything else. The Jew,
with his belief in colonies of the spirit, his desire to help victims, will
always be concerned with responsibilities. Often he will blame himself.
Allbee gives Asa something to brood about by suggesting that he has
victimized a gentile. Critic Geismar is surely correct in indicating that
Allbee is more Jewish than Asa—more aware of victimization and
blame. He even "delights" in old-world customs, festivals and songs,
constantly referring to them.

Because of Allbee, Asa discovers his Jewishness, enacting existentialist Jean-Paul Sarte's definition:

> What is it, then, that serves to keep a semblance of unity in
> the Jewish community? To reply to this question, we must come
> back to the idea of *situation*. It is neither their past, their religion,
> nor their soil that unites the sons of Israel. If they have a common
> bond, if all of them deserve the name of Jew, it is because they

have in common the situation of a Jew, that is, they live in a community that takes them for Jews.

Asa remembers the "old" ways of his parents—of the Jewish past—only after he is placed into his *situation*. What is ironic is that New York—the place of alienation—is, to quote Allbee, a "very Jewish city." Bellow suggests that once a Jew is so reminded, he assumes a historic role; he acts in the way his fellow Jews have always acted. Asa, for example, suffers more: he feels more guilt; he is more alone. This helps explain Bellow's ambivalence toward his own Jewishness: like Asa he seems to resent enacting a role thrust upon him. Being a Jew means for him that he is an "ideal construction"—if not of the Lord, then of the community. Bellow finds it difficult to grow within "anterior" limits.

Because Asa has no real belief in God, he must assert that his present position is the result of chance: "And what more was there for him to say than that his part in it was accidental? At worst an accident, unintentional." Often he thrusts responsibility onto fate, feeling relieved in being helpless and dumb. Only gradually does Asa accept universal order—but he does not see it as divinely ordained. Things seem to be "exactly human." All men react as he does when placed in *such a situation*—there are no values in a type—be he Jew or gentile. When Allbee suffers, he resembles Asa—this means that everybody is Jewish (or that nobody is). Bellow does not offer a comforting message in *The Victim*. By showing that Allbee and Asa are equally human, he implies that Jewishness is less significant than universal truth. He has written a plea for assimilation. But he has not solved the tensions of being a Jew.

The Adventures of Augie March continues this escapist pattern. Although we get a close view of Jewish customs, foods and proverbs, especially in the early chapters, we do not completely understand the nature of Jewishness. *Augie March*, unlike the earlier two novels, is a picaresque comedy. Augie ranges far and wide, trying to find his identity. He meets many bizarre characters who "adopt" him; but he resists their advances.

Perhaps Bellow implies that the March family merely accepts historical type-casting; it becomes another masquerade for them. Here is Grandma Lausch: "But she never went to the synagogue, ate bread on Passover, sent Mama to the pork butcher where meat was cheaper, loved canned lobster and other forbidden food, she was not an atheist and free-thinker." But *is* she Jewish? *Why* is she Jewish? Bellow suggests that the family knows that it is "different" only when the "others" say so: "And sometimes we were chased, stoned, bitten, and beat up for Christ-killers, all of us, even Georgie, articled, whether we liked it or not to this mysterious trade." We would expect Augie to resemble Asa Leventhal, but in this "carefree" world he simply admits: "I never had any special grief from it, or brooded, being by and large too larky and boisterous to take it to heart . . ." Anti-Semitism needs no more explanation, he continues, than other juvenile delinquency. He even laughs at Anna Coblin's Orthodox beliefs: she "had the will of a mar-tyr to carry a mangled head in Paradise till doomsday, in the suffering mothers' band led by Eve and Hannah." She is "silly," directing Augie to the "great eternal things."

Despite the fact that Augie does not care about anti-Semitism or Orthodox rituals, he looks at the world with Jewish irony. Almost any passage indicates his skeptical admiration of greatness. When he thinks of Einhorn, for example, he said that he "isn't kidding" when he enters him in the list of great men, along with Caesar, Machiavelli and Ulysses. Einhorn is great because he is able to endure the onslaughts of existence—endurance is a quality always admired by Jews living in exile. But Augie knows that even endurance can be laughed at: Ein-horn, after all, achieves greatness by means of trickery. Endurance and wisdom are not accepted as solemn truths—they are viewed as "cheap items," even by the great men themselves. Realizing that he cannot achieve greatness for himself, Augie wants only to go his own erratic way. He is a "trader dealing in air," facing life with an "ironic shrug." He is an "anti-hero," "archetypal," *dos kleine mentshele* (the little man)! Augie resembles the Jewish folk-character who is "long-suffering, persistent, lovingly ironic."

The great sense of the "sanctity of the insulted and the injured" is always present in Augie's remarks. Here too he follows his co-religionists. He defends the Marches, Grandma Lausch—the poor versus the silly materialists. He defends his imbecile brother George, his blind mother—the crippled.

The Adventures of Augie March escapes from confronting many problems Jews must face—how to live in a "new world," the right way to approach God—at the same time that it is infused with Jewish humor and legend. It is a strange mixture, perhaps more than any other of Bellow's novels, because it sees Jewishness in a nostalgic, folksy way, disregarding the tensions of *The Victim*. It is inappropri-ate to call it either an American novel *or* a Jewish one. It is, paradoxi-cally, unprovincial as it exalts provincial feelings.

Seize the Day is a powerful Jewish work. It is a short novel which deals with one day in the life of Tommy Wilhelm. The setting is New York (as in *The Victim*); the plot evolves about Tommy's desire to "beat" the market and to find himself; but the main interest is his

cosmic awareness. If such a phrase has any meaning, this work suggests
that Bellow removes his rose-colored glasses and scrutinizes the tensions of Jewish life. He uses the same devices as before; Tommy
Wilhelm, *dos kleine mentshele*, employs Yiddish phrases and jokes,
but he is concerned, in part, with probing the identity of the Jew in
America. *Seize the Day* asks as does *The Victim:* What is a Jew? Why
is someone a Jew?

Tommy Wilhelm is torn by his three selves: "Tommy," "Wilky,"
and "Velvel." Tommy is his desired American self—the goodlooking
actor who, unfortunately, discovers that he has no real talent and
turns to selling products. He is inauthentic, running away from the
old world. Wilky is the name his father calls him—his real name—to
control him. Wilky is the bleak, "inescapable self." These names represent two conflicting aspects of the hero's personality—freedom and
determinism:

> Wilhelm had always had a great longing to be Tommy. He had
> never, however, succeeded in feeling like Tommy and in his soul
> had always remained Wilky . . . He had cast off his father's
> name, and with it his father's opinion of him. It was, he knew it
> was, his bid for liberty, Adler being in his mind the title of the
> species, Tommy the freedom of the person. But Wilky was his in-
> escapable self.

The inescapable self is Jewish. Wilky knows that he looks like his
ancestors—that he has some of their beliefs in the family sense, the
sanctity of the insulted and injured, the Messianic vision. When
Wilhelm prays, he resembles the suffering ghetto inhabitants.

But even Wilky may not be his true soul. Wilhelm remembers that
his grandfather called him Velvel. Velvel represents the cozy affection
of his heritage, the real closeness. What is interesting, then, in *Seize
the Day* is that Bellow uses three names to symbolize the Jew—Tommy
(the assimilationist), Wilky (the inescapable heritage) and Velvel (the
loved heritage).

Wilhelm chooses to be Velvel. More and more he thinks in Jewish
terms, finding "power and glory" in rituals. Old Rappaport asks him
at one point whether he had reserved a seat in the synagogue for Yom
Kippur. Although he answers no, he expresses his longing to pray for
his dead mother. He realizes that he does not know the Hebrew words.
In the family structure grandfather is Orthodox, father has no religion, mother is "Reformed," and he is ambivalent toward Jewishness.
At last he thinks of part of the Hebrew memorial service—he begins to
resemble his grandfather. And this resemblance is strengthened when
he stumbles into a funeral parlor where a Jewish ceremony is in

progress: "Men in formal clothes and black homburgs strode softly back and forth on the cork floor . . . The white of the stained glass was like mother-of-pearl, the blue of the Star of David like velvet ribbon." Here he identifies not only with the corpse but with all his co-religionists. He cleanses himself. When he cries, his name is Velvel.

The surprising thing in Bellow's fiction is that he does not approach his Jewishness in any consistent way. *Seize the Day* confronts it more than does *The Adventures of Augie March;* it is his most forceful or most loving acceptance of his heritage. *The Victim* is, of course, another acceptance, but its message is escapist.

Henderson the Rain King is a comic romance set in an imaginary, fantastic "Africa." What does Henderson want? He seeks divine self-knowledge, and he comes close to it by going through odd rituals with animals and even odder conversations with the philosophical African king, Dahfu. We would expect Bellow's pilgrim's progress to offer another view of the Jewish theme in his latest novel. But Henderson is gentile. He even has a dispute with a Jewish friend—which compels him out of crazy spite to start raising pigs.

The only Jewish vision in *Henderson* is indirect—perhaps it lies hidden in the flaming love expressed throughout the novel. Bellow seems to accept Reichianism which, as Theodore Solotaroff writes, resembles Hasidism.

Bellow uses a wealthy Protestant to express a boundless love for the universe. He has come a long way from Asa's victimization. Jewishness is transformed in the wilds of Africa. Bellow no longer feels trapped in assuming an historical or cultural role: he expands his Jewishness until it reminds us of Bernard Malamud's remark: "All men are Jews." Is such a remark an escape from—or a confrontation of—his heritage?

Israel—Reborn

Eretz Yisrael in Jewish Tradition
Emanuel Rackman

THE concept of *Eretz Yisrael* began with God's promise to Abraham, who traversed its length and its breadth; it was confirmed to Isaac, who never separated himself from its soil; and it meant home for Jacob all the time that he was in flight from Esau, as well as thereafter when he asked his sons in Egypt to inter him in the cave of Machpela. Even for the Israelites in bondage to Pharaoh, and for their children who were liberated, the conquest of the land was the ultimate step in their redemption.

Why did God choose the land of Israel for His people? It was a land flowing with milk and honey, rich in mineral resources, a beautiful land so varied in its terrain as to be a microcosm of the entire earth. According to the Rabbis, men sought God on the mountain peaks of Jerusalem even before Abraham. The land was conceived as holy before it was conquered by Moses and Joshua.

After the conquest and for many centuries, the land was the place where the Hebrews were to live and fulfill the mandates of Torah. According to Nahmanides, the Torah was intended to be nothing more than a constitution for the Jewish polity in Canaan. Whatever observance of the Torah there was to be elsewhere was only for the sake of keeping the people perpetually prepared for their return. Even those who differed with Nahmanides and ascribed to Torah a more universal significance admitted that scores of commandments were applicable only to the Holy Land: the so-called *mitzvot ha-tluyot ba-aretz.*

To return to their ancestral home and fulfill these special commandments became the dominant hope after the Exile. In prayer and study, our ancestors described the joys associated with the Temple, whose service could not be held anywhere else in the world. The offering of *bikurim,* the first fruits, was studied on every Pentecost festival, and Jews were wont to dream of their own ascent to Jerusalem in the Messianic era, and the re-enactment of this joyous ceremony was actually one of the first to be reinstituted in modern Israel by religious and secularist Jews alike.

Of all the commandments applicable to the land none captivated the imagination of scholars and saints in exile more than the system of land tenure and cultivation involving the jubilee and sabbatical years. This system helped the land retain its holiness and was to save the people from being expelled. Since the land was God's—sanctified by

Him and reserved for His people—Jews were not to till the soil or sow the seed for one year in seven. Every fiftieth year there was to be a redistribution of the land to its original owners; Jews "were to proclaim liberty throughout the land, to all the inhabitants thereof," the verse now found on the Liberty Bell in Philadelphia but originally ordained for the Holy Land.

God had promulgated special laws for a place that had special significance. When Jews ignored their mandate, the prophet Jeremiah predicted their destruction and their loss of the land. But interest in the laws of the jubilee and sabbatical years never ceased. The sounding of the shofar at the conclusion of every fast of Yom Kippur was the annual reminder of the emancipation of slaves at the end of the Day of Atonement in a jubilee year.

Once God chose the land for His people and charged it with His holiness, it had a special role in the fulfillment of His ultimate purpose for all mankind. For that reason, while idolatry, from Judaism's point of view, is a crime everywhere, it is especially heinous if practiced in Israel, and homicide and sexual improprieties are especially contaminating to its soil. God's attachment to this land makes it necessary that higher moral standards prevail there—not only for purposes now discernible but also for the future destiny of humanity.

It is there that the Messianic age is to be heralded. On its mountains God will ultimately judge between the nations. Even for the resurrection of the dead, which can only be realized in the age known as *olam haba* (the world-to-come), the land of Israel will have a special quality.

From the verse in Deuteronomy (11:12), "a land, with which the Lord thy God is concerned, perpetually are the eyes of the Lord thy God upon it, from the beginning of the year to the end of the year," the Rabbis derived the belief that God has a special relationship to the land. It was a mitzvah to reside there—even if one could perform none of the applicable commandments. The mere act of residence brought one closer to God: the land in its entirety was His altar. Burial in the land was regarded as burial on an altar of atonement.

Husbands and wives in the Diaspora could force each other to move to Israel. Even a slave could run away from his master and take up residence in Israel; all he had to do was give his master a promissory note for the amount of loss sustained by this act of self-liberation. If a man craved the holiness of a Nazirite he had to ascend to the Holy Land to fulfill his vow. Moreover, to buy land in Israel on the Sabbath one might use the services of a non-Jew, though this normally would constitute a breach of the Sabbath.

The Talmud tells of Rabbis who kissed the rocks of Israel and

rolled in her sands when they reached its border en route from Babylon or other countries. Though Babylon had many great academies in
the third and fourth centuries, the Babylonian Talmud records with
approval the prohibition that Palestinians were not to leave the Holy
Land to take up permanent residence even in Babylon. Virtually the
only reason justifying emigration from Israel was self-preservation.

To reduce the habitability of the land was a sin. Even to demolish a
house in order to replace it with a garden was not permitted because
one or more families were thus denied an opportunity to settle there.
To such an extent did the Rabbis give expression to their passion for
the preservation of everything in Israel that they ruled that while
outside of Israel one may occasionally remove a mezuzah from his door
when changing his place of residence, one may never do so in Israel.
Every home must be held in immediate readiness for someone to move
in. Moreover, while outside of Israel one may wait thirty days before
affixing a mezuzah, in Israel one must affix the mezuzah immediately.
In the performance of the mitzvah of dwelling in Israel one never
considers oneself a transient!

Prayers giving expression to the yearning for *Eretz ha-z'vi*—the
beautiful land—are found in the Talmud; and several were composed
long before the destruction of the Temple. After the destruction, Jews
did not thank God for a land they possessed but for a land to which
they hoped to be restored.

In two prayers in the Pentateuch we find special blessings for the
land. One was recited when all the tithes and heave-offerings were
finally disposed of, the other when the first fruits were brought to the
Temple. Another occasion for praying for the land is suggested in the
verse in Deuteronomy which ordains grace after meals. For that reason, the second paragraph of the grace, still recited today, thanks God
both for food and for the sacred soil of Israel.

In an ancient prayer which the High Priest recited at the conclusion
of the sacred service on the Day of Atonement, we also find references
to the land. However, it is after the destruction of the Temple that
prayers for its restoration and the return of the Jewish people to Zion
became the most important theme of the liturgy. Even prayers for
God's forgiveness were almost invariably linked with the thought that
once we were forgiven our redemption would follow. Thus the reten-
tion of prayers for dew and rain chanted on the first day of Passover
and the eighth day of Tabernacles are only seasonal ties with *Eretz
Yisrael.*

But there were ties repeated three times each day in the "Eighteen
Benedictions," when Jews pleaded for the privilege of beholding God's
return to Zion with their own eyes. This prayer was recited facing in

the direction in which Jerusalem lay. On Mondays and Thursdays Jews recited special penitential prayers, *ve-hu rahum,* pleading with God to call a halt to their shame and restore His glory to His land and shrine. On New Moons, Sabbaths and festivals, they recounted the offerings which Scripture had prescribed for the occasion. With words descriptive of the Temple service they hoped to receive credit themselves "as if" they had personally brought the sacrifices. And in awe and trepidation, in the midst of *Kedushah,* as they sang to God with words which express God's immanence and transcendence, Jews wept: "When wilt Thou rule in Zion, soon in our own day, forever."

During the Middle Ages, many hymns expressed the longing for a return to Zion. Judah Halevi's odes to Zion are classics, chanted at the close of the morning service on Tisha Ba'av.

Medieval Jewish philosophers like Saadia and Maimonides never tried to rationalize or validate the conceptions of the "chosen people" and the Holy Land. Since they were writing to meet the challenges of Christian and Mohammedan writers—principally the latter—they could assume the authenticity of the Bible which vouched for God's special relationship to the land and people of Israel. The only question that might arise was whether the Jews had not forfeited their privileged position by rejecting Jesus or Mohammed.

The basic issue therefore was: who was entitled to possess the sacred patrimony? In the Middle Ages much blood was shed in wars and crusades to resolve this question. Saadia interpreted all the mitzvot as means to happiness which Jews were to bring to all mankind. While Saadia had no personal association with the land and remained in Babylon, Maimonides did live there for a brief interval. The day of his arrival with his family was celebrated by them for years thereafter with feasting and prayer and the distribution of gifts to the poor. In Maimonides' classic work codifying Jewish law he cited with approval many of the rules found in the Talmud concerning the sanctity of the land of Israel and the importance of residing there. Yet, in his philosophical classic, *Guide for the Perplexed,* the land is not as central as it actually was in Jewish thought and hope.

On the other hand, the philosopher Halevi, in the *Kuzari,* undertook to avenge his people's honor, and one incident in European history provided him with the sought-for background. A Slavic nation, the Khazars, had embraced Judaism in the eighth or ninth century; Halevi retells the story of how the king of the Khazars, wanting to choose a religion for his people, called in a rabbi, a priest and a Mohammedan teacher. After hearing the three debate the merits of their respective religions, the king chose Judaism.

From the dialogue between the king and the rabbi one senses

Halevi's passion for the land of Israel. Indeed, in his old age he set out
for the land. Legend has it that he reached his destination but upon
debarkation was trampled in the sands he bowed down to kiss.

The king of the Khazars said to the rabbi:

> If this be so (all that you said about *Eretz Yisrael*), then you
> fall short of the duty laid down in your law, by not endeavoring to
> reach that place and making it your home in life and death . . .
>
> You believe that the divine providence will return there where
> it dwelt for five hundred years. That is sufficient reason for man's
> soul to retire there and find purification near the homes of the
> pious and the prophets . . .
>
> Your bowing and your kneeling in the direction of Israel is
> either hypocrisy or thoughtless worship. If you really meant it
> you would go there.
>
> Your first forefathers chose that place as an abode in preference
> to their birthplace. They lived rather as strangers in the land of
> Israel than as citizens of their own countries. This they did even
> at a time when the Divine Presence had not yet revealed Himself
> and the land was full of unchastity, impurity and idolatry. Your
> fathers, however, had no desire other than to remain there. Nor
> did they leave it in time of drought or famine except with God's
> permission. Finally they directed their bones to be buried there.

The question raised by the king of the Khazars was not easily answered, but it troubled many. The Tosafists—who wrote brilliant
notes on the texts of the Talmud and on Rashi's commentary—also
dealt with the issue. One expressed the view that in their day it would
be most hazardous to make the trip, wherefore the obligation to go was
suspended. Another stated that since it was then impossible for reasons
of survival to observe all the commandments applicable to the land,
the mitzvah of residing there had lost most of its significance. Though a
minority view, many Jews did feel that rather than go to the land and
find that necessity would oblige them to violate many of the applicable
rules, they should rather choose to observe the fewer mitzvot of the
Diaspora.

What is important is that there was soul searching; the seeds of
modern *aliyah* were sowed not in the late eighteenth century but in
the twelfth and thirteenth centuries. One of the first of these pioneers
was Nahmanides, an outstanding teacher of Jewish law, philosophy
and mysticism. Nahmanides went to Israel after a bitter polemic with
an apostate, and in the three years spent there prior to his death he
reorganized the Jewish community of Jerusalem. There he also wrote
his commentary on the Pentateuch, a mine of material on the holiness

of the land of Israel. Thus, for example, on the verse, "And Jacob came in peace to the city of Shechem which is in the land of Canaan, after he had departed Padan Aram (in Mesopotamia), and encamped before the city and bought a parcel of land where he had spread his tent" (Genesis 33:18), Nahmanides said, "He did not want to sojourn in the city but he wanted to sleep on his own property his first night in the land of Israel. That is why he camped in the field but purchased a lot, thereby performing an act of possession in the land."

Another distinguished "displaced person" was Rabbi Joseph Karo, who went to Israel from Turkey almost three centuries later. In Safed he wrote the great code of Jewish law, the *Shulhan Arukh*. Nahmanides, Karo and hundreds of others who went to the land of Israel became mystics and developed the two greatest movements in modern Jewish history—Hasidism and Zionism.

The love of God is of primary importance in the life of the mystic, and the literature of mysticism is a series of variations on this one theme. God's gifts to the people were the Torah and the land. Therefore to study His Torah and to dwell upon His land helped one to come physically and spiritually closer to Him. It was like attaching oneself to an extension of His being.

Said Rabbi Nahman of Bratislav: "In physical reality one doesn't see any difference between the land of Israel and the other countries of the earth. But he who is privileged to believe in the holiness of the land of Israel can detect at least a bit of the difference." Rabbi Nahman also observed that the first commandment given to Abraham was to leave his home and go to the land of Israel.

From the yearning of the Kabbalists and their spiritual heirs, the Hasidim, came also the belief that the hour of redemption was near. That is why there were several instances in the Middle Ages and modern times when Jews believed that the Messiah had actually come.

The rationalists and legalists were less impulsive, and perhaps less passionate in their love of God and the land. But in their continued dedication to the Law they also nurtured the hope that would not die. In the modern period Jews and the Jewish community were governed less and less by their own law—the law of the Torah—and more and more by the law of the state in which they lived. The study of Torah became progressively irrelevant to daily living. Its goal was either *Torah lishmah*—Torah for its own sake—or Torah for a projected Jewish commonwealth still to be established.

In more recent times, one group of rabbis, including many who never identified with the World Zionist Organization and even opposed it, undertook the intensive study of those parts of the Torah dealing with the ancient Temple service. Despite their refusal to honor Zionist leaders who were not "religious," they felt that the new ferment signified that the Messianic era was imminent. And they wanted to be prepared with a mastery of all the knowledge that a rebuilt Temple would entail. Much more than in the Middle Ages the Talmudic scholars of the modern period concerned themselves with that sixth of the Talmud known as *Kodshim* ("Things Holy"). As the mystics inspired the homeward movement, the rationalists and legalists were preoccupied with the laws that would have to be followed after the return.

Yet the major contribution of the legalists—over a period of more than half a millennium—was to shape and popularize the conception that every Jew has a share in *Eretz Yisrael*. This led to the establishment of the Jewish National Fund, whereby the land of Israel was bought by Jews to be held in perpetuity for the Jewish people. This institution was not the product of nineteenth-century socialism, as so many mistakenly believe. Millions of Jews who responded to its appeal, especially on the Fast of Av, did so out of the conviction that everyone has a share in *Eretz Yisrael*.

Certain legal rules helped induce this conviction. There was, for example, the manner of conveying title known as *Kinyan Agav*. By this method one could transfer ownership to movable things even when the objects were not sold in the presence of the vendor and purchaser. What one did was to sell one's land—a tiny piece of it— and with the land one sold the movable objects as well. Title to both realty and personalia then passed simultaneously.

But what if one had no land? The presumption was conclusive that every Jew had four square ells in the land of Israel. Even after he had sold it, he had more left. No matter how often he sold by means of the *Kinyan Agav* he could not expropriate himself vis-à-vis *Eretz Yisrael*.

This assumption regarding the inseparability of the Jew from the land became the basis for still another rule which may now give comfort to the intransigent zealots in Israel who refuse to recognize the State of Israel. No matter where Jews live, outside of Israel they must obey the law of the state which is their host. So Jeremiah ordained. There may be limitations: we need not obey the state if it promulgates immoral or discriminatory legislation. Generally, however, we must obey the law even if it contravenes the mandates of the Torah.

Rabbi Nisim (fourteenth century) expressed the rationale of the rule: we must obey the law of every host country because our residence there is conditional upon our obedience to its law.

However, this is not true of the land of Israel. No Jew resides in Israel conditionally or by the grace of someone else. He has an absolute right to live there. And no king, president, parliament or other constituted authority can say to a Jew, "Either obey our statutes or go forth to exile." One cannot order a Jew out of the territory to which he has an inalienable right. The zealots in Israel today rely upon this insight of Rabbi Nisim to resist what they regard as an administration of sinners.

The legal as well as mystical tradition reached a climax in the writings of Rabbi Abraham Kuk, leader of his people in the critical years between the two World Wars. In one Responsum he concerns himself with the manner in which a Jewish community shall take title to land. Shall it do so as a partnership? Are members of a kibbutz who take such a title partners?

Rabbi Kuk observed that many people may view their community as a partnership—as a joint enterprise to improve the lot of every member of the group. However, a Jewish community in Israel is more than a partnership and its property is more than partnership property. "The corporate entity of the Jewish community has a reality independent of the totality of its individual constituents." The Jewish community has a reality that transcends the present; the partnership is with those already born and those unborn. That is why it is a partnership that never terminates with death. Individual Jews may die; even individual communities may be wiped out. But the eternal mission of the Jewish people charges its very being and its land with purpose and holiness.

Therefore, property owned by a Jewish community in Israel is not property in which every individual Jew has an undivided share. It is rather property that belongs to *Klal Yisrael* and is vested with the spiritual character of the Jewish community. To convey title to such land requires rules different from those applicable to partnerships.

The modern philosopher Martin Buber distinguishes between a collectivity and a community. He too would like to regard a kibbutz as more than a collective which is a group of individuals each of whom has a partnership interest in the group's property. A community, on the other hand, has a transcendent purpose and its property is charged with that purpose—*Zweckvermogung,* the German legal philosophers call it. Indeed, the source of this conception can be found in the Mishnah.

While the Law does much to give the land a position of centrality in the Jewish tradition, the Law requires the land for its fulfillment.

In the seventeenth century an attempt was made in Israel to revive this ceremony. The controversy that ensued is relevant to the issue that Israel faces today—shall it reconstitute a Sanhedrin? Only in Israel can there be final word on the Law. And howsoever Jews may differ in their attitudes toward a central rabbinic authority in Jerusalem, the fact is that only in Israel can there be any such authority.

Israel—The Emergence of a Society

Abba Eban

THE central theme in the life of the Jewish people in this decade has been the revolutionary movement which has brought about the restoration of Israel's statehood. The echoes set up by this event are far deeper and stronger than can be explained in terms of Israel's physical attributes. There is a broad universal recognition among our own contemporaries that Israel's significance is not to be measured in terms of its eight thousand square miles or its two million people, but that this is a people very small and meager in geography but very great indeed in history. It is in such terms that we should contemplate both the achievement and the frustration, both the victories and the set-backs, both the exaltations and the apprehensions which mark modern Israel today.

In this emergence of a new society the most prominent attribute is the transformation of the land itself. This little strip of territory, most of it arid and ravaged by centuries of neglect, poised between the Mediterranean and the Jordan, occupying that historical crossroads where the three continents of the ancient world converged, looking out westward to Europe, northward to Asia and southward to Africa, has within the period of our statehood undergone a notable and visible transformation. Never since the psalmist first sang of our green pastures and peaceful waters three thousand years ago has such a carpet of rich fertility covered so large an area of this sacred land.

The desert and the wilderness are not the essential attributes of Israel's geography; they are the artificial creation of human neglect. All the experience of modern Israel in the revival of the ancient grace and fertility of its landscape has fully confirmed the pastoral roman-ticism which marks the ancient Hebrew poetry and which made Israel a byword throughout history as a land that flowed with milk and honey, a land whose fertility and abundance were inscribed in match-less and eternal language upon the literary records of the past.

No less significant is the transformation of a people. This is an immigrant pioneer society. Two out of every three in our country were not there when its independence was proclaimed on that unforgettable morning in May 1948. They come from disparate backgrounds of social and economic development, from Western and Eastern Europe, North Africa, Arab lands, from societies plunged into the ninth century in respect of their cultural and social development.

This is a pattern of social diversity which has had no parallels or precedents in modern history. Perhaps the only approximation to this process of creating a unified culture, a symphony of divergent elements from so many backgrounds and creeds, lies in the American Revolution and War of Independence and in those great streams of pioneer immigration which built up the strength of the American republic in the eighteenth, nineteenth and early twentieth centuries.

Yet within Israel the diversity is more extreme; the divergence between an Israeli citizen from Western Europe and his fellow from the Yemen represents a far broader gulf than has ever existed between the various elements out of which the democratic structure of the United States was constituted. The bringing-together process has taken place on a far narrower compass of space and with a far greater intensity of time than that which brought about the construction of an American society by immigration and pioneering throughout the past two and a half centuries.

The unifying element in this pageant of divergence is the sense which is shared by all of our immigrants and established community —of belonging to the same history, of being identified with the destiny of the same historic process. An Israeli is one for whom the central purpose of history has been the great march of the Jewish people for three thousand years and its fulfillment in the renewed cycle of its independence in its homeland. One who is identified personally with that vast process of continuity of life and aspiration is in every sense a citizen of this history, and therefore the divergences are bridged by a community of experience reaching deep back into religion and into language. The schools, the educational system and the citizen army of Israel are perhaps the most effective elements in unifying into the discipline and loyalty of a new nationhood so many peoples.

In order to understand the true significance of Israel, it is necessary to say a word about the more intangible and imponderable elements of the country's contemporary life and experience. What does modern Israel mean? To what does it aspire? What are its roots and what are its horizons in terms of the mind and of the spirit? This is perhaps the central question which future generations will ask about a people whose aristocratic tradition derives far more from its spiritual contributions than from any attributes of material greatness in the past or in the present.

Israel's new culture is still in the early stage of its emergence. All we can do at this juncture is to isolate and describe the elements which flow into its formation. By far the first and most fundamental element in the formation of modern Israel's culture is our sense of lineal descent from the ancient Hebrew kingdoms which proclaimed to mankind the authentic message of individual conscience, social justice and universal peace. Israel is not a new Esperanto nation writing its history upon a clean slate. One cannot begin to understand its associations or its memories without going deep back into the history of this people and this land. And the history of this people and land intersect in the Biblical epoch, the vivid memories of which exercise a far more active control upon modern Israeli life than most external observers have understood or believe. It was not an accident that from the first day of our statehood we expressed the emblems of sovereignty in terms which recalled the earlier period of Israel's independence; that the coins and the stamps of our republic all evoked memories of the Biblical period and of the two Jewish commonwealths which had preceded the revival and restoration of our statehood in this generation.

Here the question of language exercises its mystic and unfathomable influence. It is a matter of deep moment in spiritual and historical terms that our vernacular is the same language as that which prevailed in the life of the two previous eras of Israel's independence. It is a matter of great moment for every citizen of Israel to know that he speaks the tongue in which Isaiah prophesied the vision of universal peace, in which Amos declaimed against social injustice, in which Ezekiel looked out across the valley at the inscrutable mysteries of renewal and resurrection.

This sense of belonging to that incomparable tradition accompanies the life of modern Israel and springs out of its very depths. There is no more potent attribute in creating this link of conscious connection between modern Israel and Israel of old than this unique episode in the preservation and the revival of this most eloquent language ever uttered upon the lips of men.

Archeological discovery has in recent years further stimulated our people's consciousness of belonging to that tradition. The awesome experience of discovering in the depths of the Dead Sea Valley authentic documents of Hebrew and Aramaic literature belonging to that immortal period of Israel's creativeness have all had their effects in emphasizing the Biblical element in the cultural consciousness of modern Israel. It is this which gives depth to our nationalism.

The second element which goes into Israel's national culture is the experience derived and crystallized by the Jewish people throughout its particular history in the development of its own culture, experience and folk culture in the lands of dispersion. The rabbinic and Talmudic literature, the post-Biblical Hebrew poetry and philosophy, the attachments of the Jewish people to the arts and sciences of the Western world are all part of the reservoir from which modern Israel draws its sustenance.

And third is the broad humanism and technological advance of

Western Europe which constitute by far the predominant element in Israel's cultural life. It is true that our immigration contains a very large factor of Oriental derivation, but it is the cultural fact that it is they who assimilate to the existing European patterns of Israel's political and technological outlook. The victory in the great battle for the soul of Israeli culture belongs inexorably to the West which had already created the patterns and the outlooks of modern Israel before the Eastern immigration came to its shores.

We stand upon an eminence of history from which we look back three thousand years toward antiquity and forward toward the awesome challenge of atomic generation. There is no other people in history whose continuous historical experience covers the entire span of human progress from ancient Biblical ethics to modern nuclear science.

The Biblical tradition, the Jewish heritage accumulated through two millennia of exile, the technology and political institutions of the West—these are the three elements out of whose effervescence Israeli culture will arise.

Nation of Creative Rebels

Alfred Jospe

THERE is a Hebrew term which describes what I feel is essentially the spirit of Israel and its people. It is the word *hutzpah,* by which I mean the spirit of creative defiance. It is the spirit of Abraham arguing with God that He has no right to destroy Sodom and Gomorrah, to disregard the merits of the righteous, few though they may be. It is the spirit expressed in the famous Kaddish of Rabbi Levi Yitzhak of Berditchev who takes God to task for neglecting His people Israel and for delivering His first-born into the hands of God's enemies.

Erich Fromm, discussing the meaning of the Sabbath ritual, defines work as man's interference, constructive or destructive, with the physical world, while rest (as on the Sabbath) is a state of peace between man and nature.* *Hutzpah,* as I see it, is the rejection of such peace between man and nature. It is the drive to touch, to build, to transform, to change the physical world as well as man's inner world. It is the spirit of rebellion which refuses to acquiesce in the status quo and is ready to defy the forces of man, nature, history, yes, even God, in order to reach out for something better, more complete and greater than oneself.

This spirit of defiance is probably the dominant characteristic of the spirit which has brought Israel into being and sustains it today.

Israeli life is characterized, first of all, by a defiance of nature. The Negev is an outstanding example. On 280 kilometers of utterly depressing desolation, traversed only by a narrow black-top road, all one sees is sand, rocks, sky, loneliness and erosion which has bitten deeply into the rocky ground. There are just a few inches of rain during the year. The lifelessness is only slightly relieved by the luminous colors of strange rock formations.

And yet, Israel has transformed its South into an area alive with self-confidence, vibrating with the expectation of growth. There are new cities.

There are many other large sections, besides the Negev, that have been carefully nursed and beautifully developed. The spirit is the same everywhere. There is a vision to whose realization people inch closer through each day's hard work: the desert and other parts of the country are a rich potential, bursting with minerals or the promise of fruit waiting to be brought forth, lacking nothing but water to yield unheard-of crops. And water they will bring, tomorrow, the day after, in five or ten or twenty years; but bring it they will. The Israelis defy

* See pages 138–141.

nature in order to conquer it. By redeeming a land from the erosions of nature, they seek to redeem a people from the ravages of history.

Israel's defiance of nature is accompanied by its rebellion against history. Many Zionists had always accepted and affirmed Herzl's felicitous dictum that the Jews are a *people, one people.* In Israel one discovers that Jews are not one people but many peoples, with countless racial strains, with radically different cultural patterns and philosophies of life and attitudes toward work, religion, family and society—and that there are Jews who look and behave unlike anything we may have thought a Jew could ever be or look like.

Israel's Jewish population today is composed of two major elements. About half came from the Middle Eastern countries, the other half from Europe, in the main from Eastern and Central Europe. Two thousand years ago these groups had a common home base, but history separated and isolated them. They were dispersed on different continents and became acculturated to the peoples among whom they lived. And when, in our own day, their descendants arrived in Israel, the cultural and emotional baggage they brought contained many items that had been shaped by or taken from the culture of their non-Jewish environment.

From 1882 to 1948—the era of pre-State development—the overwhelming majority of immigrants had come from Eastern and Central Europe. The culture they developed in their new home was essentially a Hebraized version of whatever their European culture had been. The German Jews, who arrived in large numbers after 1933, imported the culture of the German middle class: its books and love for art, its social patterns and intellectual ambitions, the culture, skill and managerial competence of the *Herr Doktor.* The Jew from Russia or Poland brought along the *shtetl:* he imported Yiddish and the religious values and habit patterns of the ghetto, or the secularized Messianism of the Russian socialist which he sought to translate into reality in the communal settlements of Palestine. His culture was largely the culture of the *shtetl* translated into Hebrew.

After the State had been established, hundreds of thousands of North Africans and Orientals came from the coastal plains of North Africa, the rocky remoteness of the Atlas mountains, the vast emptiness of the Sahara. They came from the crowded *mellahs* of Morocco and Algeria, from Egypt, Syria, Iraq, Yemen: Arab or Arabized Jews who were endangered by the hatred of the Moslem world and had to be evacuated.

The differences between East and West are enormous. Some of the newcomers look as if they had come straight out of the pages of the Bible. Others look like Ali Baba and the forty thieves, with their baggy pants and colorful but dilapidated Oriental clothing.

There is a difference in color. The scale ranges from the flaxen hair, blue eyes and "cream and peaches" complexion of many young sabras of European parentage to the light brown of immigrants from Casablanca or Agadir, to the near-black of the Falasha or Indian Jew from Cochin China.

But the differences between East and West go far deeper. A major difference exists with regard to what students of the Arab world call "familism." In the Middle East the individual is deeply attached to his family and, in fact, subordinated to it to a degree that is inconceivable in the Western world. Specifically, as Raphael Patai has shown in *Cultures in Conflict*, the Middle Eastern family has several distinct features. It is patrilineal: every person is regarded as belonging only to the family of his father. It is patrilocal: the newly married couple takes up residence in the house, tent or compound where the husband's father and his family live. It is patriarchal: the father has all the authority over the family, and all its members must subordinate themselves to his authority. And it is endogamous: the preferred marriage is within a very close circle of blood relatives.

In the Western world home and family are a point of departure for the children; in the East they are a point of steady return. Our basic aim of education is to make the child gradually independent of his family; to train and equip him to become a person in his own right, establish his own family, live his own life potential to the fullest. In the East, education aims to retain the individual as an obedient member of the family or tribal unit.

Again the groups differ radically in their approach to education. In the Western world we offer it free and make it compulsory. Orientals are accustomed to consider education voluntary and restricted to boys, preparing them for participation in the life of the community. Even after their arrival in Israel, many Oriental parents retain a strong emotional block against having their daughters sit together with boys in one classroom.

Israel's ethnic diversity and cultural multiplicity are symptoms of the ravages which history has wrought on the body and soul of the Jewish people, and Israel today represents a rebellion against those ravages. What Israel must do is mold a people out of these diverse elements which had been separated not only by thousands of miles geographically but also by two thousand years of history.

It was inevitable that Jews, coming from different countries and social settings, would import not only the good habits but also some of the cultural and social prejudices of their countries of origin. Hence, even Israelis are not wholly free from fear of the different, the dislike of the unlike. In one of the small settlements which had taken in a number of dark-complexioned families from Iraq, a youngster, recently arrived with his parents from South Africa, refused to attend school with what he thought were "black" children. Similar tensions exist elsewhere. The newcomers frequently feel unwelcome, unwanted and hence insecure and inadequate. No matter how successful and well-integrated they become, some continue to feel that they are second-class citizens as compared with the "white" Ashkenazim who had settled and built the country before statehood and who now occupy or control all decisive positions.

These tensions will probably continue for a long time because of the fertility of the "Easterners" who will soon outnumber the people from the West. Orientals in general have an extraordinary birthrate by Western standards. Even if the natural increase of the Ashkenazi population were to be augmented by an annual immigration of five thousand Jews from America, the Oriental population would still grow much faster by natural reproduction. The question which troubles many people is whether the country will ultimately remain Western—not alone in its political orientation but in its mores, religious notions and practices, social habits and cultural stance.

Today, the West—that is, Europe—is still the dominant factor. It sets the standards to which to aspire. It tries its utmost to speed the process of absorption, acculturation and integration—all different terms for the same overriding objective: the Westernization of the newcomers. The reshaping process begins in school, where the children are Hebraized and absorb not only the customary subject matters but are also trained in discipline, cleanliness and punctuality. Another unifying influence is the army, which every young man and woman enters at eighteen, the boys for two and a half years, the girls for two years. The army is probably the single most potent factor in breaking down barriers among the different elements.

There is also a process of Westernization by legislation. Not long ago, the government passed a law setting the minimum marriage age of seventeen for girls. This departs from Jewish tradition, which permits a girl to marry at twelve plus one day. At the same time, however, the law breaks with Oriental tradition generally.

An attempt is also made to create a new nation—or people—even in the true biological sense of the word. Intermarriage between East and West is encouraged in every possible way. Israel's 1960 beauty queen was the daughter of a German immigrant and a Yemenite woman. On Lag ba'Omer, 130 weddings took place in Tel Aviv, about twenty between Ashkenazim and Sefardim; each of the latter couples received a wedding present of one hundred Israel lira from the municipality.

Whether these and similar factors will ultimately assure Israel's Westernization keeps some of Israel's keenest minds guessing. The

general trend is toward Westernization. Pronounced ethnic and ge-
netic differences will continue to exist, however, and Israel's culture
will have a distinctive Oriental coloration, especially in decorative art,
folk music and religious custom. In all other areas, it is hoped that the
West will emerge dominant, for Israel's political, social and scientific
Westernization is the only assurance that its rebellion against history
will succeed and that it will not be separated from the West by an
unbridgeable culture gap.

Defiance of the Jewish past is a third rebellion. Some people, especially the strict Orthodox elements, define it as the rebellion of the
godless against God—a denial of the validity of religious faith. But
what is really happening in Israel is largely a rebellion against what
many people consider the mentality of the ghetto, fortified by an
outraged reaction to what they feel are the coercive claims of the
clerical custodians of institutionalized religion in Israel.

The ghetto and institutionalized Judaism are the inheritance of the
Jewish past with which Israelis, especially the young generation, have
to come to terms—and often are utterly unable to do so. Actually, the
conflict is rooted in the very origin and nature of the Jewish people.
Historic Judaism is the fusion of two motives: Egypt and Sinai, the
one constituting Israel as a separate people, the other defining the
purpose of this people's existence. In the traditional view both belong
together. The Torah needs the people for its fulfillment in time and
space; the people needs the Torah as its guide toward the realization
of its national destiny. Jewish tradition hopefully claims that "Israel
and Torah are indivisible."

That Israel and the Torah are one is a statement of faith, however,
not of fact. Jewish life has always been characterized by the tension
between these two elements—the tension between Egypt and Sinai,
between *am* and *kadosh,* body and soul, the struggle for physical survival and the claims of the spirit, between life for its own sake and life
"for the sake of heaven."

Our conflicts and debates today are merely a symptom of this persistent tension. Are we to be a people like all other peoples, or are we
an *am s'gulah,* unlike any other people, carrying the burden of a
special divine vocation setting us apart from all other peoples?

In Israel, the battlelines are clearly drawn. Tremendous emotional
forces are involved in this clash. On the one side, the traditionalists—
of numerous shadings—insist, often vehemently, that Jewish identity
can be defined only in religious categories and that religion, in turn,
can be defined solely in terms of Torah from Sinai and the *Taryag
Mitzvot.* In their view, there can and must be no separation of church
and state in Israel, no matter how much Israel were to pattern itself

after the Western democracies in all other respects. In a Jewish state the law of the State must be Jewish—God's immutable and irrevocable law as revealed to Moses and interpreted by the rabbinic authorities. The creed and code of *Medinat Yisrael* must be grounded in the Torah, they say, and the State must use its power of legislation and enforcement to safeguard and compel public obedience to the ritual and sacerdotal practices of a timeless faith. The unyielding acceptance and continuation of the patterns of the past are the only guarantee that Israel's society will be a Jewish society and Israel a Jewish state.

On the other side are the men and women, often equally unyielding, who reject the pattern of the past precisely because they feel that in order to survive they must build a future that is different from the past.

The young Israeli finds it difficult to understand his forefathers— the tailors, peddlers, *melamdim,* the whole gamut of *luftmentshen* of Eastern Europe. He cannot understand how, during the nineteen hundred years of the Diaspora, his forefathers let themselves be passively massacred on the rack and in gas chambers. The young man or woman who, machine gun in hand, smuggled the pitiful survivors of concentration camps ashore in the dark of night under the eyes of hostile British patrols, or who stood guard against the murderous invasions of Arab *fedayeen,* cannot see any heroism in martyrdom. He fires back if he is attacked. This determines his attitude toward the last nineteen centuries of Jewish history. Whatever may have happened culturally and intellectually during those nineteen hundred years, to him they are primarily a record of cowardice and weakness. He knows little if anything about the successive flowering of Jewish centers in Babylonia, Spain, Poland, Germany; their philosophies and theologies, their Halakhah and ways of life, are, to him, merely compensatory ideologies, an "ersatz" for the lost national status of the past.

For this reason, many Israelis reject the men who represent exactly what they rebel against—the bearded Orthodox Jews with their Yiddish, their habits, their mentality, their observances—these, say many Israelis, are the language and mores of the ghetto. They, particularly, resist any attempt to bind them in what they feel is the strait jacket of a narrow ecclesiastical definition of Jewishness. They insist that Jewishness encompasses more than religion, that what makes them Jewish is not an assent to some obscure metaphysical notions or outdated rites but the same factors which, for instance, make England Anglo-Saxon: their country, their language, the literature and art they produce, the way they eat, drink, work, rest, procreate and deal with the fundamentals of birth and death.

Hence Israelis demand that in Israel, too, a man's religion should be his personal affair, that individual freedom of thought and belief should be inviolate, that the invasion of the civil code by the ritual code should be stopped, and that the complete separation of state and church should be enforced.

A second factor adds fuel to this rebellion. Many young people consider the Israel rabbinate obscurantist. They resent the intervention in politics by the so-called religious parties. They see religious groups, admittedly small yet vociferous and influential far beyond their actual numbers, which decry the very existence of the State as an unwarranted invasion by secular men of God's plan for Israel's Messianic redemption. They see a rabbinate which seems to concern itself primarily with banning the pig, rioting over Sabbath observance and demonstrating against mixed bathing in the Jerusalem swimming pool; and they feel the ecclesiastical authorities live in a world that is out of touch with modern realities. Joseph Badi, in his book *Religion in Israel Today*, concludes that "the synagogue today stands apart from the world. The rabbis are city or town employees and . . . they busy themselves only with ritual matters. Neither the synagogues nor the rabbinate as a whole have anything to do with youth work or education." The *Jerusalem Post* says: "When most of the young people come into contact with the rabbinate (e.g., at family ceremonies) their attitude tends to be one of more or less amused tolerance. It would be difficult for any rabbinate in the modern world to reach many of the young people: but with its present mentality, the Israel rabbinate is in danger of being regarded as little more than a museum piece."

Does the so-called rebellion against God mean that the young Israeli has ceased to be a Jew? The answer depends on what one's definition of a Jew is. If Jewish identity can be expressed solely in terms of prayer, in visits to the synagogue, in the observance of the dietary laws and all other Halakhic precepts, many young Israelis have in fact ceased being Jews, even though they still require the services of a rabbi at their wedding since there is no civil marriage in Israel.

But have they really stopped being Jewish? Whatever our definition of Jewish identity may be, we cannot write off the vibrant Jewishness found in Israel: the Jewish consciousness of the people, their love of their land, their sense of kinship with Jews everywhere.

We cannot write off the fact that the young Israeli knows his Bible better than does the Orthodox Jew of the Diaspora. As someone once said, a boy in an Israeli grade school can recite by heart more passages from the prophets than a professor of theology in Europe. And the Bible means something to him. It is not dead, a document of a forgotten past. It is his history book, the history book of his people.

We cannot write off the fact that the young Israeli speaks Hebrew, which is not merely the living language of a living people today but just as much the language of Jewish tradition. Every word is freighted with overtones that echo the emotions and experiences of thousands of years of Jewish life. Every word reverberates something of the spirit that fought for expression in the Bible, inspired our prayers, formed our traditions and molded the attitudes of our people.

Above all, we cannot write off the young Israeli as no longer being a Jew even in religious terms. There are undoubtedly genuine secularists in Israel. The writer Yizhar may be right when he characterizes some segments of the youth population as the "espresso generation." There is no all-pervasive quest for religious values. Yet one can often sense a deeper quest underneath this so-called rebellion of the godless. One cannot write off, for instance, the spirit of religious quest and affirmation which surges out of Hannah Szenes' poem, *Eli, Eli.*

> *My God,*
> *May there never be an end*
> *To the sand and the sea,*
> *To the whispering of the water,*
> *To the glistening of the skies,*
> *To the prayer of man.*

This is religion too, an outcry and outreach springing from the same depths of the human heart which may have motivated the psalmist three thousand years earlier. It may not be continuous with the formalized expressions and canons of the Jewish past; but this is exactly the question which Israel poses: can a Jew be defined only in terms of the standards and criteria of the past, or is there room for new expression? Are Jews today supposed to be merely custodians, the curators of a past which they did not create but which nevertheless makes a claim upon them, or may they also be creators, seeking to give expression to man's deepest impulses, aspirations and commitments in a new language and in new forms?

It is doubtful whether a full reconciliation of the opposing views can ever be achieved. No culture is ever free of conflicts and tensions. In the pluralistic society of Israel, these conflicts will probably continue to exist both as creative tensions and as one of the dissonances in the emerging culture of a people. While pledged to safeguard its civil code from the intrusion of the ritual code, Israel will have to come to grips with the spirit of its own past that defines the purposes and meaning of its national existence.

Image of Israel

Oscar I. Janowsky

I SPENT five months in Israel and met numerous visitors who were
fascinated by what they saw in the country. My mission was to study
the welfare policies of the new state, but as I read far too many, and
dry, government reports and interviewed scores of officials, I could not
get the tourists out of my mind.

What is it that intrigues them?

Israel is no utopia, and its people are no saints. Poverty is evident
there as elsewhere, and one is not enchanted even with picturesque
mendicity or slums.

There is political bickering, status seeking and vanity, as in all
human societies, and one is not captivated by these qualities. I spent a
few days at a fashionable hotel on the coast, and that experience
certainly does not evoke enthusiastic memories.

To be sure, the Israelis are very friendly. They are warm, eager to be
helpful, and everyone is an amateur guide. They are proud of their
achievements and want you to share their enthusiasm. Compulsive
speakers, they often overreach themselves.

I was crossing the intersection at Terra Sancta in Jerusalem, where
there is considerable traffic by local standards. My gray hair induced a
gentleman to take my arm in a spirit of helpfulness. When we had
negotiated the crossing, he asked:

"You are a visitor?"

"Yes."

"Where from?"

"America."

"From New York or Brooklyn?"

"From New York."

He looked squarely at me and challenged:

"Here it is better than in New York."

"Why?" I asked, and braced myself for a spiritual harangue.

"Here," he said, "we are building." And his eyes turned proudly to
the imposing unfinished structure across the street and the large crane
perched overhead. I parried to draw him out.

"And you think that in New York we do not build? We have a few
tall buildings, too, and such cranes are not uncommon either."

He was perplexed and quickly shifted his ground. It was a hot day, a
hamsin having followed a heat wave. The desert *hamsin* blows up fine
particles of sand which dry your throat, and the heat goes to your

head. He coughed lightly, tugged at his open collar, and said stubbornly:

"But here the climate is better."

This gentleman really evoked the image most characteristic of the country. The Israelis are building with a dynamism, daring and intelligence which impress the visitor. And they are transforming the country.

Nature has not been kind to this strip of soil, rock and desert which has been idealized through the ages. The land is small, and by modern standards quite barren. Only a few years ago, the visitor was dispirited by the wastes of the Negev, the waterless southland where nomads roamed, the rock-strewn valleys, the coast disfigured by sand dunes, the hills rising bare, harsh and cheerless.

Soon after the war, a wealthy American industrialist had visited the country and returned unimpressed. He saw no rich soil beckoning to homesteaders, no mineral resources to lure prospectors, no ready market for quick returns.

"There is nothing there," he told me with contemptuous finality. Yes, nothing but people, and he had not had the vision to see that desperate and courageous men and women can meet the challenge of insufficiency, that inhospitable soil and climate can respond to patient toil and modern scientific knowledge.

The land has responded and its face is being transformed. Hundreds of new settlements dot the hillsides, and below, in the valleys, fields which were waste only yesteryear are heavy with life-sustaining crops.

The landscape is changing: a treeless country twenty years ago, with human beings panting for shelter from the hot sun, the hand of man which in the past denuded the land is now laboriously investing it with nature's garments. Trees line the highways, and the craggy hillsides, so long wholly bare or sprinkled here and there with lonely and shriveled olive trees, are beginning to be wrapped in a mantle of green.

Even the Negev, mute and forbidding for centuries, is astir with new life. Buses, lorries and passenger cars speed along the new highways and planes whir overhead, transporting people and goods to outposts at Sodom or Eilat. The desert itself is no longer entirely a waste to be spanned in haste. The eye is startled by the sudden appearances of islands of habitation like Sde Boker, man-made oases literally wrung from the wilderness. In the distance, such a settlement has the deceptive quality of a mirage in the overwhelming grey-brown desolation which surrounds and envelops it. But it is reality.

Water is the wand that works the magic. Twenty-five years ago, I stood at the monastery atop Mt. Tabor with a French-speaking monk and, as we surveyed the valley below, he said in a voice barely audible, "The Jews will win this land. They have bored down a thousand meters and found water."

The borings have multiplied and the ubiquitous pipelines convey the life-giving water from afar to the parched land. Everywhere, along the roads and into the fields, these fingers of metal reach out like rays of sunshine to probe and quicken and fructify the barren soil.

I traveled by bus to Eilat in October, an eleven-hour stint which no visitor in his right mind should undertake during that season. I paid the penalty in discomfort, but I had no regrets. The image of Israel would be incomplete without that experience.

I savored something of the hardship endured by the pioneers, and I saw the desert in slow and halting retreat before the onslaught of human knowledge, dedication and toil. A stretch of land is in full bloom under the covering shield of sprinklers. Beyond is the grim expanse of sand, with pillars of dust rising and mockingly performing a devil's dance among the rocks and stones. And the fringes of this wasteland are already yielding, as men are gathering stones, moving boulders and preparing the soil for cultivation.

Next year another field will be fruitful, another settlement will arise, another group of human beings, unwanted or unwelcome in their native lands, will have something to cling to as home.

The results of this dynamism have been phenomenal. In 1949, Israel produced foodstuffs sufficient to supply fifty per cent of the needs of the population of one million; ten years later, when mass immigration had doubled the population, the small arid country with scarce resources was able to supply seventy per cent of the foodstuffs for its two million inhabitants.

The world today is attuned to economic development, and visitors to Israel are fascinated by the image of man struggling to bend nature to his will. Economic development, just increased production and consumption of goods, would win acclaim. But, Israel's efforts do not end with material growth. Something more is communicated to the visitor.

The multiplication of goods and services without a sense of direction may create the illusion of progress and result only in waste. Richly endowed countries may be able to afford this. Israel cannot. Therefore gadgetry and conspicuous consumption are not the aims of Israel's dynamism, at least not yet. It is motivated by a broader purpose. Israel appears to be striving (in the illuminating phrase of Lewis Mumford) to convert energy into human welfare and culture.

In many parts of the world, the early stages of economic development brought misery in their train. Wealth accumulated, but the masses were mired in poverty, disease, ignorance and squalor.

Israel's economy has not been reared on cheap labor, Jewish or Arab. Its architects have not been dominated by the desire for quick returns. The passion for human liberty and equality stirs large segments of Israel's population. The conviction is strong that social stability and social change must rest on respect for human personality, individual freedom and democratic processes. This is what captivates the American visitor.

Public elementary education (universal, free and compulsory) was decreed in 1949, and in ten years school enrollments increased from one hundred thousand to five hundred thousand. Secondary education is still neither free nor compulsory, but the needy are assisted by graded reductions in tuition fees. Higher education and research facilities of superior quality are available at The Hebrew University, the Weizmann Institute, the Technion, Bar-Ilan University, and others.

Learning and knowledge are prized in the country. Of the many homes I visited, very few were without substantial libraries, and the books were not tooled sets meant only for décor. They were read and studied.

Every Saturday morning a study circle used to meet in a private home in Jerusalem, with the late President of Israel (Ben Zvi) in attendance. I found there a serious group of scholars, most of them private citizens, and even the President's guard sat before an open volume and followed the discussion.

Every other Saturday evening, a Bible study group meets at the home of former Prime Minister Ben Gurion. The chairman is a member of the Supreme Court, and every participant, in turn, prepares a paper and leads the discussion. I visited this study circle during a period of tense political controversy which rocked the country, but the then Prime Minister and his colleagues were concerned with the nature and sources of monarchy in ancient Israel, the time of Saul and David. This devotion to learning is part of the image of Israel.

Housing is a critical problem in a small country with mass immigration, and sustained efforts have been made to cope with it. Eight years ago, one-quarter of a million people lived in improvised, ramshackle immigrant quarters. Two years later, more decent housing had been found or built for all but fifty thousand, and each year brings improvement.

Old-age pensions have been provided through compulsory state insurance, and maternity grants and compensation for victims of work accidents are also available. Health insurance is not a state function, but more than three-quarters of the population are insured against sickness through non-government, mainly trade-union, funds.

The achievements in public health by government and private

agencies deepen one's faith in human intelligence. A million people were dumped into this tiny and poor country. Many were broken in body and spirit; more were illiterate, ignorant of the elementary requirements of hygiene and sanitation, prone to infectious diseases and weakened by substandard living in backward countries. This mass immigration threatened to undermine the health standards painfully achieved in preceding years. Infant mortality, for example, leaped from twenty-nine to nearly fifty-two per thousand of live births. (During 1949–50, the infant death rate in the improvised immigrant settlements was 157 per thousand!) But the menace was mastered, and today the infant death rate approximates the figure achieved prior to mass immigration.

There are lights and shadows in the image of Israel that haunt the visitor long after his return home. I recall a social visit to an average middle-class home. Of those present, two couples were natives of Czechoslovakia, one each of Poland, Germany and Austria, and a Yugoslav wife was accompanied by her Dutch husband.

I found myself in animated conversation with the Yugoslav lady, an intelligent, handsome and well-informed person. She gestured to make a point by raising her arm. The sleeve fell, and there was the concentration camp number burned into the skin.

Many Israelis are undergoing surgery to remove these savage symbols. A surgeon placed in the palm of my hand a strip of human skin which he had preserved, number and all. The sensation is still acute and chills the body.

A man in the late thirties, a neighbor and friend in Jerusalem, twenty years ago saw his mother struck down and the entire family carted off to perish in a concentration camp. He fled from Czechoslovakia to Russia, from Russia to Rumania, where he was jailed, starved and beaten. Through a succession of near-miracles, he reached Palestine and found a home there.

The wife of a hotel attendant lost her toes in concentration camp experiments. When the camp was liberated she was hospitalized and told a leg would have to be amputated. She reminisced with me in a simple matter-of-fact manner. "I didn't care," she said. "I was happy because the torture was over."

In Nazareth I met a young man who had been in Auschwitz as a boy. After the war he attempted to enter Palestine as an illegal immigrant, was intercepted and imprisoned in Cyprus. He escaped somehow, got to Palestine, served in the War of Independence, was captured by the Arabs and remained a prisoner of war for a year. He now has a good job, a fine family and a small but cheerful apartment. He walks with a decided limp.

In Haifa I went on board a ship which had brought about a hundred immigrants from a country behind the Iron Curtain. I talked to the people, and they were happy to have left, as they put it, "the Communist paradise." When Israeli officials in uniform arrived, a pall of silence fell on the immigrants, and one could see the anxiety in their eyes. They had to be reassured that the men were "merely officials."

I traveled with one group of these immigrants to the settlement where dwellings had been prepared for them. An adolescent boy asked whether the three small rooms of the apartment would be shared by three families, and I can still see the reserved happiness on the faces of the entire family when they were told that they would have the apartment to themselves. The women were to be employed in a chocolate and a textile factory in the vicinity and the men on the roads. All were eager to begin at once to build their new lives.

Every image has its characteristic feature. In the image of Israel, the epitome is a lonely youth in the vicinity of Bet Katzir, a settlement near Lake Kinneret. The bank east of the lake is Israeli territory, but the overhanging mountain is beyond the frontier and well fortified. As I traveled along the road, I had the uneasy and fatalistic feeling that a volley from the mountain could easily dispose of the car and its occupants. Yet in the field east of the road and nearer to the mountain, I can still see an Israeli youth serenely guiding his tractor, virtually under the muzzles of enemy guns, to the last tillable foot of Israeli soil.

One stands in awe before such physical courage and spiritual strength. A whole people is in the process of regeneration. Risen from the ashes of the crematoria, liberated from the stagnant ghettos of Asia and Africa, this people has surmounted despair and is transforming barren soil into a viable homeland. One has the faith that such spirit will overcome all obstacles and will endure.

An Emerging Israeli Literature
Bernard Cherrick

WHEN we talk about Israelis, we must bear in mind that we are discussing a population made up of various strata, with widely different cultural and educational backgrounds. The range is from Second *Aliyah* men and women from the ghettos of Eastern Europe to German immigrants of the thirties who were quite divorced from Jewish interests, to the later mass immigration from Yemen, Iraq and North Africa.

It is only now, out of this melee, that a first generation of sabras with characteristics of its own is emerging. It is largely to this group that one has to look for what is happening with contemporary Israeli culture. These young people are either going to reject what the earlier generation laid down or they are going to accept it partially. Whatever the outcome, the sabra generation will shape the future of Jewish culture in Israel.

Clearly, not everything in Israel is to be examined by what it contributes to the overall Jewish cultural heritage. An independent country must necessarily be creative in areas which have nothing to do with the Jewish heritage. It has always been said that atheism in Hebrew is as much atheism as in any other language. If an Israeli writes a book on an anti-religious theme, the fact that he is a sabra and writes in Hebrew does not make the book any more a part of Jewish culture than if he were a Jew living in America and had written the book in English. The question is even more complicated when we discuss music. If a great Israeli composer like Paul Ben Chaim composes a symphony with a broad theme which has nothing to do with Jewish life or even contemporary Israel, it is not part of Jewish culture but it is surely part of Israeli culture.

In the realm of literature, there is much more evidence of a creative emerging Israeli culture. Three definite schools of writers show specific Israeli traces and tendencies.

First is the *galut* or "old" school, among whom Shmuel Yosef Agnon is probably the best known and the greatest master of prose. But Agnon was already a mature man when he came from Eastern Europe; he cannot really be called an Israeli writer. He has, from time to time, adopted an Israeli theme for his works, but he is at his greatest when writing in Hebrew of the medieval poets, the Talmud or the Hasidim, and when he is writing about life in the little village of Eastern Europe.

Among the *galut* poets are Uri Zvi Greenberg and Shin Shalom. Although Greenberg has identified himself with the current life of Israel, his style and tone reflect his training, background and expressions, his reaction to Jewish history and his concern for what is happening to Jews in the rest of the world. In all this he belongs to the older school of current Israeli writers who are very popular and whose works appear in week-end literary supplements and monthly literary journals, of which there is a great profusion in Israel. Greenberg's poems, for example, appear in the newspaper *Ha-aretz.* Despite their popularity, this older generation is passing in Israel.

There is a second school made up of a generation also born in the *galut,* who came to Israel at a younger age than did the Agnons and Greenbergs. Coming in their late teens or early twenties, they became identified with the upbuilding of Palestine just before or immediately after World War I. They were young enough to become halutzim and spend their formative years attached to the soil and in the kibbutzim. They worked on the road and became active members of the early *shomrim* (watchmen), the predecessors of Haganah, who guarded the new colonies against Arab marauders. But their identification with the developing life of the new country notwithstanding, they had lived in their countries of origin long enough to have had some part of their formative education there. They retained nostalgic memories of the "old country," its yeshivas and *shtetlakh.* Because of this, they relate not only to modern Israel but also to the whole Jewish people. From the point of view of an emerging Israeli culture, these writers do not completely reflect the country and its natural background. Belonging to this school are the short story writer Yehuda Yaari, the late Yitzhak Shenhar, better known as Shenberg, and Leah Goldberg, who, though primarily a poet, is also a playwright.

Somewhere between the first and second schools is Nathan Alterman, the talented political poet who has satirized so much of the political development of mandatory Palestine and the growth of Israel. Alterman is certainly of the *Eretz Yisrael* landscape and the greatest part of his later poems deal with aspects of life in Israel.

It is the third group, however, the sabra writers, who must be considered as the major factor in shaping the future of Israeli literature. They share a great deal of similarity in their backgrounds because the country is so young and so small. The recent political history of Israel and its struggle for existence are so ever-present that most young people still retain vivid memories. In fact, they may well be called Israel's "angry" young men and women.

Because their lives have been spent completely in Israel, most of them are utterly divorced from Jewish life outside. Indeed, no major novel or piece of writing of the young Israeli generation is concerned with Diaspora Jews. Occasionally one runs across a short story which deals with Jewish types who are not of current Israel—usually the grandfather who has come to live in Israel but who has remained foreign to the country and represents the *galut* to the young sabra. For him *galut* and ghetto tend to be synonymous; he has no conception of Diaspora which is not *galut*.

The young Israeli understands a Jew who is persecuted or who has to be rescued; there is no sacrifice too great for that. He is willing to be parachuted into enemy territory and to carry on activities behind the enemy lines. But Jews of the Diaspora have no meaning to him. He expects Jews who are free to do so to come to Israel. He does not understand the Jew who remains abroad, and he is little interested in him.

This attitude has given rise to an extreme though small group of writers who at one time were called "Canaanites" after the pre-Israelite settlers of the country, and at other times the "Semitic Group," identifying themselves as Israelis who belong to the Semitic peoples of the Middle East. They do not consider themselves Jews, and would have nothing to do with other Jews, arguing that "the Jew and the Hebrew are not and cannot be identical."

In their view, Jewish history stopped, more or less, with the Bible and started up again in 1897, or possibly in 1948. Zionists are anathema to them even though it is far from clear how history can start again in 1948 without the Zionist movement and everything before it. But these Canaanites or Semitics are an interesting phenomenon, often attracting the best of the young writers but never retaining them for very long.

Milder offshoots of this attitude toward Diaspora Jews and Zionism are widespread among the sabra generation of writers and among young Israelis generally. To counteract this Israeli schools have introduced *Toda-a Yehudit,* or the "Jewish consciousness" element. This is basically an attempt to balance the ultra-nationalist feeling that disregards everything that does not happen in Israel, of Israel, or about Israel.

The average young writer of Israel, however, is neither a Canaanite nor a traditionalist. He was born in the late twenties or after, possibly in a kibbutz, or else, at an early age, he joined some kind of halutz youth movement and spent his holidays and vacations working in a kibbutz. At the age of ten or eleven he might have been a runner in Haganah, carrying secret messages.

The sabra writer may have taken part in the Jewish Brigade during the second part of World War II, later in fighting against the British as part of the Jewish underground movement, *Aliyah Bet,* the "illegal" immigration movement that was being carried on from Europe. Or else he belonged to the parachutists who were dropped into German-occupied confines as volunteers to rescue Jews.

Then came the experience in the War of Independence, the second war experience for the older sabras. They took part in the fight in the Negev or in Galilee, or lived through the siege of Jerusalem in 1948.

During this period the sabra writer found that he had creative ability. While fighting in the War of Independence or even earlier, he was writing and even publishing his first poem, short story, or novel.

Unlike the normal pattern by which young writers receive academic training, discipline and background in world literature and general education before having wide experiences in life, the procedure was reversed in the case of most young Israelis. They did their fighting and often some of their creative writing first, and then they came to Hebrew University to discipline themselves in Hebrew and to acquire a background in Hebrew literature as well as in English, French or other literatures and general history.

As a sabra, at home, the Israeli writer is free of the malaise characteristic of most Jewish writers of Eastern Europe or of other countries. He is militant, almost aggressive in his independence. He is affirmative and feels sure of himself—characteristics which show in his style and in his character portrayals. Unlike the Hebrew and Yiddish writers of an earlier generation who were much more familiar with the confining walls of the ghetto than with the beauties of mountain, valley or dale—the sabra writer is concerned deeply with and is part of nature. He is also politically and socially minded. He uses a colloquial Hebrew which is earthy, vigorous, natural and filled with new vocabulary which expresses modern life but which at the same time goes back to the Bible as a reservoir of language.

Furthermore, the sabra writer does not reflect the historical experiences of earlier generations. The Bible is his only contact with earlier Jews. "Before our parents all was dark" is his guiding line.

The sabra has gone through several stages in his writings. In his earlier stages he tended to glorify life in the kibbutz, in Haganah and the War of Liberation. His heroes were inclined to be excessively good, and the virtues and valor of labor were extolled. Next came the theme of the ingathering of the exiles, with stories about the Magic Carpet from Yemen and other such heroic episodes. This was followed later by a reversion to aspects of Jewish history. Moshe Shamir's novel, *King of Flesh and Blood,* for example, deals with the Maccabees and the Second Commonwealth, while his *The Poor Man's Lamb* is set during the period of King David.

But today the sabra theme is anger, and present-day sabra literature is inclined to be the literature of protest. The writer sees the conflicts of kibbutz life as well as the problems confronting individuals during the War of Liberation. Not every soldier was a hero nor is every kibbutz a utopia. The writers are disturbed by what they consider lack of character among young Israelis and their lack of interest in ethical values, and they write out of their disillusionment.

S. Yizhar, a nephew of Moshe Sharett, is a good example. His works, which last year were among the most widely read, depict the bitter conflict between the demands of national exigencies and human conscience. One of his characters states: "The time will come on returning from work, tired and worn-out, one will enjoy meeting a fellow man, or walking silently along—just walking, leaving silence to envelop everything and permitting nobody to break or interrupt the silence . . ."

One of his soldiers is far from heroic: "Fear possessed him: a strange fear, a sense of the abysmal nothingness of your being, with a double will: to forget and to remember, such a kind of shadow of death, while whenever you try to see ahead, a falling into nothingness, and a desperate confusion hurtling down."

Yizhar also depicts the reaction of one of his characters who has to conquer an Arab village. He is deeply disturbed when he sees the refugees: "I have never been in the Diaspora. I have never known what it means, but people have talked to me—have told me, and ingrained into my ear 'galut' but at this moment its real meaning has dawned upon me: such is *galut*."

Moshe Shamir, born in 1921, is rated tops among young sabra writers. *He Walked in the Fields,* one of his best-known works, deals with the problems of kibbutz life and the "fall" of the hero's family life there. The son of the kibbutz comes back from school to find his father in the army and his mother in the midst of love affairs. *With His Own Hands* is an outstanding novel, dealing with the depths and struggle of the young soldier, Alek, from babyhood to youth. It is semi-autobiographical, written out of the memory of the author's brother, who was killed by the Arabs in a convoy to Jerusalem. It gives a picture of the attitudes, actions and anger of the younger generation.

Another major sabra writer is Yigal Mossensohn, an angry young man and an excellent storyteller, whose themes are also like those of his fellow sabras. *The Way of Man* is a critical novel about the kibbutz and Haganah, while *Casablanca* stresses the problems of North Africa immigrants. Mossensohn has also written a large number of plays, some quite controversial, as well as children's stories.

Benjamin Tammuz is especially noted for his introspective short stories, often told from the point of view of the adolescent and occasionally presenting semi-beatnik types. The literary editor of *Ha-aretz*, Tammuz is also the creator of Uzi, a famous comic strip character in Israel.

Among the leading young poets is Yehuda Amichai, whose second volume of poetry was acclaimed as "a major poetic event."

> *I've seen that you can live and get along*
> *And decorate the lion's den, if*
> > *there's no other place.*
> *I don't give a damn if I have to die alone*
> *But I want to die in my own bed.*

An innovator in poetic forms, some of his works are based on medieval Spanish poets. Others reflect war weariness.

> *Once I ran away but I don't recall*
> > *when and from which deity,*
> *Therefore I swim through my life*
> > *as Jonah in his dank whale*
> > *throughout the deep sea.*
> *I have come to terms with my fish*
> > *because I am in the bowels of*
> > *the world.*
> *And so is he. I won't be abandon-*
> > *ing him. He won't be digesting*
> > *me.*

His work expresses the angry generation—who are devoid of the old values to guide them.

Haim Guri is another important sabra writer. His is the typical biography already familiar to us. Born in 1923, he went to school in Tel Aviv and spent time in a kibbutz. In 1947 he went abroad on a Haganah mission to Hungary and Czechoslovakia. Then he spent time in Eilat in the Negev, and later went to Hebrew University where he studied Hebrew literature and French. His major contribution is in army and folk songs and lyrical soldier's poems interpreting the ideas of his generation.

There are many more—including poets like Yitzhak Shalev, Amir Gilboa and Abba Kovner and, in prose, Aaron Meged, Mathi Meged and Mordecai Tabib. Whether angry or not, the sabra writers promise much for the future of Israeli culture.

VII

Jewish Life
in the United States

Can American Jewry Be Culturally Creative?
Salo W. Baron

AMERICAN Jews are now deeply concerned, more than ever before, with the problem of revamping and reshaping the Jewish tradition so that it can once again become a living entity. Can we in the United States, upon whom the mantle of leadership has fallen—perhaps too suddenly, too unexpectedly, too unpreparedly—take the place of the great Jewries of Eastern and Central Europe in creating a cultural center for the Jewish people in the Western hemisphere?

Time and again we hear pessimistic predictions, reinforced by similar statements emanating from Israel, that American Jewry has no cultural future. Three centuries of Jewish American life, these observers point out, have created relatively little. Indeed, it is disconcerting that over two hundred years—or more than two-thirds of the whole period during which Jews have lived in the United States—elapsed before the first Hebrew book, exclusive of reprints of Bibles and prayer books, was written and published here.

What has happened since is a little more encouraging. We have witnessed, in the last century, a heartening growth of the Yiddish press, the Yiddish theater, Yiddish poetry and songs. Simultaneously, we have seen the rise of Hebrew culture and of Jewish scholarship in English equal in caliber to any produced in Europe and Palestine during the twentieth century.

But can we truly claim this as an American phenomenon? There is no denying the fact that the main protagonists in the culture drama were people born and bred in the Old World. The major contributions to Hebrew and Yiddish culture in the United States have been made by Jews born and educated in Poland, Lithuania, the Ukraine, Germany and England.

Then too, it is often said in Israel as well as in the United States that American Jewry is too materialistic, too concerned with monetary values, to be creators of culture. Everyone admits of course that American Jews, in raising money and developing new techniques of fund-raising not only for themselves but for the whole Jewish world, have established a philanthropic structure the like of which has never before been seen. It is also freely conceded that American Jews, despite the fact that they have come from all over the world, each bringing different traditions, biases and animosities, have built a communal structure of imposing dimensions, and have developed new institutions, adapted to new forms of living—all on a voluntary basis, and without government support or official status. In a real sense, American Jews are communal pioneers working out a network of Jewish centers and YM-YWHA's to meet American needs, organizing fraternal orders and *landsmanschaften,* and generally setting the pace in organizational forms for the Jewries of the free world.

But culturally, it is held, we are still at the beginning. Some people even warn that we may be at the end. As soon as the influx of European Jews tapers off, they say, as soon as the main reinforcements from the reservoirs of Jewish cultural strength stop, American Jewry will prove how impoverished are its own cultural resources.

Before condemning our cultural insufficiency, however, we should consider the development of great cultural centers throughout the history of the Jewish people. How long did it take them to flower? Babylonia, for example, which created the great Babylonian Talmud, was unquestionably creative during the First Exile, but this was only a temporary phenomenon. As soon as the Babylonian exiles returned to Palestine, the large majority of their fellow Jews who were left behind ceased to function as a great cultural force. Josephus, in his first book on the great war, addressed himself to the Babylonian Jews, whom he speaks of as numbering in untold multitudes. Though it is estimated that more than a million Jews, or one-eighth of the total Jewish population of the world, lived in Babylonia in the days of Josephus, they created nothing culturally.

And yet, it was Babylonian Jewry which furnished cultural manpower for Palestine; this was true time and again, not only in the days of the Exile but in later periods as well. A Palestinian historian recorded in the third century that three times the Torah was in danger of being forgotten in Palestine, and three times Babylonian Jews came and saved it—first, Ezra; the second time, Hillel; and the third, Rabbi Hiyya. In other words, there existed in Babylonia scholars and rabbis, but they were inarticulate; they were not yet culturally creative as they were to become a century or two later, when they produced the Talmud.

A similar situation existed in Spain. This became a great Jewish cultural center only during the Golden Age in the tenth, eleventh and twelfth centuries, and yet there is evidence of Jewish communities in Spain as early as 300 C.E., and probably earlier. It is even surmised that Paul wanted to go to that country in order to address Jewish communities and speak in synagogues. But had a catastrophe occurred and wiped out Spanish Jewry before 900 C.E., there would have been no record of any cultural activity. And this despite the fact that the Spanish Jews were numerous, fought enthusiastically for their religion against the Visigothic kings, enduring two expulsions and many forced conversions, and emerged, nevertheless, strong and powerful. But culturally, we have no record of their activity, no book or poem. After six or more centuries of organized communal life, Spanish Jews were still culturally uncreative. Then all of a sudden, following the tenth century, a galaxy of creative personalities arose like Solomon ibn Gabirol, Judah Halevi, Moses and Abraham ibn Ezra. The great Golden Age of Spain was at hand, the like of which Jewry has not experienced since.

The same thing happened in Germany. In the fourth century, Emperor Constantine the Great addressed two decrees to the Jewish community of Cologne, which were incorporated into the Theodosian code of law. Organized Jewish communities existed from about 300 on, and yet nothing is heard from German Jewry before the tenth century, shortly before Rabbenu Gershom. From 300 to 900, Hebrew literary documents are completely absent, and we might well have doubted the very presence of Jews in Germany were it not for some incidental references in non-Jewish sources. But in 900 or soon thereafter, they started a new life and produced law books, commentaries and homilies, poetry and chronicles, making medieval German Jewish history of central significance in world Jewish history.

And in Eastern Europe, we have Jews in Khajaria in the eighth and in Kiev in the tenth centuries, the latter even boasting a "Jewish gate." Yet, Polish and Ukrainian Jewries were culturally inarticulate until they found their voice late in the fifteenth and early sixteenth centuries, when a great cultural outpouring took place. In the middle of the sixteenth century, Polish Jewry produced some of the greatest Jewish scholars, and from that time on, Poland, like Germany, became a great center of Jewish culture.

What is clear from the example of these four great centers of Jewish culture in the past is that it takes time for any culture to grow. Centuries must pass before the Jewish community can take sufficient root in any new country to develop its own attitudes, which become in turn a basis for creativity. Three hundred years of American Jewish life do not necessarily prove that we must remain culturally uncreative. Compared with these centers of the past we have accomplished much.

But we must also look at the reverse side. We face conditions today which threaten Jewish cultural creativity and even survival. These may be simply stated as a new development under Jewish emancipation, which created a new major crisis in Jewish history, one of unprecedented virulence since the First Exile. After the first fall of Jerusalem, the Jews had lost their country, their independence, their temple and their territorial moorings, and had to go into exile. This forced them into the permanent status of a minority facing varying majorities. It took several centuries from the Babylonian Exile to the late Pharisaic age before a real answer was developed to the question as to how a Jew could live in his own minority community in the Diaspora as well as in Palestine.

Because the Jews were able to develop a way of living their daily lives much as they would have done had they remained in Palestine, centered around their own cultural and religious institutions, and maintaining their own social welfare system, they were able to survive in Babylonia, in Spain, in Poland and in Germany—in fact, wherever they happened to find themselves. Though interterritorially dispersed, they were able to maintain their group solidarity and unity.

Now, however, under Emancipation, the Jews are accepted as Americans and Englishmen as well as Jews. They are no longer isolated minorities facing majorities, but they have become part and parcel of the majority nation. With Emancipation, Jews have had to give up much of their autonomy and their "separatism." As they have become integral parts of the ruling nations, some part of their heritage has had necessarily to be pushed into the background. In the West they emerged as one religious denomination among other religious denominations.

In Northern Europe, Jews were recognized as a nationality among other nationalities. If the Soviet Union, for example, had continued along the lines of its first decade during and after the Lenin regime— with the recognition of Jewish national minority rights and with a national school system in Yiddish, a Yiddish press and theater—one might really have witnessed there the emergence of a Judaism devoid of religion, Hebrew, the Zionist Messianic ideal, that is, a purely secular, Yiddishist national entity. Under such conditions, a Russian Jew, as was already noticeable in the twenties and early thirties, began looking down upon the American Jew as assimilated, sending his children to English-speaking schools, speaking English.

If that had developed undisturbedly, we might have had two types of Judaism, a national secular Yiddish Judaism of Eastern Europe, and the religious, Zionist, Hebraic Judaism of the Western world. And each would claim superiority over the other. Unfortunately, the last twenty years have seen a great change in the Soviet Union, and have put an end to the possibility of the evolution of any really flourishing national secular Judaism as such.

Our question today is whether Jews can be culturally creative under Emancipation. Can they be creative within their own as well as within the majority culture? Certainly there will be Jewish poets and writers, artists, musicians, scientists and scholars. If the pattern follows past experience, Jews will undoubtedly contribute more than may be expected from their ratio in the total population. But will they have enough energy of a cultural nature left to cultivate their own Jewish heritage? We can find no answer in history because history has had no precedence of real emancipation.

Fifty years ago, a short time in history, half of world Jewry lived in Czarist Russia, another significant proportion in Rumania, the Ottoman Empire and North Africa—all under conditions of non-emancipation. Even though one-third of world Jewry lived in the United States and other free countries at that time, most of them had been born and bred under conditions of non-emancipation, and could hardly have been expected to have changed overnight merely because they had left their *shtetlakh* in the Ukraine or Poland for Chicago or New York. In 1917 with the Russian Revolution, and in 1919, with the peace treaty, it began to look as though world Jewry might at last be truly emancipated once and for all. The great counter-movement of Nazism, however, arose to deny not only Emancipation but also the very right of Jews to exist.

Consequently, Emancipation really had no chance to show its good or its bad effects until after World War II. Only in our own day have we had the opportunity to observe the effect of real freedom—in this country and elsewhere. As a result, we have seen a tremendous rate of assimilation, and simultaneously we have also witnessed certain elements of religious and cultural revival which pessimists had previously considered impossible.

What are our chances today for cultural creativity? It is of vital importance to realize that a drastic revision of our cultural patterns is absolutely necessary under the revolutionary pace of Emancipation. We just cannot continue completely along traditional lines.

We need a new program of Jewish cultural activity in our time. Precisely what form this should take has not yet been determined. There are many different answers stemming from many groups and movements—which in itself is a sign of vitality. In this country we find constant struggle, even within Orthodoxy, Conservatism, Reconstructionism and Reform. Outside of these four religious movements, there have been numerous other attempts to come to grips with cultural problems. Such differences of opinion are vital.

When the American Jewish community begins to become conscious —as it appears to be on the way of doing—of its great obligations toward the whole structure of Jewish education, and when it concentrates on raising a generation in the direction of a new American Jewish type of cultural creativity, I for one would be willing to predict that two centuries from now, on the completion of five centuries of American Jewish life, we might have as flourishing an American Jewish culture as that of Spain's Golden Age.

The American Jewish Community
Harold Weisberg

WE HAVE reasonable cause for dissatisfaction with what is convention-
ally assumed to be valuable in the American Jewish community. Far
from undergoing a significant revitalization of their culture, religion
and standards of value, American Jews seem to be growing increasingly middle class in thought and deed, and their communal and
organizational success appears to be fundamentally a triumph of mass
culture and leisure. In fact, the established and flourishing agencies of
post-war Jewish community revival—the synagogue, center, welfare
funds, community councils, fund-raising drives and membership campaigns—may well be responsible, unwittingly, for a serious debasement
of character and culture in our community.

It is a truism to note the continuing decline of many dominant
Jewish cultural traits. However emotionally we may use the term
"assimilation," it is undeniable that we continue to assimilate American culture at a steadily increasing rate—so much so, in fact, that we
have all but lost what I wish to term the "natural" Jewish community
and culture and have replaced them by the "organizational" community and culture.

By "natural," I mean that aspect of culture which requires no un-
derpinning of ideology, no conscious campaign for continuity, no organized program for survival. It is the day-to-day intercourse of society
transmitted neutrally through habit, custom and tradition. Today we
have instead a culture and society which conducts its business under
the auspices of a set of public organizations (often overlapping in
their activities), each of which requires formal membership and claims
to offer some ideology to justify its existence. All these organizations
together constitute the culture of the community.

This is vastly different from the over-romanticized *shtetl*, for example, where the natural culture dominated the pattern of Jewish
communal living. One did not elect to speak Yiddish, one did not send
his child to heder in order to emphasize the continuity of the Jewish
tradition, and one did not join one or more organizations in order to
identify with the Jewish community. The culture was neutrally transmitted and carried on. It was a manifestation of the daily business of
existence, in which a particular language, an educational system, marriage customs and a social structure were taken for granted—just as in
the United States one learns the language, customs and habits without
a conscious effort to "participate in American culture" or develop a

theory of democracy. The natural culture is the culture of the street, group associations and ordinary but often crucial affairs of society.

By contrast, what is natural in the contemporary American Jewish community is largely non-Jewish: the American language, American shopping habits, American city or suburban neighborhood culture. These come to us without the aid of consciously organized programs, special modes of celebration and long hours of instruction.

But whatever is Jewish in the culture of the Jewish community seems to require conscious pursuit and continuous programming under the auspices of one or more Jewish organizations. The dominant elements in our daily experience—how we make our living, the kind of jokes we laugh at, the television programs we watch, the newspapers and magazines we read, the public school we attend, and our encounters in the shopping center, the street and the voting place are predominantly American and natural. Superimposed on or added to this culture—as a kind of adjunct—is the organizational Jewish culture which tries to accomplish, through organized planning and programming, what is natural in American culture.

We parcel out our Jewish culture to a number of organizations. Religion is "done" under the auspices of the synagogue. Fighting anti-Semitism is "done" under the auspices of various community relations groups, and recreation is "done" under the auspices of a community center or country club. The Jewish organizations provide the culture itself; their activities *are* the Jewish culture.

American Judaism might be mischievously but not incorrectly defined as the set of activities which takes place in the buildings and under the auspices of various Jewish organizations. We go to a building to practice Judaism, or we attend some public function to manifest Jewish culture. Presumably the organizations are supposed to effect a carry-over of culture to the home and the family. But we are primarily an organization-centered community, practicing its culture in and through organizations and rapidly transferring this culture away from the home, the street or local neighborhood, to the organization, its facilities, professionals and ideologies. No doubt this development cannot be helped, but its consequences and their effect on Jewish life cannot be ignored.

Among such consequences is the gradual sloughing off of many distinctive cultural traits of earlier natural Jewish communities. For one thing, Yiddish as a "second" or "first" language of American Jews is on its way out. If it hangs on, it is like a dispossessed tenant waiting for the sheriff to forcibly move him out into the street. It will not do to argue that there is more than a passing interest in Yiddish literature and language these days among intellectuals and some suburban Jews.

The interest is in translations, and the fact that there are Yiddish language courses in some colleges only indicates that it is by now sufficiently petrified to be worthy of academic consideration. Hebrew has not replaced Yiddish, and I doubt that it ever will. Furthermore, the loss of Yiddish is symptomatic of comparable losses in the distinctive and peculiar habits, intonations, sounds, smells, stories, ironies and customs which clustered around the language. It indicates the extent of the breakdown of the natural culture. For example, is there a Jewish folk culture in America? Are there "Jewish types" or folk characters—*schlemiels* and classic *luftmentshen*—in America? The prototype of the American Jew is instead a nice clean-looking "white Protestant" kind of Jew, presumably sophisticated, efficient and successful.

Another index of what is taking place can be noted in the neighborhood changes of the Jewish community. The older city neighborhoods had some kind of natural Jewish culture. There was what could be called a "Jewish street." Aside from pushcart vendors and *knishe* odors, whose passing we do not have to regret, there were Jewish book stores (places where one bought *s'forim*—copies of the Bible, Mishnah, Talmud and the *Shulhan Arukh,* rather than the gaudy Hanukkah menorah and Bar Mitzvah present establishments of today), the sounds of Yiddish, and manifestations of genuine piety. By way of contrast, the contemporary neighborhood is Jewish usually by virtue of a large concentration of Jewish population and possession of vast Jewish organizational structures and paraphernalia staggering to the eye and the pocketbook. We live in rather "decent" neighborhoods (even those of us who have not succumbed to suburbia) where there is no peculiar Jewish language of the street, no unique neighborhood culture, and where Jewish foods come packaged and precooked. What is "Jewish" about the new neighborhood is the organizational plant and activity, the pattern of meetings and drives, lectures, dances and fashion shows. In our daily living we dress, eat, talk and act like most other Americans.

This organizational culture is accompanied by the development of a predominantly middle-class sectarian Judaism. There is strong evidence that we have not only absorbed practically the whole of middle-class culture, but in the very practice of organizational Judaism we foster its growth. We prize success, almost any kind of success, as of greatest value. We confuse sentimentality with religiosity and the mediocre with the extraordinary. Demanding active participation in a variety of community tasks, we have made of those community tasks themselves a final goal of community life. We prize the man of action, the leader who gets things done, the man who can produce a crowd, raise the most funds, recruit the most members. What excites us most in Jewish life is the pattern of activity, tasks, jobs to be done, quotas to be met, meetings to attend.

All of this is usually done in a group, under the auspices of an organization, and largely unconcerned with the values or the ends the tasks allegedly serve. The communal organizations not only fail to discourage middle-class and mass cultural values but their very success depends on furthering them.

This shows up most clearly in the synagogue. We are supposed to be living in the midst of a substantial theological revival, but this theology, which goes under various names—from neo-orthodox to existentialist—is employed as an ideological prop for the activities, programs and services of temples and synagogues. But it is basically a middle-class religion which is being offered. Whatever the faults of the new theologies—and they are many—most have stressed the personal qualitative elements of religious worship, the need for deep religious conviction and a sense of holiness and piety.

But our synagogues and temples, despite a torrent of words to the contrary, stress the very values that their theological ideologies are committed to oppose. The synagogues are large and comfortable. The services are conducted by professionals who do not simply perform the services, but spend almost an equal amount of time instructing the congregation when to rise and when to sit down, what page has just been finished and where to turn next. The congregation itself is largely ignorant of the order of the service and the meaning of the prayers. The translations are often very poor, and the "activity" of worship consists in the dull, monotonous recital of responsive readings, punctuated occasionally by a choral rendition or "congregational sing-ing." Worse yet, the tone of the service is "spiritual." There is a deathly silence in the synagogue. The rabbi in his clerical robes is grave, solemn, introspective, forbidding, but rarely warm. He may preach to a sea of mink and persian the virtues of humanity and piety. He may cite a homily, quote a text and emphasize the value of *kedusha*. But he is betrayed by his surroundings: appeals to piety in the modern luxurious synagogues have a hollow sound, as do exhorta-tions to virtue, sermons on humility, withdrawal or contemplation.

In other community activities the influence of mass culture is also quite profound. The use of prestige promotion, the "soft" and "hard sell," the "gimmick" devices and mass communication techniques characterize much of the content of Jewish organizational activity. It will not do to say that these are necessary in the promotion of worthy causes. The means unfortunately cannot be overlooked. They influ-ence and in many respects overwhelm us. The crux of the matter is that without the techniques of mass culture and the standards of middle-class culture, Jewish organizational life would collapse and with it much of what passes for Jewish culture. A Jewish community without "drives," meetings, functions, testimonial dinners, planning sessions and campaigns is impossible to contemplate. There would be nothing for Jews to do.

The American Jew, as we noted earlier, is just like all other middle-class Americans, perhaps more so. What is now alleged to be distinctively Jewish about him is his religion. Since his natural culture has largely disappeared and has been replaced by American natural culture, what remains of his "Jewishness" is centered completely in organizations. The American Jew is a member of a religious community, the "third" faith. It sharply separates the domain of the religious from the domain of ordinary affairs, it practices "religion" mainly under the auspices of some religious institution, and it activates its religious life only at specified times or particular occasions. Whether we approve of this condition or not, and no matter what "culture content" we read into Jewish religion, the Jewish community is identified as a religious community.

In the midst of all the meetings, campaigns and other activities, a time does come when one begins to question the purpose, point and price of this organizational culture. There are always the children asking questions, there is an adult education course which raises doubts, and, most important of all, there is often a choice to be made between competing synagogues or other institutions. The synagogue service may not inspire, the children may not be satisfied with a conventional explanation of the absence of a Christmas tree, we may begin to feel a touch of cultural claustrophobia and wonder whether the standard routines of the Jewish community are not a bit too confining, and our daughter may want to know why dating the Sullivan boy is taboo. Starting from such specific questions, doubts may grow and problems of Jewish survival and continuity begin to disturb us.

This unrest is most acute among the younger members of the community, the college population and the young married people, who are increasingly products of the organizational community and quite remote from the natural Jewish culture of a generation or two ago. We are not now dealing with children of immigrant families who rebelled against the natural Jewish culture of their parents and have, in many respects, recently "returned," but rather with the children of those who have returned and built the organizational community. These young people do not come to their Judaism or Jewishness in the street or neighborhood, and through natural and normal means of cultural transmission. They have to learn their Jewishness through schools, camps and youth activity programs. They do not go to schools and camps merely to "get a Jewish education"; they go or are sent in order to learn to be Jews. They are to be made *into* Jews, not educated *as* Jews. Moreover, the Judaism they develop or are exposed to is quite fragmentary in character—a ritual here, a wedding there, perhaps a seder, and of course the ubiquitous Bar Mitzvah. But there is no continuity of culture, no organic relationships among the fragmented activities and practices.

This creates a number of problems, not the least of which is that the more sensitive young people quickly realize that the Jewish organizational community is essentially an adjunct to the natural American culture. It does not seem to be integrally related to the dominant, momentous options of their lives. Gradually they come face to face with the crucial and inescapable questions: "Why be a Jew?" "What is the value of Judaism?" "Why should I continue to identify with the Jewish community?"

In other words, they want some ideology to justify their Jewish identification. Many of these young people find sufficient satisfaction in the general American culture and are disturbed by the apparently "useless encrustation" of a Jewish organizational culture upon the natural American culture. While these are perennial problems they are complicated by the fact that the organizational culture, in many respects, unwittingly encourages dissatisfaction and a search for ideologies. On the one hand, its adult courses, lectures and sermons suggest a spirit of inquiry, analysis of Jewish life and quest for ideologies. On the other, we are constantly reassured that the answers will always be affirmative, that Judaism is true and good and noble, that the Jewish way of life is of superlative worth, that Judaism is first among its peers.

The truth is, however, that the answers cannot always be affirmative. Indeed, I suspect that the search for a suitable Jewish theology is bound to be frustrating. For example, when a sensitive and inquiring young Jew analyzes contemporary American Jewish life, instead of ethical and religious distinctiveness, he is likely to discover a complacent middle-class community, stressing activity and organization. There will be no great religious or spiritual heroes to inspire him, no dedicated way of life to motivate him, no cause—save organized philanthropy and experiencing Israel's accomplishments second-hand—to thrill him. The Judaism he will discover will be ordinary, mediocre, *parve* and at root often boring.

Moreover, in seeking some ideology to justify continued Jewish identification, young people are further confused by the repeated promises of golden destinies for American Judaism. They are informed that if only they would read and study, take adult courses, seriously analyze and carefully appraise their Jewish tradition and its contemporary manifestations, they would find Judaism a rewarding way of life and the experiences of Jewish communal life satisfying and fulfilling. But these promises are betrayed by the kind of community that actually exists, which has little in it that is great, ennobling or inspiring.

The consequences are not difficult to foresee. We are on the verge of a great disappointment. Our predictions about the future are catching up with us; the "revival" has apparently failed to develop that kind of Judaism which would permit us to continue as an important ethical and religious community.

The question will always lurk: "Why be a Jew?" While a sense of inevitable submission will take hold of many, others—and an increasingly large number—will rebel and break. Few, however, will willingly and affirmatively accept the organizational community. They may identify formally and may even be "active," but deep emotional conviction will undoubtedly be lacking. Worse yet, many will hanker after some invisible and unattainable ideology which will make it all clear and at last put to rest the lurking doubts and confusions. They will take their ideological pulse daily to see if and why they continue to live as Jews.

The organizational community will no doubt prosper for many years to come. But even if it appears to be flourishing, it will not reflect the glory of Israel's past nor promise a great and ennobling future. It will neither inspire nor transform, but reflect, affirm and promote the mass culture which threatens us all.

No doubt these are harsh words and dire predictions. They are meant to be. No doubt, too, the inevitable question of alternative suggestions and programs will arise. As we have said earlier, the preceding is put forth in the name of analysis and in the hope that more reflection on the status of Jewish life may help to lead us to a more positive Judaism.

A Layman's Look at Jewish Education
Label A. Katz

IT IS still the fashion abroad to find fault with Americans, to challenge us as a materialistic people in passionate pursuit of wealth and leisure, proud of our gadgets, expensive cars and homes. Culturally, Americans are supposed to be quite primitive, with little understanding or appreciation of art, music, literature or the other attributes of a sophisticated cultural life.

American Jews are appraised in the same cavalier fashion. We have more wealth than is good for us. That we are a generous community will be grudgingly admitted—but with the qualification that we could do better. Culturally, we are often adjudged ignorant of and unconcerned with Jewish values, Jewish education, Jewish study and learning.

Before taking a fresh look at American Jewish life, we must confess that in the material aspects, Jews tend to identify with the prevailing American way of life. But otherwise, we do have distinctive forms which make us unique: religious expression, social organization, a system of values and customs, a host of institutions growing out of our communal life, and the tasks which we, as a group, consider essential.

Contrary to the charge, we are a literate and intelligent community. In the roster of leadership in Jewish organizations are men and women of high educational and professional attainments—judges, doctors, professors, rabbis and teachers, business men, leaders in the arts and sciences, social welfare and government. As for the rank and file: a study of New York City in 1952 showed that twenty-six per cent of the Jewish male population twenty-five years and older had attended college. The percentage of college graduates is even higher in smaller communities: in Nashville, for example, forty-four per cent of the Jewish males over eighteen had attended college.

Recent studies of San Francisco and Washington, D.C. indicate that the ratio of college graduates among American Jewish women is also high, almost double that of the total white female population. In New Orleans the proportion in the professions had grown from fifteen to twenty-one per cent of the Jews gainfully employed since World War II. It is doubtful if any other Jewish community, including Israel, has attained as high a level of education.

It is far easier to be critical when discussing Jewish culture in contemporary American Jewish life. The indictment is familiar: lack of support of cultural efforts, of literature and the arts; shallowness of religious commitment; inadequacy of Jewish education and its irrelevancy to present-day Jewish life; neglect and ignorance of Hebrew, Jewish history and traditional values.

Jewish education as we know it today has serious deficiencies. About twenty per cent of the Jewish children of elementary school age receive no Jewish education whatsoever. Another forty per cent are exposed to *some* Jewish education at *some* time during their young years. Only forty or possibly forty-five per cent of the children are currently enrolled in Jewish schools.

The time spent by most children who attend Jewish schools is insufficient. More than forty-five per cent of those who receive a Jewish education attend Sunday school; forty-seven per cent afternoon schools (two to five sessions a week); less than eight per cent attend all-day schools. This means that a large majority of the children receive only two to six hours of instruction a week.

The children do not remain in school long enough to be seriously and positively affected. At best, the average Jewish child attends about three years of his childhood in a weekday school, or about six to seven years in a Sunday school.

The problem of teachers is even more depressing. Low salaries, unattractive conditions and discouragement have resulted in a serious teacher shortage. Many of those who remain in the field are not fully qualified.

Of our Sunday school teachers, nine per cent have had no Jewish schooling at all, and another fifty-eight per cent no more than an elementary Jewish education. More than three-quarters of the Sunday school teachers have no Jewish teaching license.

Even the weekday Jewish teachers—those in so-called intensive Jewish education—leave much to be desired: forty per cent have no Jewish teaching license; about thirty-eight per cent do not consider Jewish education their main occupation, often devoting their best energies to other callings.

The situation with respect to Hebrew is equally bleak. If language is an integral part of the culture and genius of people, our lack of fluency in Hebrew is a gross deficiency.

Only the wilfully blind would argue that all is well with American Jewry as a cultural community. And yet it is important to note lights as well as shadows.

The vast network of institutions and agencies that minister to the needs of American Jews, cooperate in the development of Israel and extend overseas aid are also elements of culture. They represent ideas, attitudes and values which are deeply rooted in the Jewish heritage. Hospitals, homes for the aged, child-care agencies and family-welfare establishments that serve community needs are part of our cultural growth.

Most important, the American Jewish community must be viewed in the perspective of a young community, barely emerging from the agonizing struggles of immigration and adjustment. In 1840 there were only fifteen thousand Jews in the United States; in 1880 there were still fewer than two hundred and fifty thousand. The millions arrived between 1880 and the first World War, an immigrant generation that expended its best energies in the bitter struggle for a livelihood.

Our immigrant parents attempted to reproduce the cultural institutions of the Russian-Polish ghetto, but without determining their suitability for the new environment. Habits and customs of the Old Country, its ideas, ideals and values, appeared irrelevant and useless to the native-born children who prized only acceptance in American society and culture. These new Americans shunned the synagogue, spurned the Jewish school and ignored Jewish scholarship, literature and language. A whole generation had to pass before harmonious adjustment between American and Jewish institutions could be effected.

It is only in our day that American Jewry has achieved psychological security and a measure of social homogeneity—two conditions necessary for cultural progress.

Young communities do not blossom into great cultural centers in two or three generations. Babylonia became a great Jewish cultural center in the third century C.E., in the time of Rav and Samuel. But Jews had lived in Babylonia since the destruction of the First Temple, and it took Babylonian Jewry eight hundred years to mature as a center of Jewish learning and culture.

Jews were established in Spain in significant numbers by the fourth and fifth centuries. But it took five or six hundred years before Jewish intellectual life there first reached a level of importance.

Certainly our young American Jewish community has not yet reached the level of the great Jewish cultural centers of the past. But neither are we in a cultural vacuum. We have our rabbinical seminaries, even some Jewish colleges and universities; we have academies of research and learned societies, libraries and museums; we have books, newspapers and periodicals of Jewish interest; radio programs, lectures, forums—and even some music and dance recitals. We have zealous groups that devote themselves to Hebrew and to Yiddish.

The evidence is conclusive that American Jews want Jewish identification and religious affiliation. They want Jewish education for their children, a better and more meaningful education than what they received. They want Jewish content and orientation in their Jewish institutions and associations. The mass flight from Jewishness has ceased. The great majority of the present generation accepts its Jewishness and seeks to render its commitment meaningful. It is disturbed by its lack of Jewish knowledge and bewildered by the holocaust which took the lives of millions of Jews. It has identified itself with the restoration and rebuilding of Israel. It is concerned with communal needs and overseas aid.

Synagogue affiliation has increased greatly. Although this may not represent piety or the pursuit of godliness, it unquestionably signifies the urge for Jewish identification, and, no doubt, concern for Jewish education.

Our deficiencies in Jewish education notwithstanding, there are also trends of great promise in this area. Enrollments have multiplied, increasing from 1948 to 1958 by over 130 per cent. Today there are five hundred and fifty thousand children in Jewish schools.

The growth of the Jewish day school movement is another indication of a deepening desire for intensive Jewish education. In 1942, there were thirty-three such schools, seven of them outside metropolitan New York. By 1958, 214 day schools in twenty-four states and the District of Columbia were in existence, with a total enrollment of over forty-two thousand.

The day school is a controversial issue. There is strong opposition to it based largely on the principles of public education in the American society. Some Jewish community leaders are disturbed by any separation of Jewish children from the public school. This is another problem: the fact that it is raised at all, however, points up Jewish growth in American society.

The concern of American Jewry reaches beyond formal education for children. Adult education and that of Jewish college youth have received considerable and increasing attention. Synagogues, temples, Jewish centers and national organizations have in recent years sponsored lectures, adult classes, study circles, institutes and other means of reaching the more intelligent elements of the Jewish community. Especially significant is the ferment in the Reform movement, whose rank and file are popularly supposed to be unconcerned with Jewish knowledge. In 1960, the Union of American Hebrew Congregations responded to a demand from its membership for more adult education by charting a program which calls for an adult school of Jewish studies in every temple. Similar accelerated programs are being nationally promoted by both Conservative and Orthodox movements—and by such mass movements as B'nai B'rith.

Fifteen years ago a serious clash developed over the recommendation for a positive Jewish purpose in Jewish community centers. An important segment believed then in the "non-sectarian Jewish center." Today, this is no longer an issue. The Jewish purpose of the center is recognized as axiomatic.

Perhaps the most promising trend of all is the growing recognition that Jewish education and Jewish cultural activity are not peripheral concerns within the organized Jewish community. Before World War I, Jewish federations did not recognize education as their responsibility. Even as late as the thirties there was heated controversy in federation and welfare fund circles over the question of whether it was right to divert funds—as the critics put it—from social service needs to educational and cultural purposes.

Today, central community agencies recognize the claims of Jewish education and cultural activity to a share of the community funds; both the dollar allocations and the proportional slice of the community pie have increased during the past twenty years, despite the continuously pressing needs of Israel, overseas relief and local social service programs. In 1937, less than six per cent of the federation monies allocated to local needs went to Jewish education; by 1957 it had risen to more than ten per cent.

We can no longer be importers of the wisdom that flourished from the great *shtetl* centers of East Europe. Nor can we be a cultural satellite of Israel. Culture reflects the life of a people, and Israeli life patterns are not likely to be reproduced in America. Our cultural future must be built by ourselves. The crucial fact, however, is that American Jewry is concerned with its cultural advancement. We are a Jewish community not by chance but by choice.

My Credo as Jew and American

Herbert H. Lehman

As AN AMERICAN, I view with alarm the decline in our country of the spirit of liberalism and the shrinking of its ranks during the past few years. People are so concerned with the problem of mere survival and the threat of annihilation which nuclear energy presents that everything else seems to dwindle in importance. The young men of our nation are greatly worried because they know that they must interrupt their lives to go to the military. We are all full of anxiety because there may be an explosion at any time. The prosperity which we have enjoyed until recently has brought about a kind of self-righteousness and the loss of moral perspective. As a result, ideas and ideals have lost their clear shape; the fire of positive conviction is no longer evident.

We are almost in danger of forgetting what liberalism is. In essence I believe it means to do justice in every situation, to use every effort and legitimate means to insure equality to all people. It takes for granted the inherent rights of every human being to enjoy equal opportunity in every field, decent living and working conditions, adequate provision for the moral and spiritual development of his children, and free association with our fellow men as equals under the law and in the sight of God. Above all, liberalism means a concern for the everyday needs of people.

None of these blessings, however, is self-executing. To make this liberal credo of kindliness, justice and decency in human affairs effective in our society requires constant vigilance.

Many of my political critics have called me a social-worker type. I have never denied this because there is much truth in it. I suppose my whole life has been in one way or another a seeking to advance the cause of liberalism and human welfare. Social responsibility has been a key concept in my thinking—the obligation upon each of us to fight against discrimination and for the rights of all men. My entire public career has been based on my firm belief that there is a responsibility on the part of society to protect the individual when he can not protect himself and to provide a government with a heart.

My memory goes back to the time when much of the social and economic security which we now enjoy did not exist. For example, American children used to work twelve to fourteen hours a day. Coal miners slaved without safety regulations for a pittance, and millions of our people in needlework and other trades toiled long hours in unsanitary, stifling sweatshops.

My own interest in social questions was awakened early in my youth. I grew up in an atmosphere of concern for the welfare of others. My parents and older brothers and sisters (I was the youngest of eight children) were very much involved in social welfare and charitable causes. As a child I was taken to see the slums of New York and the sweatshops, and all of this made a deep impression upon me.

My father Mayer Lehman had come over from Germany in 1848 as a young man and, like so many German Jews of that period, settled in the South. He married my mother in New Orleans just one hundred years ago, and they moved to Montgomery, Alabama, where he engaged in the cotton business. Ours was a warmly Jewish home. My father was religiously inclined, read Hebrew fluently, and conducted the seder and other Jewish festivals at home. He helped establish the Orthodox synagogue in Montgomery, which held services in German, and was a regular attendant on the Sabbath and the Holy Days.

During the Civil War, my father was in the Confederate service and as part of his duties was sent by Jefferson Davis to inform General Grant that the state of Alabama had set aside five hundred thousand dollars' worth of cotton to be sold in the North, the proceeds of which were to be used for the care of Alabama prisoners of war incarcerated in northern prisons. My father got as far north as Richmond and met with General Grant; but the latter refused the request for free access through the lines.

After the war, when our family moved to New York and my father became involved in business activities (he was one of the founders and most active members of the Cotton Exchange), he always took an active interest in philanthropy and Jewish communal affairs. Among his many civic responsibilities he served as director of Mount Sinai Hospital and on the boards of various other hospitals and child-care institutions. My older brother Arthur was also very active, serving later as president of the Federation of Jewish Philanthropies.

Irving Lehman, my brother, who was later to head the judiciary branch of New York State at the same time I was Governor, also had many Jewish interests. From his boyhood, he was always militantly proud of being a Jew, and he had a great influence on me. We enjoyed a very close relationship, and when I was in Albany we never missed a single Sunday morning without phoning each other and discussing the problems of the world.

A second major influence that gave direction to my life grew out of a long and close association with a group of liberals, chief among whom was Lillian Wald, the dedicated and devoted head of the Henry Street Settlement. She had come down to New York from Rochester as a young girl in 1893 or 1894, and had taken a small apartment on the lower East Side. With the training she had as a nurse, she started working among the people in the neighborhood. That was the beginning of the Visiting Nurses Service. A great friend of Jane Addams, the pioneer settlement worker in Hull House, Chicago, she soon broadened her work.

I first met Miss Wald and became a great admirer of hers while I was still in college, in 1897. I was already interested in social questions at that time, and remember writing an essay on immigration in which my views were not too different from those I hold today. But it was Miss Wald who sharpened my interest and helped focus it on the social problems that cried out for solution. When I left college, she invited me to take over a boys' club at the Settlement, known as the Patriots, which I led for five or six years.

Miss Wald was a great community leader and became involved in many city-wide efforts to improve the physical conditions and standards of labor, and I too developed a strong concern in these areas.

I soon became acquainted with Robert Wagner, then in the state legislature, and in 1912 I met Franklin Roosevelt, who was also in the Albany Senate. In the liberal group were Mrs. Belle Moskowitz and Mrs. Mary Simkovitch. Spending a great deal of time with social workers and labor leaders, I came to know Samuel Gompers and leaders in the garment industry, who were struggling against the sweatshops and for fair wages and better and safer working conditions. All these personalities had a growing influence on me.

In 1914, at the outbreak of World War I, I helped to found the Joint Distribution Committee, which came about as a merger of three Jewish groups—the Reform, the Orthodox, the Conservative—and certain labor and socialist forces, each of which had previously organized a separate relief effort which sent supplies to Europe. That merger was the beginning in the Jewish community of the movement to unify in all matters relating to charity.

By 1921, the active emergency relief program of the JDC had pretty well ended, but people were still prostrate economically in Poland, Hungary, Rumania, Lithuania, Latvia and other East European countries. I was appointed chairman of the Reconstruction Committee of JDC which had a fund of five million dollars for reconstruction work.

All this was good preparation for my political career, which began in 1928, when I was elected Lieutenant Governor of New York State. During my fourteen years in Albany, where I served two terms as Lt. Governor under Roosevelt and four terms as Governor, I placed great stress on unemployment insurance, social security, workmen's compensation, emergency unemployment relief and other things that affected day-by-day life of people. I was particularly concerned with care of the mentally ill, of which there were over one hundred thousand in the state hospitals, and saw to it that several large bond issues were authorized for rebuilding hospitals devoted to that purpose. In 1935, the only year my party had majorities in both houses of the state legislature, we enacted laws that George Meany (then head of the State Federation of Labor) described as "the greatest code of labor and social legislation" ever passed by any state in the nation. I take particular satisfaction in recalling that much of the legislation we put through in New York became a model for later federal laws as well as for those passed by other states.

Perhaps the work that has given me the deepest satisfaction and which I consider the highlight of my career was my service in the United Nations Relief and Rehabilitation Administration, which I headed for almost three years as Director General. At the request of President Roosevelt, I resigned as Governor three weeks before the end of my fourth term, in December 1942, to do the preparatory work for the creation of UNRRA, which was formally established by an agreement signed by forty-four nations at the White House the following November. President Roosevelt sponsored my election because he was cognizant of my interests and my experience—thanks to our years together in Albany—and also because he wanted Hitler and the Nazis to know that he was appointing a Jew to bring relief and rehabilitation to the people and areas they had ravaged. My appointment was to be a symbol to the world. I know it was recognized as such in Germany and throughout the world.

This vast operation involving the resettlement of millions of displaced persons and the rehabilitation of totally devastated areas in Europe and in Asia was undoubtedly the greatest relief effort in the history of the world. It was an indescribably farflung operation with missions in about twenty-five different countries. We dealt with countries having a population close to a billion people, several hundred million of whom were suffering from various forms of want. Fortunately we had available four billion dollars with which to work, and it was a tremendous challenge to act as steward for so important a trust.

During this period, I made eight trips across the Atlantic, and wherever I traveled in Italy, Greece or North Africa, I could see the results of our work. We literally saved hundreds of thousands from starvation. The help which we gave in certain countries, I am sure, was the one thing which kept them out of Communist control. I believe that today, behind the Iron Curtain, particularly in Yugoslavia, Poland and Czechoslovakia, where people were most appreciative of our work, there are many millions of people who are still friendly to the West because of UNRRA.

I of course came in contact with many Jewish survivors, and it was a very moving experience. I remember too attending services in July 1945 in the beautiful synagogue in Athens, and learning with great sadness how sixty thousand out of eighty thousand Jews had been killed in Greece. I remember hearing from Archbishop Damiskinos, Regent of Greece during the King's exile in London, how he had sent word to the invading Nazis that the synagogue was under the protection of the Church and must not be touched. Fortunately, he succeeded in prevailing on the Nazis to let it stand intact.

When I resigned from UNRRA in 1946, I was approaching seventy. Several years later, after I had been elected to the Senate, what I had learned and experienced during my UNRRA years about the plight of refugees put me in the forefront of the fight, which still needs to be waged today, against the McCarran-Walter Immigrant and Naturalization Act of 1952. This indefensible and evil act reflects a racist philosophy of fear, suspicion and distrust of foreigners, and must be repealed or drastically revised in conformity with bills I introduced for four successive years. It grew out of an incredible philosophy, based on belief in blood-stocks and Nordic superiority, that forgets the fact that America was settled and peopled entirely and built to greatness by immigrants from many lands. I felt then as I feel now that what has made America great is not the racial or national ancestry of our inhabitants, but the very mixture and molding of many cultures and blood strains, and the fusing of these streams, in a climate of freedom and opportunity, into a mighty river of energy and individual dignity.

There were other battles too—against economic monopoly, juvenile delinquency, slums and inadequate housing, growing mortality from cancer, heart ailments and other diseases, and inadequate school facilities and teachers. Most crucial of all was the fight for civil rights, spearheaded by the problem of school integration. While we have made a great deal of progress in this area, the road ahead is still long and full of stones.

How does all this relate to my Jewishness? My Jewish heritage has unquestionably affected my political and social thinking. All through my years of public life I have felt strongly the importance of keeping faith with the ethics of Judaism, and its basic concept that "creed without deed" is meaningless. As a Jew and as a human being, I have accepted no boundaries except those of justice, righteousness, humility and charity.

Because of the sufferings and oppression under which Jews have lived for countless centuries and the injustices and crimes committed against them in many parts of the world, we inevitably value our freedom, and should automatically be willing to battle against discrimination and loss of human liberty. This accounts in great part for my own natural interest and devotion to liberal government. I am only one of many Jews in the United States and other countries who are active in the fight for justice and equal rights for all. It is an inherent passion with us because our people have suffered so greatly over the centuries.

In a very real sense, the aims and ideals of the Jewish religion are identical with the purposes of democracy. I have always felt that any man who is really religious in any faith could never consciously and sincerely oppose the bases of democracy. The sense of duty and right, the passion for freedom and justice, and the faithful obedience of the Law and the Word of God are basic tenets of the Jewish heritage and are also the heart and soul of America.

In these difficult days of declining liberalism, it is important for us as Americans and as Jews to try to regain the moral perspectives first charged by our Jewish heritage. Our mission is to fight against injustice when practiced against any minority, anywhere in the world. We Americans of Jewish faith have a special obligation consistent with our ancient heritage to be messengers of peace.

New Jewish Writers in America

Leslie A. Fiedler

FOR THE first time in the history of the United States, the leading writers at the center of the literary scene are American Jews. They speak for America to their fellow Jews, to their gentile compatriots and to the whole world. For better or for worse, in the fifties and on into the sixties, major writers in America destined to be remembered are of Jewish descent.

Ernest Hemingway and William Faulkner and F. Scott Fitzgerald are the literary names we remember of the twenties; those of the past decade who are apt to be known by serious readers are Saul Bellow, Bernard Malamud, Philip Roth, J. D. Salinger, Norman Mailer, Herbert Gold, Irwin Shaw and Herman Wouk. Among poets who occupy a distinguished position on the American scene second only to the writers of fiction are Delmore Schwartz, Karl Shapiro and a number of younger versifiers such as Howard Nemerov, Allen Ginsberg.

Jews also play a leading role among the critics who help direct American taste by introducing new writers to the public and spreading their fame. Lionel Trilling has for years played a key role not only as a critic but more recently as one of the three judges and owners of the Mid-Century Book Club. Alfred Kazin, Irving Howe and Philip Rahv are also prominent American Jewish critics.

Of perhaps even greater importance is the role of American Jewish editors in helping to create standards in book publication and in editing magazines such as *Partisan Review,* an influential force in American letters despite its small circulation. Moreover, Jews have moved into academic life; a large proportion are now found in college departments of English literature, for decades a kind of gentile preserve.

What is significant about Jews occupying these positions in American intellectual and cultural life? A Jew writing in America today is not doomed to be a parochial writer because he is Jewish and because his themes come from Jewish life. If he wants to reach a wider public he does not have to turn his back on or deny his Jewish background. As a matter of fact, Jewish writers, insofar as they are Jewish, have at present wide appeal; the more Jewish they are the more universal their appeal seems to be. It is in this sense that Jewish writers are in the position of creating for all Americans—Jew and gentile alike—the most useful, the most livable, the most viable images of what it means to be an American in the sixties.

In some ways the Jewish writer has benefited by a general relaxation in the cold war between gentile and Jew in America. It has become fashionable recently, in certain middle-class quarters at least, to be pro-Jewish. Philo-Semitism is required in intellectual circles the way anti-Semitism used to be required.

Today, Jews in the United States are not merely allowed but required to create the image of the American people for the world. This means, among other things, that Jewish writers must leave behind them the memories of the time when they were purely parochial writers. When they wrote just for their own group, their primary duty was to project an image of the Jew for that group to live by. Indeed, one of the tasks of Jewish writers in the thirties and forties was to rescue the American Jew from the undignified position of having to live by images of himself invented by gentiles. The Jew might wince at certain travesties of what it meant to be a Jew created by gentiles, or he might be grateful for more favorable images created by kinder gentiles, though even those images were condescending and sentimental. Yet there were no other images in literature of subtlety and depth.

One of the very first Jews to exist in American literature was created in the sixties of the nineteenth century by a strange writer now almost forgotten, George Lippard, in a weird and disorderly book, *The Monks of Monk Hall*. This character was named, with obvious symbolism, Solomon von Gelt, endowed with the first Jewish accent that anyone ever attempted to put down in American literature, and portrayed as a member of a gang of secret criminals who presumably controlled life in Philadelphia.

The 1920's left us one image of a Jew which continues to live in American literature, the figure of Robert Cohen in Hemingway's *The Sun Also Rises*. This is a rather vicious portrait of a Jewish Princeton-*nik*, amateur boxer, boy scout who never grew up, outsider among the outsiders, trying hard to "make" it, but never quite succeeding.

As for poetry, the image of the Jew most characteristic of the twenties is perhaps that portrayed by Ezra Pound—the Jew as the usurer and secret enemy of culture, the fantasy Jew of an anti-Semite. Before Hitler, anti-Semitism was a tolerated minor vice among the gentiles who happened to have been the best writers of the period. Even as late as the thirties, the accounts of Jewish life provided by Thomas Wolfe reflect a bias which helped make him favorite reading for the Nazis. Certainly, his country boy's view of his urban Jewish students at New York University makes a not too friendly series of portraits.

The one notable exception, a novel written by a Jew before the modern period and projecting a real image of the Jew, is *The Rise of David Levinsky* by Abe Cahan. This is a truly great book—but it

stands alone. Today, however, images of the Jew are created by Jews
—by Malamud, Saul Bellow and Philip Roth. It is hard to say whether
we are better served by our own in terms of our status in the community, but at least the creating of our literary images has passed into our
own hands. We do not have to worry about coming to terms with
somebody else's image of ourselves.

It is therefore no longer the task of the Jewish writer to create
images of the Jew primarily for the Jewish community. Neither is it
his task to create favorable images of the Jew for the sake of gentile
neighbors. His is not a public relations job, which, however important
in itself, must not be confused with the function of literature. Sometimes Jewish organizations nudge and heckle the Jewish writer to
create images of good Jews, and blame and vilify him when he does
not. Some second-class writers accept this public relations job as primary, but no first-rate writer can consider his principal function to be
that of improving Jewish relations with gentile neighbors. His is a task
much more important, and consequently much more difficult to
conceive.

When we think of the nineteenth century in America, certain great
figures live in our mind—Captain Ahab in *Moby Dick,* or Mark
Twain's Huckleberry Finn. What appears likely at this moment is that
the great fictional figures who come to stand in the public mind for
America in the twentieth century may perhaps be figures of Jews, and
certainly figures created by Jewish writers.

How does this happen? What set of circumstances has turned Huckleberry Finn into Augie March?

The Jew as now seen by the imagination of the Western world is
the prototype, the key example, of the urban man, the lonely man.
Accidents of Jewish history have brought it about that the Jew has in
fact been the fully citified, the fully urbanized man, and, therefore,
the first man who is lonely in the peculiar and particular way in which
only people who live in big cities and industrialized societies can be
lonely.

But the Jew is thought of in the world's imagination not only in
terms of urbanization; he is also thought of in terms of what the Jew
has traditionally called *exile* and what the critics and philosophers
nowadays call alienation. The Jew is the alienated man, the outsider,
the stranger. As such, he becomes a universal symbol in a time when
we have come to feel that all human beings are strangers in the world
they inhabit. There is no one at this moment of history who does not
feel alienated, in exile and a stranger. This is the human condition in
the mid-twentieth century.

As the world has become increasingly industrialized, urbanized and atomized, as man everywhere begins to feel that he has been torn up from his past, the roots dangling, he begins to be conscious of himself in the same way as the Jew in his long exile. All men begin to feel as if their essential condition is exile; and, therefore, they begin to look to the Jewish writer to express this feeling, since the Jews are experts in exile, loneliness, alienation.

In America, another factor enters. American cultural life and literature through the nineteenth century were dominated by a group of writers of Anglo-Saxon ancestry, coming chiefly from New England and its outposts. Our literature was then primarily New England literature. A Jewish or Italian school boy in Newark, Brooklyn, Cleveland or Chicago reciting "barefoot boy with cheeks of tan" was projecting an image of memories and aspirations divorced from his life. But in the twentieth century a revolution took place against the bondage to the cultural heritage of a group who had the peculiar notion that what had been the values of their kind in England and in America for fifty or seventy-five years were universal and lasting values.

Led by writers like Theodore Dreiser and Sherwood Anderson, American literature and American thought turned toward the West, away from the big cities of Boston and New York and toward the small towns, away from the old world and toward the new. In turning away from Europe and American ties to Europe, American literature became anti-cultural and anti-intellectual as well as anti-European. This literary revolt began before World War I and the figure out of the American minorities who attracted writers was the Negro; for the Negro symbolized to them the opposite of the cultured, paleface Calvinist—a life of impulse as opposed to one of reason.

But this anti-intellectualism soon wore itself out. After a while, writers wanted to turn back, not to Boston, but to Europe and culture. With this swing back to pro-intellectualism the Jew took over the place which the New England Anglo-Saxon had once held.

It so happens that in American life there have been only two or three groups with deep intellectual roots. Aside from the first immigration of New Englanders, most of the people who came to America were culturally dispossessed, even in the Old Country. America is made up of men who had little share in the traditions of the country from which they came. Those who belonged to the upper levels of society did not usually emigrate. In the main it was not the Italian who knew Italian culture who came to America; it was the Italian peasant who knew scarcely anything. It was not the Irish intellectual who came in large numbers to America; it was the poor Irishman who had scarcely gone to school.

One of the few groups who came to America with a tradition and intellectual training, a respect for knowledge and some learning, was the Jews. Some were emancipated secularists and their culture was a compound of European culture at the time of their emigration. They brought with them socialism, an interest in literature, Russian and German in particular. Indeed, for a time, every Jew who wanted to become a poet thought he ought to begin by translating Heine into English.

Other Jews who came to America were still involved in the old Jewish learning, the Bible and Talmudic studies. It was easy for their sons to turn the tradition of Talmudism into the tradition of academic scholarliness, to move from the synagogue to the university. Abe Cahan remarked on how City College in New York became the synagogue of the emancipated Jews in America.

One of the reasons why Jewish intellectual leadership seemed more acceptable, toward the middle of the twentieth century, than the old Anglo-Saxon intellectual leadership was that the latter had been cautious and timid, afraid to deal with the more gross and earthy aspects of life. In the Jewish tradition there is a kind of stubborn earthiness to which Jews have always clung. The Jew has traditionally had one foot not only on the ground, but in the universe that encircles it. The Jew, though he is interested in culture, is rarely genteel; but he is not merely coarse either. He does not swing from the side of complete gentility to complete grossness, but manages to hold the two extremes together. This is one of the contributions which the Jew has to make to literature.

An eminent Jewish writer in the thirties who has testified on this score is Nathanael West, author of two of the best books of this period, *Miss Lonely Hearts* and *The Day of the Locust,* the most convincing novel ever written about Hollywood. In a very early book, *The Dream Life of Balso Snell,* West has one character try to identify a peculiar quality of the Jews, and he quotes a sentence actually spoken about Semitic people in general and the Arabs in particular by the great English explorer Doughty: "The Semite stands in dung up to his eyes but his brow touches the heaven."

This is a quality which Jewish writers have often had in the past and which they continue to have, and which sometimes upsets people who do not understand it. Philip Roth is an excellent example. Another example is *Call It Sleep* by Henry Roth, one of the most beautiful Jewish books ever written by an American-Jewish writer, long neglected and just recently republished. Such writers are not afraid of the brutal facts of life, yet at the same time they manage to touch certain spiritual heights.

For better or worse, Jews have inherited the leadership in the second turning back to Europe; and the Jewish writer continues, up to our own period, to be the chief mediator between Europe and America. That American literature has again become, in our time, a genuine part of world literature is largely the work of Jewish authors, Jewish poets, Jewish fictionists and Jewish critics. It is the Jews who have brought America and Europe together again; just as it is the Jews who have translated into American terms the great intellectual movements which moved from Europe to the United States.

Finally, one thing should be clear: the American Jewish writer is not transmitting Judaism in the specific sense of the word. Few Jewish writers have been moved by religious Judaism, few are Jews in a deeply religious sense. And few serious writers outside of Ludwig Lewisohn and Maurice Samuel have been Zionists.

The only specifically Jewish movement which has attracted serious American writers at all is Hasidism. And this comes to them not directly out of the old Hasidic tradition but via intellectual interpretations of it by Martin Buber and others. Hasidism is attractive to modern secular Jews because it has been fitted into a recent philosophical family of ideas which has come out of post-war Europe—existentialism.

What are the chief intellectual currents out of Europe which have come alive in the work of American Jewish writers? The first two movements and the two greatest which have moved through Jews into American literature are Marxist economics and political theory and Freudian psychology. Jews have also been the instrument through which existentialism and such European literary movements as surrealism have been introduced to American audiences. In fiction, for instance, as early as Ludwig Lewisohn and Ben Hecht, the ideas of Freud were being made a part of the American mind; Lewisohn wrote the first Freudian history of American literature.

In the thirties, Jewish writers like Mike Gold and Isidore Schneider and even Nathanael West were recording instruments through whom Marxist ideas were brought into American literature. *Partisan Review* has been a chief literary organ in America through which Marxist, Freudian and existentialist ideas have been developed.

Jews in America have also been the intermediaries through whom the great European writers were introduced in America, so that the recent literary tradition speaks to us with traces of a Yiddish accent. James Joyce, the Irish writer who lived most of his life in Switzerland and France, has been popularized in America largely by Jewish writers from Harry Levin to Richard Elman, who has just completed a biography of Joyce. Certainly the Jewish writer Kafka, who for a while was one of the major influences on certain younger writers, came into

America through such American fictionists as Isaac Rosenfeld, Paul Goodman and others.

Most recently, the ideas which younger Jewish American writers have been expounding are a strange compound in which the basic element is derived from Zen Buddhism. Jews are always apostles of new ideas; it is no surprise that they are apostles of Zen, the religion for the movement of the un-churched everywhere. From Salinger in the *New Yorker* to Norman Mailer and the beatniks and hipsters, the ideas of that oddly revived decadent Japanese sect have become a property in American literature.

The latest exponent is Karl Shapiro who, having been converted to these shadowy notions, is busy expounding them in prose and spreading them in poetry. But Zen Buddhism is combined in the strange new ideology of certain American writers in general and some Jews in particular with a peculiar outgrowth or offshoot of Freudian psychology expounded by Wilhelm Reich, whose teachings have influenced Saul Bellow, Karl Shapiro, Norman Mailer and Paul Goodman. At one time an eminent follower of Freud, Reich developed the notion that psychological attitudes become built into the body, into posture and facial expressions, and that if you want to cure anybody of any profound psychological disturbance or illness you have to treat it through the body as well as through the mind.

But Reich believes also that mental health depends upon what he calls full genitality, or the ability to achieve a complete and satisfactory orgasm, which he claims is beyond the reach of most people. In a weird way, he has touched the mind of American writers more deeply than any psychologist in many decades. In *Henderson the Rain King* by Saul Bellow, when the hero penetrates into the heart of darkest Africa, he comes to the kingdom of a tribal chief and he discovers that the chief has a library of Reichian literature. Played out as comedy by Bellow, the notion that sex means salvation is combined more seriously by types like Norman Mailer with the tenets of Zen Buddhism into a strange compound which does not yet have a name (*beat* and *hip* are approximations only) though it has many exponents among Jewish writers ranging from Allen Ginsberg to J. D. Salinger.

It is an odd paradox that Jews, who have been the leaders in the past in bringing intellectualism back to America, have now become part of the vanguard of a movement which is primarily anti-intellectual. The combination of Zen and Reich leads to a creed which asserts that the way is to be found not by the human intelligence but in the body, not in heder or school but in bed.

A recent book by Karl Shapiro, *In Defense of Ignorance,* attacks the intellectual tradition in American life; and a magazine published by

Saul Bellow is called *The Noble Savage,* a kind of joke perhaps, though by implication extolling the virtues of going back to the brute and instinctual life.

The most interesting fact about Jewish writing at the present time is that it is successful. But this fact is as much curse as blessing, since in America "nothing fails like success." Some Jewish writers have begun to sense that their ostensible success may be the outward sign of an inward failure. Precisely at the moment that serious Jewish literature has come to play a central part in American life, when for the first time serious Jewish writers have a general audience and are being heard everywhere, tne larger Jewish community is being assimilated to the values of an alrightnik society in America. Just when Jews are beginning to be listened to in some quarters because they represent a dissenting minority, a kind of lonely group which stands for values not of This World, most of the Jewish community is enthusiastically disappearing into This World. It has become, that is to say, okay to be a Jew in America now.

In certain small communities, as a matter of fact, one is almost required to be a Jew, a member of the Jewish community. At this moment the Jewish community lives a life which is the contradiction of all the values for which the Jewish writer stands, and it celebrates belongingness instead of alienation and loneliness. The Jewish community has cast out its writers so that it may freely indulge in small talk in place of the argument about ideas which used to be the heart of Jewish culture.

All of us are tempted to yield to something which does not seem assimilation in the old sense, but is in reality the worst kind of assimilation: the sham of worship without conviction—under the auspices of the motto, "let everyone go to the church of his choice this Sunday or Saturday, it doesn't make a bit of difference!" The equation of all religions and the notion that merely going to synagogue or temple or church is the center of religious life destroy many of the meanings of the Jewish tradition in which the sages of our past and the writers of the present are chiefly interested. At the moment when the Jewish writers are becoming more and more influential, the Jewish community is ironically turning away from intellectual life to sociability. It has become as hard to be a dissenter in the Jewish community as any place else.

The situation has, in one sense, never been worse for the serious Jewish writer. Certain positions which, when they were taken by Jewish writers and intellectuals back in the twenties and thirties, were radical and revolutionary, have turned into conventions and platitudes. Nowadays when somebody makes a speech against conformism one yawns just as much as when somebody makes a speech in favor of it. Anti-conformity has become a higher kind of conformism.

Intellectual curiosity, the intellectual hunger which was in the Jews when they came to this country, has been turned into the yearning to get a Ph.D. and to settle into the modest comfort of a teaching job in college. The Jews are now not so much intellectuals as they are academics. Their interest in ideas has become professional, and they have become peddlers of ideas. More and more Jewish young people go into university teaching, but the place where Jewish students go now is not City College but Amherst, Princeton or Harvard.

The radicalism with Marxist roots which shook people during the thirties has become a polite, standardized accepted leftism; just as the sexual revolution which people fought for back in the twenties has become conventionalized into a kind of Freudianized broad-mindedness. Everybody understands that the working man has rights and that sex plays a role in bringing up children. It has all become commonplace, all the fury of the two great Jewish prophets of nineteenth-century Europe, whom certain American Jews brought to the United States in hopes of redeeming all, gentile and Jewish.

How does one revolt today? Allen Ginsberg blasts society and two weeks later is invited to give a speech before the class in contemporary literature at City College, explaining what it means to be *"beat."* But, "explained" so nothing means anything. A Jew "explained" is not a Jew; a revolution "explained" is a bore. That is what our daring fathers and grandfathers wished for less daring us. And now that we have it, what? This is what I mean by "nothing failing like success."

What then remains for the Jewish writer? To be a writer and to be a Jew—to be a Jewish writer. But that is not easy. To be a Jewish writer means to be an outsider, to assume the prophetic role; that is, to assume the role of one step ahead of the moral order in which he lives. And the prophetic writer is driven to blast and excoriate and caricature the community, which is in the process of making the kind of capitulations just described.

Philip Roth, for instance, in the title story of *Goodbye Columbus,* shows what suburban Jewish life has actually become—what a dead, valueless, overstuffed thing it is. An extra refrigerator is stuffed full of extra food, but there is nothing left in the mind. But when the Jewish writer tries to tell the truth and reveal to the Jewish community what is really wrong with it, he is in trouble. The people he is attacking never read him. The people who read him applaud what he is doing. He is finally driven to the logically absurd position of maintaining the old Jewish tradition, the tradition of dissent, outsidedness, the prophetic tradition itself by attacking the lost value in which ordinary Americans think they believe: education.

But this is a chief value of the Jewish tradition! Reading the literature written by Jewish American writers and their friends one discovers that the chief activity of their characters seems to be running away from school. It is a petty enough way of manifesting independence, playing hooky as a way of life. Running away from school is running away from heder, too—and where does one run? In attacking schools and academic thought one attacks intelligence—and in attacking intelligence, one attacks the stereotype if not the fact of Jewishness.

One runs from his Jewishness—to what? To becoming a naive and lusty American like Henry Miller (this is the way of Karl Shapiro) or to remodel himself on the Negro hipster (this is the way of Norman Mailer); to become an imaginary goy, white or black.

One of the most interesting things that has happened recently in Jewish-American fiction is that the Jewish writer has come to think that he has to project himself in the form of a gentile character. In Saul Bellow's *Henderson the Rain King,* the protagonist, who in earlier works has always been a Jew, has been transformed into a large, vital, muscular, vulgar (utterly unconvincing) goy.

The hero of Norman Mailer's most recent book likewise is gentile, a character called Serges O'Shaughnessy. Originally, when Mailer planned the whole group of books, the huge work which he is writing, he had intended to present what happened in his fictional world as a long dream dreamed by a little Jewish writer who had not quite "made" it. And this device would have made clear what O'Shaughnessy in fact is—a phantasmal projection of the Jew's desire to be a noble savage, that is, a real American.

Here is a second paradox parallel to the first. At the moment that the bourgeois gentile community looks for images of its life in versions of Jewish alienation, the Jewish bourgeois community swaps exile for belongingness. At the moment the gentile intellectual sees himself as an imaginary Jew alienated, abstruse, sensitive, committed to ideas, the Jewish intellectual plunges into a deliberately induced nightmare in which he inhabits the form of a muscular, fully genital goy.

And perhaps we are ready for the next generation; a generation able to point out that "genital" is our time's pun on "gentile," as "gentle" was the pun of an earlier time. Neither "gentleman" nor "genital-man" because he is not "gentile-man," the Jew must be content simply to be a "Jew," even when he can no longer define his Jewishness. And even if we could imagine the American writer capable of asserting that he is the last Jew—we cannot help imagining him asserting his Jewishness in that very act.

VIII

Dilemmas, Challenges, Reappraisals

Three Who Faced a New Age

Seymour Siegel

THE nineteenth century was the century of ideologies. Most of the systems of thought and programs of action which move men today were formulated during that crucial hundred year period.

The theory of democracy was consolidated in the United States; the philosophy of Marxism was presented to the growing European proletariat; the foundations of Nazism and Fascism were being laid in the German reaction and in Nietzsche's call for a transvaluation of values; liberalism gained a foothold in England; liberty, fraternity and equality—though distorted by Napoleon's grand adventure—still gripped the minds of Frenchmen and other Europeans; the discoveries of Darwin confronted a startled world; and in 1897 an obscure Viennese physician. Sigmund Freud, published his first article about the mysterious workings of the human psyche.

In the Jewish world—especially in Western and Central Europe—ideologies and programs were being born. The foundations of the old Jewish life were being shaken and new voices were being heard. The *Haskalah* arose as did also the Reform movement, the Conservative (positive-historical) school, the neo-Orthodox party, Zionism and Jewish socialism. In the Pale of Settlement, where the majority of East European Jews dwelt, Hasidism was experiencing its golden period; the foundations of the great Lithuanian yeshivot were being laid, and the fervent and introspective circles of the *Mussar* movement were spreading their teachings among students of the Talmud. The great communities of the New World—especially in the United States—began to influence world Jewry, and the nineteenth century saw the founding of both the Hebrew Union College in Cincinnati and the Jewish Theological Seminary in New York.

The focus for the birth of new ideologies and reformulations of old ones was Germany. There Napoleon's victories had given the Jews a taste of freedom and had all but crumbled the old ghetto walls. A land of thorough Jewish learning and high general culture, it was the natural place for the rethinking of Jewish fundamentals. In Germany —in Solomon Schechter's colorful expression—the method of the West met the madness of the East.

Three main problems faced Jewish leaders—especially in Western and Central Europe. The first was to gain complete political emancipation for the Jews. For centuries the Jewish communities had lived under civil disabilities and deprived of elementary civil rights. They were, for the most part, enclosed in ghettos and restricted in their movements; even the number of marriages was decided by the authorities. Napoleon and his armies had changed these conditions radically, but after his defeat the problem was to consolidate the gains already won and to fight for new ones.

The second problem was to integrate the Jew into the new society. Judaism, with its many restrictions and rules governing conduct, posed grave problems for those Jews who wished to participate in the educational, commercial and cultural activities of a predominantly Christian society. A poignant yet illuminating *she'lah* (question of ritual law) was posed to Rabbi David Tzvi Hoffmann by a young man studying in a commercial school in Germany and obliged to attend classes on Shabbat. He went to classes but did not take notes. His mother—anxious that he succeed—urged him to take notes. When he refused she threatened suicide. What should he do? the boy asked the rabbi. The rabbi counseled him to continue his Sabbath observance.

A third problem, of a theologico-philosophical character, was posed by the new understanding of religion revealed in comparative studies, especially by historical research. Interestingly enough, the Jewish literature of the period was not as concerned with the new discoveries in natural science as it was with the suppositions of social science and the humanities, which suggested that every human phenomenon, including religion, religious rites and rituals, should be viewed under the aspect of history. Once one views dogmas, customs, laws as having grown and developed under specific circumstances at specific times, belief in relativism is inevitable. That which history creates can be dismantled by history. Dogmas and rituals can make no absolute claim. The systems of religions did not appear in the world complete at one moment in time, but were instead the result of long periods of development and change. This new outlook, of course, struck at the heart of traditional Judaism, which had viewed itself as a complete structure of belief and practice having its source in the supernatural and not subject to natural development.

There were other problems as well. But the emancipation of the Jews, their integration into the general society and culture, and the problem of history were the most important ones.

Three Jewish thinkers—Abraham Geiger, Zechariah Frankel and Solomon Schechter—coped with these problems. Each was both a theoretician and a man of action as well. Geiger and Frankel worked in Germany, while with Schechter the scene shifts to the New World. These three faced the challenge of the modern world and left their stamp upon Jewish life.

Abraham Geiger was born in 1810 in Frankfurt. A child prodigy, he could read the Bible at three, the Mishnah at four and the Talmud at six. He received a thorough education in the Jewish classics. He studied in the Universities of Heidelberg and Bonn. He was a rabbi first in Wiesbaden, then in Breslau, Frankfurt and Berlin. His works are classics of Jewish historical research, especially his monumental *Urschrift und Uebersetzungen der Bibel ihrer Abhsengigkeit von der innern Entwicklung des Judentums* (The Original Text and Translations of the Bible in Their Relation to the Inner Development of Judaism). One of the founders of "Jewish Science," Geiger was convinced that Judaism had to be reformed; to be freed from the chains of the past so that it could develop and adjust itself to the radically new conditions of that new era. He organized a group of like-minded rabbis to carry out his program and is considered the father of Reform Judaism.

As a great historian of Judaism Geiger was conscious of the historical character of Jewish religion. He pointed out again and again that Jewish faith and practice had evolved throughout the centuries. Geiger formulated his ideas using the simile of a husk and a kernel; Judaism consists of a kernel of ethical monotheism, a pure conception of God and His ethical will, which has been expressed at different times in various kinds of external forms or "husks." The husks change or are abandoned, and new ones come into being to express the ideas of Judaism. The Law or Jewish observance is the main content of the husks.

According to Geiger, Judaism has actually undergone four periods. First was the period of revelation, the Biblical age, when the ground-ideas of Judaism were discovered. The second period was that of tradition, the period of the Talmud, when the "primary concern became, not to create new things, but to preserve the acquired heritage, to collect it, sift it, supplement it and adapt it for every conceivable situation in life, an effort which might entail complete change in one instance, and the ferreting out and confirmation of the smallest and pettiest details in another." The third period, beginning in the sixth century and extending into the eighteenth century, was that of "rigid legalism," a period of stagnation when custom became frozen and inner development ceased. Geiger believed that his own time was a fourth epoch in Jewish history—namely, the time for "critical" study, when Judaism would free itself from the shackles of tradition.

This picture of Jewish history, which Geiger developed in many articles and lectures, formed the basis for a thoroughgoing reform of Judaism—especially in its outward forms. Judaism's husk had always been in a state of change and flux, and Judaism could be saved only by finding new forms to express the inner basis of Judaism—ethical monotheism.

Geiger's ideas were related to his program of painstaking and detailed historic research, which legitimized reform by showing that change had always been the hallmark of Judaism. Geiger's own contribution to the study of Judaism was extremely important: he founded a journal to stimulate historical and theological studies and was the author of many articles and books.

Geiger believed that a cardinal goal for the reformulation of Judaism was to denationalize it. This was related to the Jewish aspiration to become part of the general culture, and to the belief that the growth of religious liberalism in the West would usher in a period of tolerance and tranquility. The days of the Messiah were close at hand —a Messiah not sent by the Almighty in a miraculous way, but a redeemer representing the forces of enlightenment and good will who would soon gain the upper hand in Europe. Jews should consider themselves not a foreign element within the body politic but rather an integral part of the nations and societies within which they live. All prayers for a return to Palestine should therefore be removed. References to Zion as the Jewish homeland should be removed from the prayer book and the syllabus of instruction in Jewish schools. *Galut* is not an evil but a blessing, for exile makes possible the expansion of Judaism into a universal religion. "Exile is the geographic coefficient of universalism." Geiger predicted that the older forms of Judaism would disappear as would Catholicism—once Enlightenment became universal.

Thus Geiger laid the foundations for a complete reform of Jewish religion and practice. He theoretically sanctioned the abandoning of such ancient rituals as tefillin and circumcision since they were merely husks around the true kernel of Judaism, husks whose usefulness had been outlived. He thought of Jews not as members of a world-wide people but as a group holding in common certain theological principles and which should become part of the nations among whom it lived. The times called for the giving up of quaint national characteristics and anachronistic hopes such as the return to Palestine.

Geiger was the product of his times. Unfortunately, the period of progress was not to be long-lived; Jewish national aspiration could not be stifled, and other ideologies developed which sought to keep Jewish tradition alive and thriving. All of Judaism, however, is in Geiger's debt for his contributions to the study of Jewish history and for asking some of the right questions.

Zechariah Frankel (1801–1875), like Geiger a mighty figure in the

history of *Jüdische Wissenschaft,* participated in a rabbinical confer-
ence arranged by Geiger in Frankfurt-on-Main in 1845. But he was out
of sympathy with the direction of the discussions and the mood of the
participants. Before an abrupt departure, he delivered an address describing his conception of "positive-historical" Judaism.

Agreeing with Geiger that Jewish faith and practice are the result of
historical development, Frankel contributed important studies on the
history of the Mishnah and the character of the Jerusalem Talmud.
Where he parted company with Geiger was in his attitude toward that
which history had created. While Geiger felt that the Judaism which
had been created by history could now be dismantled, Frankel dis-
agreed and his viewpoint was called "positive-historical." In his view,
the value created by history becomes permanent, and man must relate
to it positively. For example, even according to the strictest legal
interpretation it is not necessary to pray in Hebrew. Whereas Geiger
felt that the language of the country should be substituted for Hebrew, Frankel insisted that since Jewish history had created the
Hebrew liturgy, and since Jews had expressed their deepest feelings
and longings in the holy tongue, it was not possible to eliminate
Hebrew from the services.

Differing from Orthodoxy, Frankel insisted that Judaism has
evolved, grown, and is the product of history. But unlike Reform, he
felt that law or custom created by history should be hallowed and
preserved—and not radically changed. Modern Reform was possible
(Frankel called himself a moderate Reformer), and minor changes in
customs and ceremonies might be made. But such changes should be
instituted gradually and in accordance with the will of the people who
are still loyal to the tradition. In Frankel's outlook one can find the
influence of the German romantic view, especially the influence of the
German legal thinker Friedrich Carl von Savigny and the philosopher
and writer Gottfried von Herder. The latter taught that the folk, the
people, are the creators and bearers of value: not abstract rationalism
should dictate the legal structure of a community, but the spirit of the
people as it unfolds throughout the centuries! This emphasis on the
folk and its historical creation is evident in Frankel's thought. History
is the locus of the people's creativity and therefore must be studied.
That which the spirit of the people has created should be cherished
and preserved.

Frankel's thought is based also on the theological premise that the
people of Israel—the people of the covenant—reflects the divine intent
in its history, in its evaluation of novelty, in its adaptation to unprecedented conditions. The original content of revelation is supple-
mented, shaped and broadened by the continuing revelation which is

expressed through the people's will and creativity. "For the adherent of this school (that is, the positive-historical school) the sanctity of the Sabbath reposes not upon the fact that it was proclaimed on Mount Sinai," says Louis Ginzberg, "but on the fact that the Sabbath idea found expression in Jewish souls."

When the Breslau Seminary was organized and Frankel was appointed its director, he was able, together with great scholars like Heinrich Graetz, to build a major academic institution. Through the Seminary positive-historical Judaism became a strong and influential force in Western and Central Europe and also in the great new burgeoning Jewish community being formed in the New World. Fortunately, the shaping of the American Jewish community was then in the hands of Solomon Schechter, an outstanding, multifaceted personality.

Schechter was a figure "comparable in depth of understanding, breadth of learning, originality of thought, force of personality, genius for organization, brilliance of vision, and religious insight," in the words of Louis Finkelstein, "to the foremost personalities of post-Talmudic times."

He received his early childhood education in Rumania, and later studied in Vienna under the pioneers of Jewish scholarship, Meir Friedmann and I. H. Weiss. After studying in German universities, he was called to England through the initiative of Claude Montefiore. He taught at Cambridge, where he became the center of a group of remarkable writers and students of Judaism. There too he mastered English and became a superb stylist in that language. He uncovered the famous Genizah in Cairo, bringing to light a "hoard of Hebrew manuscripts" which have immeasurably enriched Jewish studies, and winning renown as one of the greatest Jewish scholars of his time.

In the 1880's a group of Conservative rabbis and laymen, in reaction against the excesses of the American Reform movement, organized the Jewish Theological Seminary in New York to train traditional religious leaders; after a promising beginning it began to flounder for lack of leadership. At that juncture, in 1902, a group of influential laymen brought Solomon Schechter to New York to become its president. In less than thirteen years, he had left his indelible stamp on American Judaism.

Schechter's program was a continuation of the positive-historical school of Frankel. He outlined his program in a few paragraphs which serve as an introduction to his *Studies in Judaism:*

> The historical school, according to the best of my knowledge, never proposed to the world a theological program of its own . . . In a general way, however, its approach to religion can be defined

as an enlightened skepticism joined with a firm conservatism, which does not lack the mystical moment as well . . . its theological position might thus be defined: Not the Scriptures—given by Revelation—is of primary importance to the Jew. But Scripture as it repeats itself in history. In other words, as it is interpreted by Tradition . . . Since the interpretation of Scripture or its Secondary Meaning is, for the most part, the result of historical factors, the result is that the main authority is taken from Scripture itself, and is transferred to a Living Body, which, thanks to its being close to the ideal strivings of each epoch and its religious needs, can determine the Secondary Meaning. This Living Body is not represented by any one part of the people or by any religious authority, but by the conscience of Catholic Israel as it is expressed in the Universal Synagogue.

The emphasis on "catholic Israel" (a phrase coined by Schechter) became the identifying mark of his work. When Schechter arrived in America, he found, on the one hand, the old-line Reform congregation (very different from those of today) which had abandoned Hebrew, prohibited any mention of Zion, worshipped on Sunday and spoke of the Talmud in almost Pauline terms (Schechter, in fact, called them amateur Christians). On the other hand were the large immigrant masses organized into their Orthodox synagogues, where English was suspect and where modern scientific study of Judaism was looked upon with horror. (Schechter called this artificial ignorance.)

His aim was to include all Jews in an effort to revive Judaism so that it could function in the modern world.

I would consider my work, to which with the help of God I am going to devote the rest of my life, a complete failure if this institution (referring to the Seminary) would not in the future produce such extremes as on the one side a raving mystic who denounces me as a sober philistine, and on the other hand an advanced critic who would rail at me as a narrow-minded fanatic.

The notion of "catholic Israel," while vague and undefined, furnished a formula for change and modification of Jewish law and ritual. The conscience of those committed to the Law would reflect the kind of changes which must be undertaken.

Schechter championed the Zionist cause against the leaders of his time. His statement in support of Jewish national aspirations was in those days most courageous. But it expressed his overwhelming appreciation of the spirit of the Jewish people and his support of the program to establish a spiritual center in Palestine.

Like Geiger, he stressed the importance of research in Judaism;

indeed, one of his first addresses in America was entitled "The Emancipation of Jewish Science." The Seminary became an important center for the study of the Jewish past as a guide to the Jewish present.

Schechter also championed the cause of rabbinic Judaism against its detractors—both among Jews and Christians. In his work *Some Aspects of Rabbinic Theology,* he contributed insights into the nature of rabbinic piety. Railing against those who repeated the clichés about "the dark night of legalism" or the cold, unfeeling character of Talmudic Judaism, he pointed out the importance of a living Judaism which consisted of a tangible form of practice and ritual.

Schechter created the United Synagogue of America and established the Jewish Theological Seminary of America as a leading center for the training of Jewish religious leaders. He did not succeed in his hope of unifying American Jewry around the banner of Conservative Judaism. But Schechter's vision of a modern yet traditional Judaism is gaining adherents. It is interesting to note that Reform Judaism has changed radically since the early years of the century, and has come closer to the center. The same is true of Orthodox Judaism, at least its largest section.

The three men whose thought has been described here were all products of a traditional, vibrant and learned Jewish atmosphere. They faced the new world and tried to guide their fellow Jews through the pitfalls in their path. They stressed the importance of authentic, objective learning as indispensable for the growth of Judaism. As far as practical programs are concerned, Geiger differed with both Frankel and Schechter; he advocated radical reforms, though he did not actually put them into practice. Frankel and Schechter saw the necessity for change, but felt it should be gradual and reflect the conscience of the Jewish community. While Geiger opposed Jewish nationalism, Schechter and Frankel saw that Jewish religion without the Jewish community was a disembodied spirit.

All three thinkers were vague about the nature of Jewish authority. Both Schechter's concept of "catholic Israel" and Frankel's trust in the "spirit of the people" require a good deal of definition and refinement. Nor did these men deal with the challenges to religion posed by science. They lived before the insights of existentialists and phenomenologists of religion revolutionized our concepts about the nature of faith and ritual. Yet they were pathfinders for those who seek their way as Jews in the new perplexing world.

The Bible for Moderns

Robert Gordis

THE time has come for Jews to reclaim the Bible. Jews particularly and the entire modern world have lost touch with the Bible to their infinite hurt and great loss. They have tended to honor it rather than to understand it. What the French philosopher Voltaire said a hundred and fifty years ago—"the Bible is more celebrated than known"—is still true today.

What has made it difficult for the Bible to be appreciated in our time? Unfortunately, the Book of Books is not only the world's most printed, but also worst printed book. Most Bibles are printed in two columns with numbers down the margin as in a catalog. Prose and poetry, history and fiction, the philosophic discussions and proverbs, speeches and narratives are all bunched together, all printed in a very forbidding type which repels rather than attracts the reader.

Then too, the Bible is an ancient book which cannot be read without some background in the language and customs of the period. In our own day, for example, all of us know the difference between a simple colloquial phrase like "calling somebody up" or "calling somebody down." But five hundred years from today when archeologists excavate the ruins after the fourth atomic war and discover some scraps of American literature, they would not know the difference—without notes telling them that "calling up" means one thing and "calling down" means another.

Just as we constantly use all kinds of phrases and allusions which are part of our civilization, so too did the writers of the Bible employ the language and expressions of their time. The Bible belongs to all men and all ages but it arose in a specific locale and age thousands of years ago. And therefore it just cannot be read any more than one can read Chaucer or Shakespeare or any other ancient writer without some understanding of the background involved.

In a strange way, too, the Bible has tended to be misunderstood precisely because it is a sacred book. Jews as well as Christians tend to approach it with a sense of awe rather than with anticipation and excitement. We tend to forget that the Bible became holy because it is great, and we make the mistake of thinking that it is great simply because it is holy. We approach the Bible knowing that it is respectable, and because it is respectable we do not find it exciting. That is fatal. The Bible represents the work of a group of highly gifted men and women who over a period of a thousand years wrote a great

345

library of classics. A classic is not a book which belongs on a shelf, but it is a book which is perpetually modern.

The old attitude toward the Bible, one shared by Jews as well as Christians, may be described as dogmatic. It believes that throughout history God at particular moments selected certain men to whom He dictated His will word for word. The Rabbis, for example, commenting on the last twelve verses of the Bible which describe Moses' death, raise the question: "How could Moses himself have written the description of his death?" And the answer is given in the Talmud in a beautiful and touching legend: "God was dictating the story of Moses' death and Moses was writing with a tear in his eye." He had no choice, God was dictating it.

This view that the Bible represents the actual dictation of the word of God to man is very important, and is still held today by millions of people. For thousands of years our ancestors took the Bible literally to be the word of God, and to their steadfastness we owe its preservation at a time when most other great books written in the ancient and medieval world were destroyed. The Bible was preserved both in the Hebrew original and in other translations only because men were persuaded that it was God's word. They made every sacrifice for it, dragging it out of burning buildings, carrying it in the face of pogroms and cherishing it above all other possessions.

It was this love which preserved the Bible and prevented it from being lost through neglect or changed by scribes. Revisions and errors were thus prevented for thousands of years because people zealously guarded the Book word for word, letter for letter, through the ages. We owe to this literal interpretation the preservation of the Bible itself.

Though people took the Bible to be the word of God, they constantly interpreted it and tried to keep it abreast of new ideas. For example, the phrase, "an eye for an eye and a tooth for a tooth," occurs several times in the Five Books of Moses and represents an important juridical and legal principle: the idea that if a man injures his neighbor he is to be punished only in the same proportion as was originally the case.

In an earlier more primitive period, if a man took out his neighbor's eye the penalty was death. The concept of "an eye for an eye" represented a great step forward in the civilizing of the human race. As time went on, however, people realized that even that was going too far. Suppose a man did take out somebody's eye by accident? The idea of reciprocating by removing his own eye now impressed people as being too heavy a penalty, and so they were sure that could not be the intent of the Torah. Hence, nearly two thousand years ago, the Rabbis of the

Talmud actually interpreted that principle to mean monetary compensation; while the letter of Torah still read "an eye for an eye," Jewish law interpreted that to mean an estimate of the damage in financial terms.

As a result of all this interpretation and reinterpretation, a rich literature on the Bible came into being. The *Aggadah,* for example, is a vast compilation of legendary, ethical and moral literature scattered through the pages of the Talmud and the Midrashim. A great body of medieval philosophy of the Jewish people was also produced, beginning with Philo of Alexandria in the second century and going right down through the medieval philosophers of Spain, each of whom attempted to interpret the Jewish religion and adapt it to the conditions of his time.

During the past few hundred years, we have come to understand that in order to read the Bible we must see it in the perspective of modern thought. No less religious than the traditional view, the new approach interprets the Bible not as the literal word of God but as the resultant of a partnership between God and man. If we want to know the Bible we must recognize not only its divine source, but also its human conditions, its human background. During the past few hundred years many new branches of science and knowledge have come into being which make it possible for us to understand the Bible better than the Rabbis and scholars were able to do centuries ago. Just as a dwarf standing on the back of a giant can see further than the giant himself, so we today, who have the benefit of all the knowledge of the generations gone by, are able to look deeper into the Bible than were our forebears.

Among these recent studies is the science of comparative philology. There was a time when people thought that Hebrew was a unique language, in a class by itself. We know today, however, that languages are related just as are human beings. The Indo-European group includes most European tongues, while the Semitic group takes in Hebrew, Arabic, the Ethiopic language of the Abyssinians, Aramaic, Syriac, Assyrian, Ugaritic and a handful of other languages which scholars have rediscovered. Our understanding of Hebrew, the language of the Bible, is now vastly deepened through our knowledge of other Semitic languages.

Equally important is the field of comparative religion. A great deal of light is thrown on the Bible and Biblical religion by what we have discovered about the nations surrounding the Holy Land. Jews learned from their neighbors, sometimes accepting and at other times rejecting or modifying what they learned.

As an illustration, the old Jewish custom of *pidyon haben,* the custom of the redemption of the first-born, which goes back to the Bible and which is an obligation of Jewish law, cannot be understood except against the background of ancient religion. In former times, when the first child was born the parents would express their thanksgiving to God by sacrificing that baby. The Bible warned again and again against passing a child through the fire, and burning him as a sacrifice to the god Molech. The Jewish religion, always very realistic, did not try to uproot this practice of thanksgiving, but ordained that gratitude for the birth of a child should be expressed by redeeming him through the five shekels that are offered up to the *kohen* or priest as the representative of the God of Israel.

Perhaps the single most important and interesting branch of modern Biblical research is archeology, the science of discovering the past through digging up ancient civilizations. When scholars went to Palestine and the nearby countries of the Fertile Crescent, they discovered that they could resuscitate ancient civilizations in a simple manner. It is like taking off layers of onions, each successive civilization covering over an earlier one.

That was exhibited by the Scottish archeologist Macalister, who in 1908 and 1909 excavated Gezer, a city in the south which is mentioned several times in the Bible. Once he and his trained archeologists began removing layers, with every ten or fifteen feet they were traveling a couple of hundred years back into time. On top of Gezer was an Arab village; then they found a Second Commonwealth Jewish city, which had been burned; underneath that was the First Temple city of the First Commonwealth period. And then they went down layer after layer below the Jewish settlement to the Canaanite period, and even earlier. It was like letting a shaft down not merely through space but also through time. As they went down some eighty feet they were actually going back nearly thirty-five centuries.

What Macalister found in Gezer, other scholars of all nationalities and religions have been able to do in dozens of other cities. They have discovered how our ancestors lived, the layout of their houses, some of their religious customs and practices. Knowing this background has illuminated our reading of the Bible.

Modern scientific research also helps us to understand the question of miracles in the Bible—which has disturbed many a thoughtful reader and student. These are infinitely less difficult to accept than those in other religious texts because by and large Judaism does not depend on them. In the miracle of the crossing of the sea, for example, most scholars today are convinced that it was not the Red Sea the Israelites were crossing but rather a series of low-lying marshes northeast of Egypt called the Serbonian Lakes. It happens to be a matter of common record that often the water recedes and it is possible to get over, and at other times the water gets deep and cannot be crossed. The Bible itself explains the miracle of the crossing of the Red Sea by saying that a strong wind arose and parted the waters, and the Israelites got over, and then by the time the Egyptians arrived, the waters had receded and blocked their passage.

This modern tendency to explain how things happened is important. From the standpoint of Judaism a miracle is still a wonderful thing, but it does not have to be a break in the laws of nature. A miracle may be defined broadly as a unique, unexpected event at the right time for the right purpose. When the Israelites were escaping out of Egypt, the miracle which happened then made it possible for them to escape and found a great new religion and people.

Everybody knows the Negro spiritual about how the walls of Jericho came tumbling down. The Bible says that when Joshua marched around the city walls for seven days, he blew the trumpets and the walls fell down. This makes a vivid story, but the interesting fact is that when the English archeologist John Garstang, in charge of the Ministry of Excavation during part of the British Mandatory Regime in Palestine, actually excavated the city of Jericho, he did discover that fire had broken out underneath, and that the walls had collapsed. On the basis of purely scientific evidence, Garstang came to the conclusion that the walls of Jericho had burned to the ground about the year 1400, the date which agrees almost to a decade with that given in the Bible. The issue of date is still being discussed by scholars, but the approach is clear.

Suffice it to say that archeology has helped us to validate by modern scientific research matters of religious faith. A knowledge of the sciences of comparative philology, comparative religion, ancient history, archeology and textual criticism gives us a clearer grasp of what the Bible has to say.

With the path thus cleared and with this perspective made more simple and appealing, what then can we moderns find in the Bible? As a great Jewish Bible scholar of the twentieth century put it, the Bible is more than a collection of tracts or sermon texts; it is the national literature of the Jewish people. Everything in it is suffused by the spirit of religion because religion was coextensive with life itself. Moreover, the Bible is for us the record of God's revelation of His will to dedicated and inspired men, who strove, struggled and sacrificed for righteousness and truth, and in the process created beauty as well.

By reading the Bible we can gain insights about the eternal issues of life and death, the meaning of suffering, the purpose of life, the pattern of existence, the relation of the individual to his fellow man, his people and history. We can discover the great social, economic and political teachings which the Bible proclaimed first for our ancestors, for us and for all mankind in the days to come. An inexhaustible source of inspiration, guidance and insight, the Bible is, in the deepest sense, a religious book.

The Bible is also a great literary collection of masterpieces: the great speeches in the Book of Deuteronomy and in Jeremiah, the matchless love poetry of the Song of Songs, the moving religious poetry of the Psalms, the Book of Job, which Carlyle called "the grandest book written by human pen," the penetrating biographies and masterpieces of historical writing as in Samuel and Kings that modern psychologists and scholars have not been able to surpass. Thomas Mann, perhaps the greatest novelist of the twentieth century, wrote in six volumes a profound novel called *Joseph and His Brothers*. The Bible tells that story in some fifteen chapters in Genesis; Tolstoy, the Russian novelist, called the story of Joseph the greatest narrative ever written. The Bible offers much more—short stories, proverbs, laws, even medical commentaries. There is material dealing with every phase of human life. Nothing is too high, nothing too low. Nothing is too close or too remote for the great collection of authors represented in the Bible.

Finally, we have in the Bible not only a vital religious source and not only a superb collection of literary material, but also the most important source of history of the Jewish people. In its pages are laid down the lines of its character, its early struggles, its emergence out of tribalism, its understanding of the nature of the world, its concept of nationhood and international morality, its faith in man as co-partner with God in building the world.

While it is perfectly true that our attitude toward the Bible is not identical with that of earlier ages, and that we read it in the light of modern scientific research, we can still echo the words of our sages in speaking of the Torah: "Turn it over and over, for everything is in it. Grow old and gray in it, but do not swerve from it, for there is no better portion than this."

Why a New Translation of the Bible?
Harry M. Orlinsky

THE Jewish people have always understood the importance of making the "Holy Writings" available in translation for those who could not understand the original Hebrew text. About 2200 years ago, the Jewish community in Alexandria was, in some respects, similar to American Jewry at the turn of our century. Grown to great proportions in population and status, it had begun to give up the Hebrew language in favor of the Greek vernacular. A translation into Greek of the Five Books of Moses, the most authoritative part of what then constituted the Holy Writings, became necessary.

This is the origin of the famous Greek translation now called the Septuagint, probably the most important ever made by Jews. Translation into Greek of the other sacred Books, which ultimately came to constitute the remaining two divisions of the Hebrew Bible—the Prophets and the Hagiographa—took place during the second and first centuries B.C.E.

In Western Asia, especially in Babylonia and Judea, Aramaic rather than Greek was the popular vernacular among Jews. By the second century C.E., there existed several Jewish Aramaic versions of the Bible, the best known being the Targum Onkelos on the Pentateuch.

As the earlier Christian Jews became less Jewish and more Christian, and after the sovereign Jewish state was destroyed by Rome in 70 C.E., the Septuagint version came to be rejected by the Jews and accepted by the Christians. Early in the second century, a pagan convert to Judaism, Aquila by name, made a new Greek translation of the Hebrew Bible, incorporating the Jewish interpretation current in his day. Interestingly, Aquila's translation was still in use in the synagogue in the days of Byzantine Emperor Justinian I, in the sixth century, and fell into disuse only after the seventh century, when Arabic replaced Greek and Latin.

In the tenth century less than a thousand years ago, the Jews of Babylonia and other parts of the great Moslem domain were most at home in Arabic, and their outstanding Jew, Saadia Gaon, prepared an Arabic translation of the Hebrew Bible.

Saadia's primary goal was to achieve *intelligibility,* and his translation, while not a paraphrase, was not literal either. Saadia did not hesitate to add a word not found in the Hebrew original, or to telescope several Hebrew words, in his desire to make the meaning clear.

His translation is still used by Yemenite Jews in Israel, who brought it together with their Hebrew Torah and Targum from Yemen.

In the fifteenth and sixteenth centuries, Jewish translations into many vernaculars began to come thick and fast, encouraged in no small measure by the invention of printing. In addition to Greek and Persian translations, there were several Spanish versions.

The *Tzenah U-Renah,* the Bible of every good Jewish woman in Central and Eastern Europe, came into being the following century, along with other Judeo-German or Yiddish translations of parts of the Bible, among them the translation by Joseph Witzenhausen, published in Amsterdam in 1679.

These translations, made by Jews for Jews, reflected the social ferment of gentile society. Christians, to whom the Hebrew Bible was the important Old Testament forerunner of the New Testament, also made translations and revisions, even more than the Jews, to conform to their needs, in the various vernaculars of Asia, Africa and Europe—Latin, Coptic, Armenian, Syriac, Ethiopic, the German of Luther, Dutch, Danish, Swedish, Norwegian. English translations were made by Tyndale and Coverdale. The King James (so-called Authorized) Version of 1611 had a greater influence than any translation since the Septuagint and the Vulgate, and also influenced most subsequent Jewish versions of the Hebrew Bible.

A great impetus to the Jewish versions which began to appear increasingly in the eighteenth and nineteenth centuries was the renewed study of the Bible, with a rationalistic emphasis, in Jewish circles. Partly under the influence of Protestant Biblical criticism of the eighteenth and nineteenth centuries, and partly as an inner development, both of which were brought about by the advent of the Industrial Revolution and the new economic and political orders which followed in its wake—Jewish study of the Bible along more scientific lines once again came into its own.

Among the many scholars who engaged in such study were Moses Mendelssohn and his school of Biurists, Heinrich Graetz, Samuel David Luzzatto and Meir Leibush Malbim.

Out of these new conditions and studies emerged many varied Bible translations and revisions, including the scholarly French Bible (completed in 1851) and a more popular French version, of which only the Pentateuch appeared, done by members of the French rabbinate.

Three translations in German, by Philippson, Hexheimer, and Fürst, appeared between 1856 and 1874. Two Dutch versions, one of the entire Bible, were issued. Luzzatto's pupils translated the entire Bible into Italian in 1875. The Russian, Hungarian and Yiddish languages were likewise enriched by Jewish versions of the Bible, in whole or in part.

Isaac Delgado in England—"teacher of the Hebrew language"—published in 1789 an English translation of the *Humash,* a correction of the King James in three main areas: "wherever it deviates from the genuine sense of the Hebrew expressions, or where it renders obscure the meaning of the text, or, lastly, when it occasions a seeming contradiction."

Fifty years later, Selig Newman published his *Emendations of the Authorized Version,* and twenty-five years afterwards Abraham Benisch produced a fresh English version of the Hebrew Bible. Michael Friedlander prepared a somewhat modified revision of the Authorized Version in 1884.

In this country, a very important English version of the Bible was produced by Isaac Leeser, in 1853. For over fifty years it was virtually *the* English Bible for English and American Jewry, and it is still in use today. There is much merit in Leeser's Bible and, not infrequently, its translation is superior to that adopted in the Jewish Publication Society edition of 1917.

Forty years after Leeser's Bible appeared, the Jewish Publication Society, at its second biennial meeting, resolved to produce a new English version of the Bible. In 1894 the Society formally adopted a plan which revolved about a revision of Leeser's Bible. Within two years, each Book in the Bible was assigned to a different Jewish translator—all American scholars, except for Rabbi Joseph H. Hertz of England. Marcus Jastrow was made editor-in-chief, with Kaufmann Kohler and Frederick de Sola Mendes as his two assistant editors.

The quality of the would-be translators was uneven, with not one Bible specialist in the entire group! When Jastrow died, he was replaced by Solomon Schechter.

The committee did not function smoothly and rapidly enough, and in 1908 the entire project was reorganized. Cyrus Adler became chairman of a seven-man committee, with Max Leopold Margolis, Professor of Biblical Philology at the newly-founded Dropsie College, as editor-in-chief. The entire scholarly work was done by Professor Margolis, probably the only scholar in the world who controlled so many of the pertinent sources directly and methodologically; and his manuscript was the basis for all the committee's deliberations.

The translation made its debut in 1917. "It aim(ed)," the preface asserted, "to combine the spirit of Jewish tradition with the results of Biblical scholarship, ancient, medieval and modern. It gives to the Jewish world a translation of the Scriptures done by men imbued with the Jewish consciousness, while the non-Jewish world, it is hoped, will welcome a translation that presents many passages from the Jewish traditional point of view."

What prompted the revision of Leeser, and then the more independent new translation?

The key word, as it was with Saadia Gaon, is intelligibility. Professor Margolis—see his little book *The Story of Bible Translations*—makes clear that the translator's "principal function is to make the Hebrew intelligible. Faithful though he must be to the Hebrew idiom, he will nevertheless be forced by the genius of the English language to use circumlocution, to add a word or two, to alter the sequence of words, and the like . . ."

The problem is that intelligibility inevitably changes from generation to generation. In the past decade or so, Jews all over the world complained that the JPS translation, made more than fifty years ago, was no longer as intelligible as it should be. Leeser's Bible flourished in usefulness for some fifty years, until new conditions brought the JPS version of 1917 into being. That version could not have been expected to maintain undisputed popularity forever.

The new JPS translation now in preparation was undertaken for two principal reasons. The English language has undergone rapid change, far more since the days of World War I than it had through the entire nineteenth century, and our knowledge of the background and text of the Hebrew Bible has increased so enormously that many scores of passages in the older translations are now understood differently and more correctly than before.

The English of the JPS translation of 1917 was patterned after that of the King James Version of 1611 and of the British Revised Version of 1881. Nearly everyone praised the King James Version for "its simplicity, its dignity, its power, its happy turns of expression . . . the music of its cadence, and the felicities of its rhythm." But we have come to recognize that new generations of people were growing up whose home, school and religious upbringing was such that the English of the King James and Revised Versions was frequently unintelligible to them, to the point where the Bible had become almost a foreign book.

The American Revised Version of 1901, the Revised Standard Version of 1952, and, most recently, the British 1961 version (New English Bible: New Testament) all demonstrate this much needed adaptation.

But while many Protestants and Catholics have rejected the English of the older authorized versions, Jews have clung to their outmoded English in both the Leeser and JPS versions. For example, in Deuteronomy 24:11, and elsewhere, the older English versions, followed by the JPS, read "thou shalt stand without," when "you shall stand outside" would be closer to the original and would make the meaning clearer.

In Judges 12:9 we are told that Ibzan of Bethlehem, a Judge in Israel, "had thirty sons, and thirty daughters he sent abroad, and thirty daughters he brought in from abroad for his sons." "Abroad," to most of us, means "a foreign country." But this is clearly not what Judge Ibzan did: he did not intermarry his children with the Canaanites. The Hebrew expression in this context means simply "outside his clan."

In Numbers 12:8 the Lord says to Aaron and Miriam about their brother Moses—as rendered in JPS—"with him do I speak mouth to mouth, even manifestly, and not in dark speeches." The latter half is not clear and something like "plainly and not in riddles" would clarify this passage for the average reader of our own time. These are but a few examples of renderings which no longer convey the meaning required by the original Hebrew text.

An English translation of the Hebrew Bible intended for modern readers should not retain obsolete Old English forms and endings. When, in the JPS rendering, the angel of the Lord, in Genesis 16:8, asks Hagar, Sari's handmaid, "Whence camest thou, and whither goest thou?," the Hebrew text and the modern reader would both be better satisfied with "Where have you come from, and where are you going?" The pronouns *thou, thy* and *thine* ought not to be retained, except perhaps where the Deity is addressed. The plural nominative *ye* could be eliminated. Whenever possible, double prepositions such as *unto* and *into* should be replaced by the simpler forms *to* and *in,* and cumbersome forms like *whosoever, whatsoever, according as,* should be simplified to *whoever, whatever, as.* The same holds true for *wherein, whereby, thereabout.*

In short, a translation for our times must be simplified and modernized, without loss, as far as possible, of the majesty and dignity of the King James Version.

Of even greater significance is the accurate rendering of the Hebrew text. Bible scholars today recognize the correct meaning and nuance of a word better than their predecessors, thanks largely to the increased knowledge which archeology and refined methodology have made available.

Thus, we know that the famous expression in Psalm 137:5 should not be rendered, as in JPS and earlier Christian versions, "If I forget thee, O Jerusalem, let my right hand forget her cunning." There is no word for "her cunning" in the original Hebrew and the JPS translation does not indicate the existence of this serious gap.

Several emendations have been proposed, to produce "(my right hand) shall be forgotten" or "shall grow (become) lean." From the Canaanite texts which have come to light in the past two decades, it is fairly clear that the preserved Hebrew word should be rendered "waste away," as Israel Eitan argued long before these Canaanite texts were discovered.

Various objects used in the daily life of the Israelites can now be identified with greater certainty than was possible in the pre-archeological and pre-exploration days of World War I. The results must be reflected in the new JPS translation. For example, the word *hamman,* found eight times in the Bible and translated in the 1917 JPS version, in keeping with the American Standard Version, as "sun-pillar," is really an "incense altar (or stand)." We know this because a few years ago an altar of incense which had this very word inscribed on it was excavated at Palmyra, in Syria.

In general, we now have much more scientific knowledge for a correct and intelligible understanding of the Hebrew text. Until World War I and the consequent rediscovery of an important part of the ancient Near East through exploration and excavation, scholars generally felt free to reconstruct the history of ancient Israel, even where the Biblical record was neither altogether clear nor adequate. From about 1875 to 1925, many competent scholars belittled and even disregarded the given Biblical data. Such a skeptical and even cynical attitude toward the worth of the Bible as an historical document was expressed as recently as 1945 by Bertrand Russell in his *A History of Western Philosophy:*

> The early history of the Israelites cannot be confirmed from any sources outside the Old Testament, and it is impossible to know at what point it ceases to be legendary. David and Solomon may be accepted as kings who probably had a real existence, but at the earliest point at which we come to something certainly historical, there are already two kingdoms of Israel and Judah (in the ninth century) . . .

The first thousand years of Jewish history is thus glibly written off as "legendary"!

We know better today. The vast collections of archeological and inscriptional material have established the Bible as one of the most important and reliable documents in history. But it is not alone the substantial reliability of the Bible as an historical document which has thus been confirmed. The very *text* of the Hebrew Bible, which Jewish scribes and scholars had copied by hand and transmitted for fifteen hundred years, after the Second Jewish Commonwealth was destroyed by Rome in the year 70, is coming once again to be appreciated.

The nineteenth century, and the first part of the twentieth, witnessed an unprecedented tendency among scholars to emend the Hebrew text of the Bible whenever it did not appear intelligible or satisfactory in their eyes. The best known and widely used critical edition of the text of the Hebrew Bible, Rudolf Kittel's *Biblia Hebraica,* recommended several thousand changes in the traditional Hebrew text.

In contrast to this tendency, there is now available the evidence of a text of Isaiah which came to public light just over ten years ago—the Dead Sea Scroll of Isaiah.

The text of this manuscript abounds in so many errors, and is so inferior to the text preserved by the Masoretes—the Jewish scholarly scribes of the first millennium and a half of the Common Era—that scholars now realize how remarkably careful and trustworthy the Masoretes were in preserving accurately the text of the Holy Scriptures. It would seem to be self-evident that the preserved, masoretic Hebrew text must form the basis of any modern, revised Jewish translation of the Bible. While it may be necessary sometimes to emend the masoretic text, emendations should be held to a minimum, and in no case should an emendation be introduced if it lacks the support of a pertinent ancient Near Eastern text, or of an ancient primary version, such as the Septuagint.

The late Professor Margolis established the principle that "a judicious handling of the ancient versions often brings to light superior readings. But whether by the aid of the versions or by mere conjecture, the business of textual emendation requires a sure tact which few possess."

I have been asked frequently whether the new Protestant Bible, the Revised Standard Version (RSV), on which I have worked actively seven years, would be suitable for English-reading Jews.

All translations which shed light on the Hebrew Bible should be utilized. Thus, Hai Gaon of Pumbeditha, nine hundred years ago, when confronted with an exceptional difficulty in Psalm 141:5, did not hesitate to consult the Christian interpretation on the ground "that scholars in former times did not hesitate to receive explanations from those of other beliefs."

On the other hand, it is my opinion that Jews should use a translation which relies on the Jewish scholarly interpretation of the Septuagint, Targum, Rashi, Ibn Ezra, David Qimhi, the Malbim, and other great Jewish commentators. For example, in the very first chapter in Genesis, verse 2, the RSV reads the "Spirit of God," with capital "S"—as though the Christian concept of the Holy Spirit had been meant by the author of the Hebrew text. As the preface of the old JPS translation put it:

> The repeated efforts by Jews in the field of Biblical translation show their sentiment toward translations prepared by other denominations. The dominant features of this sentiment, apart from the thought that the Christological interpretations in non-Jewish translations are out of place in a Jewish Bible, is and was that the Jew cannot afford to have his Bible translation prepared for him by others. He cannot have it as a gift, even as he cannot borrow his soul from others. If a new country and a new language metamorphose him into a new man, the duty of this new man is to prepare a new garb and a new method of expression for what is most sacred and most dear to him.

That is why the JPS has now embarked on a new translation. The past fifty years have witnessed great changes. A new American Jew has emerged, one raised neither on the language of Shakespeare, King James, or on the Hebrew text of the Bible. He requires a different garb and a different method of expression for what is most sacred and most dear to him. We need a new version of the Hebrew Bible so that its teachings may be as fully intelligible as possible to our people. In all periods and in all lands wherever Jews found themselves, such revisions were made in the past. The Jewish Publication Society is engaged in this same task for our day.*

* Since the writing of this article, *The Torah*, the new translation of the Five Books of Moses, has been published (1962) by the JPS. Dr. Orlinsky is editor-in-chief.

Jewish Law and the Modern Jew
Theodore Friedman

FOR most of its three-thousand-year history, Judaism expressed itself, in thought and deed, in terms of Jewish law (Halakhah). The initial impulse that launched Judaism and the Jewish people was more than a new vision of God. To be sure, monotheism was a radically new departure in the ancient world, perhaps one of the greatest revolutions in man's way of thinking of himself, society, the world and God. But even a cursory perusal of the chapters of the Book of Exodus (19–20), in which the events at Sinai are recorded, reveals that the monotheistic faith came embodied in a code of Law whose observance was henceforth to be the self-accepted task of the people of Israel in its newly won character as a "kingdom of priests and a holy people."

The central task of the rabbis of each succeeding generation was to interpret the Law. Their business was to pore unceasingly over the evergrowing legal literature, that they might be equipped to shed light on questions brought to them. These, for the most part, were routine situations anticipated by Halakhah. But since life is a swift-moving current, new situations were constantly arising for which the Law offered no clear-cut precedents.

So the rabbis resorted to legal fiction. To the Biblical law forbidding the taking of interest, the Rabbis of the Talmud added restriction upon restriction. With the rise of modern capitalism, any literal fulfillment of the Law would have virtually excluded Jews from industry and commerce. The rabbis, in the sixteenth century, thereupon devised a legal fiction (*Shtar Heter Iska*) which theoretically made the lender of money a partner in the enterprise, and thus entitled to a share of the profits. To this day, strictly observant Jews will place their money only in banks, if owned by Jews, which have executed such legal form.

Another contemporary illustration comes from Israel. Theoretically, despite the lapse of centuries since Jews engaged in agriculture in the land of Israel, the Biblical law of the sabbatical year (in which the land must be permitted to lie fallow) never lapsed. According to traditional calculation, 1907 was a sabbatical year. To permit the land to lie fallow would have been economically disastrous to the struggling colonists. The late Rabbi Abraham Kuk, then Rabbi of Jaffa, wrote a learned opinion declaring that the land could be tilled if it were first sold to a non-Jew, then resold to the previous owner at the end of the year. This legal fiction is still used in Israel. The Chief Rabbinate executes the fictitious sale of the entire country to an Arab.

Where no legal fiction was available, and where the exigencies of the situation were such as to require an interpretation of the Law other than an habitual one, learned rabbis were not found lacking.

Talmudic law does not deal with the question of the Jewish apostate. Apparently, there were few such cases in Talmudic times. In later generations, the question arose: how was a Jewish apostate to be regarded? Was he, despite his formal conversion to another faith, still a Jew?

The early authorities adopted an equivocal position. Rashi (eleventh century) was the first Jewish legal authority to take the position, for which he found Talmudic warrant, that apostasy does not nullify one's status as a Jew. In the light of the regnant circumstances—periodic persecution and forced conversion—this otherwise quixotic position must be judged both reasonable and humane. It was engendered by the hope that a refusal to shut the door to the Jewish apostate might conceivably induce him to return to the fold.

When "the gates of interpretation" were closed, the rabbis possessed the authority to issue legal enactments which would "temporarily" suspend the law. These enactments (*Takkanot*) could expressly forbid (or permit) acts, the Law notwithstanding. The basis for the prohibition of polygamy, for example, is a tenth-century enactment of Rabbenu Gershom, one, incidentally, that was never officially recognized by Oriental Jewry. Jewish law reveals a long series of such enactments going back to its earliest rabbinic beginnings.

It would, of course, be erroneous to conclude that in every age the official expounders and interpreters of the Halakhah were always eager to bring the requirements of the Law into realistic alignment with changing social, economic and cultural conditions. Actually, as the Law developed over the centuries, the power of adaptation waned, and the growing rigidity of Halakhah, in the hands of its official expounders, leads to the core of the present-day problems of Jewish law.

Law, by its very nature, is conservative. It tends to give legal status, hence sanctity, to accepted modes of practice. Thus, in Halakhah, a custom observed by the pious (*minhag vatikin*), though it has no basis in the recorded sources of the Law, is regarded as binding. In the sixteenth century, Rabbi Solomon Luria, after proving conclusively that there is no halakhic basis for keeping one's head covered even while engaged in prayer, concluded his legal opinion:

> But what can I do if the people consider it prohibited (to be with uncovered head)? I am not permitted to be lenient in this

matter in their presence . . . Nevertheless, it seems to me that even if there were no prohibitions in this matter, and even if piety were not involved . . . a scholar ought to be careful inasmuch as the people consider bareheadedness to be light-minded and frivolous as if one had violated Jewish law.*

Moreover, thanks to an ingrained habit of thought prompted by a number of Talmudic sentences, each generation regarded itself less worthy and less pious than those preceding. The Talmudic precept that no court can nullify a decision of another court unless it be "greater in wisdom and number" seemed to offer solid legal ground for a growing conservatism that shrank from the task even of extending Talmudic precedent to situations not too dissimilar in essence from those actually cited in the Talmud.

A most instructive insight in this regard is offered by the Talmudic treatment of rabbinical authority to annul a marriage. The Talmud describes five instances, each of varying circumstances, in which the rabbis exercised the prerogative of declaring a marriage null and void, even though, according to the Torah, such marriage would be considered valid.

The early rabbinic authorities (the *Geonim*) were inclined to extend this prerogative and grant the rabbis of each generation the right to issue such enactments as they might deem necessary in order to safeguard the sanctity of marriage. Where an act of marriage was performed in disregard of these enactments, such marriage could be annulled by the rabbis. Medieval authorities, on the other hand, notably Rabbi Solomon ibn Adret of fourteenth-century Spain, were prone to restrict this rabbinic authority only to those cases specifically mentioned in the Talmud. In the nineteenth century, Rabbi Moses Sofer, one of the leading Halakhah authorities of his time, took the position that in no instances, even including those described in the Talmud, do latter-day rabbis have the authority to annul a marriage.

Another factor contributing to the diminishing authority of latter-day rabbis and to the growing conservatism of the Law was that Jewish piety characteristically expressed itself in an almost ever-growing extension of the prohibitions ordained by Halakhah.

At first these self-accepted extensions of the Law were the practice of individuals or small groups of pietists. But in a society dominated by the ideal of piety, many of these voluntarily assumed extensions of the Law became common practice and, in time, an intrinsic part of Halakhah.

For example, a Talmudic rabbi cites the practice of his father to

* Quoted in *The Responsa Literature* by Solomon Freehof (Jewish Publication Society of America, 1955).

abstain from eating dairy products after meat for a period of twenty-four hours. "In this regard, I am like vinegar compared to wine, for I wait only from one meal to the next." In his time, the waiting period between eating meat and dairy products was clearly not subject to rigid regulation, but was left to the individual's personal discretion. Some early authorities defined the waiting time between one meal and the next as six hours. Others insisted that the Talmudic statement is to be regarded as an expression of individual piety and that the requirements of the Law are fully satisfied if the meal is merely formally concluded before dairy products are partaken of. The *Shulhan Arukh* (sixteenth century), following a similar opinion codified by Maimonides, declares a six-hour waiting period to be required. Rabbi Moses Isserles, in his gloss on the *Shulhan Arukh's* decision, notes that many observe the custom of waiting one hour between the eating of meat and dairy products, but those who are fastidious in observing the Law wait six hours. "It is proper," he concludes, "that this latter practice be observed." What began as the practice of a single individual or small group of pietists turned into codified law incumbent upon all.

The establishment of the State of Israel has shown that a secular state governed by secular law is sometimes beyond the scope of Halakhah. By the time Halakhah had entered upon the main phase of its development, Jewish autonomy had already been radically reduced. The authority of the state and the duties of the citizen to the state were areas beyond the interest of the codifiers. Rabbi Joseph Karo knew that the Jews of Palestine, for all their internal autonomy, had to conform to the requirements of the public law of the Turkish Empire. The *Shulhan Arukh* therefore offers no guidance on how a modern state can be conducted in accordance with the principles of Halakhah.* This is, in part, a direct outcome of the fateful shrinkage in the operative scope of Halakhah.

Before the modern era, Jews seldom had recourse to the secular courts for litigation with fellow Jews. Threats of excommunication were not infrequently issued against such action. Halakhah dealt with the laws of partnership, estates, liens, with at least as much detail as it did with such purely ritual matters as dietary laws, circumcision and marriage.

One of the four sections of the *Shulhan Arukh* (*Hoshen Mishpat*) deals exclusively with what might be termed civil law. Until modern times, European Jewish communities enjoyed an internal autonomy at times so broad as to include police power. The rabbi or *dayan* (expert in Halakhah) was called upon to adjudicate civil matters among Jews

---

* True, Maimonides in his code does offer a section on *Hilkhot Melakhim* (Laws of Kings), but it presumes the coming of the Messiah, a scion of the House of David who will be crowned king.

as frequently as for decisions in matters of ritual. With Emancipation, the civil jurisdiction of the rabbinical court ceased and, at virtually one fell swoop, a whole section of Halakhah fell into disuse.

The present state of affairs in Israel, where only matters of personal status (e.g., marriage and divorce) are subject to rabbinic jurisdiction, is a tacit acquiescence on the part of the Orthodox community in this truncation of the Law brought about by historic circumstances. There are at present no serious efforts for the alignment of the current civil law of Israel with the main traditions and institutions of Jewish civil law, or the substitution of the latter for the former.

It might be argued that in accepting the limitations, and thus shortening its lines, the area of Law that remains could be more effective. To a limited extent, this is true. In American Jewish life, maintaining the dietary laws has become a principal concern of the Orthodox rabbinate in its preaching and efforts for community administration and control. Other aspects of the Law, however, e.g., the Biblical prohibition against shaving, form no part of its active agenda.

In reality, the practice of Halakhah has been reduced to a relatively small group of American Jews. Much religious observance among American Jewry today is purely pragmatic.

Yahrzeit and Kaddish, for example, possess scant halakhic warrant, yet many American Jews observe both with a high degree of zeal and regularity. The wearing of tefillin, on the other hand, is a law of the Torah; yet, often enough the man who attends services twice a day to recite Kaddish would not think of putting on tefillin for the recitation of the morning service. The factors at work in the American environment strongly militate against creating a consciousness of Judaism as a system of sacred law. And the gap is enormous between official pronouncements of rabbinic bodies and the actual practices of the laymen, Orthodox, Conservative or Reform.

Yet no interpretation of Judaism, if it be historically grounded, can dispense with mitzvot, the performance of which is both the content and method of Judaism. A Judaism without mitzvot—concrete, historically conditioned acts and practices by which the Jew at once deepens his sense of God-awareness and his membership in the people of Israel in its character as "a kingdom of priests and a holy nation" —is inconceivable.

I have deliberately refrained from qualifying or categorizing the mitzvot into the familiar categories of ceremonial, ethical and religious. How does one categorize the mitzvah of Sabbath observance in which the religious, social, ethical and ritualistic motifs are organically interwoven? Is the mitzvah of circumcision purely ritualistic? The Torah informs us that it is intended as the sign of God's covenant with Abraham; that covenant was directed to "the end that he (Abraham) may command his children and his household after him, that they may keep the way of the Lord, to do righteousness and justice" (Genesis 18:19). Further, the basic religious purpose of the covenant is clearly set forth in the preamble of the mitzvah of circumcision—"to be a God unto thee and to thy seed after thee."

Is there a scale of values in Judaism as to the relative importance of the ethical and ritual? Indeed there is. The prophets once and for all time established in Judaism the principle of the primacy of the ethical: "It hath been told thee, O man, what is good and what the Lord doth require of thee, only to do gently, and to love mercy, and to walk humbly with thy God" (Micah 6:8). But it would be an egregious error to conclude, as is commonly done, that such prophetic utterances meant to imply any derogation of the purely ritual. The mere fact that in their Messianic views the prophets anticipated the exaltation of the house of the God of Jacob is sufficient to refute such view.

It follows then that authentic Judaism, in the future as it did in the past, will concern itself with the full gamut of the mitzvot, mindful, of course, that where there is a conflict of values, primacy will be accorded, in keeping with traditional teaching, to the ethical requirements of Halakhah.

The proposition remains axiomatic. Judaism is a religion of Law, a religion in which spiritual feeling, aspirations and commitment are expressed through concrete acts. The impulse that gave rise to both the creation and observance of the Law is divine in nature. The particular form which the Law took was subject to all the influences of time and place that impinge on the human mind in its effort to express its hunger for holiness.

Some of these forms are so remote from modern consciousness as to be powerless to re-kindle in us the spiritual strivings which once inspired them. These may well lapse into disuse, for where the Law is no more than form it awakens in us neither ethical nor religious import. Fortunately, Jewish traditional practices offer a plenitude of opportunity for ethical and religious expression. Moreover, a reawakened religious consciousness can in time be expected to find new occasions and opportunities for the development of new forms.

The first task must be the determination of what is intact with the possibility for spiritual life in the domain of Jewish law and what is empty husk. This process involves reading the literature of Halakhah as carefully as the rabbis of Halakhah read the Bible. If they dared to say that "the words of Scripture are rich in one place and poor in another," dare we not say the same of their words, and act in accordance with them?

Needed: Dynamics of Judaism
Louis L. Kaplan

THE rise of the American Jewish community, numbering more than five million souls and enjoying equality of political, cultural and economic rights, marks a turning point in the two-thousand-year history of the Diaspora. Hitherto, Jews were regarded as aliens by the governments and peoples in whose midst they lived, and thought of themselves as being in exile even when they acquired wealth and positions of trust and responsibility, as under the eastern and western Caliphates. Less than a hundred years ago, Benjamin Disraeli, who as Queen Victoria's Prime Minister helped build the British Empire, was nevertheless known as the "alien patriot."

This situation has been radically altered. In the United States, Jews did not have to wage a struggle for full citizenship, nor was it granted them by any special act of emancipation passed by Congress. The Constitution conferred these rights on all citizens. This is not to say that anti-Semitism has disappeared or that there will not continue to be enclaves of economic and social prejudice and discrimination. The fundamental difference is that Jews in America are not the objects of government mercy. We are here not on sufferance but as of right. We can and do resist—perhaps with insufficient courage and determination—infringements of our rights.

Such active, personal involvement in the affairs of government and society, not on the part of a few court-Jews but by all American Jews, flows from the conviction that we are not in exile but that America is our home. Vis-à-vis Israel, we may be part of the Jewish Diaspora in that our ties with the historic Jewish people and all it represents in the spiritual history of mankind are indissoluble.

Jewish identification now has a different character from what it had in the past. We are no longer members of a people in exile, since we need not continue to labor under that status, if we do not wish to. Nor are we Jews only by religion, unless by "religion" we understand the all-encompassing range of Jewish religion, which is co-extensive with life.

We are members of an historic people that more than three thousand years ago accepted a covenantal responsibility to develop a collective life as well as the life of each individual member in accordance with certain ethical and moral principles. This remains the unfinished task to which the Jewish people is committed.

Happily for American Jews, these ethical and moral principles are implicit in the American design and have become woven more and more into the fabric of national life. It is this, and not simple patriotism, which makes it possible for Jews to give themselves without reservations to America. We have the difficult and exciting task of living fully in two cultures simultaneously. The spectre of dual loyalties which haunts the minds and hearts of some Jews is of their own making.

American education and experience are altering the substance of Jewish life and the character of its institutions. Free association with other religions and with secular schools of thought have had a marked effect on the content and forms of Jewish religion and religious institutions in America. Since the rise of Christianity and Islam, Judaism was at best a tolerated faith, at worst proscribed—and always the object of scorn and repressive legislation. From time to time there were public disputations under royal or church command, but, in the main, contact was confined to compulsory Jewish attendance at conversionary sermons.

Today, philosophical and theological dialogues are taking place between Jewish teachers and those of other religions, and conscious or unconscious influences are manifest. So great is the resultant state of flux that Jewish Orthodoxy has become militant, Reform clamors for regulatory codes of law, Conservatism is pulled simultaneously to the left and right. Reconstructionism has become a movement instead of a philosophy, and secular Judaism flirts with religious ceremonies.

On the ideological level, the interaction with Christian religious thought, with scientific humanism and secularism, has led to the development of Jewish theological writings which fill a great need for Jews and other thoughtful Americans. In the realm of organization, however, our religious institutions betray more deliberate imitation than creative originality, and the models date back a generation.

At a time when American and world Protestantism have brought their ecumenical efforts from one success to another, and large denominations long engaged in theological controversy have been able to effect religious mergers, American Judaism is torn by divisive denominationalism and parochialism. In the Catholic Church, the most divergent and often contradictory views of Dominicans and Jesuits, conservatives and liberals, have found ways of living together in mutual respect and accommodation. But in American Jewish life, the separatist trend is on the ascendancy.

It is not the lack of religious uniformity which needs to be decried, for nothing would be more stultifying or less Jewish than such uniformity. Judaism was never monolithic. It was hospitable to dissenters, and their views were recorded in the official literature which has been

studied down the centuries with reverence and affection. The Deuter-
onomist's view of the operation of God's justice stands in the same
Bible with Jeremiah's anguished question, "Wherefore do the wicked
prosper?" and with Job's relentless pursuit of God until He answers
him out of the storm in terms we wish we understood. On the pages of
the Mishnah and Talmud appear side by side the differing and dis-
putatious opinions of Shammai and Hillel, Rav and Samuel, Abbaye
and Rava.

But is it really too much to ask of American Jews that they accept
difference without rancor and place devotion to the totality of Jewish
life above parochial loyalties?

One suspects that vested organizational interests are more responsible for the heightened denominationalism than ideological differences,
real though these may be. Is there one large Orthodox, Conservative or
Reform synagogue in which half of the members have the same God
concept or are committed to the same pattern of religious observance?
It is far easier to achieve such a consensus on *non*-observance. Many
years ago Solomon Schechter said that the difference between Orthodox and Reform Jews is that Orthodox Jews don't observe two days
and Reform Jews don't observe one day. Divisive denominationalism
in a period of Christian ecumenicity, theological dialogues and the
political concept of a United Nations is a costly cultural lag.

No less disturbing is the over-emphasis on the cultic aspects of Jewish religion, the observance of certain forms and ceremonies. Judaism
was never a mere religious cult of Bar Mitzvah and Confirmation, of
Kaddish and *yahrzeit,* of candles and kiddush, of kashrut and prayers.
It includes all these and more, but as vocalization and musical nota-
tions in the text of its spirit. Without the letters which form the words
and concepts that instruct and inspire, that call for conviction and
command commitment, the vowels and notes remain a spurious code
that neither invite deciphering nor communicate meaning.

The pulpits of our synagogues resound with the message of the
prophets but the activities bear the hallmark of the priests. One is
tempted to paraphrase: "The voice is the voice of Israel, but the hands
are the hands of Jacob." The constant barrage on the centrality of the
synagogue may or may not be effective advertising, but it is a distortion of the Jewish religion. Judaism has always held that the *Jewish
home* and the *Jewish family* are institutions of far greater significance
than the synagogue, life-long *study* a higher form of worship than
prayer, and deeds of loving-kindness the supreme *imitatio dei.* "As He
is merciful, so be thou merciful."

Judaism is not synagogue-centered as Christianity must, of necessity, be church-centered. Paradoxically, while many church leaders,

notably Reinhold Niebuhr and Bishop Pike, today summon Christians to give expression to their noblest and highest religious idealism through civic, labor and other non-church institutions, Jewish teachers beat the drums for a return to the synagogues, with their largely social and secular programs.

The synagogue needs to be saved from its current success. It must again become the power-station where Jewish idealism is energized so that Jews and society can move forward. Prayers are not a payment for past favors or a requisition for present and future needs. They are, or should be looked on as, a "signing in" for duty, to help man confront himself as he is and as he *ought to be*.

Worship experience must be a means of bringing to its full potential the divine spark in each person so that he may work cooperatively and effectively with his neighbors to improve the community. Instead of taking the market place or the country club into the synagogue, the ideals of the true synagogue must be carried into our daily work.

How can American Jews meet these challenges? For one thing, the system and program of Jewish education in America need drastic improvement. To be content with a two-to-six-hour study week for five or six years at the elementary level is to make a mockery of the Jewish past. The possibility of any worthy future depends on serious Jewish study on the secondary and college levels and throughout adult life. The Torah was not given to children alone, though a Midrash would have God prefer them as surety for its preservation.

Nor was the Torah given as a completed revelation. Side by side with the Written Torah was the Oral Torah, which is still being pondered and enriched. Above all, this Torah was given to be embodied in the history and life of our people.

We live today in a world of danger and destiny, risk and responsibility, oppression and opportunity. Jews in America, Israel and wherever freedom thrives are part of this world and cannot stand apart from the struggle to expand the areas of freedom in society, political, economic and social, as well as in the mind and heart of man. Ours is a heritage of courage in the face of death and a life-worse-than-death, of faith in God if need be, as Judah ibn Verga said, in spite of what He permits to be done to the faithful, of faith in man to rise again though he fall again, and of faith in the world as the home where our lives must be built.

Judaism is more than a technique for Jewish survival, though it be true that without Judaism there is no Jewish people even as without the Jewish people there is no Judaism. Judaism is nothing less than a view of the universe, of man's place in this universe in all his interrelationships with God, nature, his fellow men and with the animal kingdom. It is a philosophy of life and history, tested and tried in the experience of a particular people.

This historic experience was not accumulated in a vacuum. From the very beginnings, the Jewish people was in touch with the great centers of power and civilization. Babylon and Egypt, Assyria and Persia, Greece and Rome, paganism and Hellenism, Christianity and Islam—all were confronted by Israel's evolving life and thought and, in turn, all had their impact on the development of Judaism. Time and again, we were overpowered by their physical might, and the peripheral were overcome by the blandishments of the current culture. But always the loyal center rose to the occasion and met the challenge, with martyrdom and exile if need be, and with renewed intellectual ferment.

Judaism was neither self-insulating nor a blank, open book in which every passing scribe could write at will. Abraham and Moses knew the Babylonian and Egyptian Creation epics and faint echoes of these mythological tales may be found in the Bible. But Genesis is in no way a parallel account. It is a *protest* against the crude, polytheistic and demonic mythology of the time. Some of the civil laws of Exodus were anticipated in the Code of Hammurabi but in no other code, ancient or modern, were the duties to love the stranger and to provide for his well-being mandatory. No people of antiquity or of our own times has thought of itself as chosen by God, not for world dominion but for moral responsibility.

And from Moses until today, Jewish scholarship was ever sensitive to any new burgeoning of intellect and spirit. Always there were the servile and self-abasers who wished to refashion Judaism to fit the reigning *zeitgeist*. Their efforts passed into history with that *zeitgeist*. The most discerning sought to separate the wheat from the chaff and bent their efforts to transplant that which was of true worth in the foreign culture into the soil of Judaism, certain that it would take root there and grow. Nor did they eschew the opportunity of bringing Jewish truths to bear on the dominant culture in a fruitful interaction. Thus, Judaism was enriched without being torn from its own roots.

Our present task is to effect a creative *interaction* between the emerging values in democratic scientific, twentieth-century America and the historic insights and tested ideals of Judaism.

Jews were the first people in history to learn, even if they did not always remember, that nations do not exist to exercise power. Belief in their national destiny, heightened though it was by the doctrine of divine election, was purified in the fires of prophetic chastisement and refined in the crucible of exile so that they came to understand that their national life must be directed to ethical and spiritual ends, not to lordship and dominion.

America is in travail today, partly at least because of its possession of unprecedented power and wealth. It stands poised on the threshold of a new era in the history of nationalism. Without abandoning national sovereignty, it can make its power and wealth work through the United Nations so that the prophetic vision of a family of nations living in peace and in mutual assistance may be brought nearer to realization. As American Jews it must be our obligation to help lead America toward this understanding of its national destiny.

A high level of consumption, not to say waste, has become the familiar image of America. This has led some religious and intellectual circles to indict American society as being grossly materialistic. We are told that only a return to "spirituality" will save us.

This dichotomy of matter and spirit is alien to Judaism, which has always viewed the body, no less than the spirit, as the work of the Creator. Bible and Talmud, Halakhah and *Aggadah,* rationalism and the Kabbalah have all insisted that the essence of spiritual life is to be found in raising the physical act to the dimension of the spiritual by sanctifying and hallowing it.

In our own day, Rabbi Abraham Kuk, poet and mystic, strove with all his might against those mistaken pietists in and out of Palestine who failed to see a religious quality in the work of the impious halutzim. "Segregated holiness" was his label for spirituality separated from nature and physical life.

Even in its view of the Messianic age, Judaism remained true to this acceptance of nature and the material world. Jewish Messianism was *this*-worldly. The utopia of the "end of days" envisioned by prophets and sages was not to be in heaven but here on earth. To prevent a wedge of hostility from being inserted between the material and the spiritual, to use America's material for ethical and spiritual ends, is an insight that we can bring from Judaism.

Judaism also has something to contribute to the creative use of the increased leisure that most Americans now enjoy, thanks to the progress of technology. Recreational agencies and their staffs have been girding their loins for an assault on the great opportunities that beckon. Far too much of their thinking, however, is predicated on the assumption that in the not too distant future our leisure-time activities will be more important than the *work* we do.

With famine, disease, illiteracy and want afflicting a vast majority of the world's peoples, it is frighteningly frivolous to suggest that leisure-time activities may soon be more important than the work that needs to be done.

Judaism has never been very hospitable to the play-and-sport motifs in human life. It outlawed hunting and frowned upon athletic games of prowess. It sanctioned swimming, since life might depend on the possession of this skill. It knew the joys of music and dancing. But in the main it viewed life seriously and saw the earth as an unfinished creation awaiting man's dedicated labors for its fulfillment.

Today, this approach may appear somber and neglectful of man's legitimate needs for physical recreation and play. To give these precedence over work, however, is dangerous to the national health and well-being of America and damaging to the face which we present to the world.

"By three things is the world sustained," said Simeon the Just, "Torah, work and acts of loving-kindness." *Avodah* has here been rendered as *work* and not as "divine service" or "worship," since in Judaism Torah includes "worship" even as study of Torah is itself the highest form of "worship." Judaism also teaches that "Torah which is not associated with work must sooner or later become irrelevant and lead to evil."

Ben Gurion's impassioned and often raucous and misunderstood calls for halutzim from free America to help integrate the hundreds of thousands of backward Oriental and North African Jews into a modern democratic society might be welcomed as an opportunity for religious service of the highest order and not looked upon as political disloyalty to America. Were the late Dr. Tom Dooley and his associates in their crusade to bring medical aid to Asia's millions, or the thousands of Christian missionaries in all parts of the world disloyal?

Moreover, it is not only in underdeveloped countries that such opportunities for self-redemptive labor can be found. There are areas in our own land that sorely need creative and enterprising work.

Language study is another important area in American life in which Jewish historic experience may be of service. Jews have often been a polylingual people, always adopting the language of the country in which they settled but retaining a considerable familiarity with Hebrew and, to a lesser extent, with Aramaic. We even Hebraized the adopted vernaculars and thus produced a family of new languages—Jewish Aramaic, Judeo-Arabic, Judeo-French (Rashi), Ladino or Judeo-Spanish, and Yiddish (Judeo-German).

By contrast, most Americans, having had no historic necessity to master languages other than their own, have been notoriously monolingual. The absence of adequate language instruction and proficiency in American high schools and colleges has produced adverse effects in our diplomatic and international relations. Though Hebrew has not been and is not likely to become an important factor in American foreign policy, the maintenance of the study of Hebrew by Jewish schools on the elementary, secondary and college levels has served to keep at least one small door open for foreign language study.

Today many voices heard in the land decry American linguistic isolationism. American Jews may well set an example, encouraged by their historic openness to other languages and cultures and aided by aptitudes developed through custom and use.

Clearly, a vital, dynamic Judaism has much to contribute to the development of American life and thought. It is essential, however, that this relationship continue to grow in new ways, if it is to meet the needs of the future.

Our Changing Jewish World
Cecil Roth

DURING the last few years the general geography of the Jewish world has been fundamentally altered. The first enormous change has been the tragic obliteration of East European Jewry, which less than twenty-five years ago was the great hope and guarantee for the future of Jews of the entire world. Even when the possibilities of assimilation or the disappearance of Jewish communities were discussed, it was always assumed that the vast reservoir in Eastern Europe would preserve Jewish values intact.

We know only too bitterly what happened. The great mass of Jews in the former Russian Empire together with great numbers in the Austro-Hungarian Empire were divided into two parts after World War I. Those who remained outside Russia were entirely destroyed, and what is left is only the palest shadow of the Jewish life that existed before. There are a few thousand Jews left in Poland, but little of Jewish life. A synagogue or a Jewish museum may be open here and there, and a rabbi may continue to study, but by and large Judaism has disappeared.

In the Soviet Union a large number of persons still bear the name Jew on their passports. But the Judaism which is left is an almost negative and disappearing quantity. Every now and again somebody reports that the synagogue of Moscow was filled on a certain Jewish holiday. But what does that mean in a community of a half million Jews, especially when those in attendance are mainly elderly?

There is no point in deceiving ourselves: Judaism in the former Russian Empire, under Soviet rule, is finished. There is no hope for its future, and an odd episode or individual here and there can hardly demonstrate the reverse.

One area where there may be greater hope is in the south of Russia, where there are more Jews and a greater degree of Jewish religious life than had formerly been thought possible. Synagogues are open and frequented, as I am informed, even on week days, and Jewish traditions are observed. But this community, in Bukhara and the neighboring region, constitutes only a small minority of Russian Jewry.

With the destruction of East European Jewry comes also the end of Yiddish supremacy. Before World War II a majority of the world's Jews could probably speak and understand Yiddish, or were at least immediately descended from Yiddish-speaking ancestry. Nazi persecutions dealt Yiddish a mortal blow and it is hardly possible that in the next generation any large section of the Jewish people will speak Yiddish in a natural, familiar fashion. That language, unfortunately, is going the way of Judeo-Italian, Judeo-Spanish and other Jewish dialects which flourished earlier.

Another tragic change is the gradual elimination of Jews from the Arab world. Up to a generation ago there were large, flourishing Jewish communities in the Arab countries.

As a result of the anti-European and anti-colonial movements throughout the Arab world as well as of Arab-Israel hostilities, few if any Jews now live in Arabia, Iraq and Egypt, and the exodus is now spreading all over North Africa—Tunis, Algiers and Morocco. It will surely gather increasing momentum. More than half the Jews of the Arab-speaking world have already left that area; the rest are planning departure.

As for Western Europe, the Jewish communities that still exist are in many cases much smaller than before World War II. They still maintain a show of activity: some synagogues have reopened, some communal organizations function. But in several countries they cater only to the elderly and may lose their *raison d'être* once that generation passes away.

In Yugoslavia, for example, there is a confederation of Jewish communities, synagogues have been reopened and rededicated. But Jewish religious life, as we conceive it, barely exists. On the New Year three years ago, in the once famous community of Sarajevo there were about fifteen persons in the synagogue. On the Day of Atonement at Belgrade with a community of a thousand Jews, perhaps one hundred drifted in and out, sometimes only for a few minutes. The same can be said of Bulgaria, perhaps of Czechoslovakia, and of some communities in Italy.

There is of course the possibility of a revival previously unimagined. At the beginning of this century the face of the Jewish world was changed fundamentally by the immigration of Jews from Eastern Europe which revitalized English Jewry, fashioned the great American Jewish center, and brought into being Jewish communities in many other parts of the world.

A new Sefardic immigration from North Africa has already reached various European countries as well as Israel. In England, for example, the Jewish Temporary Shelter, which maintains a hostel in the East End of London to help Ashkenazi immigrants from Eastern Europe, during the last year housed mainly Sefardim from India, Egypt and North Africa. Within the last few years the Sefardic community in London has almost doubled.

In France a large influx of immigrants from North Africa is changing the face of Jewish communal life. The ancient Jewish community Avignon, which had nearly ceased to exist, is now a viable community again because of these immigrants. Some of the splendid old synagogues in Paris were given over two years ago to the North African immigrants. Immigration is continuing more and more—from Morocco, Tunis and most recently Algiers.

French Jews anticipate with some nervousness the addition of one hundred to one hundred and fifty thousand Algerian Jews in addition to the three hundred thousand Jews already in the country, thus adding fifty per cent to their numbers within a period of a few years exclusive of the Egyptian, Moroccan and Tunisian Jews who have already settled.

Perhaps one of the most important changes of our time is the emergence of Anglo-Jewry, the Jewry of the English-speaking lands. The American Jewish community is now numerically the greatest in the world, and there are more Jews speaking English (in the U.S.A. and the British Empire) than speak any other language. Indeed, English is nearly as widely spoken among Jews today as Yiddish was yesterday.

Another contemporary phenomenon of vast importance is the emergence of a new Spanish-speaking Jewry. A generation ago perhaps half a million Jews knew Ladino, the old medieval Spanish spoken by the Sefardim, the exiles from Spain in the Mediterranean basin. But of those who spoke modern Spanish in Latin America, there were no more than a few thousand. Today the number of Jews speaking Spanish in Latin America and elsewhere will soon touch the million mark. We are witnessing the growth of a Spanish-speaking Jewry much larger than the Spanish-speaking Jewry of the Middle Ages.

One of the strengths of Jews in the past was that they were widely scattered. When storms raged locally, there was always some land of refuge in which to take shelter. When Jews were expelled from England in 1290, Spain, Germany and France lay open. When they were cast out from Spain in 1492 Turkey was a refuge. When the persecutions of 1648 took place in Eastern Europe, Western Europe and Germany were havens. After 1882 England and Russia were open.

But today there are only two nerve centers of Jewish life: the United States and Israel. Our interests are now concentrated to a degree that was never before the case during the whole history of the Diaspora.

The United States thus takes on enormous importance—not merely for American Jewry but for world Jewry. Having overcome the problem of poverty and enjoying economic well-being, American Jews played a large role in the creation of Israel as well as in preserving what was left of European Jewry after World War II.

My first visit to America was in 1925, and my recollection is that American Jewry then presented a depressing picture. The synagogues of the old type were full of greybeards and the younger generation was getting away from Jewish life as fast as it could. To meet a younger man who was vitally interested in Judaism, who read Jewish literature, who responded to Jewish values, was most unusual. On the West Coast the degree of intermarriage had risen to a very high per cent.

Certainly the picture today is more promising. There has obviously been a great revival of interest in Jewish values and Jewish religious institutions. Whether the magnificent temples are synonymous with real religious revival and represent self-sacrifice on the part of those who conceived them, whether they have the same religious content and religious fervor as the prayer halls of the fathers of their builders, is less certain. But there can be no question that a great part of American Jewry is deeply attached to Jewish values and Judaism as it conceives them, and is willing to give of its time and money to perpetuate the heritage of its fathers.

Judaism has always been a religion of optimism. A fundamental of our belief is that the Messiah is to come. The implication of this in the present troubled times is that we believe humanity is going to survive. However perilous the future of the world may seem today, it is far less so than that of the Jewish people in the tragic period between 1939 and 1945.

But out of that depth of disaster we were able to snatch one of the greatest of our achievements—the State of Israel. This is the lesson of Jewish history and of Judaism for the world as a whole in this desperate hour.

About the Contributors

ADLER, MORRIS

Rabbi, Congregation Shaarey Zedek, Detroit; author of *The World of the Talmud;* Chairman, B'nai B'rith's Commission on Adult Jewish Education.

AGUS, JACOB B.

Rabbi, Beth El Congregation, Baltimore; author of *The Evolution of Jewish Thought, The Meaning of Jewish History,* etc.

ALBRIGHT, WILLIAM F.

Archeologist and Professor Emeritus, The Johns Hopkins University; author of *The Archeology of Palestine, The Biblical Period from Abraham to Ezra,* etc.

BARON, SALO W.

Professor Emeritus of Jewish History, Columbia University; author of *Social and Religious History of the Jews,* etc.

BOKSER, BEN ZION

Rabbi, Forest Hills Jewish Center, New York; author of *Judaism and Modern Man, The Wisdom of the Talmud,* etc.

BOROWITZ, EUGENE B.

Professor of Education and Lecturer in Jewish Religious Thought at New York School of Hebrew Union College—Jewish Institute of Religion.

CHERRICK, BERNARD

Executive Vice President, The Hebrew University; former Minister, New Synagogue, London.

COOPERMAN, HASYE

Chairman, Department of Literature, New School for Social Research; author of *The Chase* and *Men Walk the Earth.*

DAVIES, W. D.

Edward Robinson Professor of Biblical Theology, Union Theological Seminary; author of *Paul and Rabbinic Judaism, Christian Origins and Judaism,* etc.

DRESNER, SAMUEL H.

Rabbi, Congregation Beth El, Springfield, Mass.; editor, *Conservative Judaism.*

EBAN, ABBA

Former Israeli Ambassador to U.S.; presently Deputy Prime Minister of Israel; author of *Zionism and the Arab World, Voice of Israel,* etc.

FEUCHTWANGER, LION

Author of many novels, including *Power, Josephus, The Oppermanns, Jeptha and His Daughter, Jew Süss, The Ugly Duchess.*

FIEDLER, LESLIE A.

Professor of English, Montana State University; author of *An End to Innocence, Love and Death in the American Novel,* etc.

FRIEDMAN, THEODORE
Rabbi, Congregation Beth El, South Orange, N.J.; co-editor, *Jewish Life in America*.

FRIMER, NORMAN E.
New York Metropolitan Regional Director, B'nai B'rith Hillel Foundations; author of *Judaism and Ethics* and other monographs.

FROMM, ERICH
Psychiatrist and author of *The Sane Society, Escape from Freedom, The Forgotten Language, Art of Loving, The Heart of Man*, etc.

GOLD, HENRY RAPHAEL
Psychiatrist and psychoanalyst; author of many articles on the psychiatric values of Judaism.

GOLDIN, JUDAH
Professor of Judaic Studies, Yale University; author of *The Living Talmud* and *The Period of the Talmud*.

GOODENOUGH, ERWIN
Professor of Religion, Yale University; author of works on Philo, *Jewish Symbols in the Greco-Roman Period*, etc.

GORDIS, ROBERT
Rabbi, Temple Beth-El, Rockaway Park, N.Y.; author of *Judaism for the Modern Man, A Faith for Moderns, The Root and the Branch—Judaism in the Free Society*, etc.

GREENBERG, SIDNEY
Rabbi, Temple Sinai, Philadelphia; editor of *A Treasury of Comfort, Modern Treasury of Jewish Thought*, etc.

HERTZBERG, ARTHUR
Rabbi, Temple Emanu-El, Englewood, N.J.; Lecturer in History at Columbia University; author of *The Zionist Idea, Judaism, The Outbursts That Await Us*.

HINDUS, MILTON
Professor of English Literature, Brandeis University; author of many literary studies.

JACOBS, LOUIS
Rabbi, The New London Synagogue, London; author of *Jewish Values, We Have Reason to Believe*, etc.

JANOWSKY, OSCAR I.
Professor of History, City College of New York; author of *Foundations of Israel: Emergence of a Welfare State;* editor, *The American Jewish Community—A Reappraisal*.

JOSPE, ALFRED
National Director of Programs and Resources, B'nai B'rith Hillel Foundations; author of *Judaism on the Campus, Religion and Myth in Jewish Philosophy, Handbook for Student Leaders*, etc.

KALLEN, HORACE M.
Professor Emeritus, New School for Social Research; author of *Cultural Pluralism and the American Idea, Judaism at Bay*, etc.

KAPLAN, LOUIS L.
President, Baltimore Hebrew College; Regent, University of Maryland; chairman, Editorial Committee, *Jewish Heritage*.

KATZ, LABEL A.
President of B'nai B'rith (1959–1965); co-chairman of COJO, member of the National Cabinet of the United Jewish Appeal, etc.

LEHMAN, HERBERT H.
Former Governor of New York and U.S. Senator; an outstanding champion of liberal and humanitarian causes.

LELYVELD, ARTHUR J.
Rabbi, Fairmount Temple, Cleveland; contributing author to *Religion and the State University*, etc.

LEVINTHAL, ISRAEL H.
Rabbi, Brooklyn Jewish Center, N.Y.; author of *Judaism—An Analysis and Interpretation* and *Point of View—An Analysis of American Judaism*.

LISITZKY, EPHRAIM E.
Hebrew poet and teacher for many years in New Orleans; author of *In the Grip of Cross-Currents*.

MALIN, IRVING
Instructor of English Literature, City College of New York; fellow of the National Foundation for Jewish Culture; co-editor of *Breakthrough*.

MARK, YUDEL
Author of numerous articles on Yiddish literature; editor of the *Great Dictionary of Yiddish Language* and philological journal *Yiddishe Sprakh*.

ORLINSKY, HARRY M.
Professor of Bible, Hebrew Union College–Jewish Institute of Religion, N.Y.; Editor-in-Chief, New Translation of Hebrew Bible for Jewish Publication Society; author of *Ancient Israel*.

PATAI, RAPHAEL
Research director, Herzl Institute; co-author with Robert Graves, *Hebrew and Greek Myth Contrasted;* author of *Sex and Family in the Bible and Middle East, Cultures in Conflict*, etc.

RACKMAN, EMANUEL
Assistant to President, Yeshiva University; rabbi, Congregation Shaaray Tefila, Far Rockaway, N.Y.; author of *Israel's Emerging Constitution*, etc.

REIK, THEODOR
Psychoanalyst and author of *Jewish Wit, Listening with the Third Ear, Of Love and Lust, The Compulsion to Confess*, etc.

RIVKIN, ELLIS

Professor of History, Hebrew Union College; author of *Leon de Modena and the Kol Sakhal* and *The Hidden Revolution: Analysis of Pharisaism as an Historical Phenomenon.*

ROTH, CECIL

Author of more than twenty-five books on Jewish history, including *A Bird's-Eye View of Jewish History, The Marranos, Jewish Contribution to Civilization,* etc.

SANDMEL, SAMUEL

Provost, Hebrew Union College; author of *A Jewish Understanding of the New Testament,* etc.

SCHULWEIS, HAROLD M.

Rabbi, Temple Beth Abraham, Oakland, California; co-author *Approaches to the Philosophy of Religion* and contributing author to *Mordecai M. Kaplan: An Evaluation.*

SIEGEL, SEYMOUR

Associate Professor of Theology, Jewish Theological Seminary, and Assistant Dean of its Herbert Lehman Institute of Ethics.

WEISBERG, HAROLD

Dean of Graduate Faculty, Brandeis University; former Director, Department of Adult Jewish Education, B'nai B'rith.

WEISS-ROSMARIN, TRUDE

Editor, *The Jewish Spectator;* author of *Judaism and Christianity, Highlights of Jewish History,* etc.

WERBLOWSKY, RAPHAEL ZVI

Associate Professor of Comparative Religions, The Hebrew University; Visiting Professor of Religion, Brown University (1963).

WERNER, ALFRED

Senior Editor, *Art Voices;* contributing editor, *Arts Magazine;* author of *Modigliani the Sculptor, Jules Pascin,* etc.

WIESEL, ELIE

Novelist-author of *Night, Dawn, The Accident, The Town Beyond the Wall.*

ZOHN, HARRY

Associate Professor of German, Brandeis University; author of *The World Is a Comedy* and *Wiener Juden in der Deutschen Literatur.*

Index

Abraham, 17, 19, 24–5, 36–7, 89, 91, 118, 120, 121, 131, 145, 146, 170, 176, 177, 190, 193, 199, 267, 272, 279, 363–4, 369
Aging, Jewish view of, 142–6
Agnon, S. Y., 293, 294
Akiba, Rabbi, 30, 58, 74
American Jewish community: 235 ff., 301–17, 342–4, 365–72, 375–6; and Israel, 11–6; materialism of, 301–2, 313
American Jewish culture, 301–5, 306 ff., 313 ff., 324–33
Amos, 92, 111–2, 113–4, 115–6, 117, 131, 277
Anti-Semitism: 89, 184, 191 ff., 197, 225, 233, 260–1, 307, 325, 365; in Middle Ages, 178–84
Archeology and Biblical history, 23 ff., 176, 277, 348, 349, 356

Baal Shem Tov, 47, 74, 217, 231, 255, 256
Baeck, Leo, 38, 87, 91
Bar Mitzvah, 66, 308, 311, 367
Bellow, Saul, 246, 257–63, 324, 326, 330, 331, 333
Ben Gurion, David, 11, 12, 13, 15, 70, 290, 371
Bible: 19, 25, 27, 34 ff., 39, 44, 80–3, 90, 103 ff., 133 ff., 138 ff., 142 ff., 147, 174 ff., 183–4, 185, 188, 196, 199, 270, 285–6, 296, 308, 339, 364, 370; as history, 23–9; for moderns, 345–8; impact of, 15; modern scholarship and study of, 347 ff., 356; new translation of, 351–8; translations of, 351 ff.; see Torah
Biblical criticism, 135, 138
Blood accusations, 181 ff.
B'nai B'rith (b'nai b'rit), 18, 91, 221–2, 316
Bovo-Bukh, 61–2
B'rit: see Covenant
"Bube-Mai'seh," 61–2
Buber, Martin, 103, 106–10, 274, 329

Cahan, Abe, 325–6, 328
Chagall, Marc, 242, 253–6
Charity: 69, 196; see Philanthropy
Chosen People: 88–91, 131–7, 168, 189, 257, 270; see Election
Christianity: 27, 33, 177, 366, 369; and Judaism, 88 ff., 159–72, 232; attitude toward Jews, 178–84; differs from Juda-

ism, 148, 149, 185–96, 197 ff., 367–8; Jewish view of, 191–6, 197 ff.
Conservative Judaism, 337, 342–4, 366
Conversion, 5 ff., 89, 197–202, 244
Covenant, 13 ff., 17, 18, 89, 91–2, 96, 116, 120, 131, 267 ff., 341, 363–4
Creation, 39–40, 45, 47, 99, 147
Crucifixion, 159–66, 169, 172, 178, 183

Daniel, Father, 5–10
David, King, 18, 19, 26, 88, 89, 93, 94, 95, 112–3, 117, 146, 164, 290, 296
Dead Sea Scrolls, 174, 277, 357
Deeds, good: see Mitzvah
Deutero-Isaiah, 95, 104, 114, 117
Deuteronomy, 35, 80, 129, 134, 138, 146, 151, 268, 269, 350, 367
Diaspora Jewry: 198, 268, 304, 365, 373–6; relations to Israel, 11–6, 295

Education, Jewish attitudes toward: see Learning
Election: 88 ff., 96; see Chosen People
Elijah, 69, 88, 113, 121
Emancipation, 14, 304 ff., 337 ff.
Enlightenment: 70, 205, 206, 340; see Haskalah
Eretz Yisrael, concept of, 267–74, 294
Essenes, 29, 30
Ethics: 188, 193, 364; see Moral teachings
Evil, problem of, 106, 125–30
Exodus, 17, 25, 42–3, 92, 113, 116, 137, 138, 189, 359, 369
Ezekiel, 45, 111, 116, 277
Ezra, 161, 302

Family, Jewish view of, 144 ff., 281, 367
Folklore, medieval, 178 ff.
Frankel, Zechariah, 338, 340–1, 344
Freud, Sigmund, 25, 148, 221–6, 238, 329, 330, 337

Geiger, Abraham, 87, 338, 339–40, 341, 343, 344
Genesis, 24, 26, 35, 45, 71, 104, 145, 146, 147, 198, 350, 355, 364, 369
Ginsberg, Allen, 324, 330, 332
God: and Jewish people, 13 ff., 18; and Kabbalah, 47 ff.; and Land of Israel, 267 ff.; and Pharisees, 28 ff.; arguments for existence of, 97 ff., 133 ff.; as center of man's life, 75, 76; belief in, 103 ff.,